"I like the layout and design. The reading level is easy, yet not condescending. The book is engaging. There is wonderful information presented in a concise, understandable, practical, usable manner. It is such a **positive and practical text.** Compared to other texts, I'd give it a definite thumbs up."

Jeanine Long, Southwest Georgia Technical College

"[S]tudents with every type of learning style will be able to learn and apply the concepts in [this text] in a lasting manner."

Lanita Legan,
Texas State University

"User-friendly, interesting to read… full of tips and strategies students can use."

Katherine Hansen,
Minnesota State University

"I think the text is excellent and supports lifelong learning. The writing style… suggests a conversation between the text and its reader. Clear, 'fresh,' comprehensive and focuses on the 'whole' student. Sound theoretical base."

Christine A. Lottman, University of Cincinnati

"*Keys to Success* is an invaluable resource. It walks the reader through transitioning to college and demonstrates how to build intelligence that will help in all college classes."

David G. Horn, Student, Denison University

"I like the message that success is earned and takes work – that message seems clearer in this text than many others."

Jean E. Abshire, Indiana University Southeast

"Unlike other textbooks that focus on lecturing with a certain heaviness, Carter's *Keys* is more interactive. Never once while reading did I feel discouraged; rather, *Keys* inspired and encouraged me to take the next step in my academic career with confidence."

Laura Daugherty, Student, University of Colorado—Boulder

ABOUT THE AUTHORS

CAROL CARTER was a C student in high school. During her senior year, she got a wake-up call when her brother told her that she had intelligence, but she wouldn't go far in life unless she believed in herself enough to work hard. She began college knowing she was "behind the 8-ball" in terms of her skills. What she lacked in experience, she made up for with elbow grease and persistence. She maximized her strength as an interpersonal and intrapersonal learner. The work paid off and she graduated college with honors and a desire to help other students.

Carol is committed to helping students turn on their brains, get motivated, and discover their abilities. As president of her own company, LifeBound, she teaches study, interpersonal, and career skills to middle school and high school students in order to help them become competitive in today's global world. She trains and certifies coaches in academic coaching skills, and focuses on at-risk students with her volunteer teaching at the federal prison and her LifeBound work in the Denver housing projects. "All students are at risk for something whether it is academic, emotional, social, or economic," says Carol. "If each of us is allowed to be human and accept our flaws, we can overcome our limitations and be the best for ourselves and others."

Carol also speaks on educational topics nationally and internationally, and is pictured here with some students at the Aziza Schoolhouse in Phnom Penh, Cambodia. Her first book, *Majoring in the Rest of Your Life*, launched her writing career and opened the door to her work on the *Keys to Success* series.

JOYCE BISHOP has taught college students for more than 20 years. After struggling with a learning disability as a student, she focused on her visual and logical-mathematical learning abilities and went on to earn a Ph.D. in psychology. Right now, she is in her dream job as Staff Development Coordinator at Golden West College, training other faculty in effective teaching and learning strategies and also in how to teach online. For five years Joyce was voted "favorite teacher," and she was Teacher of the Year for 1995 and 2000.

Joyce and her husband, Dave, a former high school principal, started a program 17 years ago for girls who have no family support or whose families are unable to help them through school. Since that time, the Pathways to Independence nonprofit foundation has sent 215 young women to college, and 175 have graduated into gainful employment. While the girls have come from backgrounds as diverse as prison, extreme poverty, abuse, or psychological disorders, Joyce and Dave have been their champions. This photo is of Joyce with one of her Pathways graduates, Valerie, who obtained her degree in nursing and is now working at a major university hospital as a pediatric nurse. "It is so inspiring to see what these girls do with their lives," says Joyce, "once they know that they can do anything."

SARAH LYMAN KRAVITS lives the strategies for success that she writes about. As an author and mother of three children aged 8, 5, and 2, she faces the challenges of time management, goal achievement, and fulfilling responsibilities (not to mention eating right and getting enough sleep). In her writing and research, she works to keep up with technology and the growth of knowledge. In her relationships with work colleagues all over the country as well as with friends and family, she strives for integrity, effective communication, productive teamwork, and, most of all, flexibility. Creativity also plays a dominant role. Along with her husband, an actor on Broadway and a musician, she promotes creative ideas and actions in the home (and needs lots of creativity in order to manage children's strong wills and unique personalities).

Unlike Carol and Joyce, Sarah thrived in school from an early age based on her strength in verbal-linguistic and logical-mathematical learning. A few years after graduating from the University of Virginia as a Jefferson Scholar, she worked as program director for LifeSkills Inc., a nonprofit organization that aims to further the career and personal development of high school students. This work led her into coauthoring her first student success text and the realization that she was driven to empower students to reach their goals. "Lifelong learning is the essential success skill," says Sarah. "I would happily trade places with my readers to have the chance to challenge my mind in a college classroom again. Learning gives you a chance to go beyond just thinking about your dreams so that you can make them happen."

KEYS TO SUCCESS

Building Analytical, Creative, and Practical Skills

Brief Fifth Edition

CAROL CARTER

JOYCE BISHOP

SARAH LYMAN KRAVITS

PEARSON

Prentice
Hall

Upper Saddle River, New Jersey
Columbus, Ohio

Library of Congress Cataloging-in-Publication Data

Carter, Carol.
  Keys to success : building analytical, creative, and practical skills / Carol Carter, Joyce Bishop,
Sarah Lyman Kravits.—Brief 5th ed.
    p. cm.
  Includes bibliographical references and index.
  ISBN-13: 978-0-13-512846-6 (pbk.)
  ISBN-10: 0-13-512846-3 (pbk.)
1. College student orientation—United States—Handbooks, manuals, etc. 2. Study skills—Handbooks, manuals, etc.
3. College students—United States—Life skills guides. 4. Career development—United States—Handbooks, manuals,
etc.   I. Bishop, Joyce (Joyce L.), 1950–   II. Kravits, Sarah Lyman.   III. Title.
  LB2343.32.C37 2009
  378.1'70281—dc22

                                                                                      2007051148

Vice President and Executive Publisher: Jeffery W. Johnston
Executive Editor: Sande Johnson
Developmental Editor: Charlotte Morrissey
Managing Editor: Pamela D. Bennett
Project Manager: Kerry J. Rubadue
Production Coordination: Thistle Hill Publishing Services, LLC
Editorial Assistant: Lynda Cramer
Design Coordinator: Diane C. Lorenzo
Cover Designer: Candace Rowley
Cover Image: Jupiter Images
Operations Specialist: Susan Hannahs
Director of Marketing: Quinn Perkson
Marketing Manager: Amy Judd
Marketing Coordinator: Brian Mounts

This book was set in Sabon by S4Carlisle Publishing Services. It was printed and bound by R.R. Donnelley/Willard.
The cover was printed by Phoenix Color Corp./Hagerstown.

Credits and acknowledgments appear on page 309, which constitutes an extension of the copyright page.

Pearson Education Ltd.   Pearson Education Australia Pty. Limited
Pearson Education Singapore Pte. Ltd.   Pearson Education North Asia Ltd.
Pearson Education Canada, Ltd.   Pearson Educación de Mexico, S.A. de C.V.
Pearson Education—Japan   Pearson Education Malaysia Pte. Ltd.

10 9 8 7 6 5 4 3 2 1
ISBN-13: 978-0-13-512846-6
ISBN-10:   0-13-512846-3

FOREWORD
by the Student Editors

College is a time of self-discovery and growth, a time to understand how education serves you in school and out, a time to chart the course for your future. The knowledge you gather will change the way that you see yourself, society, and the world. Through this knowledge, you can find and travel your own path in life.

We have each had our unique struggles in finding our paths. We have worked at becoming better students, we have tried to stay dedicated in the face of challenges, we have adapted to people and academic subjects, and we have kept a lot of balls in the air as we worked to manage our academic, work, and personal lives. Through it all we picked up on some helpful strategies that we want to share with you.

Stay on top of your time. Most students have to stretch to make time for classes, homework, and studying. Your course schedule has to fit into your family time, work schedule, and social life. Remember not to overload yourself and spread yourself too thin among all of your responsibilities, and make sure to prioritize your course work. And study for tests ahead of time—tests sneak up on you quickly, and cramming doesn't always work (we know this from experience).

Examine choices carefully. Unlike high school where you more or less followed a standard curriculum, you now have much more freedom to make choices about nearly every aspect of your education, including your major, classes, instructors, and even schedules. Make sure that you are prioritizing the classes you need. Meet with academic advisors and instructors, look at your needs and strengths, and take time to make the choices that work best for you.

Connect with people and organizations. Befriend your classmates because college relationships are special and also because those relationships will often help you learn the material better than you would learn it on your own. Get involved with organizations to expand your horizons, give back to others, and enhance your résumé (or grad school application).

Use your resources. Math and language labs, computer labs, tutors, advisors, libraries and librarians, and instructors are all there to help you and make your college experience the best that it can be.

This class will help you lay the foundation that will carry you through to your degree and on to your professional life. *Keys to Success* has helped us learn, grow, and make effective choices now, and has given us tools to keep growing in the future. Now it is your turn—use it well, and best wishes for an incredible college experience.

DARREN LOVE
COURTNEY MELLBLOM
CHERYL WHITLEY

REAL PEOPLE, REAL PERSPECTIVES

Peer-to-Peer Perspectives from Students

Perspectives from Academics and Workplace Professionals

BRIEF CONTENTS

DEDICATION

We dedicate the brief fifth edition of *Keys to Success* to the memory of the students and faculty at Virginia Tech who were victims of the tragic campus shootings on April 16, 2007. May their unfulfilled goals and dreams inspire students everywhere to push harder to grasp their own dreams and to believe in education as the answer and the hope.

CONTENTS

CHAPTER 8
WELLNESS, MONEY, AND CAREERS: BUILDING A SUCCESSFUL FUTURE 252

NOTE: Every effort has been made to provide accurate and current Internet information in this book. However, the Internet and information posted on it are constantly changing, so it is inevitable that some of the Internet addresses listed in this textbook will change.

PREFACE

Many students beginning college—or returning after many years—wonder if they have what it takes to succeed. What is the recipe for success in college and beyond? Does a top SAT score, straight-A report card, or high IQ predict success? Do low grades or scores signal that you'll stumble?

Among the ideas presented by the many people who have researched this question, one approach stands out from the rest. Psychologist Robert Sternberg coined the term *successful intelligence* to indicate that intelligence is much, much more than the kind of "book smarts" that can be measured by IQ or similar tests. Rather, it is the ability to use a combination of **analytical, creative,** and **practical** abilities to reach your most important goals.

What are the analytical, creative, and practical processes that underlie intelligence?

This Is Intelligence: Analysis

Analytical intelligence is highly valued as a crucial component of academic success. More commonly known as critical thinking, it is the ability to assess, analyze, compare, and evaluate information.

This Is Intelligence: Creativity

Creative intelligence is the ability to innovate, generate a variety of ideas in response to problems, or think out of the box. It also involves shifting perspectives and risk taking.

This Is Intelligence: Practical Application

Practical intelligence is more than "street smarts" or common sense. It also includes an awareness of oneself and others in situations and the translation of that knowledge into action. It is developed primarily through experience, observation, and practice.

Keys to Success Focuses on Successful Intelligence

Why is successful intelligence such an effective theme for a student success text? Here are some key reasons:

- It delivers strategies that work for *all kinds of students,* not just those with strong analytical skills who tend to do well in school.

- Research proves that teaching and learning with successful intelligence *improves achievement* across cultures, socioeconomic status, age, and gender.[1]
- It recognizes that *intelligence is dynamic* and can be developed, which *encourages lifelong learning,* a key ingredient for success in the modern world.
- It *promotes goal achievement* in college and beyond, supporting our tried-and-true emphasis on success in college, career, and life.

Having introduced successful intelligence as its theme in the brief fourth edition, *Keys to Success* takes its integration to new heights this time around, with tools in each chapter to help you build analytical, creative, and practical intelligence:

- **NEW!** At the beginning of the chapter, a mind map preview surveys the successful intelligence skills you will be working on.

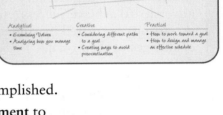

- **REVISED!** Throughout the chapter, **Get Analytical, Get Creative,** and **Get Practical** exercises build those specific skills in the context of chapter material.

- **NEW!** As you finish the chapter, a **Successful Intelligence Wrap-Up** hits the high points of what you explored and accomplished.

- **NEW!** Chapters 1 and 8 contain a **pre- and post-course assessment** to help you measure yourself as a "self-activator" who will put successful intelligence strategies into action.

- **REVISED!** Each end-of-chapter exercise set begins with **Successful Intelligence: Think, Create, Apply,** an exercise that synthesizes the three aspects of successful intelligence by applying them to chapter content.

- **NEW!** Each chapter has a link to Successful Intelligence Connections Online, an audio feature on the text's Companion Website that will help you apply successful intelligence to specific chapter topics.

Keys to Success Features Help You Grow

Complementing the successful intelligence theme, additional features of this text will help you achieve your goals in college, career, and life.

Practical Strategies and Advice. Practical intelligence is in high demand in college and in the workplace. Instructors and students all over the country said they wanted more practical advice and application—and here it is in the form of topics and text features:

- Reflecting psychologist Daniel Goleman's latest research on **social intelligence** as well as his ongoing work with **emotional intelligence**, *Keys to Success* offers practical tools to help you master your feelings and make the most out of your relationships with others. New material on social intelligence, and expanded material on emotional

1. E. L. Grigorenko, L. Jarvin, and R. J. Sternberg, "School-Based Tests of the Triarchic Theory: Three Settings, Three Samples, Three Syllabi." *Contemporary Educational Psychology,* 27, April 2002, pp. 167–208.

intelligence, is highlighted in chapters 1, 4, and 8, and both social and emotional intelligence are referenced throughout the text.

- Near the beginning of each chapter, **Real Problems, Practical Answers** offers advice from a peer, an instructor, or a professional in response to a student question.

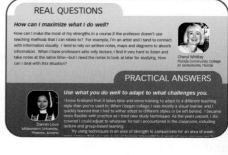

- In this information age, **information literacy** is crucial for success. Chapter 4 has a new analytical thinking example showing different ways in which to critically evaluate information.

- Test taking and time management are high on the list of important practical skills. At the end of each of the two parts in *Keys to Success,* **Get Focused! features** help you build these crucial skills.

- At the end of chapters 3, 6, and 8, a **Personal Triumph case study** showcases an extraordinary student who overcame adversity to achieve success. Accompanying these stories are art pieces created by students who have overcome challenges of their own.

A Text-Wide Focus on How You Learn. This text gives you tools to find out how you learn best, as well as strategies for applying this information in practical ways:

- The first of **chapter 3's self-assessments** helps you explore your strengths in eight ability areas that psychologist Howard Gardner calls the **multiple intelligences:** verbal-linguistic, logical-mathematical, bodily-kinesthetic, visual-spatial, interpersonal, intrapersonal, musical, and naturalistic. The other, the MBTI-based **Personality Spectrum,** helps you explore how you relate to others.

- In chapters 5 through 8, you will find **Multiple Intelligence Strategies grids** with strategies, related to a chapter topic, geared toward each of the eight intelligences. Enhanced for this edition, each grid has a new column that demonstrates possible ways to apply multiple intelligence-based strategies to a particular academic discipline (each chapter features a different discipline).

- Beyond the Multiple Intelligence Strategies grids, material in other chapters (particularly chapters 3 and 8) shows how you can apply what you know about how you learn to situations such as career exploration and communication.

End-of-Chapter Exercises. In addition to the **Successful Intelligence: Think, Create, Apply** synthesis exercise, the end-of-chapter exercises promote development of a skillset necessary to compete in a knowledge economy and global marketplace: group problem solving (**Teamwork: Create Solutions Together**), journaling and practical writing (**Writing: Journal and Put Skills to Work**), and preparing for a successful career (**Personal Portfolio: Prepare for Career Success**).

Keys to Success Is Better Than Ever

The new edition of *Keys to Success* includes improved presentations of critical college, career, and life success topics. Highlights include the following:

- **Quick Start to College,** new to this brief fifth edition, is focused on helpful information to get you in the groove as you begin school.

- An overhaul of **chapter 1 (Welcome to College)** involves an expanded introduction of successful intelligence, three successful intelligence self-assessments, and careful selection of supporting topics such as academic integrity and working with others.

- **Chapter 3 (Diversity Matters: How You Learn and Communicate)** is newly streamlined in its explanations of multiple intelligences and the personality spectrum, more clear in its treatment of the accompanying assessments, and more practical in helping you apply what you learn from the assessments to your experiences in school, work, and life. The chapter now also encompasses the coverage of diversity and communication, highlighting the fact that how you learn is just one of many aspects of personal diversity.

- **Chapter 4 (Critical, Creative, and Practical Thinking)** has been strengthened to help you understand and use the different aspects of successful intelligence.

- Study skills enhancements in **chapters 5 through 7 (Reading, Listening/Note Taking/Memory, and Test Taking)** include revised coverage of SQ3R, memory, and test taking, as well as new material on text notes and highlighting and on combining text and class notes.

- **Chapter 8 (Wellness, Money, and Careers)** contains the latest information on eating well and drugs, as well as an increased emphasis on practicality in money management and career planning advice.

Keys to Success Is Your Tool for Life

Broadening your definition of intelligence may change how you view your abilities and what you expect of yourself in college, in the workplace, and in your personal life. Successful intelligence can empower you with tools you never knew you had. Take action with what you learn about yourself and success in this text. Think and act analytically, creatively, and practically in the coming years as you work hard to achieve your goals and find a learning path that is uniquely your own.

Students and instructors: Many of our best suggestions come from you. Send your questions, comments, and ideas about *Keys to Success* to Carol Carter at *caroljcarter@lifebound.com.* We look forward to hearing from you, and we are grateful for the opportunity to work with you.

ACKNOWLEDGMENT

Keys to Success, Brief Fifth Edition: An Exceptional Development Process

When we introduced the theme of Robert Sternberg's *Successful Intelligence* with the brief fourth edition of *Keys to Success,* our users let us know that we had something special happening. Our goal for the brief fifth edition became the enhancement of this cutting-edge theme, with particular attention to its practical application in college, the workplace, and life.

To that end, Prentice Hall enlisted the involvement of Glenn and Meg Turner of Burrston House in our revision process. The Burrston House instructor and student focus groups, as well as instructor contacts who responded to extensive surveys, brought to us an extraordinary wealth of information about our materials and about what students and instructors need today. Glenn and Meg synthesized this information and presented insightful views that greatly informed the revision process.

With the Burrston House participants, our excellent team of reviewers who gave extensive feedback, and three savvy student editors, we received input on both text and design from more than 80 individuals on the revision of this edition. *Keys to Success,* Brief Fifth Edition, has risen to new heights in large part due to their efforts, and we are immensely grateful. We also especially thank our editor Sande Johnson for her advocacy and her driving this process to such a successful conclusion, and our developmental editor Charlotte Morrissey for somehow providing both in-depth content feedback as well as minutely detailed process management.

Finally, we thank Robin Baliszewski, Jeff Johnston, and Prentice Hall President Tim Bozik for their support and vision of what *Keys to Success* can accomplish.

Chicago Focus Group
Deryl Davis-Fulmer, Milwaukee Area Technical College
Valerie Jefferson, Rock Valley College
Georgia Kariotis, Oakton Community College
Antoinette McConnell, Northeastern Illinois University
Jacqueline Robinson, Milwaukee Area Technical College
Manuel Salgado, Elgin Community College
Arturo Vazquez, Elgin Community College
Tania Wittgenfeld, Rock Valley College

Denver Focus Group
Martha Martin
Joe Ritchie, University of Central Florida
Karen Schulz, University of Baltimore
Rose Stewart-Fram, McLennan Community College
Cheri Tillman, Valdosta State University

Ft. Lauderdale Focus Group
Raishell Adams, Palm Beach Community College–Palm Beach Gardens
Susan Bierster, Palm Beach Community College–Lake Worth
Kobitta Chopra, Broward Community College
Alice Godbey, Daytona Beach Community College
Roselee Helfand, Broward Community College

Cynthia Johnson, Palm Beach Community College–Lake Worth
Frank Kurtz, Broward Community College
Nick Nunes, Daytona Beach Community College
Amoy Reid, Broward Community College
Cathy Seyler, Palm Beach Community College–Palm Beach Gardens
Pamela Shaw, Broward Community College–South Campus
Ione Turpin, Broward Community College
Joy Vaughan-Brown, Broward Community College

Los Angeles Focus Group
Dirk Baron, California State University–Bakersfield
Rodolfo Frias, Santiago Canyon College
Howard Masuda, California State University–Los Angeles
Caron Mellblom-Nishioka, California State University–Dominguez Hills
Nadia Mendoza, California State University–Fullerton
Robert Roth, California State University–Fullerton
Cheryl Spector, California State University–Northridge

Orlando Focus Group
Christy Cheney, Valencia Community College–East Campus
Patsy Frenchman, Santa Fe Community College
S. Renee Jones, Florida Community College at Jacksonville–North Campus

Dana Kuehn, Florida Community College at Jacksonville–Deerwood Center
Charlene Latimer, Daytona Beach Community College–Deland
Kristina Leonard, Daytona Beach Community College–Flagler/Palm Coast
Jenny Middleton, Seminole Community College
Alan Pappas, Santa Fe Community College
Terry Rafter-Carles, Valencia Community College–Orlando
Tracy Stuck, Lake Sumter Community College–Leesburg Campus
Debbie Warfield, Seminole Community College

Student Focus Group Attendees
Golden West Community College: Marcos Cerda, Fidelio Cruz, Matthew Hendrickson, John Robledo, Vuthuyen Nong, Mayra Pena, Isabel Torres, Phuong Le, Nicole Cossani, Clara Moreno
Los Angeles Harbor College: Antonio Velasquez, Wanda Taylor
California State University, Los Angeles: Lydia C. Blanco

Brief Fifth Edition Reviewers
Jean Abshire, Indiana University Southeast
Sara Baker, Elgin Community College
Dirk Baron, California State University–Bakersfield
Lynn Berkow, University of Alaska
Ken Burns, Palomar Community College
Mary Carstens, Wayne State College
Patrick Clarke, Southern Utah University
Colleen Courtney, Palm Beach Community College
Jacqueline Crossen-Sills, Massasoit Community College
Carolyn Darin, California State University–Northridge
Billy Davis, Florida Community College at Jacksonville-South Campus
Joseph Fly, South Plains College
Jean Gammon, Chattanooga State Technical Community College
Katherine Hansen, Minnesota State University-Mankato
Madeline Hart
Noreen Lace, California State University–Northridge
Lanita Legan, Texas State University
Linda Lemkau, North Idaho College
Jeanine C. Long, Southwest Georgia Technical College
Christine A. Lottman, University of Cincinnati
Judith Lynch, Kansas State University
Patricia A. Malinowski, Finger Lakes Community College
John Mancuso, Art Institute of New York City
Howard Masuda, California State University–Los Angeles
Gladys Montalvo, Palm Beach Community College
Nanci C. Nielsen, University of New Mexico–Valencia Campus
Patricia Parma, Palo Alto College
Carolyn Patterson, Texas State Technical College–West Texas
Allison Perrin, South Plains College
Kim Smokowski, Bergen Community College
Rose Stewart-Fram, McLennan Community College
Cheri Tillman, Valdosta State University
Ronald Weisberger, Bristol Community College

Reviewers for Previous Editions
Peg Adams, Northern Kentucky University
Veronica Allen, Texas Southern University
Fred Amador, Phoenix College
Angela A. Anderson, Texas Southern University
Robert Anderson, The College of New Jersey
Manual Aroz, Arizona State University
Glenda Belote, Florida International University
Todd Benatovich, University of Texas at Arlington
John Bennett Jr., University of Connecticut
Ann Bingham-Newman, California State University–Los Angeles
Mary Bixby, University of Missouri–Columbia
Barbara Blandford, Education Enhancement Center at Lawrenceville, NJ

Jerry Bouchie, St. Cloud State University
D'Yonne Browder, Texas Southern University
Mona Casady, Missouri State University
Kara Craig, University of Southern Mississippi
Leslie Chilton, Arizona State University
Jim Coleman, Baltimore City Community College
Sara Connolly, Florida State University
Janet Cutshall, Sussex County Community College
Valerie DeAngelis, Miami-Dade Community College
Joyce Annette Deaton, Jackson State Community College
Rita Delude, NH Community Technical College
Marianne Edwards, Georgia College and State University
Judy Elsley, Weber State University in Utah
Ray Emett, Salt Lake Community College
Jacqueline Fleming, Texas Southern University
Ralph Gallo, Texas Southern University
Skye Gentile, California State University–Hayward
Bob Gibson, University of Nebraska–Omaha
Jennifer Guyer-Wood, Minnesota State University
Sue Halter, Delgado Community College
Suzy Hampton, University of Montana
Karen Hardin, Mesa Community College
Patricia Hart, California State University–Fresno
Maureen Hurley, University of Missouri–Kansas City
Karen Iversen, Heald Colleges
Laura Kauffman, Indian River Community College
Kathryn K. Kelly, St. Cloud State University
Quentin Kidd, Christopher Newport University
Nancy Kosmicke, Mesa State College
Patsy Krech, University of Memphis
Paul Lede, Texas Southern University
Frank T. Lyman Jr., University of Maryland
Marvin Marshak, University of Minnesota
Kathy Masters, Arkansas State University
Barnette Miller Moore, Indian River Community College
Rebecca Munro, Gonzaga University
Sue Palmer, Brevard Community College
Bobbie Parker, Alabama State University
Curtis Peters, Indiana University Southeast
Virginia Phares, DeVry of Atlanta
Brenda Prinzavalli, Beloit College
Margaret Quinn, University of Memphis
Corliss A. Rabb, Texas Southern University
Eleanor Rosenfield, Rochester Institute of Technology
Rebecca Samberg, Housatonic Community College
Karyn L. Schulz, Community College of Baltimore County–Dundalk
Jacqueline Simon, Education Enhancement Center at Lawrenceville, NJ
Carolyn Smith, University of Southern Indiana
Joan Stottlemyer, Carroll College
Jill R. Strand, University of Minnesota–Duluth
Toni M. Stroud, Texas Southern University
Cheri Tillman, Valdosta State University
Thomas Tyson, SUNY Stony Brook
Eve Walden, Valencia Community College
Marsha Walden, Valdosta State University
Rose Wassman, DeAnza College
Angela Williams, The Citadel
Don Williams, Grand Valley State University
William Wilson, St. Cloud State University
Michelle G. Wolf, Florida Southern College

Student Editors
Darren Love
Courtney Mellblom
Cheryl Whitley

The rest of the *Keys,* Brief Fifth Edition story—Our heartfelt thanks to these individuals who also facilitated this edition's leap forward:

- Robert J. Sternberg, Dean of the School of Arts and Sciences at Tufts University, for his groundbreaking work on successful intelligence and for his gracious permission to use and adapt that work as a theme for this edition.
- Those who generously contributed personal stories, exhibiting courage in being open and honest about their life experiences:

    Kevin Abreu, Montclair State University; Stephen Beck, Learn-to-Learn Company; Joyce Bishop, Golden West College; Peter Changsak, Sheldon-Jackson College; Darrin Estepp, Ohio State University; Victoria Gough, Glendale Community College; Jennifer Joralmon, Paradise Valley Community College; Darren Love, Midwestern University; Parisa Malekzadeh, University of Arizona; Joe A. Martin Jr., Professor of Communications, University of West Florida; Courtney Mellblom, California State Polytechnic University; Morgan Paar, Academy of Art University; Shyama Parikh, DePaul University; Antoine Pickett, Resident Engineer, Federal Aviation Administration; Benjamin Victorica, University of Florida; Cheryl Whitley, Florida Community College; Tonjua Williams, St. Petersburg College
- Cynthia Nordberg, Dr. Frank T. Lyman, Prof. Beth Berry, and Prof. Jennifer Joralmon for their invaluable advice and assistance.
- Student artists Matthew Denman, Jen Fisher, Abigail Holtz, and Elie Sanon for their artwork accompanying the Personal Triumph features and their Personal Triumphs on the Companion Website. Thanks also to Susan Denman, Dana Kuehn, and Linda Russ for their help in securing artwork.
- Martha Martin, for her significant contribution to the new Instructor's Manual and PowerPoints, and Christy Cheney and Terry Rafter-Carles, for their work on the Test Item File and the Companion Website.
- Our production team for their patience, flexibility, and attention to detail, especially Pam Bennett, Candace Rowley, Kerry Rubadue, Angela Urquhart and the team at Thistle Hill, and typesetters S4 Carlisle Publishing Services.
- Our marketing gurus, especially Amy Judd, David Gesell, and Joe Hale, who leads a savvy team of sales directors including Matt Christopherson, Patty Ford, Connie James, and Deborah Wilson.
- The Prentice Hall representatives and the management team, led by National Sales Manager Brian Kibby, who deliver our message to its intended recipients—instructors and students.
- Our families and friends, who have encouraged us, advised us, and put up with our commitments.
- We extend a very special thanks to Judy Block, whose research, writing, and editing work was essential and invaluable.

UPPLEMENTAL RESOURCES
for *Keys to Success*

INSTRUCTOR SUPPORT

Resources to simplify your life and engage your students:

Book Specific

Instructor's Manual with Test Bank	0-13-512847-1
PowerPoint CD	0-13-512895-1
TestGen	0-13-512892-7
Faculty Development Workshop: Integrating Successful Intelligence	0-13-514245-8

Online Faculty Training

Hone your teaching skills and build community with other instructors with the first-of-its-kind **Keys Online Faculty Training Course** *with author Joyce Bishop!*

Online Instructor Faculty Training—Join the *Keys* author online faculty training sessions, available to all adopters through Course Compass, at your convenience. Ask questions. Share ideas. Troubleshoot. Be part of this collaborative community—learn what other *Keys* adopters are doing; be able to share exercises, syllabi, and teaching strategies; and observe an actual online student success course taught by Joyce Bishop. Request your unique pass code from your local representative.

Online Resources

Easy access to online, book-specific **teaching support** *is now just a click away!*

Instructor Resource Center—Register. Redeem. Login. Three easy steps that open the door to a variety of print and media resources in downloadable, digital format, available to instructors exclusively through the Prentice Hall IRC. Visit www.prenhall.com for additional information.

Online Instructor Resources include: Online Instructor's Manual, Test Bank, PowerPoints, Faculty Development Workshops, OneKey Course Cartridge, and more.

Online Course Management Through OneKey

*Teaching an online course, offering a hybrid class, or simply introducing your students to **technology** just got a whole lot easier!*

OneKey

All you and your students need to succeed. Powered by Blackboard, WebCT, or Course Compass, OneKey is Prentice Hall's course management resource for instructors and students. This platform provides access to online teaching and learning tools—24 hours a day, 7 days a week. OneKey means all your resources are in one place, with one passcode for maximum convenience, simplicity, and success.

What's Key?

This powerful, ***integrated course management*** resource for *Keys to Success* contains the following:

- Online instructor's resources: Computerized Test Bank, PowerPoints, Instructor's Manual and more
- Pearson's Research Navigator™
- Text-specific Companion Website
- Prentice Hall Planner for Student Success
- Student Reflection Journal for Student Success
- Ten Ways to Fight Hate
- Student Success SuperSite (publisher-provided course website)
- Strategies for Success CD
- Understanding Plagiarism
- Supplemental Videos: Students will be engaged by the video clips on Technology, Math and Science, Managing Money and Career, Learning Styles and Self-Awareness, Study Skills, and Peer Advice, which reinforce the course content.

Visit www.prenhall.com/onekey, and scroll through the gallery option to Student Success for additional information. Note the videos housed on our OneKey sites are now available on DVD, 0-13-514249-0.

Research Resources

*Reinforce strong **research skills**, encourage **library use**, and **combat plagiarism** with this tool!*

Prentice Hall's Research Navigator—Designed to help students with the research process—from identifying a topic to editing the final draft. It also demonstrates how to make time at the campus library more productive. RN includes 4 databases of credible and reliable source material to get your research process started: The EBSCO/Content Select, *New York Times*, Link Library, and the *Financial Times*. Visit www.researchnavigator.com for additional information.

Video Resources

*Choose from a wide range of **video resources** for the classroom!*

Prentice Hall Reference Library: Life Skills Pack, 0-13-127079-6, contains all of the following videos:

- Learning Styles and Self-Awareness, 0-13-028502-1
- Critical and Creative Thinking, 0-13-028504-8
- Relating to Others, 0-13-028511-0
- Personal Wellness, 0-13-028514-5

Prentice Hall Reference Library: Study Skills Pack, 0-13-127080-X, contains all of the following videos:

- Reading Effectively, 0-13-028505-6
- Listening and Memory, 0-13-028506-4
- Note Taking and Research, 0-13-028508-0
- Writing Effectively, 0-13-028509-9
- Effective Test Taking, 0-13-028500-5
- Goal Setting and Time Management, 0-13-028503-X

Prentice Hall Reference Library: Career Skills Pack, 0-13-118529-2, contains all of the following videos:

- Skills for the 21st Century—Technology, 0-13-028512-9
- Skills for the 21st Century—Math and Science, 0-13-028513-7
- Managing Money and Career, 0-13-028516-1

Prentice Hall Full Reference Library Pack, 0-13-501095-0, contains the complete study skills, life skills, and career skills videos on DVD.

OneKey Video Pack, 0-13-514249-0, contains Student Advice, Study Skills, Learning Styles, and Self-Awareness, Skills for the 21st Century—Math, Science, and Technology, and Managing Money and Careers videos on DVD.

Faculty Development Video Resources

- Teacher Training Video 1: Critical Thinking, 0-13-099432-4
- Teacher Training Video 2: Stress Management & Communication, 0-13-099578-9
- Teacher Training Video 3: Classroom Tips, 0-13-917205-X

Faculty Development Series Workshops

- Carter: Faculty Development Workshop DVD, 0-13-199047-0
- Faculty Development Workshop on integrating Successful Intelligence, 0-13-514245-8

Current Issues Videos

- ABC News Video Series: Student Success, 2/E, 0-13-031901-5
- ABC News Video Series: Student Success, 3/E, 0-13-152865-3

Assessment

*Through partnership opportunities, we offer a variety of **assessment** options!*

LASSI—The LASSI is a 10-scale, 80-item assessment of students' awareness about and use of learning and study strategies. Addressing skill, will, and self-regulation, the focus is on both covert and overt thoughts, behaviors, attitudes, and beliefs that relate to successful learning and that can be altered through educational interventions. Available in two formats: Paper, 0-13-172315-4, or Online, 0-13-172316-2 (Access Card).

Noel Levitz/RMS—This retention tool measures Academic Motivation, General Coping Ability, Receptivity to Support Services, PLUS Social Motivation. It helps identify at-risk students, the areas with which they struggle, and their receptiveness to support. Available in Paper or Online formats, as well as Short and Long versions. PAPER Long Form A: 0-13-072258-8; PAPER Short Form B: 0-13-079193-8; Online Forms AB&C: 0-13-098158-3.

Robbins Self Assessment Library—This compilation teaches students to create a portfolio of skills. S.A.L. is a self-contained, interactive library of 49 behavioral questionnaires that help students discover new ideas about themselves, their attitudes, and their personal strengths and weaknesses. Available in Paper, 0-13-173861-5; CD-Rom, 0-13-221793-7; and Online, 0-13-243165-3, (Access Card) formats.

Readiness for Education at a Distance Indicator (READI)—READI is a Web-based tool that assesses the overall likelihood for online learning success. READI generates an immediate score and a diagnostic interpretation of results, including recommendations for successful participation in online courses and potential remediation sources. Please visit www.readi.info for additional information, 0-13-188967-2.

Diversity

*Teaching tolerance and discussing **diversity** with your students can be challenging!*

Responding to Hate at School—Published by the Southern Poverty Law Center, the Teaching Tolerance handbook is a step-by-step, easy-to-use guide designed to help administrators, counselors, and teachers react promptly and efficiently whenever hate, bias, and prejudice strike.

Custom Publishing

*For a truly tailored solution that fosters campus connections and increases retention, talk with us about **custom publishing**.*

Pearson Custom Publishing—We are the largest custom provider for print and media shaped to your course's needs. Please visit us at www.pearsoncustom.com to learn more.

STUDENT SUPPORT

Tools to help make the grade now, and excel in school later.

*We offer an **online study aid** to help students fully understand each chapter's content, assess their knowledge, and apply what they've learned.*

Companion Website—The text-specific website includes an online glossary of key terms, practice quizzes of objective and subjective questions, e-journaling activities, real student stories, and audio files from the authors. Please visit the site for this text at **www.prenhall.com/carter.**

*Our **Student Success SuperSite** is a one-stop shop for students to learn about career paths, self-awareness activities, cross-curricular practice opportunities, and more! This course-specific, rather than text-specific, website provides materials to supplement your student success course.*

SuperSite—**www.prenhall.com/success**

*We recognize students may want a **choice** of how their text is delivered.*

CourseSmart eTextbooks Online—Provides an alternative to the traditional print version of the text. The entire book can be purchased in an online format for 50% off the cost. Now students have a choice! Please visit www.coursesmart.com for additional information.

Where the web meets textbooks for STUDENT SAVINGS.

***Time management** is the #1 challenge students face. We can help.*

Prentice Hall Planner—A basic planner that includes a monthly and daily calendar, plus other materials to facilitate organization (8.5 × 11).

Premier Annual Planner—This specially designed, annual 4-color collegiate planner includes an academic planning/resources section, monthly planning section (2 pages/month), and weekly planning section (48 weeks; July start date), which facilitate short-term as well as long-term planning (spiral bound, 6 × 9).

***Journaling** activities promote self-discovery and self-awareness.*

Student Reflection Journal—Through this vehicle, students are encouraged to track their progress and share their insights, thoughts, and concerns (8½ × 11, 90 pages).

*Learning to adapt to the **diverse** college community is essential to students'
success.*

10 Ways to Fight Hate—Produced by the Southern Poverty Law Center, the
leading hate-crime and crime-watch organization in the United States, this
guide walks students through 10 steps that they can take on their own campus
or in their own neighborhood to fight hate every day, 0-13-028146-8.

*The **Student Orientation Series** includes short booklets on specialized
topics that facilitate greater student understanding.*

S.O.S. Guides—Connolly: *Learning Communities*, 0-13-232243-9, and
Watts: *Service Learning*, 0-13-232201-3, help students understand what
these opportunities are, how to take advantage
of them, and how to learn from
their peers while doing so. New to
the series is Hoffman: *Stop
Procrastinating Now!: 10 Simple
& SUCCESSFUL Steps for Student
Success*, 0-13-513056-5.

Quick Start to College, with its coverage of some basic information you need at the beginning of your course work, is designed to help you feel more in control as you start this important journey toward the achievement of a college education. As you read, consult your college handbook and/or website to learn about the specific resources, policies, and procedures of your college.

Start by learning what your college expects of you—and what you have a right to expect in return as a consumer of education. Continue on, to explore the people and resources that can help you while you are enrolled. Finally, consider the financial aid possibilities that can help you pay for it all.

What Your College Expects of You

If you clarify what it means to be a college student right at the start, you will minimize surprises that may be obstacles later on. What is expected of you may be different from anything you encountered in high school or in other educational settings. Because expectations differ from college to college, use the material that follows as general guidelines.

Follow Procedures and Fulfill Requirements

Understanding and following college procedures will smooth your path to success.

Registration

Registration may take place through your school's computer network, via an automated phone system, or in the school gym or student union. Scan the college catalog and Web site and consider these factors as you make your selections:

- Core/general requirements for graduation
- Your major or minor or courses in departments you are considering
- Electives that sound interesting, even if they are out of your field

Once you choose courses, but before you register, create a schedule that shows daily class times to see if the schedule will work out. Meet with your advisor for comments and approval.

Graduation and Curriculum Requirements

Every college has degree requirements stated in the catalog and Web site. Make sure you understand those that apply to you. Among the requirements you may encounter are these:
- Number of credits needed to graduate, including credits in major and minor fields

- Curriculum requirements, including specific course requirements
- Departmental major requirements

School Procedures

Your college has rules and regulations, found in the college handbook and on the Web site, for all students to follow. Among the most common procedures are these:

Adding or dropping a class. This should be done within the first few days of the term if you find that a course is not right for you or that there are better choices. Withdrawals after a predetermined date, except those approved for special cases, receive a failing grade.

Taking an Incomplete. If you can't finish your work due to circumstances beyond your control—an illness or injury, for example—many colleges allow you to take a grade of Incomplete. The school will require approval from your instructor and you will have to make up the work later.

Transferring schools. Research the degree requirements of other schools and submit transfer applications. If you are a student at a community college and intend to transfer to a four-year school, take the courses required for admission to that school. In addition, be sure all your credits are transferable, which means they will be counted toward your degree at the four-year school.

Understand Your School's Grading System

GRADE POINT
AVERAGE (GPA)

A measure of academic achievement computed by dividing the total number of grade points received by the total number of credits or hours of course work taken.

When you receive grades, remember that they reflect your work, not your self-worth. Most schools use grading systems with numerical grades or equivalent letter grades (see Key QS.1). Generally, the highest course grade is an A, or 4.0, and the lowest is an F, or 0.0.

In every course, you earn a certain number of college credits, called *hours*. For example, Accounting 101 may be worth three hours. These numbers generally refer to the number of hours the course meets per week. When you multiply each numerical course grade by the number of hours the course is worth, then take the average of all these numbers and divide by the total number of credit hours you are taking, you obtain your **grade point average,** or GPA.

Learn the minimum GPA needed to remain in good standing and to be accepted and continue in your major. Key QS.2 shows you how to calculate your GPA. You can also use Web resources such as www.back2college.com/gpa.htm to calculate your GPA electronically.

KEY QS.1 Letter grades and equivalent numerical grades per semester hour.

Letter grade	A	A−	B+	B	B−	C+	C	C−	D+	D	F
Numerical grade	4.0	3.7	3.3	3.0	2.7	2.3	2.0	1.7	1.3	1.0	0.0

KEY QS.2   An example that shows how to calculate your GPA.

COURSE	SEMESTER HOURS	GRADE	POINTS EARNED FOR THIS COURSE
Chemistry I	4	C (2.0 points)	4 credits × 2.0 points = 8
Freshman Writing	3	B+ (3.3 points)	3 credits × 3.3 points = 9.9
Spanish I	3	B− (2.7 points)	3 credits × 2.7 points = 8.1
Introduction to Statistics	3	C+ (2.3 points)	3 credits × 2.3 points = 6.9
Social Justice	2	A− (3.7 points)	2 credits × 3.7 points = 7.4
Total semester hours **Total grade points for semester**	**15**		**40.3**

GPA for semester (total grade points divided by semester hours): 40.3 divided by 15 = 2.69
Letter equivalent grade: C+/B−

Make the Most of Your School's Computer System

A large part of college communication and work involves the computer. In a given day you might access a syllabus online, e-mail a student, use the Internet to tap into a library database, write a draft of an assignment on a computer, and send a paper draft to an instructor electronically. Most dorm rooms are wired for computers, and an increasing number of campuses have wireless networks. Some schools are even moving to a "paperless" system where all student notifications are sent via e-mail, requiring every student to activate an e-mail account and check it regularly. Here are some suggestions for using your computer effectively:

- *Get trained.* Register for an e-mail account at your school and connect to the college network. Take classes to master word processing, data and spreadsheets, and the Internet. You may want to get trained in course management systems such as Blackboard if your school uses one.
- *Use computers to find information.* Frequent the college Web site and use library databases. If they are available, download podcasts of lectures.
- *Be a cautious user.* Save Save your work periodically onto a primary or backup hard drive, CD, or flash drive. In addition, install an antivirus program and update it regularly.
- *Stay on task.* During study time, try to stay away from Internet surfing, instant messaging, visiting Facebook pages, and playing computer games.

One of the most important directives for college students communicating via computer is to *follow guidelines when contacting instructors via e-mail.* When you submit assignments, take exams, or ask questions electronically, rules of etiquette promote civility and respect. Try these suggestions the next time you e-mail an instructor:

- *Use your university account.* Instructors are likely to delete unfamiliar e-mails from their overloaded e-mail in-boxes. "Helen_Miller@yourschool .edu" will get read—but "disastergirl@yahoo.com" may not.
- *Don't ask for information you can find on your own or bother your instructor with minor problems.* Flooding your instructor with unnecessary e-mails may work against you when you really need help.
- *Write a clear subject line.* State exactly what the e-mail is about.
- *Address the instructor by name and use his or her title.* "Hello Professor Smith" or "Hi Dr. Reynolds" is better than "Hey."
- *Be clear and comprehensive.* First, state your question or problem and what you want to achieve. For example, "In my essay, I believe I covered the key points. I would like to meet to discuss your critique." Next, if necessary, support your position, using bullet points if you have a number of support statements. Finally, end by thanking the instructor and signing your full name.
- *Avoid abbreviations and acronyms.* Write as though you were crafting a business letter, not a social e-mail to a friend.
- *Use complete sentences, correct punctuation, and capitalization.* Be sure to reread your e-mail before sending, so that you have a chance to correct any mistakes.
- *Give the instructor time to respond.* Don't expect a reply within two hours. If you hear nothing after a couple of days, send a follow-up note that contains the full text of your first message. A note that simply says "Did you get my last e-mail?" won't be helpful if for any reason your instructor didn't receive or read the first one.

Get Involved

Extracurricular activities give you a chance to meet people who share your interests and to develop teamwork and leadership skills as well as other skills that may be important in your career. In addition, being connected to friends and a supportive network of people is one of the main reasons people stay in school.

Some freshmen take on so many activities that they become overwhelmed. Pace yourself the first year. You can always add activities later. As you seek the right balance, consider this: Studies have shown that students who join organizations tend to persist in their educational goals more than those who don't branch out.[1]

Connect with People and Resources

During your first weeks of school—as you navigate through what may seem like a maze of classes and business offices—it is important to know that instructors, administrators, advisors, and a range of support staff are available to help. Groups and organizations also provide support and opportunities to broaden your experience. Tap into the following resources at your school.

Instructors and Teaching Assistants

The people who teach your courses—instructors and teaching assistants—are your most available human resources at college. You see them from one to five times per week and interact with them more directly than with any other authority on campus. They see your work and, if your class size is small, they hear your ideas and consequently may get to know you quite well. Instructors are potential resources and necessary allies in your education.

What kind of help might you seek from an instructor or teaching assistant?

- Clarification on material presented in class
- Help on homework
- Information about how to prepare for a test
- Consultation on a paper you are working on
- Details about why you received a particular grade on a test or assignment
- Advice about the department—courses, majoring—or related career areas

When you want to speak personally with an instructor for longer than a minute or two, choose your time carefully. Before or after class is usually not the best time for anything more than a quick question. When you need your instructor's full attention, there are three ways to get it: Make an appointment during office hours, send e-mail, or leave a voice mail message.

- *Office hours.* Instructors keep regular office hours. Generally, these appear on your syllabus and are posted on instructors' office doors and on instructors' or departmental Web pages. Always make an appointment for a conference. Face-to-face conferences are ideal for working through ideas and problems (for example, deciding on a term paper topic) or asking for advice (for example, looking for guidance on choosing courses in the department).
- *E-mail.* Use e-mail to clarify assignments and assignment deadlines, to ask questions about lectures or readings, and to clarify what will be covered on a test. Using the e-mailing guidelines presented earlier in Quick Start will increase the likelihood of receiving a positive response. Instructors' e-mail addresses are generally posted on the first day of class and may also appear in your handbook or syllabus.
- *Voice mail.* If something comes up at the last minute, you can leave a message in your instructor's voice mailbox. Make your message short, but specific ("This is Rick Jones from your ten o'clock Intro to Psychology class—I'm supposed to present my project today, but have a fever of 102 degrees"). Avoid calling instructors at home unless they give specific permission to do so.

If you are taking a large lecture course, you may have a primary instructor plus a *teaching assistant* (TA) who meets with a small group of students on a regular basis and grades your papers and exams. You may want to approach your TA with course-related questions and problems before approaching the instructor. Because TAs deal with fewer students, they may have more time to devote to specific issues.

Academic Advisors

In most colleges, every student is assigned an advisor who is the student's personal liaison with the college. (At some schools, students receive help at an advising center.) Your advisor will help you choose courses every term, plan your overall academic program, and understand college regulations, including graduation requirements. He or she will point out possible consequences of your decisions ("If you put off taking biology now, you're facing two lab courses next term"), help you shape your educational goals, and monitor your academic progress.

Although you are responsible for fully understanding graduation requirements—including credit requirements—and choosing the courses you need, your advisor is there to help you with these critical decisions. You will most likely be required to meet with your advisor once each term; however, you can schedule additional meetings if and when you need them.

MENTOR

A trusted counselor or guide who takes a special interest in helping you reach your goals.

Mentors

You may find a mentor during college who can give you a private audience for questions and problems, advice tailored to your needs, and support, guidance, and trust. In return, you owe it to a mentor to respectfully take advice into consideration. A mentor might be your advisor, an instructor in your major or minor field, or a resident assistant (RA). Some schools have faculty or peer mentoring programs to match students with people who can help them.

Tutors and Academic Centers

Tutors can give you valuable and detailed help on specific academic subjects. Most campuses have private tutoring available, and many schools offer free peer tutoring. If you feel you could benefit from the kind of one-on-one work a tutor can give, ask your instructor or your academic advisor to recommend a tutor. If your school has one or more academic centers, you may be able to find a tutor there. *Academic centers*, including reading, writing, math, and study-skills centers, offer consultations and tutoring to help students improve skills at all levels.

Administrators

Every college needs an administrative staff to operate smoothly and efficiently. One of the most important administrative offices for students is the Office of the Dean of Student Affairs, which, in many colleges, is the center for student services. Staff members there can answer your questions or direct you to others who can help. You will also encounter administrative offices involved with tuition payments, financial aid, and registration, as follows:

- The *bursar's office* (also called the office of finance or accounting office) issues bills for tuition and room and board and collects payments from students and financial aid sources.
- The *financial aid office* helps students apply for financial aid and understand the eligibility requirements of different federal, state, and private programs (see chapter 8 for more details on financial aid).

- The *registrar's office* handles course registration, sends grade reports, and compiles your official *transcript* (a comprehensive record of your courses and grades). Graduate school admissions offices require a copy of your transcript, as do many prospective employers.

Student-Centered Services

A host of services helps students succeed in college and deal with problems that arise. Here are some you may find.

Academic computer center. Most schools have computer facilities that are open daily, usually staffed by technicians who can assist you. Many facilities also offer training workshops.

Student housing or commuter affairs office. Residential colleges provide on-campus housing for undergraduate students. The housing office handles room and roommate placement and deals with special needs (for example, an allergic student's need for a room air conditioner) and problems. Schools with commuting students may have transportation and parking programs.

Health services. Health services generally include sick care, prescriptions, routine diagnostic tests, vaccinations, and first aid. All clinics are affiliated with nearby hospitals for emergency care. In addition, psychological counseling is sometimes offered through health services or at a separate facility. Many colleges require proof of health insurance at the time of registration.

Career services. This office helps students find part-time and full-time jobs, as well as summer jobs and internships. Career offices have reference files on careers and employers; they also help students learn to write résumés and cover letters and search job sites on the Internet; and they hold career fairs and provide space for employers to interview students on campus.

Services for disabled students. For students with documented disabilities, federal law requires that assistance be provided in the form of accommodations ranging from interpreters for the hearing impaired to ramps for students in wheelchairs. If you have a disability, visit this office to learn what is offered, and remember that this office is your advocate if you encounter problems.

Veterans' affairs. The Office of Veterans' Affairs provides veterans with services including academic and personal counseling and current benefit status, which may affect tuition waivers.

Resources for Minority Students

The term *minority* includes students of color; gay, lesbian, and bisexual students; and students from underrepresented cultures or religious backgrounds. Along with activities that appeal to the general student population, most colleges have organizations and services that support minority groups, including specialized student associations, cultural centers, arts groups with a minority focus, minority fraternities and sororities, and political-action groups.

Many minority students seek a balance, getting involved with members of their group as well as with the college mainstream. For example, a student may join the Latino Students Association as well as clubs for all students such as the campus newspaper or an athletic team.

Explore and Apply for Financial Aid

Financing your education—alone or with the help of your family—involves gathering financial information and making decisions about what you can afford and how much help you may need. *The first important step is to never assume you are not eligible for aid.* Almost all students are eligible for some kind of need-based or merit-based financial assistance.

Types of Aid

Aid comes in the form of student loans, grants, and scholarships.

Student loans. As the recipient of a student loan, you are responsible for paying back the amount you borrow, plus interest, according to a predetermined payment schedule that may stretch over a number of years. The federal government administers or oversees most student loans. To receive aid from any federal program, you must be a citizen or eligible non-citizen and be enrolled in a program that meets government requirements. Individual states may differ in their aid programs, so check with the financial office for details. Key QS.3 describes the main student loan programs.

Grants. Unlike student loans, grants do not require repayment. They are awarded to students who show financial need and can be funded by federal, state, or local governments as well as private organizations. Key QS.4 describes federal grant programs.

Scholarships. Scholarships are awarded to students who show talent or ability in specific areas (academic achievement, sports, the arts, citizenship, or leadership). They may be financed by government or private organizations, schools, or individuals.

 KEY QS.3

Get the details on federal student loan programs.

LOAN	DESCRIPTION
Perkins	Low, fixed rate of interest. Available to those with exceptional financial need (determined by a government formula). Issued by schools from their allotment of federal funds. Grace period of up to nine months after graduation before repayment, in monthly installments, must begin.
Stafford	Available to students enrolled at least half-time. Exceptional need not required, although students who prove need can qualify for a subsidized Stafford loan (the government pays interest until repayment begins). Two types of Staffords: the direct loan comes from federal funds, and the FFEL (Federal Family Education Loan) comes from a bank or credit union. Repayment begins six months after you graduate, leave school, or drop below half-time enrollment.
PLUS	Available to students enrolled at least half-time and claimed as dependents by their parents. Parents must undergo a credit check to be eligible, or may be sponsored through a relative or friend who passes the check. Loan comes from government or a bank or credit union. Sponsor must begin repayment 60 days after receiving the last loan payment.

KEY QS.4

Get the details on federal grant programs.

GRANT	DESCRIPTION
Pell	Need-based; the government evaluates your reported financial information and determines eligibility from that "score" (called an expected family contribution, or EFC). Available to undergraduates who have earned no other degrees. Amount varies according to education cost and EFC. Adding other aid sources is allowed.
Federal Supplemental Educational Opportunity (FSEOG)	Need-based; administered by the financial aid administrator at participating schools. Each participating school receives a limited amount of federal funds for FSEOGs and sets its own application deadlines.
Work-study	Need-based; encourages community service work or work related to your course of study. Pays by the hour, at least the federal minimum wage. Jobs may be on campus (usually for your school) or off (often with a nonprofit organization or a public agency).

Applying for Federal Aid

Anyone who wants to apply for federal aid needs to fill out the Free Application for Federal Student Aid (FAFSA) form either on paper or electronically. The form can be found at your library, at the Federal Student Aid Information Center, through your college's financial aid office or Web site, or via the U.S. Department of Education's Web site at www.ed.gov/finaid.html.

In recent years the FAFSA form has come under fire for its length (8 pages with 101 questions) and complexity, involving detailed and often hard-to-compile financial information. It is easy to be intimidated by the amount of work involved and to simply give up on the process altogether. The U.S. Department of Education, concerned about the low number of eligible students who apply for federal aid, has become aware of this "fear factor" that keeps people from making the most of this resource and is attempting to make the process more user-friendly.

The Department of Education has a new online tool called FAFSA4caster (FAFSA Forecaster). You or your parents can enter financial information into the tool and receive an estimate of the amount of federal aid you would qualify for, as well as an estimate of the amount of money that you would have to put in (the "expected family contribution"). The tool will also store your answers to FAFSA questions and transfer them to the FAFSA form when you make your actual aid application, reducing the form length by about half. Even with these changes, the process can still be challenging, so don't hesitate to ask for help from your financial aid office.

Additional information about federal grants and loans is available in the current version (updated yearly) of *The Student Guide to Federal Student Aid*. This publication can be found at your school's financial aid office, or you can request it by mail or phone (800-433-3243). The publication is also available online at http://studentaid.ed.gov/guide.

Managing the Application Process

The key word for success in this process is *early*. Research early; get forms early; apply early. The earlier you complete the process, the greater your chances of being considered for aid, especially when you are applying for part of a limited pool of federal funds granted to your college.

It can take work to locate financial aid opportunities; many aren't widely advertised. Start digging at your school's financial aid office and on the school Web site. Visit your library, bookstore, and the Internet for ideas. Funding guides catalog thousands of financial aid offers, and the Internet features online scholarship search services. Think carefully about what you should apply for and why, and get insight from someone in the financial aid office as you consider the options.

Your role in this process does not stop here. If you do receive aid from your college or elsewhere, follow all the rules and regulations, including remaining in academic good standing and meeting yearly application deadlines (in most cases, you will have to reapply *every year* for aid). Finally, take a new look at what's available to you each year; you may be eligible for different grants or scholarships at various points in your college career.

You are beginning the journey of your college education and lifelong learning. The work you do in this course will help you achieve your goals in your studies, your personal life, and your career. Psychologist Robert J. Sternberg, the originator of the successful intelligence concept that is the theme of *Keys to Success*, said that those who achieve success "create their own opportunities rather than let their opportunities be limited by the circumstances in which they happen to find themselves."[2] Let this book and this course help you create new and fulfilling oppurtunities on your path to success.

Endnotes

1. Alexander W. Astin, *Preventing Students from Dropping Out,* San Francisco: Jossey-Bass, 1976.
2. Robert J. Sternberg, *Successful Intelligence: How Practical and Creative Intelligence Determine Success in Life*, New York: Plume, 1997, p. 24.

PART
I

Defining Yourself and Your Goals

WELCOME TO COLLEGE

Opening Doors to Success

"Successfully intelligent people . . . have a can-do attitude. They realize that the limits to what they can accomplish are often in what they tell themselves they cannot do, rather than in what they really cannot do."

ROBERT STERNBERG

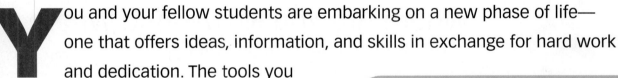

ou and your fellow students are embarking on a new phase of life—one that offers ideas, information, and skills in exchange for hard work and dedication. The tools you acquire in college will help you succeed in an ever-changing world where technology and the global marketplace are transforming the way you live and work. *Keys to Success* will help you learn successfully, graduate, and reap the personal and professional rewards of a solid education. This chapter gets you started with an overview of how being a "successfully intelligent," responsible, and forward-thinking student will help you face challenges head-on and achieve more than you ever imagined.

In this chapter you explore answers to the following questions:

- Where are you now—and where can college take you? 4
- How can successful intelligence help you achieve your goals? 7
- What actions will prepare you for college success? 11
- How can you work effectively with others? 20
- How can the things you learn now promote life success? 24
- Successful Intelligence Wrap-Up 26

Analytical

- Evaluating your starting point as you begin college
- Analyzing how successful intelligence can help you achieve goals
- Considering how specific actions promote success in college

Creative

- Creating new ideas about college goals
- Developing a fresh understanding of your ability to grow
- Creating ways to benefit from failure

Practical

- How to follow the code of academic integrity
- How to work with others effectively
- How to become a lifelong learner

Where Are You Now—And Where Can College Take You?

Reflect on the road that brought you to this day. You completed high school or its equivalent. You may have built life skills from experience as a partner or parent. You may have been employed in one or more jobs or completed a tour of duty in the armed forces. You have enrolled in college, found a way to pay for it, signed up for courses, and shown up for class. And, in deciding to pursue a degree, you chose to believe in your ability to accomplish goals. You have earned this opportunity to be a college student!

To make the most of college, first understand its value. College is the ideal time to acquire skills that will serve you in the global marketplace, where workers in the United States work seamlessly with people in other parts of the world. Thomas Friedman, author of *The World Is Flat*, explains how the digital revolution has transformed the working environment you will enter after college: "It is now possible for more people than ever to collaborate and compete in real time with more other people on more different kinds of work from more different corners of the planet and on a more equal footing than in any previous time in the history of the world—using computers, e-mail, networks, teleconferencing, and dynamic new software."[1]

This means that you may be doing *knowledge work* and other jobs in conjunction with, or in competition with, highly trained and motivated people from around the world. Reaching your potential has never been

GLOBAL MARKETPLACE

An interconnected marketplace, where companies do business without regard to time zones and boundaries, and where companies from all over the world compete directly for business.

REAL QUESTIONS

How can I make the transition to college easier?

I grew up in a diverse community and am in the first generation of my family to attend college. In high school, making friends and fitting in was very easy for me. However, I am nervous about the college experience. One reason is that I don't have role models in my family for what college is all about, and another is that the student body at my college has a different cultural makeup than my high school and community. When I tried meeting people on campus the first day I visited, I didn't feel like I made any real connections. What can I do to make the change easier?

Kevin Abreu
Montclair State University
Montclair, New Jersey

PRACTICAL ANSWERS

Jennifer Joralmon
can Sign Language Instructor
se Valley Community College,
Phoenix, Arizona

Forge connections with organizations, role models, and fellow students.

You're asking questions and that's the best first step. I think one of the fastest ways to feel more a part of college is to visit your Student Affairs office to find a list of clubs and activities. Pick a couple that pique your interest and check them out. Meeting people who share your interests will help you feel more connected. Also, assess your academic strengths and weaknesses. If you're strong in a certain subject, such as a second language or math, visit the on-campus tutoring center and apply to become a tutor. Or, if you're weak in a subject, get the extra help early. You'll meet other students—both tutors and those who are seeking help.

Another way to ease the transition is to seek out an adult role model. As you attend your classes, find an instructor you feel comfortable with—or talk to a counselor or advisor. Ask that person questions about how to navigate college, such as how to withdraw from a class or what to do if the bookstore has run out of the text you need. Many schools, such as mine, have peer or student leadership programs where you can find an older student to explain the ins and outs of college, including which teachers and courses to seek out and which to avoid.

Above all, stick with it and remember that you're not the only one feeling awkward. I see so many students start school that way who end up having a great experience. Try some of these suggestions and experiment with your own. In fact, try introducing yourself to the person next to you in class. Who knows? That student may be feeling the same way you are.

more crucial to your success. You will be up to the task of succeeding in the global marketplace if you do the following:

- Acquire solid study skills
- Commit to lifelong learning and job training
- Persevere despite obstacles
- Perform high-quality work on a consistent basis
- Embrace change as a way of life

More education is likely to mean more income.

Median annual income of persons with income 25 years old and over, by gender and highest level of education, 2002

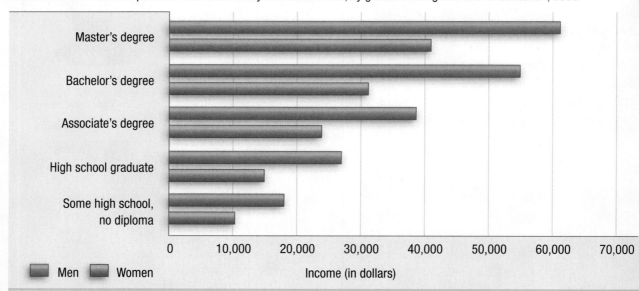

Source: U.S. Census Bureau, "Income, Poverty, and Health Insurance Coverage in the United States, 2003," *Current Population Reports*, Series P60-226, August 2004.

On a more personal level, college can help you achieve overarching "life success goals":

Life Success Goal: Increased employability and earning potential. Getting a degree greatly increases your chances of finding and keeping a highly skilled, well-paying job. College graduates earn, on average, around $20,000 more per year than those with just a high school diploma (see Key 1.1). Furthermore, the unemployment rate for college graduates is less than half that of high school graduates (see Key 1.2).

Life Success Goal: Preparation for career success. Your course work will give you the knowledge and hands-on skills you need to achieve your career goals. It will also expose you to a variety of careers and areas of academic specialty, many of which you may not have even heard of. Completing college will open career doors that are closed to those without a degree.

Life Success Goal: Smart personal health choices. The more educated you are, the more likely you are to take care of your physical and mental health. A college education prepares you with health-related information and attitudes that you will use over your lifetime, helping you to practice wellness through positive actions and to avoid practices with the potential to harm.

Life Success Goal: Active community involvement and an appreciation of different cultures. Going to college prepares you to understand complex

KEY 1.2

More education is likely to mean more consistent employment.

Unemployment rates of persons 25 years old and over, by highest level of education, 2005

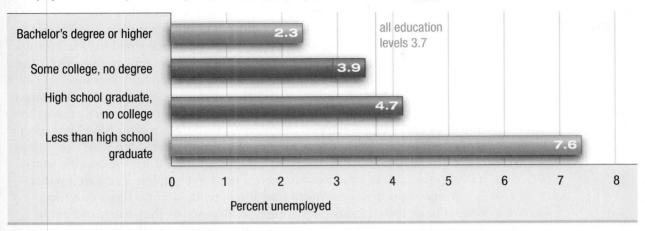

Source: U.S. Department of Labor, Bureau of Labor Statistics, Office of Employment and Unemployment Statistics, "Employment and Earnings," January 2005.

political, economic, and social forces that affect you and others. This understanding is the basis for good citizenship and encourages community involvement. Your education also exposes you to the ways in which people and cultures are different and how these differences affect world affairs. As a worker likely to encounter many cultures in the global marketplace, this knowledge will help you succeed.

Life Success Goal: Self-knowledge. Being in college gets you thinking about yourself on a big-picture level. What do you do well? What do you want out of life? What can you improve? College gives you the chance to evaluate where you are and decide where you want to be.

This course and *Keys to Success* provide the tools you need to kick off this exploration. Especially crucial is your ability to use *successful intelligence*— your most important goal-achievement tool, and the theme of this text.

How Can Successful Intelligence Help You Achieve Your Goals?

Think about how you define *intelligence*. Many people view an intelligent person as someone with "book smarts," someone who will excel in high-level analytical courses and go on to a brilliant career in a challenging profession such as science or law. Traditionally, many people have also believed that each individual is born with a fixed amount of intelligence, and that this has a significant effect on success. Another fairly common belief is that standardized tests, such as IQ (intelligence quotient) tests, accurately measure a person's intelligence and are predictors of success.

Psychologist Robert J. Sternberg has an entirely different view of intelligence. His life experiences convinced him that traditional intelligence measurements lock people into poor performances and often do not accurately reflect their potential for life success. When test anxiety caused Sternberg to score poorly on IQ and other standardized tests during elementary school, he delivered exactly what was expected of him—very little. In the fourth grade, when a teacher expected more from him than he had ever shown he could give, she provided a spark that turned his life around.

Sternberg asserts that IQ tests, the Scholastic Assessment Test (SAT), the American College Test (ACT), and other standardized tests measure inert intelligence. He further explains that those who score well on tests may have strong recall and analytical skills, but they do not necessarily have the power to make things happen in the real world.[2] No matter how high you score on a library science test, for example, your knowledge won't serve you unless you can use it to locate, in a short amount of time, the specific journals, books, and Internet resources you need to complete a research paper.

Sternberg is also convinced that intelligence is *not* a fixed quantity; people have the capacity to increase intelligence as they learn and grow. Recent studies support this perspective, showing that the brain continues to develop throughout life if you continue to learn new things.[3] To make this development happen, you need to actively challenge yourself and believe in your ability to grow. Psychologist Carol Dweck says that "people with a growth mindset thrive when they're stretching themselves."[4] Conversely, people who shy away from challenge will experience less growth. Challenge yourself, and your value to yourself and to others will grow.

> **INERT INTELLIGENCE**
> Passive recall and analysis of learned information rather than goal-directed thinking linked to real-world activities.

Defining Successful Intelligence

In his book *Successful Intelligence: How Practical and Creative Intelligence Determine Success in Life*, Sternberg focuses on what he calls *successful intelligence*—"the kind of intelligence used to achieve important goals."[5] Successful intelligence better predicts life success than any IQ test because it focuses largely on actions—what you *do* to achieve your goals—instead of just on recall and analysis.

Sternberg uses this story to illustrate the impact of successful intelligence:

> *Two boys are walking in a forest. They are quite different. The first boy's teachers think he is smart, his parents think he is smart, and as a result, he thinks he is smart. He has good test scores, good grades, and other good paper credentials that will get him far in his scholastic life.*
>
> *Few people consider the second boy smart. His test scores are nothing great, his grades aren't so good, and his other paper credentials are, in general, marginal. At best, people would call him shrewd or street smart.*
>
> *As the two boys walk along in the forest, they encounter a problem—a huge, furious, hungry-looking grizzly bear, charging straight at them. The first boy, calculating that the grizzly bear will overtake them in 17.3 seconds, panics. In this state, he looks at the second boy, who is calmly taking off his hiking boots and putting on his jogging shoes.*

The first boy says to the second boy, "You must be crazy. There is no way you are going to outrun that grizzly bear!"

The second boy replies, "That's true. But all I have to do is outrun you!" [6]

This story shows that successful problem solving and decision making require more than book smarts. When confronted with a problem, using *only* analytical thinking put the first boy at a disadvantage. On the other hand, the second boy thought in different ways; he analyzed the situation, creatively considered the options, and took practical action. He asked and answered questions. He knew his purpose. And he lived to tell the tale.

Sternberg breaks successful intelligence into three parts or abilities:

- *Analytical thinking*—commonly known as *critical thinking*—involves analyzing and evaluating information, often in order to work through a problem or decision. Analytical thinking is largely responsible for school success and is measured through traditional testing methods.

- *Creative thinking* involves generating new and different ideas and approaches to problems and, often, viewing the world in ways that disregard convention.

- *Practical thinking* means putting what you've learned into action in order to solve a problem or make a decision—and carrying what you learn from the experience with you to use with future situations. Practical thinking enables you to accomplish goals despite obstacles.

Together, these abilities move you toward a goal, as Sternberg explains:

> Analytical thinking is required to solve problems and to judge the quality of ideas. Creative intelligence is required to formulate good problems and ideas in the first place. Practical intelligence is needed to use the ideas and their analysis in an effective way in one's everyday life. [7]

Learning is not the only benefit of engaging successful intelligence. Using practical and creative skills also contributes to relationship building and a sense of fun in the classroom.

Here are two examples that illustrate how this works.

Successful intelligence in a study group—reaching for the goal of helping each other learn:

- *Analyze* the concepts you must learn, including how they relate to what you already know.
- *Create* humorous memory devices to help you remember key concepts.
- *Think practically* about who in the group does what best, and assign tasks accordingly.

Successful intelligence regarding academics—reaching for the goal of declaring a major:

- *Analyze* what you do well and like to do. Then analyze the course offerings in your college catalog until you come up with one or more that seem to mesh with your strengths.

- *Create* a dream career, then come up with majors that support it. For example, if you want to be a science writer, consider majoring in biology and minoring in journalism.

- *Think practically* about your major by talking with students and instructors in the department, looking at course requirements, and interviewing professionals in fields of interest.

Why is successful intelligence your key to success? It helps you understand how learning propels you toward goals, boosting your desire to learn. It gives you ways to move toward those goals, increasing your willingness to work hard. It helps you to maximize strengths and compensate for weaknesses, leading to a greater ability to capitalize on who you are and what you can do. It also increases your value in school and on the job: *People with highly developed critical, creative, and practical thinking skills are in demand because they can apply what they know to new situations, innovate, and accomplish their goals.*

The three elements of successful intelligence can give all kinds of learners a more positive outlook on their abilities. Students who have trouble with tests and other analytical skills can see that creative and practical thinking also play a significant role in success. Students who test well but have trouble using their knowledge to innovate and make things happen can develop a team approach to success as they work to improve their creative and practical skills. Everyone can find room, and ways, to grow.

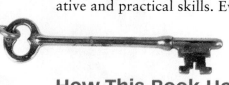

How This Book Helps You Build Successful Intelligence

Keys to Success is designed to help you build the analytical, creative, and practical thinking skills that will get you where you want to go in school and in life.

Chapter Content

Each chapter incorporates successful intelligence with the following:

- A visual overview of the analytical, creative, and practical tools that you will gather in the chapter

- Contextual connections to analytical, creative, and practical thinking

- Accounts and examples from students, professors, and professionals that show how people use various analytical, creative, and practical skills to accomplish goals

- A *Successful Intelligence Wrap-Up* that summarizes the analytical, creative, and practical skills you have explored

In addition, chapter 4—the chapter on thinking—goes into more detail about all three skills.

In-Chapter Activities

Within the text of each chapter, you will find three activities that help you build your successful intelligence skills:

- *Get Analytical* gives you an opportunity to develop your own analytical skills through your analysis of a chapter topic.

- *Get Creative* prompts you to develop your own creative skills as you think innovatively about chapter material.
- *Get Practical* provides a chance to develop your own practical skills through the experience of applying an idea from the chapter.

In this chapter, these exercises take the form of mini-assessments—tools that will help you get to know yourself as an analytical, creative, and practical thinker. With self-knowledge as the starting point, you will develop your successful intelligence throughout this book. Chapter 8 will provide an opportunity for you to assess yourself once again and consider how you have grown in each area.

End-of-Chapter Exercises

Here you have the opportunity to combine what you have learned and apply it to important tasks in several ways, as follows:

- *Successful Intelligence: Think, Create, Apply* unites the three aspects of successful intelligence.
- *Teamwork: Create Solutions Together* encourages you to apply various successful intelligence elements to a group setting.
- *Writing: Journal and Put Skills to Work* provides an opportunity to put analysis, creative thoughts, and practical ideas down in words.
- *Personal Portfolio: Prepare for Career Success* builds practical skills and a portfolio of information that promote career success.

Whereas successful intelligence is the overarching framework of how you will achieve college and life goals, many specific elements move you toward those goals day by day. Explore attitudes and actions that prepare you for success.

What Actions Will Prepare You for College Success?

Preparing for college success is as much a state of mind as it is making sure you take specific actions. The following section points to the basics you need—in actions as well as attitude—to achieve your goals. Always remember that you are your own manager, in charge of meeting your obligations and making decisions that move you toward your goals.

Be Responsible and Accountable

Your primary responsibility as a student is to pursue academic excellence—to do your very best in every course so that you come away with knowledge and marketable skills. The theme of *responsibility* stands out in how two New Mexico State University students describe the struggle to adjust to college life:[8]

Angie Miller (majoring in Biology): The hardest part of my [freshman] courses was that I had to do all my work myself with nobody telling me every day that my homework was due. . . . Also, I felt that there was more

GET ANALYTICAL!

Assess Yourself as an Analytical Thinker

For each statement, circle the number that feels right to you, from 1 for "not at all true for me" to 5 for "very true for me."

1. I recognize and define problems effectively.   1 2 3 4 5

2. I see myself as "a thinker," "analytical," "studious."   1 2 3 4 5

3. When working on a problem in a group setting, I like   1 2 3 4 5
   to break down the problem into its components and
   evaluate them.

4. I need to see convincing evidence before accepting   1 2 3 4 5
   information as fact.

5. I weigh the pros and cons of plans and ideas before   1 2 3 4 5
   taking action.

6. I tend to make connections among pieces of   1 2 3 4 5
   information by categorizing them.

7. Impulsive, spontaneous decision making worries me.   1 2 3 4 5

8. I like to analyze causes and effects when making   1 2 3 4 5
   a decision.

9. I monitor my progress toward goals.   1 2 3 4 5

10. Once I reach a goal, I evaluate the process to see   1 2 3 4 5
    how effective it was.

Total your answers here: _____

If your total ranges from 38–50, you consider your analytical thinking skills to be *strong*.

If your total ranges from 24–37, you consider your analytical thinking skills to be *average*.

If your total ranges from 10–23, you consider your analytical thinking skills to be *weak*.

Remember that you can improve your analytical thinking skill with focus and practice.

material covered in a shorter time period, so it was more study time than in high school.

   Daniel Estrada (majoring in Latin American History and Spanish):
I find that . . . the [classes are] more to my interest since I picked [them].

Now the catch is that it is not up to the instructor to keep you on task. . . . It is left unsaid that it is our responsibility to keep up with the reading, homework, and actually showing up for class.

As a student, you show responsibility by taking a series of small but important actions that are the building blocks of academic success:

- Read assigned material before it is discussed in class.
- Attend class on time and with a positive attitude.
- Complete assignments on schedule.
- Listen attentively, take notes, and participate in discussions.
- Study for exams, either on your own or with others.
- Communicate with instructors and students, and seek help from them if you need it.

A critical responsibility in each class is to thoroughly read your syllabus and refer to it frequently throughout the term. You will receive a syllabus at the first class meeting of each of your courses. Consider each syllabus as a "contract" between you and your instructor, outlining what your instructor expects of you (such as readings, assignments, and class participation) as well as what you can expect from your instructor (availability, schedule of topics, clarification of grading system).

Your syllabus will answer questions about course focus, required and optional reading, schedule of coverage, dates of exams and due dates for assignments, the components of your final grade, and more. Marking up your syllabus in your own way will help remind you of responsibilities, as will "backdating"—in other words, noting in your datebook, calendar, or PDA the interim goals you have to achieve by particular dates in order to complete more involved assignments. For example, if you have a 15-page paper due on October 15, you would enter dates in September and October for goals like choosing a topic, research, first draft, and final draft. Key 1.3 shows a portion of an actual syllabus with important items noted.

Finally, in all of your daily academic tasks, persist until you know exactly what you need to accomplish so that you can complete your work on time. Persistence is the responsible student's master key.

SYLLABUS

A comprehensive outline of course topics and assignments.

PERSISTENCE

The act of continuing steadfastly in a course of action, even in the face of obstacles or challenges.

Get Motivated

Success is a process, not a fixed mark. Motivation is what keeps the process in motion. Successfully intelligent people find ways to motivate themselves to learn, grow, and work toward what they want. Your challenge as you begin college is to identify and activate the forces that move you forward. These *motivators*—grades, love of a subject, the drive to earn a degree—can change with time and situations.

The primary key to motivation is to continually remind yourself of what you stand to gain from achieving your most important goals. A nursing student at Palo Alto College in San Antonio, Texas, understands how goals relate to motivation: "To stay motivated I will always remember that I am doing this to better myself and to learn what I need to in order to be the best nurse that I can be. Making a commitment and staying true to it is not easy, but I know that an uncommitted person will never finish anything."[9]

MOTIVATION

A goal-directed force that moves a person to action.

ENG 122 Spring 2007

Instructor: Jennifer Gessner
Office Hours: Tue & Thur 12:30–1:30 (or by appointment) in DC 305
Phone: 303-555-2222
E-mail: jg@abc.xyz

How to connect with the instructor

Required Texts: *Good Reasons with Contemporary Arguments,* Faigley and Selzer
A Writer's Reference, 5th ed., Diana Hacker

Required Materials:
- a notebook with lots of paper
- a folder for keeping everything from this class
- an active imagination and critical thinking

Books and materials to get ASAP

Course Description: This course focuses on argumentative writing and the researched paper. Students will practice the rhetorical art of argumentation and will gain experience in finding and incorporating researched materials into an extended paper.

Writer's Notebook: All students will keep, and bring to class, a notebook with blank paper. Throughout the semester, you will be given writing assignments to complete in this book. You must bring to class and be prepared to share any notebook assignment. Notebook assignments will be collected frequently, though sometimes randomly, and graded only for their completeness, not for spelling, etc.

Course coverage, expectations, responsibilities

Grading:
- Major Writing Assignments worth 100 points each.
- Final Research Project worth 300 points.
- Additional exercises and assignments range from 10 to 50 points each.
- Class participation: Based on the degree to which you complete the homework and present this in a thoughtful, meaningful manner in class.
- Attendance: Attendance is taken daily and students may miss up to three days of class without penalty, but will lose 5 points for each day missed thereafter.
- Late work: All work will lose 10% of earned points per class day late. No work will be accepted after five class days or the last class meeting.

How grades are determined for this course

Final Grade: The average of the total points possible (points earned divided by the total possible points). 100–90% = A; 89–80% = B; 79–70% = C (any grade below 70% is not passing for this class).

Academic Integrity: Students must credit any material used in their papers that is not their own (including direct quotes, paraphrases, figures, etc.). Failure to do so constitutes plagiarism, which is illegal, unethical, <u>always recognizable</u>, and a guaranteed way to fail a paper. The definition of plagiarism is "to steal and use (the writings or ideas of another) as one's own."

Reflects school's academic integrity policy

Week 4
2/1   The Concise Opinion.
               HW: Complete paper #1 Rough Draft (5–7 pages double-spaced)

Topics of that day's class meeting

Notice of due date for paper draft

2/3   How Professionals Argue
               HW: Read Jenkins Essay (p 501 of *Good Reasons) and* Rafferty Essay (p 525); compare argumentative style, assess and explain efficacy of arguments.

Notice of reading assignments to complete

Week 5
2/15   Developing an Argument
               Essay Quiz on Jenkins and Rafferty Essays
               HW: Chap 5 of *Good Reasons;* based on components of a definition of argument, write a brief explanation of how your argument might fit into this type.

Notice of quiz

2/17   Library Workday: Meet in Room 292
               PAPER #1 DUE

Notice of final due date for paper

Source: Jennifer Gessner, Community College of Denver.

Low self-esteem and fear can stall your motivation. Here are some ideas about how to overcome these roadblocks and keep moving ahead.

Build Self-Esteem

When people have faith in themselves, their self-esteem fuels their motivation to succeed. Belief, though, is only half the game. The other half is the action and effort that help you feel that you have earned your self-esteem, as basketball coach Rick Pitino explains: "Self-esteem is directly linked to deserving success. If you have established a great work ethic and have begun the discipline that is inherent with that, you will automatically begin to feel better about yourself."[10]

Although thinking positively sets the tone for success, taking action gets you there. In order to get moving in a positive direction, create personal guidelines that support your success—for example, "I turn in assignments on deadline." Then, follow up your guideline with the action you've promised to take—in this case, always turning in your assignments on time.

Face Your Fears

Everyone experiences fear. Anything unknown—starting college, meeting new people, encountering new challenges—can be frightening. The following steps will help you work through fear with courage and reignite your motivation to succeed:

1. *Acknowledge fears.* Naming your fear begins to lessen its hold on you. Be specific.

2. *Examine fears.* Sometimes one fear hides a larger one. Do you fear a test, or the fact that if you pass it you will have to take a tougher class next?

3. *Develop and implement a plan.* Come up with ways to overcome your fear, and put them to work. For example, if reading a play by William Shakespeare intimidates you, you might ask an instructor for advice, rent a film adaptation, or listen to an audio version on your iPod.

Practice Academic Integrity

Having academic integrity means valuing education and learning over grades. Academic integrity promotes learning and ensures a quality education based on *ethics* (your sense of what is right to do) and hard work. Read your school's code of honor, or academic integrity policy, in your student handbook. When you enrolled, you agreed to abide by it.

What Academic Integrity Is

The Center for Academic Integrity, part of the Kenan Institute for Ethics at Duke University, defines academic integrity as a commitment to five fundamental values:[11]

- *Honesty.* Honesty defines the pursuit of knowledge and implies a search for truth in your classwork, papers and lab reports, and teamwork with other students.

SELF-ESTEEM
Belief in one's value as a person that builds as you achieve your goals.

ACADEMIC INTEGRITY
Following a code of moral values, prizing honesty and fairness in all aspects of academic life—classes, assignments, tests, papers, projects, and relationships with students and faculty.

- *Trust.* Trust means being true to your word. Mutual trust—between instructor and student, as well as among students—makes possible the exchange of ideas that is essential for learning.

- *Fairness.* Instructors must create a fair academic environment where students are judged against clear standards and in which procedures are well defined.

- *Respect.* In a respectful academic environment, both students and instructors accept and honor a wide range of opinions, even if the opinions are contrary to core beliefs.

- *Responsibility.* You are responsible for making choices that will provide you with the best education—choices that reflect fairness and honesty.

Unfortunately, the principles of academic integrity are frequently violated on college campuses. In a recent survey, three of four college students admitted to cheating at least once during their undergraduate careers.[12] Violations of academic integrity—turning in previously submitted work, using unauthorized devices during an exam, providing unethical aid to another student, or downloading passages or whole papers from the Internet—aren't worth the price. Consequences of violations vary from school to school and include participation in academic integrity seminars, grade reduction or course failure, suspension, or expulsion.

Why Academic Integrity Is Worth It

Choosing to act with integrity has the following positive effects:

- *Increased self-esteem.* Self-esteem is tied to respectful and honorable action.

- *Acquired knowledge.* Honest work is more likely to result in knowledge that lasts.

- *Effective behavioral patterns.* When you play fair now, you set a positive pattern.

- *Mutual respect.* Respecting the work of others will encourage others to respect your work.

The risk to students who violate standards of integrity is growing because cheating is now easier to discover. Make a commitment to uphold the highest standards of academic integrity.

Understand and Manage Learning Disabilities

The following will help you understand learning disabilities and, should you be diagnosed with one, give you the tools to manage your disability successfully.

The National Center for Learning Disabilities (NCLD) defines learning disabilities as follows:[13]

- They are neurological disorders that interfere with one's ability to store, process, and produce information.

- They do *not* include mental retardation, autism, behavioral disorders, impaired vision, hearing loss, or other physical disabilities.

- They do *not* include attention deficit disorder and attention deficit hyperactivity disorder, although these problems may accompany learning disabilities.[14]
- They often run in families and are lifelong, although people with learning disabilities can use specific strategies to manage and even overcome areas of weakness.
- Persons with a disability must be diagnosed by professionals in order to receive federally funded aid.

How can you determine if you should be evaluated for a learning disability? According to the NCLD, persistent problems in any of the following areas may indicate a learning disability:[15]

- Reading or reading comprehension
- Math calculations, understanding language and concepts
- Social skills or interpreting social cues
- Following a schedule, being on time, meeting deadlines
- Reading or following maps
- Balancing a checkbook
- Following directions, especially on multistep tasks
- Writing, sentence structure, spelling, and organizing written work

For an evaluation, contact your school's learning center or student health center for a referral to a licensed professional. If you are diagnosed with a learning disability, focused action will help you manage it and maximize your ability to learn and succeed.

Be informed about your disability. Search the library and the Internet—try NCLD at www.ncld.org or LD Online at www.ldonline.org (other Web sites are listed at the end of the chapter). Or call NCLD at 1-888-575-7373. Make sure you understand your individualized education program (IEP)— the document describing your disability and recommended strategies.

Seek assistance from your school. Speak with your advisor about specific accommodations that will help you learn. Services mandated by law for students who have learning disabilities include extended time on tests, note-taking assistance, assistive technology devices (such as tape recorders or laptop computers), alternative assessments and test formats, tutoring, and study skills assistance.

Be a dedicated student. Be in class and on time. Read assignments before class. Sit where you can focus. Review notes soon after class. Spend extra time on assignments. Ask for help.

Build a positive attitude. See your accomplishments in light of how far you have come. Rely on people who support you. Know that help will give you the best possible chance to learn and grow.

Learn from Failure and Celebrate Success

Even the most successful people make mistakes and experience failures. In fact, failure is one of the greatest teachers. Failure provides an opportunity to realize what you didn't know so that you can improve.

Learning from Failure

Learning from your failures and mistakes involves careful thinking.

Analyze what happened. For example, imagine that after a long night of studying for a chemistry test, you forgot to complete an American history paper due the next day. Your focus on the test caused you to overlook other tasks. Now you may face a lower grade on your paper if you turn it in late, plus you may be inclined to rush it and turn in a product that isn't as good as it could be.

Come up with creative ways to improve the situation and change for the future. In the present, you can request an appointment with the instructor to discuss the paper. For the future, you can make a commitment to note deadlines in a bright color in your planner and to check due dates more often.

Put your plan into action. Do what you have decided to do—and keep an eye on how it is working. Talk with the instructor and see if you can hand in your paper late. If you decide to be better about noting deadlines, in the future you might work backwards from your paper due date, setting dates for individual tasks related to the paper and planning to have it done two days before it is due in order to have time for last-minute corrections.

Sometimes, however, you can't get motivated to turn things around. Here are some ways to boost your outlook when failure gets you down:

- Believe you are a capable person. Focus on your strengths and know you can try again.
- Share your disappointment with others. Blow off steam and exchange creative ideas that can help you learn from what happened.
- Look on the bright side. At worst, you got a lower grade because your paper was late. At best, you learned lessons that will help you avoid the same mistake in the future.

Your value as a human being does not diminish when you make a mistake. People who can manage failure demonstrate to themselves and others that they have the courage to take risks and learn. Employers often value risk takers more than people who always play it safe.

Celebrating Success

Take a moment to acknowledge what you accomplish, whether it is a good grade, a job offer, or any personal victory. Let your success fuel your confidence that you can do it again. Don't forget to reward yourself when you succeed. Take the kind of break you like best—see a movie, socialize with some friends, read a book for fun, declare a no-work day. Enjoy what college has to offer outside of the classroom.

Finally, being a motivated, responsible, ethical, and committed student is no easy feat. Don't hesitate to reach out for support throughout your college experience.

Assess Yourself as a Creative Thinker

For each statement, circle the number that feels right to you, from 1 for "not at all true for me" to 5 for "very true for me."

1. I tend to question rules and regulations.   1 2 3 4 5

2. I see myself as "unique," "full of ideas," "innovative."   1 2 3 4 5

3. When working on a problem in a group setting, I generate a lot of ideas. 1 2 3 4 5

4. I am energized when I have a brand-new experience.   1 2 3 4 5

5. If you say something is too risky, I'm ready to give it a shot.   1 2 3 4 5

6. I often wonder if there is a different way to do or see something.   1 2 3 4 5

7. Too much routine in my work or schedule drains my energy.   1 2 3 4 5

8. I tend to see connections among ideas that others do not.   1 2 3 4 5

9. I feel comfortable allowing myself to make mistakes as I test out ideas. 1 2 3 4 5

10. I'm willing to champion an idea even when others disagree with me.   1 2 3 4 5

Total your answers here: _____

If your total ranges from 38–50, you consider your creative thinking skills to be *strong*.

If your total ranges from 24–37, you consider your creative thinking skills to be *average*.

If your total ranges from 10–23, you consider your creative thinking skills to be *weak*.

Remember that you can improve your creative thinking skill with focus and practice.

How Can You Work Effectively with Others?

A century ago it was possible to live an entire lifetime surrounded only by people from your own culture. Not so today. American society consists of people from a multitude of countries and cultural backgrounds. In fact, in the 2000 census, American citizens described themselves in terms of 63 different racial categories, compared with only 5 in 1990.[16] Cable television, the Internet, and the global marketplace add to our growing cultural awareness, linking people from all over the world in ways that were unimaginable less than a decade ago.

Your success at school and at work will depend on your ability to cooperate with diverse people in a team setting. Valuing diversity and knowing how to work in groups are two keys to developing this ability.

Value Diversity

What does *diversity* mean?

Diversity means differences among people. On an interpersonal level, diversity refers to the differences between ourselves and others, between the groups we belong to and the groups we are not part of. Differences in gender, skin color, ethnicity and national origin, age, physical characteristics and abilities, and sexual orientation are most obvious in this level of diversity. Differences in cultural and religious beliefs and practices, education, socioeconomic status, family background, and marital and parental status are less visible but no less significant in how they define people and affect relationships.

In college you are likely to meet classmates and instructors who reflect America's growing diversity, including people in the following demographic groups:

- Biracial or multiracial individuals
- People from families with more than one religious tradition
- Non-native English speakers who may have emigrated from outside the United States
- People older than "traditional" 18- to 22-year-old students
- Persons living with various kinds of disabilities
- Persons practicing different lifestyles—often expressed in the way they dress, their interests, their sexual orientation, or their leisure activities

Being able to appreciate and adjust to differences among people is crucial to your success at school and prepares you for success in life. Former University of Michigan student Fiona Rose describes the benefits of a positive approach to diversity this way:

My years at U-M have been enhanced by relationships with men and women from all cultures, classes, races, and ethnicities. Such interactions are essential to an education. While courses teach us the history and academic value of diversity, friendships prepare us to survive and thrive in our global community. Good institutions consider not only what a potential student will gain from classes and course work, but what he or she will bring to the campus community.[17]

Diversity refers to the differences within people. Another layer of diversity lies within each person. Among the factors that define this layer are personality traits, learning style, strengths and weaknesses, and natural talents and interests. No one else has been or will ever be exactly like you.

Chapter 3 will go into more detail about diversity and communication as well as about how people learn—a less visible but no less important aspect of personal diversity. Additionally, in chapter 4 you will explore differences in analytical, creative, and practical abilities.

Develop Emotional and Social Intelligence

Successful relationships in a diverse world depend on competencies that go beyond intellectual and career skills. All relationships depend on what psychologist Daniel Goleman calls emotional intelligence and social intelligence.

Emotional Intelligence

Your emotional intelligence quotient (EQ) is a set of competencies that involves knowing yourself, mastering your feelings, and understanding how to manage those feelings when interacting with others.[18] Goleman divides these competencies into two categories (see Key 1.4):[19]

- *Personal competence:* How you manage yourself—your self-awareness, self-regulation, and motivation
- *Social competence:* How you handle relationships with others, including awareness of the needs and feelings of others and ability to encourage others to do things

Social Intelligence

When someone close to you is happy, sad, or fearful, you probably tend to experience some of the same feelings out of concern or friendship. New research shows that the human brain is hardwired to connect with other brains around it. On an MRI brain scan, the area of your friend's brain that lights up during an emotional experience also lights up in your brain as you "share" the emotion. Your nervous system has what are called "mirror neurons" that mimic an observed emotion, allowing you to "participate" in the feeling even though you did not originate it. These capacities of your nervous system are involved in social intelligence.

Goleman defines *social intelligence* as a combination of two key categories: "social awareness, what we sense about others—and social facility, what we then do with that awareness" (see Key 1.5).[20]

- *Social awareness* ranges from just sensing other peoples' emotions on a basic level to actively working to understand how other people feel. It

EMOTIONAL INTELLIGENCE
The ability to perceive, assess, and manage one's own emotions as well as understand the emotions of others.

SOCIAL INTELLIGENCE
Having an understanding of the complexity of social interaction and using that understanding to manage relationships effectively.

KEY 1.4 Become more emotionally intelligent by developing these qualities.

PERSONAL COMPETENCE	SOCIAL COMPETENCE
Self-Awareness	**Social Awareness**
• I know my emotions and how they affect me. • I understand my strengths and my limits. • I am confident in my abilities. • I am open to improvement.	• I sense the feelings and perspectives of others. • I help others improve themselves. • I know how to relate to people from different cultures. • I can sense how to serve the needs of others.
Self-Management	**Social Skills**
• I can control my emotions and impulses. • I can delay gratification when there is something more important to be gained. • I am trustworthy. • I can adapt to change and new ideas. • I persist toward my goals despite obstacles.	• I know how to work in a team. • I can inspire people to act. • I understand how to lead a group. • I know how to persuade people. • I can make positive change happen.

Source: Based on Daniel Goleman, *Working with Emotional Intelligence*, New York: Bantam Books, 1998, pp. 26–27.

also includes knowledge of how the social world works (with different understandings for different settings). Active, attuned listening is a key component.

- *Social facility* is the active and most practical component, where you put your social awareness to work to achieve a goal. It involves smooth nonverbal interaction, presenting yourself in ways appropriate to individual situations, actively shaping the course of social interactions, and acting on your sense of what others need.

Emotional and social intelligence influence your ability to communicate and maneuver in social environments and achieve your goals. You will see more about these topics in chapter 4, chapter 8, and throughout the text.

Know How to Work with Others in Groups

A real-world application of diversity in action is likely to occur in the study group setting. Students taking the same course may form a study group that meets one or more times a week or right before exams. Instructors sometimes initiate student study groups, commonly for math

KEY 1.5

Become more socially intelligent through awareness and action.

Social Awareness	Social Facility
I sense nonverbal signals about how others are feeling.	My nonverbal body language is appropriate to the situation and communicates what I am feeling.
I listen fully and tune in carefully to others.	Considering what I hear and sense from others, I present myself verbally and physically in ways that make a desired impression.
I make an effort to understand what others feel, think, and intend.	I put my understanding of others to work by using tact and self-control to shape the outcome of my interactions.
I have a sense of how the social world works, how people interact with one another.	I use my sense of the social world to note when people need support and to help them in appropriate and needed ways.

Source: Based on Daniel Goleman, *Social Intelligence: The New Science of Human Relationships*, New York: Bantam Books, 2006, p. 84.

or science courses, known as *peer-assisted study sessions* or *supplemental instruction.*

Don't wait until crunch time to benefit from studying with others. As you begin to get to know students in your classes, start now to exchange phone numbers and e-mails, form groups, and schedule meetings. When you study with one or more people, you will gain benefits like these:

- *Shared and solidified knowledge.* When students share their knowledge with one another in a group, the effort takes less time and energy than when students learn all of the material alone. Furthermore, when you discuss concepts or teach them to others, you solidify what you know and strengthen your critical thinking.

- *Increased motivation.* Knowing that you are accountable to others and that they will see your level of work and preparation, you may be more motivated to work hard.

- *Increased teamwork ability.* The more you understand the dynamics of working with a group and the more

Having a sense of how to relate to others—in other words, drawing on your social intelligence—promotes positive and productive relationships on campus.

experience you have with teamwork, the more your interpersonal skills will grow.

- *Increased awareness and understanding of diversity.* Teams gain strength from the intellectual diversity of their members. When you work with others, you are bound to come up with ideas and solutions you never would have thought of on your own.

Strategies for Study Group Success

Every study group is unique. The way a group operates depends on members' personalities, the subject you study, the location of the group, and the size of the group. No matter what your particular group's situation, though, a few general strategies apply.

Set long-term and short-term goals. At your first meeting, determine what the group wants to accomplish. At the start of each meeting, have one person compile a list of questions to address.

Determine a regular schedule and leadership rotation. Determine what your group needs and what the members' schedules can handle. Try to meet weekly or, at the least, every other week. Rotating the leadership among members willing to lead helps all members take ownership of the results.

Create study materials for one another and help one another learn. Give each group member the task of finding a piece of information to compile, photocopy, and review for the other group members. Have group members teach pieces of information, make up quizzes for each other, or go through flash cards together.

Share the workload and pool your note-taking resources. The most important factor is a willingness to work, not knowlege level. Compare notes with group members and fill in information you don't have. Try different note-taking styles (see chapter 6 for a discussion of note taking).

Know how to be an effective leader. As a leader, you need a broad perspective that allows you to envision how different aspects of a project will come together. You must define projects, assign work, and set schedules. You also set meeting and project agendas, focus the group, keep people moving ahead, set a positive tone, and evaluate results.

Know how to be an effective participant. Participants are "part owners" of the team process with a responsibility for, and a stake in, the outcome. Let people know your ideas and your opinions about decisions. Be organized and willing to discuss. Fulfill the tasks you promise to do.

As you think about your tools and how you plan to use them to achieve your goals, you may be a bit uneasy about the road ahead and its inevitable stumbling blocks. You can give yourself the best possible chance to succeed if you remind yourself of the connection between your work in school and your ability to achieve goals in your life beyond graduation.

Assess Yourself as a Practical Thinker

For each statement, circle the number that feels right to you, from 1 for "not at all true for me" to 5 for "very true for me."

1. I can find a way around any obstacle.   1 2 3 4 5

2. I see myself as a "doer," the "go-to" person; I "make things happen."   1 2 3 4 5

3. When working on a problem in a group setting, I like to figure out who will do what and when it should be done.   1 2 3 4 5

4. Because I learn well from experience, I don't tend to repeat a mistake.   1 2 3 4 5

5. I finish what I start and don't leave loose ends hanging.   1 2 3 4 5

6. I pay attention to my emotions in academic and social situations to see if they help or hurt me as I move toward a goal.   1 2 3 4 5

7. I can sense how people feel, and can use that knowledge to interact with others effectively in order to achieve a goal.   1 2 3 4 5

8. I manage my time effectively.   1 2 3 4 5

9. I find ways to adjust to the teaching styles of my instructors and the communication styles of my peers.   1 2 3 4 5

10. When involved in a problem-solving process, I can shift gears as needed.   1 2 3 4 5

Total your answers here: _____

If your total ranges from 38–50, you consider your practical thinking skills to be *strong.*

If your total ranges from 24–37, you consider your practical thinking skills to be *average.*

If your total ranges from 10–23, you consider your practical thinking skills to be *weak.*

Remember that you can improve your practical thinking skill with focus and practice.

How Can the Things You Learn Now Promote Life Success?

In his book *Techno Trends—24 Technologies That Will Revolutionize Our Lives*, futurist Daniel Burrus describes a tomorrow that is linked to continuing education: "The future belongs to those who are capable of being retrained again and again," he says. "Think of it as periodically upgrading your human assets throughout your career. . . . Humans are infinitely upgradeable, but it does require an investment" in lifelong learning.[21]

The vast majority of Americans see lifelong learning as important in their own lives. In a survey of workers aged 18 to 24, conducted by the AFL-CIO, the country's leading labor union, 85% of respondents viewed education and training as the nation's top economic priority, and 9 out of 10 believed that the key to career advancement is ongoing education and training.[22]

In other words, you will need to continue to learn and grow in order to succeed. As a college student, you are making sacrifices—including a significant investment of time and money as well as a dramatic lifestyle change—to achieve success throughout your life. You are building the analytical, creative, and practical intelligence you need to cope with a world that is changing in many ways:

- *Knowledge in nearly every field is doubling every two to three years.* That means that if you stop learning, for even a few years, your knowledge base will be inadequate to keep up with the changes in your career.

- *Technology is changing how you live and work.* The Internet and technology will shape communications and improve knowledge and productivity during the next 20 years—and will require continual learning.

- *The global economy is moving from a product and service base to a knowledge and talent base.* Jobs of the past are being replaced by knowledge-based jobs, in the United States and abroad, that ask workers to think critically to come up with solutions.

- *Workers are changing jobs and careers more frequently.* The National Research Bureau reports that currently the average employee changes jobs every three to four years, and it is estimated that a 22-year-old college graduate in the year 2000 will have an average of eight employers in his or her first 10 years in the workplace.[23] Every time you decide to start a new career, you need new knowledge and skills.

LIFELONG LEARNERS

Individuals who continue to build knowledge and skills as a mechanism for improving their lives and careers.

All of these signs point to the need to become lifelong learners. Through successful intelligence, you will maintain the kind of flexibility that will enable you to adapt to the demands of the global marketplace. If you analyze what is happening, come up with creative approaches for handling it, and make a practical plan to put your ideas into motion, you can stay on track toward your goals. Or, you may decide to shift direction toward a new goal that never occurred to you before the change. Facing change means taking risks.

Successful Intelligence Wrap-Up

You have the power to engage your successful intelligence to pursue goals that are most important to you. Although college presents challenges and risks to everyone, persistent and motivated learners can manage them effectively. Here's how you have built skills in chapter 1:

Analytical

By completing the three self-assessments, you analyzed where you are now in analytical, creative, and practical intelligence. At the beginning and end of the chapter, you explored how learning—in college and throughout life—can promote success. In learning about the theory of successful intelligence, you considered how it can enable you to reach important goals.

Creative

Reading about the global marketplace may have inspired new ideas of what you want out of college. Thinking about the three parts of successful intelligence helped to provide a new perspective of your potential as a student. Exploring strategies about learning from failure, working with others in a team, and facing fears may have helped you see connections among these topics that you didn't see before.

Practical

You examined specific practical actions that are the building blocks of college success: how to work with academic integrity, fulfill day-to-day academic responsibilities, stay motivated, and learn from failure. You also investigated emotional and social intelligence, two highly practical skills that allow you to work effectively with others. Finally, you considered specific, practical actions to take when working in a project team or study group.

Egyszer volt budán kutyavásár

(edge-zehr volt bu-darn ku-tcho-vah-shahr)

This unusual Hungarian phrase, translated literally, means "There was a dog-market in Buda only once." In modern English, you would interpret this to be a favorable opportunity that comes along only once—something that you should grasp with both hands, lest you regret not taking advantage of it later.[24]

For you, this opportunity has arrived. Make the most of all your college has to offer, and gather learning skills that you will use throughout your life. By taking the initiative to use your time well, you can build the successful intelligence that will help you realize your dreams.

"There is no elevator to success. You have to take the stairs."

UNKNOWN

Building World-Class Skills
for College, Career, and Life Success

SUCCESSFUL INTELLIGENCE
Think, Create, Apply

Activate yourself. Robert Sternberg found that successfully intelligent people, despite differences in thinking and personal goals, have 20 particular characteristics in common. He calls these characteristics *self-activators*—things that get you moving and keep you going.[25]

Step 1. Think it through: *Analyze where you are now.* Use this self-assessment to see how developed you perceive your self-activators to be *right now*.

1	2	3	4	5
Not at All Like Me	Somewhat Unlike Me	Not Sure	Somewhat Like Me	Definitely Like Me

Please circle the number that best represents your answer:

1. I motivate myself well.   1 2 3 4 5

2. I can control my impulses.   1 2 3 4 5

3. I know when to persevere and when to change gears.   1 2 3 4 5

4. I make the most of what I do well.   1 2 3 4 5

5. I can successfully translate my ideas into action.   1 2 3 4 5

6. I can focus effectively on my goal.   1 2 3 4 5

7. I complete tasks and have good follow-through.   1 2 3 4 5

8. I initiate action—I move people and projects ahead.   1 2 3 4 5

9. I have the courage to risk failure.   1 2 3 4 5

10. I avoid procrastination.   1 2 3 4 5

11. I accept responsibility when I make a mistake.   1 2 3 4 5

12. I don't waste time feeling sorry for myself.   1 2 3 4 5

13. I independently take responsibility for tasks.   1 2 3 4 5

14. I work hard to overcome personal difficulties.   1 2 3 4 5

15. I create an environment that helps me to concentrate
    on my goals.   1 2 3 4 5

16. I don't take on too much work or too little.   1 2 3 4 5

17. I can delay gratification in order to receive the benefits.   1 2 3 4 5

18. I can see both the big picture and the details in
    a situation.   1 2 3 4 5

19. I am able to maintain confidence in myself.   1 2 3 4 5

20. I can balance my analytical, creative, and practical
    thinking skills.   1 2 3 4 5

Step 2. Think out of the box: *Brainstorm over time*. Looking at the self-assessment, choose five self-activators that you most want to develop throughout the term. Then, pretend you are an instructor recommending yourself for a scholarship or a job. Write yourself a short e-mail about how strong you are in the areas of those five self-activators. Save the e-mail as a reminder of what you would like such a person to be able to truly say about you.

Step 3. Make it happen: *Prepare yourself for action*. Let this self-assessment direct your decisions about how you approach the material in this course. If you wish to procrastinate less, for example, pay special attention to the time-management information in chapter 2. To jump-start your focus, look at the self-assessment again and circle or highlight the five self-activators that you most want to concentrate on at this point.

In the last chapter of this book you will revisit this self-assessment and get more specific about actions you have taken, and plan to take, to promote personal growth.

TEAMWORK

Create Solutions Together

Motivators. Gather in a group of three to five. Together, brainstorm motivation blockers—situations or things that most often kill your motivation to succeed in school. When you have as many problems as you have group members, each person should choose one problem and write it at the top of a blank sheet of paper.

Look at the motivation blocker on your page. Under it, write one practical idea you have about how to overcome it. When everyone is finished, pass the pages to the person on the left. Then write an idea about the new blocker at the top of the page you've received. If you can't think of anything, pass the page as is. Continue this way until your page comes back to you. Then discuss the ideas as a group, analyzing which ideas might work better than others. Add other ideas to the lists if you think of them.

The last step: On your own, keeping in mind your group discussion, list three specific actions that you commit to taking in order to keep motivation high when the going gets rough.

1. _____

2. _____

3. _____

WRITING
Journal and Put Skills to Work

Record your thoughts on a separate piece of paper, in a journal, or on a computer file.

Journal entry: Reasons for college. Think about why you are here. Why did you decide to attend college, and what do you want out of the experience? What sacrifices—in terms of time, hard work, finances—are you willing to make in your quest for success?

Real-life writing: Initial impressions. Although you have not been in school for long, you already have some sense of your instructors, their style, and how classes are likely to proceed. Compare and contrast your initial impressions of two of your instructors and the courses they teach. Discuss teaching style, course expectations, degree of difficulty, how the classroom is run, and any other factor that is significant to you. Finally, note any changes you think you should make—in your in-class or study approach—based on these impressions.

PERSONAL PORTFOLIO
Prepare for Career Success

This is the first of eight portfolio assignments you will complete, one for each chapter. By the end of the term, you will have built skills that promote success in pursuing any career as you compile a portfolio of documents that will help you achieve career goals.

    Type your work and store the documents electronically in one file folder. Use loose paper for assignments that ask you to draw or make collages.

Setting career goals. Whether you have a current career, have held a few different jobs, or have not yet entered the workplace, college is an ideal time to take stock of your career goals. The earlier in your college education that you consider career goals, the more you can take advantage of how college can help prepare you for work, in both job-specific and general ways. Having a strong vision of where you wish to go will also be a powerful motivator as you face some of the inevitable challenges of the next few years.

    Take some time to think about your working life. Spend 15 minutes brainstorming everything that you wish you could be, do, have, or experience in your career 10 years from now—the skills you want to have, money you want to earn, benefits, experiences, travel, anything you can think of. List your wishes, draw them, depict them using cutouts from magazines, or combine these ideas—whatever you like best.

Now, look at your list. To discover how your wishes relate to one another, group them in order of priority. Label three computer pages or three pieces of paper Priority 1, Priority 2, and Priority 3. Write each wish where it fits, with Priority 1 being the most important, Priority 2 the second most important, and Priority 3 the third.

Look at your priority lists. What do they tell you about what is most important to you? What wishes are you ready to work toward right now? Circle or highlight the three highest-priority wishes (they will most likely appear on your Priority 1 page). Write down the trade-offs you may have to make today to make these wishes come true. Don't let yourself off the hook—be realistic and direct. You may want to look back at these materials at the end of the term to see what changes may have taken place in your priorities.

Suggested Readings

Friedman, Thomas L. *The World Is Flat: A Brief History of the Twenty-first Century*. New York: Farrar, Straus & Giroux, 2006.

Jeffers, Susan. *Feel the Fear . . . and Do It Anyway*. New York: Ballantine Books, 2006.

Kadar, Andrew. *College Life 102: The No-Bull Guide to a Great Freshman Year*. Lincoln, NE: iUniverse, 2006.

Newport, Cal. *How to Win at College: Surprising Secrets for Success from the Country's Top Students*. New York: Broadway Books, 2005.

Simon, Linda. *New Beginnings: A Reference Guide for Adult Learners*, 3rd ed. Upper Saddle River, NJ: Prentice Hall, 2005.

Sternberg, Robert. *Successful Intelligence: How Practical and Creative Intelligence Determine Success in Life*. New York: Plume, 1997.

Students Helping Students. *Navigating Your Freshman Year: How to Make the Leap to College Life*. New York: Penguin, 2005.

Tyler, Suzette. *Been There, Should've Done That II: More Tips for Making the Most of College*. Lansing, MI: Front Porch Press, 2001.

Internet and Podcast Resources

The Center for Academic Integrity: **www.academicintegrity.org**

Motivation on the Run podcasts: **http://podcasts.yahoo.com/series?s=ed9231d7be 13524016aeb51d5f40e2d1**

NPR, "For Workers, 'The World Is Flat,'" April 14, 2005, broadcast of *Fresh Air from WHYY*: **www.npr.org/templates/story/ story.php?storyId=4600258**

Student.Com—The Student Center: **www.student.com**

StudentNow—College Life, Fun, & Resources: **www.studentnow.com**

Prentice Hall Student Success SuperSite: **www.prenhall.com/success**

Success Stories: **www.prenhall.com/success/Stories/ index.html**

Check your college Web site for podcasts produced by your school.

Endnotes

[1] Thomas Friedman, *The World Is Flat,* New York: Farrar, Straus & Giroux, 2006, p. 8.

[2] Robert J. Sternberg, *Successful Intelligence: How Practical and Creative Intelligence Determine Success in Life*, New York: Plume, 1997, p. 11.

[3] Lawrence F. Lowery, *"The Biological Basis of Thinking and Learning,"* 1998, Full Option Science System, University of California at Berkeley (http://lhsfoss.org/newsletters/archive/pdfs/FOSS_BBTL.pdf).

[4] Carol Dweck, *Mindset: The New Psychology of Success*, New York: Random House, 2006, p. 22.

[5] Sternberg, *Successful Intelligence,* p. 12.

[6] Ibid., p. 127.

[7] Ibid., pp. 127–128.

[8] "Are the Classes Really That Much Harder Than High School?" New Mexico State University, June 1999 (https://www.nmsu.edu/aggieland/students/faq_classes.html).

[9] From student essay submitted by the First Year Experience students of Patty Parma, Palo Alto College, San Antonio, Texas, January 2004.

[10] Rick Pitino, *Success Is a Choice,* New York: Broadway Books, 1997, p. 40.

[11] *The Fundamental Values of Academic Integrity*, Center for Academic Integrity, Kenan Institute for Ethics, Duke University, October 1999 (www.academicintegrity.org/fundamental.asp).

[12] From "Facts About Plagiarism," 2007, Plagiarism.org (www.plagiarism.org/facts.html).

[13] "LD at a Glance," 2007, National Center for Learning Disabilities (www.ncld.org/index.php?option=content&task=view&id=448).

[14] *LD Advocates Guide,* n.d., National Center for Learning Disabilities (www.ncld.org/index.php?option=content&task=view&id=291).

[15] National Center for Learning Disabilities, "Adult Learning Disabilities: A Learning Disability Isn't Something You Outgrow—It's Something You Learn to Master" (pamphlet), New York: National Center for Learning Disabilities.

[16] "For 7 Million, One Census Race Category Wasn't Enough," *New York Times*, March 13, 2001, pp. A1, A14.

[17] Media Watch, *Diversity Digest,* Fall 1997 (www.diversityweb.org/Digest/F97/mediawatch.html#top).

[18] Daniel Goleman, *Emotional Intelligence: Why It Can Matter More Than IQ*, New York: Bantam Books, 1995.

[19] Daniel Goleman, *Working with Emotional Intelligence,* New York: Bantam Books, 1998, pp. 26–27.

[20] Quote and material for the following section are from Daniel Goleman, *Social Intelligence: The New Science of Human Relationships,* New York: Bantam Books, 2006, pp. 84–97.

[21] Cited in Colin Rise and Malcolm J. Nicholl, *Accelerated Learning for the 21st Century,* New York: Dell, 1997, pp. 5–6.

[22] Study cited in Susan Rosenblum, "Young Workers Name Lifelong Learning as Top Need for Economy of Future," *Nation's Cities Weekly*, September 6, 1999, p. 1.

[23] Jay Palmer, "Marry Me a Little," *Barron's*, July 24, 2000, p. 25.

[24] Christopher J. Moore, *In Other Words: A Language Lover's Guide to the Most Intriguing Words Around the World*, New York: Walker, 2004, p. 43.

[25] List and descriptions based on Sternberg, *Successful Intelligence,* pp. 251–269.

VALUES, GOALS, AND TIME
Managing Yourself

"Successfully intelligent people are well aware of the penalties for procrastination. They schedule their time so that the important things get done—and done well."

ROBERT STERNBERG

his chapter divides the indispensable skill of self-management into three parts: using values to guide your goal setting, working through a process to achieve goals, and managing time in a way that propels you toward your goals and helps you manage stress. It also provides ideas about how to think through the important goal of choosing a major or concentration. Your ability to manage yourself will help you cope with what you encounter, achieve your goals, and build skills that fuel your success now and in the future.

In this chapter you explore answers to the following questions:

- Why is it important to know what you value? 36
- How do you set and achieve goals? 40
- How can you begin to explore majors? 43
- How can you effectively manage your time? 46
- *Successful Intelligence Wrap-Up 55*

Analytical	Creative	Practical
• Examining values • Analyzing how you manage time • Considering what goals are most important to you	• Developing ideas for how to reach a goal • Creating ways to avoid procrastination • Brainstorming what majors interest you	• How to set effective goals • How to achieve a goal • How to manage a schedule

Why Is It Important to Know What You Value?

VALUES

Principles or qualitites that you consider important.

You make life choices—what to do, what to believe, what to buy, how to act—based on your personal values. Your choice to pursue a degree, for example, reflects that you value the personal and professional growth that come from a college education. Being on time for your classes shows that you value punctuality. Paying bills regularly and on time shows that you value financial stability.

Values play a key role in your drive to achieve important goals, because they help you to do the following:

- *Understand what you want out of life.* Your most meaningful goals should reflect what you value most.

- *Build "rules for life."* Your values form the foundation for your decisions and behavior. You will return repeatedly to them for guidance, especially in unfamiliar territory.

- *Find people who inspire you.* Spending time with people who share similar values will help you clarify how you want to live and find support for your goals.

Your value system is complex, built piece by piece over time. Many forces affect your values—family, friends, culture, media, school, work, neighborhood, religious beliefs, world events. No matter how powerful these external influences may be, however, it is your decision whether or not to adopt a value. Making this decision involves answering questions like the following to evaluate whether a given value is right for you:

- Where did the value come from?

- What other different values could I consider?

REAL QUESTIONS

How can I choose a major that is right for me?

I've just started college and my school requires that all students choose a major right away, as entering freshmen. I know this is a very important decision because it could chart the direction of the rest of my life, so I want to make sure I find what's right for me.

I've always loved being outdoors, reading, and learning other languages—and I think I would make a great teacher, but I want to do more than just teach. I see myself going toward humanitarian aid or international affairs, and then later going back to school to get an advanced degree and become a professor some day. What kind of major should I look for that will make me a marketable candidate for a fulfilling and challenging career?

Courtney Mellblom
California Polytechnic
State University
San Luis Obispo,
California

PRACTICAL ANSWERS

Antoine Pickett
Resident Engineer,
Federal Aviation
Administration
Aurora Air Traffic
Control Center,
Aurora, Illinois

Explore the possibilities carefully and follow your heart.

Many college freshmen ask this type of question. It is not an easy decision to make at such a young age. Fortunately, you seem to have a sense of what direction you want to move in. Although many people go for the quick or big bucks, the most marketable candidate for a job is one who shows a great interest and desire in what they have studied. If you follow your heart in your studies you will not go wrong.

First, I suggest that you find out more about courses that could help you explore your interest in the international arena. In fact, you could consider a major that would allow you to focus on your humanitarian interests, such as international affairs or international relations. Becoming proficient in a foreign language would also tend to make you more marketable.

Second, work backwards. Examine potential careers in the area of international affairs, talk to people who have international experience, and from there try to gain work or intern experience while you are in college to see if it truly interests you. Your proactive research should inform your decision about what major to choose.

If your eventual goal is to become a college professor, many colleges require graduate and doctoral work but do not require a teaching certificate. Later, if you decide you don't want to become a professor, you can still pursue a certificate. Your experience in the working world will make you a better teacher. As someone once said, "The error of youth is to believe that intelligence is a substitute for experience, while the error of age is to believe that experience is a substitute for intelligence." Any experience you gain will help you learn and grow.

- What might happen as a result of adopting this value?
- Have I made a personal commitment to this choice? Have I told others about it?
- Do my life goals and day-to-day actions reflect this value?

Your values often shift to fit new circumstances as you grow. For example, a student who benefits from the support of friends and family while recovering from an auto accident may place greater value on relationships than he did before.

How Values Affect Your Educational Experience

The fact that you are here in college means that you value education. Making education a priority is a practical choice that will help you do the following:

- *Keep going when the going gets tough.* "Success takes much hard work and dedication," says a student at Palo Alto College. "Since I have a hard time with writing, and I can't understand algebra, I've made a commitment to write in a journal every day and attend math tutoring at least three times a week."[1]

- *Choose your major and a career direction.* If you've always been an environmentalist, then you may choose to specialize in environmental science. If you feel fulfilled when you help people, then you might consider a career in social work.

- *Choose friends and activities that enrich your life.* Having friends who share your desire to succeed in school will increase your motivation and reduce your stress. Joining organizations whose activities reflect your values will broaden your educational experience.

- *Choose what you want to get out of school.* What kinds of skills and knowledge do you wish to build? Are you focused on building the foundation for a successful career? Your values will help you determine what you are willing to do to achieve academic goals.

Values and Cultural Diversity

At college, you may meet people who seem different in unexpected ways. Unfamiliar attitudes and behaviors are rooted in unique cultures. A *culture* is a unique set of values, behaviors, tastes, knowledge, attitudes, and habits shared by a specific group of people.

Cultural misunderstandings can interfere with relationships. As someone who accepts and appreciates diversity, your goal is to develop cultural competence.[2] Chapter 3 will go into more detail about how to be a culturally competent communicator.

CULTURAL COMPETENCE

The ability to understand and appreciate differences and to respond to people of all cultures in a way that values their worth, respects their beliefs and practices, and builds communication and relationships.

As you continue to read *Keys to Success*, think of the wisdom of cultural diversity consultant Helen Turnbull on turning differences into strengths:

> We must suspend our judgment. We should not judge others negatively because they are indirect, or their accents aren't clear, or their tone of voice is tentative, or they avoid eye contact. We must learn patience and suspend judgment long enough to realize these differences don't make one of us right and the other wrong. They simply mean that we approach communication from a different frame of reference and, many times, a different value system.[3]

Although clarifying your values will help you choose your educational path, goal-setting and goal-achievement skills will turn values into tools that help you travel that path to the end.

Explore Your Values

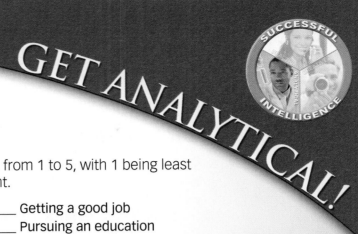

Rate each of the values in the list on a scale from 1 to 5, with 1 being least important to you and 5 being most important.

_____ Knowing yourself	_____ Getting a good job
_____ Being liked by others	_____ Pursuing an education
_____ Reading	_____ Spiritual/religious life
_____ Self-improvement	_____ Making a lot of money
_____ Taking risks	_____ Good relationships with family
_____ Time to yourself	
_____ Improving physical/mental health	_____ Community involvement
	_____ Creative/artistic pursuits
_____ Time for fun/relaxation	_____ Helping others
_____ Lifelong learning	_____ Keeping up with the news
_____ Leadership and teamwork skills	_____ Being organized
	_____ Financial stability
_____ Staying fit through exercise	_____ Other (write below)
_____ Competing and winning	_____

Write your top three values here:

1. _____

2. _____

3. _____

Now connect your values to educational goals. (*Example:* A student who values helping others chooses to study nursing.) Choose one top value that is a factor in an educational choice you have made. Explain the choice and how the value is involved:

_____

_____

Name an area of study that you think would help you live according to this value:

_____

How Do You Set and Achieve Goals?

GOAL

An end toward which effort is directed; an aim or intention.

When you identify something that you want, you set a **goal.** Achieving goals, whether they are short term or long term, involves the careful formulation and execution of a goal-achievement plan. Think of this plan as a map that defines your route to destinations nearby and far away.

Set Long-Term Goals

Start by setting *long-term goals*—objectives that you want to achieve in the next six months, year, or more. As a student, your long-term goals may include earning a degree or certificate and starting a career.

Some long-term goals have an open-ended time frame. This is especially the case with goals that involve creative expression, which depend on the time and freedom to consider different paths. For example, if your goal is to become the best jazz trombonist you can be, you will work at it over your entire life and use different methods to improve your technique. Other goals, such as completing the general education requirements at your school, have a shorter scope, a more definite end, and often fewer options for getting from A to Z.

Writing out a long-term goal statement can help you clarify the goal. Here's one example of a goal that would take forethought and years to reach:

> My goal is to build a business in which I, as a family doctor, create opportunities to expose young people in my community to the medical field. In this business, I will reach students through presentations, summer internships, and mentoring.

For a student two years away from college graduation who is pursuing this long-term goal, here is a supporting set of one-year long-term goals:

> Design courses for the year to make sure I am on track for premed course completion. Find medical practices in the area that could serve as a model for my business. Research medical schools for application next year.

Just as this set of goals is tailored to one student's personality, abilities, and values, your goals should reflect your uniqueness. To determine your long-term goals, think about what you think is important to accomplish while you are in school and after you graduate. Here are some linkages between personal values and professional goals:

- **Values:** Health and fitness, helping others

  Goal: To work for a company that produces organic foods

- **Values:** Independence, financial success

  Goal: To obtain a degree in business and start a company

Basing your long-term goals on your values increases your motivation to succeed. The more your goals focus on what is most important to you, the greater your drive to reach them.

Set Short-Term Goals

Short-term goals are smaller steps that move you toward a long-term goal. Lasting as short as an hour or as long as a few months, these goals help you manage broader aspirations as they narrow your focus and encourage

© Paul Murphy—Fotolia.com

progress. If you had a long-term goal of graduating with a degree in nursing, for example, you may want to accomplish the following short-term goals in the next six months:

- I will learn the names, locations, and functions of every human bone and muscle.
- I will work with a study group to understand the musculoskeletal system.

These goals can be broken down into even smaller parts, such as the following one-month goals:

- I will work with on-screen tutorials of the musculoskeletal system until I understand and memorize the material.
- I will spend three hours a week with my study partners.

© VisualField—Fotolia.com

In addition to monthly goals, you may have short-term goals that extend for a week, a day, or even a couple of hours in a given day. To support your monthlong goal of regularly meeting with your study partners, you may wish to set the following short-term goals:

- *By the end of today:* Call study partners to ask them about when they might be able to meet
- *One week from now:* Have scheduled each of our weekly meetings this month
- *Two weeks from now:* Have had our first meeting
- *Three weeks from now:* Type and distribute notes from first meeting; have second meeting

Your motivation is at its peak when you begin to move toward a goal and when you are about to achieve that goal. For that reason, try to pay special attention to goals that fall in the middle—for example, one-month or one-term goals on the way to a yearlong goal. If you work hard to stay motivated through the whole journey, you will have a better result.

As you consider your long- and short-term goals, notice how all of your goals are linked to one another. As Key 2.1 shows, your long-term goals establish a context for the short-term goals. In turn, your short-term goals make the long-term goals seem clearer and more reachable.

At any given time, you will be working toward goals of varying importance. Setting priorities helps you decide where and when to focus your energy and time.

Prioritize Goals

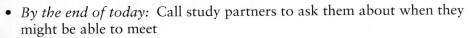

When you **prioritize**, you evaluate everything you are working toward, decide which goals are most important, and plan how to achieve them. Prioritizing helps you avoid impulsive decisions that waste energy and time. What should you consider as you prioritize?

PRIORITIZE
To arrange or deal with in order of importance.

- *Your values.* Think about what you value to establish your top goals—for example, graduating in four years or developing a strong network of personal contacts.
- *Your personal situation.* Are you going to school and working part-time? Are you taking three classes or five classes? Are you a parent with

Goals reinforce one another.

LONG-TERM		Earn a degree	
YEARLONG	Declare major		Pass classes
SEMESTER	Explore career areas	Work with study groups	Be in class and on time
ONE MONTH	Meet with academic advisor	Plan group meetings	Cut down on late-night socializing
THIS WEEK	Call advisor to set up appointment	Call friends from class about getting a group together	Study weeknights and go out on Friday nights

young children? Are you an athlete on a sports team? Every individual situation requires unique priorities and scheduling.

- *Your time commitments.* Hours of your day may already be committed to class, team practices, a part-time job, or sleep. Your challenge is to make sure these commitments reflect what you value and to establish priorities for the remaining hours. As you will see later in the chapter, setting clear priorities will help you manage your time and accomplish more.

Work to Achieve Goals

Being practical will help you achieve your goals. Remember, the more specific your plans, the more likely you are to fulfill them.

- *Define your goal-setting strategy: How do you plan to reach your goal?* Brainstorm different paths that might get you there. Choose one; then map out its steps and strategies. Focus on specific behaviors and events that are under your control and that are measurable.

- *Set a timetable: When do you want to accomplish your goal?* Set a realistic time line that includes specific deadlines for each step and strategy you have defined. Charting your progress will help you stay on track.

- *Be accountable for your progress: What safeguards will keep you on track?* Define a personal reporting or buddy system that makes accountability a priority.

- *Get unstuck: What will you do if you hit a roadblock?* Define two ways to get help with your efforts if you run into trouble. Be ready to pursue more creative ideas if those don't work.

Map Out a Personal Goal

Working backwards can help you find an interesting path toward an important goal.

Name one important personal goal you have for this year:

_____

Now imagine that you have achieved your goal and an impressed friend asks you to describe how you did it. Write three important steps you took first:

1. _____

2. _____

3. _____

Briefly describe how you followed the rest of the plan:

_____

_____

_____

Finally, tell your friend what positive results have come from achieving your goal:

_____

_____

You just created a potential plan. Consider putting it—or a plan similar to it—to work. As you begin, let the image of the success you created in this exercise motivate and inspire you.

How Can You Begin to Explore Majors?

At some point near the completion of your general education requirements, you will be asked to declare a **major** or **concentration** (for the sake of simplicity, the term *major* will appear throughout the rest of the text). Although you likely have plenty of time to make this decision, start early to

MAJOR (OR CONCENTRATION) An academic subject area chosen as a field of specialization, requiring a specific course of study.

narrow down possibilities so you can match your talents, skills, and dreams with a concrete curriculum. Choosing a major is one of the most important decisions you'll make in college because your major largely determines the courses you will take, what you will learn, and with whom you will spend school time. Your major may also influence your future career.

Thinking practically, exploring your course emphasis early on can save you time and money. Because many of the courses that fulfill requirements in one major may not count toward another, changing your major might mean that you stay in college longer and spend additional money on courses, especially if you make the change in your junior or senior year. Having a sense of what you do or do not want to specialize in will make your course selection more efficient.

With what you know about setting and achieving goals, envision declaring a major as a long-term goal made up of the multiple steps (short-term goals) that follow. Start the process now even if, as is true of many students, you don't yet know what you want to study.

Short-Term Goal #1: Use Self-Assessments to Identify Interests and Talents

When you identify your interests and talents and choose a major that focuses on them, you are likely to have a positive attitude and perform at your highest level. You may still be figuring out what inspires you, or you may have sensed a career direction since you were young. This was the case with University of Illinois student Brian DeGraff, whose interests were mechanical:

> I am amazed by how things work. The way a car can turn a tank of greasy, smelly, toxic liquid into my ride to school. People always say stop and smell the roses, but I'd rather stop and wonder why the roses smell. It was this passion that drove me to want to be an engineer.[4]

To pinpoint the areas that spark your interest, consider the following questions:

- What are my favorite courses? What do these courses have in common?
- What subjects interest me when I read?
- What activities do I look forward to?
- Am I a "natural" in any academic or skill area?
- What do people say I do well?
- How do I learn most effectively? (see chapter 3)

Short-Term Goal #2: Explore Academic Options

Next, find out about the academic choices available at your school.

Learn what's possible. Consult your college catalog for guidelines on declaring (and changing) your major. Find answers to these questions:

- When do I have to declare a major? (Generally this is required at the end of the second year for four-year programs, or earlier for associate or certificate programs.)

- What are my options in majoring? (You may consider double majors, minors, *interdisciplinary majors* incorporating more than one discipline and designed with the help of an advisor.)
- What majors are offered at my school?

If a major looks interesting, explore it further by answering these questions:

- What minimum grade point average (GPA), if any, does the department require before it will accept me as a major?
- What GPA must I maintain in the courses included in the major?
- What preparatory courses (prerequisites) are required?
- What courses will I be required to take and in what sequence? How many credits do I need to graduate in the major?

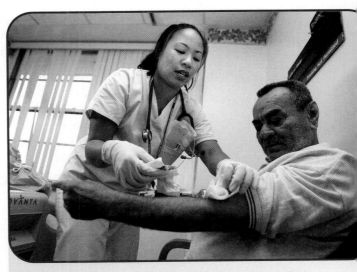

Exploring career-related interests early on can help you find a major that will support your career goals. Students interested in nursing might consider majoring in one of the sciences.

- Should I consider a minor in this academic area? (A minor has fewer requirements than a major. Many students choose a minor suited for a career. For example, a sociology major who wants to work in an inner-city hospital might consider a minor in Spanish.)

Talk to people who can help. Early on, begin discussing your major with your advisor; he or she can help you evaluate different options. You also may want to ask students who are a year or two ahead of you to describe their experiences with the courses, the workload, and the instructors.

Visit the department. When considering a major, analyze your comfort with the academic department as well as with the material. Ask the department secretary for information, sit in on a class, and consider asking an instructor in the department for an appointment. When Ashiana Esmail decided to major in Ethnic Studies at the University of California at Berkeley, she did so in part because she felt that working with a close-knit department "was better than an A+" in helping to build academic momentum.[5]

Short-Term Goal #3: Establish Your Academic Schedule

Map out your time frame. How many years do you plan to study as an undergraduate or graduate student? Do you plan to attend graduate school? If so, do you plan to go there directly after graduation or take time off? From there, get more specific about scheduling.

Set timing for short-term goals. Work with your academic advisor to pinpoint when to accomplish the short-term goals that lead to graduation. What are the deadlines for completing core requirements or declaring a major? Although you won't need to plan out your entire course load right now, drafting a tentative (curriculum)—both within and outside your major—can help clarify where you are heading. Remember, you are not expected to do this alone. Your academic advisor is there to help you succeed.

Identify dates connected to your goal fulfillment. Pay attention to academic dates (you will find an academic calendar in each year's college catalog and on the college's Web site). Such dates include registration dates, final date to declare a major, final date to drop a course, and so forth. Plan ahead so you don't miss a deadline.

Be Flexible as You Come to a Decision

Flexibility is essential when defining any important goal. Many students change their minds as they consider majors; some declare a major and then change it one or more times before finding a good fit. Once you have considered a change carefully, act on it right away by informing your advisor, completing required paperwork, and redesigning your schedule to reflect your choice.

Through this process, you will often be thinking about how well you are using your time. In fact, being able to achieve any significant goal is directly linked to effective time management.

How Can You Effectively Manage Your Time?

Although everyone has the same 24 hours every day, on some days you may feel like you have hours to spare, while on others the clock becomes your worst enemy. Thinking about time before you act empowers you to make smart choices. Consider each day as a jigsaw puzzle: You have the pieces in a pile, and your task is to form a picture of how you want your day to look.

Successful time management starts with identifying your time-related needs and preferences. This self-knowledge sets the stage for building and managing your schedule, avoiding procrastination, and being flexible in the face of change. Finally, understanding the connection between time and stress will help you keep stress levels under control.

Identify Your Time-Related Needs and Preferences

Body rhythms and habits affect how each person deals with time. Some people are night owls; others function best in the morning. Some people are chronically late; others get everything done with time to spare. Being aware of factors like these will help you create a schedule that maximizes your strengths and cuts down on stress. If you are a morning person, for example, look for sections of required courses that meet early in the day. If you work best at night, schedule most of your study time at a library that stays open late.

Take the following steps to identify your time-related needs and preferences:

Create a personal time "profile." Ask yourself these questions: At what time of day do I have the most energy? The least energy? Do I tend to be early, on time, or late? Do I focus well for long stretches or need regular breaks? Your answers will help you find your best schedule.

Evaluate the effects of your profile. Which of your time-related habits and preferences will have a positive impact on your success at school? Which are likely to cause problems?

Establish the schedule preferences that suit your profile best. Make a list of these preferences—or even map out an ideal schedule as a way of illustrating them. For example, one student's preference list might read: "Classes bunched together on Mondays, Wednesdays, and Fridays. Tuesdays and Thursdays free for studying and research. Study time primarily during the day."

Next, build a schedule that takes this information into account. Your goal should be to maximize your strengths and compensate for your weaker time-management areas.

Successful Intelligence Connections Online

Listen to author Sarah Kravits describe how to use analytical, creative, and practical intelligence to define your personal time profile.

Go to the *Keys to Success* Companion Website at www.prenhall.com/carter to listen or download as a podcast.

Build a Schedule

Schedules help you gain control of your life in two ways: They provide segments of time for goal-related tasks and they remind you of tasks, events, due dates, responsibilities, and deadlines.

Use a Planner

A planner is a tool for managing your time. Use it to keep track of events and commitments, schedule goal-related tasks, and rank tasks according to priority. Time-management expert Paul Timm says that "rule number one in a thoughtful planning process is: Use some form of a planner where you can write things down."[6]

There are two types of planners. One is a book or notebook where you can note commitments. If you write detailed daily plans, look for the kind that devotes a page to each day. If you prefer to see more days at a glance, try the kind that shows a week's schedule on a two-page spread. Some planners contain sections for monthly and yearly goals.

© Iryna Petrenko—
Fotolia.com

The other option is an electronic planner or personal digital assistant (PDA) such as a Palm Pilot, BlackBerry, or Sidekick. Basic PDA functions allow you to schedule days and weeks, note due dates, make to-do lists, perform mathematical calculations, and create and store an address book. You can also transfer information to and from a computer.

Though electronic planners are handy and have a large data capacity, they cost more than the paper versions, and their small size means they can be easily lost. Analyze your preferences and options, and decide which tool you are most likely to use every day. A blank notebook, used conscientiously, may work as well for some people as a top-of-the-line PDA.

Keep Track of Events and Commitments

Your planner is designed to help you schedule and remember events and commitments. A quick look at your notations will remind you when items are approaching. Your class syllabus is also a tool for keeping track of reading and homework assignments and test dates (see the sample syllabus on page 14).

Putting your schedule in writing will help you think ahead to prepare for crunch times. For example, if you see that you have three tests and a presentation coming up all in one week, you may have to rearrange your schedule during the preceding week to create extra study time.

Among the events and commitments worth noting in your planner are the following:

- Test and quiz dates; due dates for papers, projects, and presentations
- Details of your academic schedule, including term and holiday breaks
- Club and organizational meetings
- Personal items—medical appointments, due dates for bills, birthdays, social events
- Milestones toward a goal, such as due dates for sections of a project

It's important to include class prep time—reading and studying, writing and working on assignments and projects—in the planner. According to one reasonable formula, you should schedule at least two hours of preparation for every hour of class—that is, if you take 15 credits, you should study about 30 hours a week, making your total classroom and preparation time 45 hours.

Getting adequate study time means thinking creatively about when and where to study. This student takes time to get some work done between races at a track meet.

Surveys have shown, however, that most students study 15 or fewer hours per week, and some study even less—often not enough to master the material. As a freshman at Boston College, William Imbriale had priorities other than course work. "I got a D on my first philosophy paper," said William. "That woke me up, big time." When a professor helped him plan his time more effectively, William increased his study time and received an A− on the final paper.[7]

Working students have to fit study time in where they can. Lisa Marie Webb, a University of Utah student, prepares for class while commuting to and from her job. Athletes, too, have to work hard to fit everything in. "I get up at 6:30, go to study hall from 7:30 to 9, have class from 9:30 to 1:15, then have practice at 2," said Ohio State defensive back A. J. Hawk.[8] Situations like these demand creative time management and attention to your schedule.

Schedule Tasks and Activities That Support Your Goals

Linking day-to-day events in your planner to your broader goals will give meaning to your efforts, bring order to your schedule, and keep you motivated. Planning study time for an economics test, for example, will mean more to you if you link the hours you spend to your goal of being accepted into business school. Here is how a student might translate his goal of entering business school into action steps over a year's time:

- *This year:* Complete enough courses to meet curriculum requirements for business school and maintain class standing.
- *This term:* Complete my economics class with a B average or higher.
- *This month:* Set up economics study group schedule to coincide with quizzes and tests.
- *This week:* Meet with study group; go over material for Friday's test.
- *Today:* Go over chapter 3 in econ text.

The student can then arrange his time to move him in the direction of his goal. He schedules activities that support his short-term goal of doing well on the test and writes them in his planner as shown in the example below. Achieving his overarching long-term goal of doing well in a course he needs for business school is the source of his motivation.

Monday	Tuesday	Wednesday	Thursday	Friday	Saturday	Sunday
9 AM: Economics class Talk with study group members to schedule meeting.	3–5 PM: Study econ chapter 3.	9 AM: Economics class Drop by instructor's office hours to ask question about test	6 PM: Go over chapter 3 7–9 PM: Study group meeting.	9 AM: Economics class—Test 3:30 PM: Meet w/advisor to discuss GMAT and other business school requirements	Sleep in— schedule some down time	5 PM: Go over quiz questions with study partner

Before each week begins, remind yourself of your long-term goals and what you can accomplish over the next seven days to move you closer to them. Key 2.2 shows parts of a daily schedule and a weekly schedule.

Indicate Priority Levels

Just as your goals have varying degrees of importance, so too do your daily and weekly tasks. Prioritizing these items helps you to identify your most important tasks so you can focus the bulk of your energy and time on them. It also helps you plan when in your day to get things done. Because many top-priority items (classes, work) occur at designated times, prioritizing helps you lock in these activities and schedule less urgent items around them.

Indicate level of importance using three different categories. You can identify these categories with any code that makes sense to you—some people use numbers, some use letters (A, B, C), and some use different-colored pens. The three categories are as follows:

- *Priority 1* items are the most crucial. They may include attending class, completing school assignments, working at a job, picking up a child from day care, and paying bills. Enter Priority 1 items on your planner first, before scheduling anything else.

KEY 2.2 — Note daily and weekly tasks.

Monday, March 14

TIME	TASKS	PRIORITY
6:00 A.M.		
7:00		
8:00	Up at 8am — finish homew	
9:00		
10:00	Business Administration	
11:00	Renew driver's license @ D	
12:00 P.M.		
1:00	Lunch	
2:00	Writing Seminar (peer editi	
3:00	↓	
4:00	check on Ms. Schwartz's of	
5:00	5:30 work out	
6:00	↳6:30	
7:00	Dinner	
8:00	Read two chapters for	
9:00	Business Admin.	
10:00	↓	
11:00		
12:00		

Monday, March 28

8		Call: Mike Blair	1
9	BIO 212	Financial Aid Office	2
10		EMS 262 *Paramedic	3
11	CHEM 203	role-play*	4
12			5
Evening	6pm yoga class		

Tuesday, March 29

8	Finish reading assignment!	Work @ library	1
9			2
10	ENG 112	(study for quiz)	3
11	↓		4
12			5
Evening		↓ until 7pm	

Wednesday, March 30

8		Meet w/advisor	1
9	BIO 212		2
10		EMS 262	3
11	CHEM 203 *Quiz		4
12		Pick up photos	5
Evening	6pm Dinner w/study group		

- *Priority 2* items are important but more flexible parts of your routine. Examples include library study time, completing an assignment for a school club, and working out. Schedule these around Priority 1 items.

- *Priority 3* items are least important—the "it would be nice if I could get to that" items. Examples include phoning a friend, downloading a dozen new songs onto your iPod, and cleaning out a closet. Many people don't enter Priority 3 tasks in their planners until they know they have time for them. Others keep a separate list of these tasks so that when they have free time they can choose what they want to accomplish.

Use Scheduling Techniques

The following strategies will help you turn your scheduling activities into tools that move you closer to your goals:

Plan regularly. Set aside a regular time each day, and perhaps a longer time at the end of each week, to plan out your schedule. Being methodical about scheduling will help you reduce stress and save the hassle that might result if you forget something important. Your planner can help you only if you use it—so keep it with you and check it throughout the day.

Make and use to-do lists. Use a to-do list to record the things you want to accomplish on a given day or week. Write your to-do items on a separate piece of paper so you can set priorities. Then transfer the items you plan to accomplish each day to open time periods in your planner. To-do lists are critical time-management tools for exam week and major projects. They will help you rank your responsibilities so that you get things done in order of importance.

Post monthly and yearly calendars at home. Keeping track of your major commitments on a monthly wall calendar will give you the overview you need to focus on responsibilities and upcoming events. Key 2.3 shows a monthly calendar. If you live with family or friends, create a group calendar to stay aware of each other's plans and avoid scheduling conflicts.

Avoid time traps. Try to stay away from situations that eat up time unnecessarily. Say no graciously if you don't have time for a project; curb excess social time; declare your cell phone off-limits when you study, delegate chores. Rein in the time you spend surfing the Internet and instant-messaging with friends, because these activities can eat up hours before you know it.

Schedule down time. Leisure time is more than just a nice break—it's essential to your health and success. Even a half-hour of down time a day will

 KEY 2.3

Keep track of your time with a monthly calendar.

MARCH

SUNDAY	MONDAY	TUESDAY	WEDNESDAY	THURSDAY	FRIDAY	SATURDAY
	1 WORK	**2** Turn in English paper topic	**3** Dentist 2pm	**4** WORK	**5**	**6**
7 Frank's birthday	**8** Psych Test 9am WORK	**9**	**10** 6:30 pm Meeting @ Student Ctr.	**11** WORK	**12**	**13** Dinner @ Ryan's
14	**15** English paper due WORK	**16** Western Civ paper—Library research	**17**	**18** Library 6 pm WORK	**19** Western Civ makeup class	**20**
21	**22** WORK	**23** 2 pm meeting, psych group project	**24** Start running program: 2 miles	**25** WORK	**26** Run 2 miles	**27**
28 Run 3 miles	**29** WORK	**30** Western Civ paper due	**31** Run 2 miles			

refresh you and improve your productivity when you get back on task. Fill the time with whatever relaxes you—reading, watching television, chatting online, playing a game or sport, walking, writing, or just doing nothing.

Fight Procrastination

It's human, and common for busy students, to leave difficult or undesirable tasks until later. If taken to the extreme, however, procrastination can develop into a habit that causes serious problems, often because a procrastinator may not think through the consequences of putting something off.

This excerpt from the Study Skills Library at California Polytechnic State University at San Luis Obispo illustrates how procrastination can quickly turn into a destructive pattern:

> The procrastinator is often remarkably optimistic about his ability to complete a task on a tight deadline. . . . For example, he may estimate that a paper will take only five days to write; he has fifteen days; there is

get practical!

Make a To-Do List

Reduce stress by accomplishing practical goals. Make a to-do list for what you have to do on your busiest day this week. Include all the tasks and events you know about, including attending class and study time, and the activities you would like to do (working out at the gym, watching your favorite TV show) if you have extra time. Then prioritize your list using the coding system of your choice.

Date: _____

1. _____
2. _____
3. _____
4. _____
5. _____
6. _____

7. _____
8. _____
9. _____
10. _____
11. _____
12. _____

After examining this list, record your daily schedule in your planner (if you have a busy day, you may want to list Priority 3 items separately to complete if time permits). At the end of the day, evaluate this system. Did the list help you to manage your time and tasks effectively? If you liked it, use this exercise as a guide for using to-do lists regularly.

plenty of time, no need to start. Lulled by a false sense of security, time passes. At some point, he crosses over an imaginary starting time and suddenly realizes, "Oh no! I am not in control! There isn't enough time!"

At this point, considerable effort is directed toward completing the task, and work progresses. This sudden spurt of energy is the source of the erroneous feeling that "I work well only under pressure." Actually, at this point you are making progress only because you haven't any choice. . . . Progress is being made, but you have lost your freedom.

Barely completed in time, the paper may actually earn a fairly good grade; whereupon the student experiences mixed feelings: pride of accomplishment (sort of), scorn for the professor who cannot recognize substandard work, and guilt for getting an undeserved grade. But the net result is *reinforcement:* The procrastinator is rewarded positively for his poor behavior ("Look what a decent grade I got after all!"). As a result, the counterproductive behavior is repeated time and time again.[9]

Among the reasons people procrastinate are the following:

- *Perfectionism.* According to Jane B. Burka and Lenora M. Yuen, authors of *Procrastination: Why You Do It, What to Do About It,* habitual procrastinators often gauge their self-worth solely by their ability to achieve. In other words, "an outstanding performance means an outstanding person; a mediocre performance means a mediocre person."[10] To the perfectionist procrastinator, not trying at all is better than an attempt that falls short of perfection.

- *Fear of limitations.* Some people procrastinate in order to avoid the truth about what they can achieve. "As long as you procrastinate, you never have to confront the real limits of your ability, whatever those limits are,"[11] say Burka and Yuen. If you procrastinate and fail, you can blame the failure on waiting too long, not on any personal shortcoming.

- *Being unsure of the next step.* If you get stuck and don't know what to do, sometimes it seems easier to procrastinate than to make the leap to the next level of your goal.

- *Facing an overwhelming task.* Some big projects create immobilizing fear. If a person facing such a task fears failure, she may procrastinate in order to avoid confronting the fear.

Although it can bring relief in the short term, avoiding tasks almost always causes problems, such as a buildup of responsibilities and less time to complete them, work that is not up to par, the disappointment of others who are depending on your work, and stress brought on by the weight of the unfinished tasks. The following strategies can help you avoid procrastination and the problems associated with it:

- *Analyze the effects.* What may happen if you continue to put off a responsibility? Chances are you will benefit more in the long term from facing the task head-on.

- *Set reasonable goals.* Unreasonable goals can intimidate and immobilize you. Set manageable goals and allow enough time to complete them.

- *Break tasks into smaller parts.* If you concentrate on achieving one small step at a time, setting time limits for each step, the task may become less burdensome.

- *Get started whether or not you "feel like it."* The motivation techniques from chapter 1 might help you take the first step. Once you start, you may find it easier to continue.
- *Ask for help.* Once you identify what's holding you up, see who can help you face the task. Another person may come up with an innovative way to get you moving.
- *Don't expect perfection.* People learn by starting at the beginning, making mistakes, and learning from those mistakes. It's better to try your best than to do nothing at all.
- *Reward yourself.* Find ways to boost your confidence when you accomplish a particular task. Remind yourself—with a break, a movie, some kind of treat—that you are making progress.

Be Flexible

Change is a part of life. No matter how well you think ahead and plan your time, sudden changes—ranging from a room change for a class to a medical emergency—can upend your plans. However, you have some control over how you handle your circumstances. Your ability to evaluate situations, come up with creative options, and put practical plans to work will help you manage changes.

Small changes—for instance, the need to work an hour overtime at your after-school job, or a meeting that runs late—can result in priority shifts that jumble your schedule. For changes that occur frequently, think through a backup plan ahead of time. For surprises, the best you can do is to keep an open mind about possibilities and rely on your internal and external resources.

When change involves serious problems—your car breaks down and you have no way to get to school, or you fail a class and have to consider summer school—use problem-solving skills to help you through (see chapter 4). There are resources available at your college to help you throughout this process. Your academic advisor, counselor, dean, financial aid advisor, and instructors may have ideas and assistance.

Manage Stress by Managing Time

STRESS

Physical or mental strain or tension produced in reaction to pressure.

If you are feeling more (stress) in your everyday life as a student, you are not alone. Stress levels among college students have increased dramatically.[12] Stress factors for college students include being in a new environment, facing increased work and difficult decisions, and juggling school, work, and personal responsibilities.

Dealing with the stress of college life is, and will continue to be, one of your biggest challenges. But here's some good news: *Every time-management strategy you have read in this chapter contributes to your ability to cope with stress.* Remember that stress refers to how you react to pressure. When you create and follow a schedule that gets you places on time and helps you take care of tasks and responsibilities, you reduce pressure. Less pressure, less stress.

Analyze, and adjust if necessary, the relationship between stress and your time-management habits. For example, if you're a night person with early classes and are consistently stressed about waking up in time, use strategies such as going to bed earlier a few nights a week, napping in the afternoon, exercising briefly before class to boost energy, or exploring how to schedule later classes next term. Reduce anxiety by thinking before you act.

Following are some practical strategies for coping with stress through time management. You will find more detail on stress in chapter 8.

Be realistic about time commitments. For example, many students attempting to combine work and school find that they have to trim one or the other to reduce stress and promote success. Overloaded students often fall behind and experience high stress levels that can lead to dropping out. Determine what is reasonable for you; you may find that taking longer to graduate is a viable option if you need to work while in school.

Put sleep and down time on your schedule. Sleep-deprived bodies and minds have a harder time handling pressure effectively. Figure out how much sleep you need and do your best to get it. When you pull an all-nighter, make sure you play catch-up over the days that follow. Also, with time for relaxation in whatever form you choose, your mind will be better able to manage stress.

Actively manage your schedule. The most detailed datebook page or PDA entry can't help you unless you look at it. Get in the habit of checking at regular intervals throughout the day. Also, try not to put off tasks. If you can get it done ahead of time, get it done.

Focus on one assignment at a time. Stress is at its worst when you have five pressing assignments in five different classes all due in the next week. Focus on one at a time, completing it to the best of your ability as quickly as you can, then move to the next and the next until you're through.

Check things off. Use a physical action to indicate that you have completed a task—check off the item, delete it from your PDA task list, crumple up the Post-it Note. A physical act can relieve stress and highlight the confidence that comes from getting something done.

Sometimes stress freezes you in place and blocks you from finding answers. At those times, remember that taking even a small step is a stress-management strategy because it begins to move you ahead.

Successful Intelligence Wrap-Up

Self-management is about making well-examined choices—and you are the manager who does the choosing. Think intelligently about what you value, what goals are important to you, and how to best manage your time. Here's how you have built skills in chapter 2:

Analytical

In the *Get Analytical* exercise, you explored what you value and how your values inform educational goals. As you read the section on goals, you broke down the goal-setting process into its step-by-step parts. While exploring the topic of time management, you thought about who you are as a time manager and how that affects your scheduling and procrastination habits.

Creative

With the *Get Creative* exercise to motivate you, you came up with ideas about how to pursue an important personal goal. What you read about majors may have inspired new ideas about what you want to major in or how to construct your major. Exploring the importance of flexibility in time management showed you the key role of creativity in the face of change.

Practical

You explored the practical action of mapping out and pursuing goals step-by-step, and considered how this process applies to declaring a major. In the section on time management, you examined practical strategies for getting in control of your schedule, and created a to-do list tailored to an upcoming busy day in the *Get Practical* exercise. At the end of the chapter, you gathered practical, time-related techniques for managing the stress that all students encounter.

paseo
(pass-eh-o)

This Spanish word refers to an activity that traditionally takes place in Spanish towns in the time of evening after the afternoon *siesta*, or rest. At this late afternoon hour, families often dress up and enjoy a *paseo*—a walk outdoors in the town, to be seen and to socialize.[13]

The relaxed pace of traditional life in many European countries holds a lesson for the overscheduled, harried student. Like many other students, you may feel like you just can't afford to take a break when there is so much to do. However, you also might not be able to afford the negative effects of the stress that results when you *don't* take a break. When you manage your time effectively, you will be able to make time for relaxation, which is critical for stress reduction. So find your version of the *paseo*—a walk on the campus, a coffee shop visit, a game of soccer—and make it part of your life.

"Goals are dreams with deadlines."

DIANA SCHARF HUNT

Building World-Class Skills
for College, Career, and Life Success

SUCCESSFUL INTELLIGENCE
Think, Create, Apply

Make your first term count. Campus resources, clubs, student activity groups, and other organizations can enrich your college experience. To benefit from what your school has to offer, set a goal to get involved sooner rather than later.

Step 1. Think it through: *Analyze your college self.* Making connections with people and groups in college starts with understanding who you are as a student, both alone and in relation to your school's student body. On a separate sheet of paper, describe your particular circumstances, opinions, and needs in a short paragraph, using questions like these to think through your description:

- How would you describe yourself in terms of culture, ethnicity, gender, age, and lifestyle?
- How would you describe your student status—traditional or returning, full- or part-time?
- How long are you planning to be in your current college? Is it likely that you will transfer?
- What family and work obligations do you have?
- What is your current living situation?
- What do you feel are your biggest challenges in college?
- What do you like to study, and why does it interest you?

Step 2. Think out of the box: *Brainstorm your ideal extracurriculars.* On a second piece of paper, write ideas about how you want to spend your time outside of class. To inspire creative ideas, try using one or more of the following questions as a starting point:

- If you had no fear, what horizon-broadening experience would you sign up for?
- When you were in elementary school, what were your favorite activities? Which activities might translate into current interests and pursuits?

VALUES, GOALS, AND TIME **57**

- What kinds of organizations, activities, groups, experiences, or people make you think, "Wow, I want to do that"?
- Think about the people who bring out the best in you. What do you like to do with them? What kinds of things are they involved with?

Step 3. Make it happen: *Take practical steps toward the activities you like.* First, look in your student handbook at the resources and organizations your school offers. These may include some or all of the following:

Academic centers (reading, writing, etc.)	On-campus work opportunities
Academic organizations	Disabled student groups
Adult education center	Religious organizations
Arts clubs (music, drama, dance, etc.)	School publications
Fraternities/sororities	School TV/radio stations
International student groups	Sports clubs
Minority student groups	Student associations
	Student government
	Volunteer groups

Taking your analysis of yourself and your creative ideas into consideration, use the left-hand column on the grid that follows to list the three offices or organizations you most want to check out this term. Then—through your school publications and/or a little legwork—fill in the grid, answering the questions shown across the top for each item. The last column requires action—fill it in when you have made contact with each office or organization. Finally, if you wish to become more involved after your initial contact, go for it.

Office or Organization	Location	Hours, or times of meetings	What it offers	Phone number or e-mail	*Initial contact— date and what happened*

TEAMWORK

Create Solutions Together

Multiple paths to a goal. In a group of three or four, brainstorm important academic goals that can reasonably be accomplished in the course of one year in college. Write your ideas on a piece of paper. From that list, pick out one goal to explore together.

Each group member takes two minutes alone to think about this goal in terms of the first goal-achievement step on page 42—defining a strategy. In other words, answer the question "How would I do it?" Each person writes down all the paths he or she can think of.

The group then gathers and everyone shares their strategies. The group evaluates strategies and chooses one that seems effective. Finally, as a group, brainstorm the rest of the goal-achievement process, based on the chosen strategy or path:

- **Set a timetable.** When do you plan to reach your goal? Discuss different time frames and how each might change the path.

- **Be accountable.** What safeguards will keep you on track? Talk about different ways to make sure you are moving ahead consistently.

- **Get unstuck.** What will you do if you hit a roadblock? Brainstorm the roadblocks that could get in the way of this particular goal. For each, come up with ways to overcome the obstacle.

At the end of the process, you should have a wealth of ideas for how to approach one particular academic goal—and an appreciation for how many paths you could take in order to get there.

WRITING

Journal and Put Skills to Work

Use the tables here to record data. Answer questions and write additional thoughts on a separate piece of paper, in a journal, or on a computer file.

Journal entry: Discover how you spend your time. In the table on the following page, estimate the total time you think you spend per week on each listed activity. Then, add the hours. If your number is over 168 (the number of hours in a week), rethink your estimates and recalculate so that the total equals 168.

Now, spend a week recording exactly how you spend your time. The chart on pages 61–62 has blocks showing half-hour increments. As you go through the week, write in what you do each hour, indicating when you started and when you stopped. Don't forget activities that don't feel like "activities"—such as sleeping, relaxing, or watching TV. Finally, be sure to record your *actual* activities instead of how you want or think you should have spent your time. There are no wrong answers.

After a week, go through your filled-in chart and add up how many hours you spent on the activities for which you previously estimated your

Activity	Estimated Time Spent	Activity	Estimated Time Spent
Class		Chores and personal business	
Work		Friends and important relationships	
Studying		Communication time (phone, computer)	
Sleeping		Leisure/entertainment	
Eating		Spiritual life	
Family time/child care		Other	
Commuting/traveling		**TOTAL**	

hours. Tally the hours in the boxes in the table on page 63 using straight tally marks; round off to half hours and use a short tally mark for each half hour. In the third column, total the hours for each activity. Leave the "Ideal Time in Hours" column blank for now.

Add the totals in the third column to find your grand total. Compare your grand total to your estimated grand total; compare your actual activity hour totals to your estimated activity hour totals. Use a separate sheet of paper to answer the following questions:

- What matches and what doesn't? Describe the most interesting similarities and differences.
- Where do you waste the most time? What do you think that is costing you?

Now evaluate what kinds of changes might improve your ability to achieve goals. Analyze what you do daily, weekly, and monthly. Go back to the table on page 63 and fill in the "Ideal Time in Hours" column. Consider the difference between actual hours and ideal hours. Ask yourself questions:

- On what activities do you think you should spend more or less time?
- What are you willing to do to change, and why?

Finally, write a short paragraph describing two key time-management changes in detail. Describe what goal you are aiming for, and map out how you plan to put the changes into action.

Real-life writing: Examine two areas of academic specialty. Use your course catalog to identify two academic areas that look interesting. Write a short report comparing and contrasting the majors or concentrations in these areas, being sure to note GPA requirements, number of courses, relevance to career areas, campus locations of departments, "feel" of the departments, other requirements, and any other relevant characteristics. Conclude your report with observations about how this comparison and evaluation process has refined your thinking.

Monday		Tuesday		Wednesday		Thursday	
TIME	ACTIVITY	TIME	ACTIVITY	TIME	ACTIVITY	TIME	ACTIVITY
6:00 A.M.		6:00 A.M.		6:00 A.M.		6:00 A.M.	
6:30 A.M.		6:30 A.M.		6:30 A.M.		6:30 A.M.	
7:00 A.M.		7:00 A.M.		7:00 A.M.		7:00 A.M.	
7:30 A.M.		7:30 A.M.		7:30 A.M.		7:30 A.M.	
8:00 A.M.		8:00 A.M.		8:00 A.M.		8:00 A.M.	
8:30 A.M.		8:30 A.M.		8:30 A.M.		8:30 A.M.	
9:00 A.M.		9:00 A.M.		9:00 A.M.		9:00 A.M.	
9:30 A.M.		9:30 A.M.		9:30 A.M.		9:30 A.M.	
10:00 A.M.		10:00 A.M.		10:00 A.M.		10:00 A.M.	
10:30 A.M.		10:30 A.M.		10:30 A.M.		10:30 A.M.	
11:00 A.M.		11:00 A.M.		11:00 A.M.		11:00 A.M.	
11:30 A.M.		11:30 A.M.		11:30 A.M.		11:30 A.M.	
12:00 P.M.		12:00 P.M.		12:00 P.M.		12:00 P.M.	
12:30 P.M.		12:30 P.M.		12:30 P.M.		12:30 P.M.	
1:00 P.M.		1:00 P.M.		1:00 P.M.		1:00 P.M.	
1:30 P.M.		1:30 P.M.		1:30 P.M.		1:30 P.M.	
2:00 P.M.		2:00 P.M.		2:00 P.M.		2:00 P.M.	
2:30 P.M.		2:30 P.M.		2:30 P.M.		2:30 P.M.	
3:00 P.M.		3:00 P.M.		3:00 P.M.		3:00 P.M.	
3:30 P.M.		3:30 P.M.		3:30 P.M.		3:30 P.M.	
4:00 P.M.		4:00 P.M.		4:00 P.M.		4:00 P.M.	
4:30 P.M.		4:30 P.M.		4:30 P.M.		4:30 P.M.	
5:00 P.M.		5:00 P.M.		5:00 P.M.		5:00 P.M.	
5:30 P.M.		5:30 P.M.		5:30 P.M.		5:30 P.M.	
6:00 P.M.		6:00 P.M.		6:00 P.M.		6:00 P.M.	
6:30 P.M.		6:30 P.M.		6:30 P.M.		6:30 P.M.	
7:00 P.M.		7:00 P.M.		7:00 P.M.		7:00 P.M.	
7:30 P.M.		7:30 P.M.		7:30 P.M.		7:30 P.M.	
8:00 P.M.		8:00 P.M.		8:00 P.M.		8:00 P.M.	
8:30 P.M.		8:30 P.M.		8:30 P.M.		8:30 P.M.	
9:00 P.M.		9:00 P.M.		9:00 P.M.		9:00 P.M.	
9:30 P.M.		9:30 P.M.		9:30 P.M.		9:30 P.M.	
10:00 P.M.		10:00 P.M.		10:00 P.M.		10:00 P.M.	
10:30 P.M.		10:30 P.M.		10:30 P.M.		10:30 P.M.	
11:00 P.M.		11:00 P.M.		11:00 P.M.		11:00 P.M.	
11:30 P.M.		11:30 P.M.		11:30 P.M.		11:30 P.M.	
12–6 A.M.		12–6 A.M.		12–6 A.M.		12–6 A.M.	

Friday		Saturday		Sunday		Notes
TIME	ACTIVITY	TIME	ACTIVITY	TIME	ACTIVITY	
6:00 A.M.		6:00 A.M.		6:00 A.M.		
6:30 A.M.		6:30 A.M.		6:30 A.M.		
7:00 A.M.		7:00 A.M.		7:00 A.M.		
7:30 A.M.		7:30 A.M.		7:30 A.M.		
8:00 A.M.		8:00 A.M.		8:00 A.M.		
8:30 A.M.		8:30 A.M.		8:30 A.M.		
9:00 A.M.		9:00 A.M.		9:00 A.M.		
9:30 A.M.		9:30 A.M.		9:30 A.M.		
10:00 A.M.		10:00 A.M.		10:00 A.M.		
10:30 A.M.		10:30 A.M.		10:30 A.M.		
11:00 A.M.		11:00 A.M.		11:00 A.M.		
11:30 A.M.		11:30 A.M.		11:30 A.M.		
12:00 P.M.		12:00 P.M.		12:00 P.M.		
12:30 P.M.		12:30 P.M.		12:30 P.M.		
1:00 P.M.		1:00 P.M.		1:00 P.M.		
1:30 P.M.		1:30 P.M.		1:30 P.M.		
2:00 P.M.		2:00 P.M.		2:00 P.M.		
2:30 P.M.		2:30 P.M.		2:30 P.M.		
3:00 P.M.		3:00 P.M.		3:00 P.M.		
3:30 P.M.		3:30 P.M.		3:30 P.M.		
4:00 P.M.		4:00 P.M.		4:00 P.M.		
4:30 P.M.		4:30 P.M.		4:30 P.M.		
5:00 P.M.		5:00 P.M.		5:00 P.M.		
5:30 P.M.		5:30 P.M.		5:30 P.M.		
6:00 P.M.		6:00 P.M.		6:00 P.M.		
6:30 P.M.		6:30 P.M.		6:30 P.M.		
7:00 P.M.		7:00 P.M.		7:00 P.M.		
7:30 P.M.		7:30 P.M.		7:30 P.M.		
8:00 P.M.		8:00 P.M.		8:00 P.M.		
8:30 P.M.		8:30 P.M.		8:30 P.M.		
9:00 P.M.		9:00 P.M.		9:00 P.M.		
9:30 P.M.		9:30 P.M.		9:30 P.M.		
10:00 P.M.		10:00 P.M.		10:00 P.M.		
10:30 P.M.		10:30 P.M.		10:30 P.M.		
11:00 P.M.		11:00 P.M.		11:00 P.M.		
11:30 P.M.		11:30 P.M.		11:30 P.M.		
12–6 A.M.		12–6 A.M.		12–6 A.M.		

KEYS TO SUCCESS

Activity	Time Tallied over One-Week Period	Total Time in Hours	Ideal Time in Hours
Example: Class	IIII IIII IIII II	16.5	
Class			
Work			
Studying			
Sleeping			
Eating			
Family time/child care			
Commuting/traveling			
Chores and personal business			
Friends and important relationships			
Telephone time			
Leisure/entertainment			
Spiritual life			
Other			

PERSONAL PORTFOLIO

Prepare for Career Success

Complete the following in your electronic portfolio or on separate sheets of paper.

Knowledge, skills, and attitudes. No matter what career goals you ultimately pursue, certain knowledge, skills, and attitudes are useful in any career area. Consider this list of what employers look for in people they hire:

Acceptance

Critical thinking

Leadership

Communication

Flexibility

Positive attitude

Continual learning

Goal setting

Teamwork

Creativity

Integrity

Choose and circle three of these that you want to focus on developing this year.

Map out a plan for your progress by indicating a series of smaller goals that will lead you toward developing these skills. For example:

Skill: Teamwork

Long-term goal: To be comfortable and effective working with others

Short-term goal: I will join, or form, a study group for my economics class.

Short-term goal: I will participate in a short-term volunteering opportunity for which I am required to work in a team with others.

Short-term goal: When looking into courses with my advisor, I will consider teamwork opportunities (small group work, small seminar courses) as one of my criteria.

Suggested Readings

Allen, David. *Getting Things Done: The Art of Stress-Free Productivity.* New York: Penguin, 2003.

Burka, Jane B., and Lenora M. Yuen. *Procrastination.* Reading, MA: Perseus Books, 1990.

Charlesworth, Edward A., and Ronald G. Nathan. *Stress Management: A Comprehensive Guide to Wellness.* New York: Ballantine Books, 2004.

College Board. *The College Board Book of Majors,* 2nd ed. New York: Author, 2006.

Covey, Stephen. *The Seven Habits of Highly Effective People.* New York: Simon & Schuster, 2004.

Emmett, Rita. *The Procrastinator's Handbook: Mastering the Art of Doing It Now.* New York: Walker, 2000.

Fogg, Neeta, Paul Harrington, and Thomas Harrington. *The College Majors Handbook with Real Career Paths and Payoffs: The Actual Jobs, Earnings, and Trends for Graduates of 60 College Majors.* Indianapolis: Jist Works, 2004.

Gleeson, Kerry. *The Personal Efficiency Program: How to Get Organized to Do More Work in Less Time,* 2nd ed. New York: Wiley, 2000.

Hallowell, Edward M. *Crazy Busy: Overstretched, Overbooked, and About to Snap! Strategies for Handling Your Fast-Paced Life.* New York: Ballantine Books, 2007.

Phifer, Paul. *College Majors and Careers: A Resource Guide for Effective Life Planning,* 4th ed. Chicago: Ferguson, 2003.

Sapadin, Linda, and Jack Maguire. *Beat Procrastination and Make the Grade: The Six Styles of Procrastination and How Students Can Overcome Them.* New York: Penguin, 1999.

Simon, Sydney B. *In Search of Values: 31 Strategies for Finding Out What Really Matters Most to You.* New York: Warner Books, 1993.

Timm, Paul R. *Successful Self-Management, Revised Edition: Increasing Your Personal Effectiveness.* Los Altos, CA: Crisp Publications, 1993.

Internet and Podcast Resources

About.com—Stress Management (resources, including a variety of self-assessments): **http://stress.about.com/**

Mind Tools—Time Management: **http://mindtools .com/pages/main/newMN_HTE.htm**

Time Management Secrets with Ruth Klein podcasts: **http://odeo.com/audio/633014/view**

Top Achievement (goal-setting and self-improvement resources): **www.topachievement.com**

Troubled With (help with stress management and personal issues): **www.troubledwith.com**

Riley Guide—Values Inventories (self-assessment resources): **www.rileyguide.com/assess .html#values**

"Stress Cops" episodes on Podcast.net: **www.podcast.net/show/22377**

Prentice Hall Student Success SuperSite: **www.prenhall.com/success**

Look to your college Web site for school-specific information on declaring a major.

Endnotes

[1] Student essay submitted by the First Year Experience students of Patty Parma, Palo Alto College, San Antonio, Texas, January 2004.

[2] Mark A. King, Anthony Sims, and David Osher, "How Is Cultural Competence Integrated in Education?" March 2007, Center for Effective Collaboration and Practice (http://cecp.air.org/ cultural/Q_integrated.htm#def).

[3] Cited in Louis E. Boone and David L. Kurtz, *Contemporary Business Communication*, Upper Saddle River, NJ: Prentice Hall, 1994, p. 643.

[4] Students Speak: Excerpts from *Your Educational Experience Essays*, University of Illinois, October 2, 2001 (http://ae3_cen_uiuc_edu/stessay/ StudentsSpeak; no longer available).

[5] Cited in Terry Strathman, "What Do Students Want?" April 15, 2002, L & S Colloquium on Undergraduate Education (http://ls.berkeley.edu/?q=about-college/ l-s-divisions/undergraduate-division/ colloquium-undergraduate-education/ april-2002).

[6] Paul Timm, *Successful Self-Management: A Psychologically Sound Approach to Personal Effectiveness*, Los Altos, CA: Crisp Publications, 1987, pp. 22–41.

[7] Jeffrey R. Young, "'Homework? What Homework?' Students Seem to Be Spending Less Time Studying Than They Used To," *Chronicle of Higher Education*, December 6, 2002 (http://chronicle .com/weekly/v49/i15/15a03501.htm).

[8] Welch Suggs, "How Gears Turn at a Sports Factory: Running Ohio State's $79-Million Athletics Program Is a Major Endeavor, with Huge Payoffs and Costs," *Chronicle of Higher Education*, November 29, 2002 (http://chronicle.com/ weekly/v49/i14/14a03201.htm).

[9] William E. Sydnor, "Procrastination," from the California Polytechnic State University Study Skills Library (www.sas.calpoly.edu/asc/ssl/ procrastination.html). Based on *Overcoming Procrastination* by Albert Ellis. Used with permission.

[10] Jane B. Burka and Lenora M. Yuen, *Procrastination. Why You Do It, What to Do About It*, Reading, MA: Perseus Books, 1983, pp. 21–22.

[11] Ibid.

[12] Jodi Wilgoren, "Survey Shows High Stress Levels in College Freshmen," *New York Times*, January 23, 2000, p. NA.

[13] Christopher J. Moore, *In Other Words: A Language Lover's Guide to the Most Intriguing Words Around the World*, New York: Walker, 2004, pp. 36–37.

DIVERSITY MATTERS

How You Learn and Communicate

3

"Successfully intelligent people figure out their strengths and their weaknesses, and then find ways to capitalize on their strengths—make the most of what they do well—and to correct for or remedy their weaknesses—find ways around what they don't do well, or make themselves good enough to get by."

ROBERT STERNBERG

Diversity exists both within each person and among all people. The layers of diversity *within you*—physical being, personality, talents, skills, and thinking abilities— include your unique way of learning and communicating. This chapter builds your awareness of diversity within and without— helping you to identify how you learn, how you put your knowledge to work, how you can relate to others in a culturally competent way, and how you can practice communication strategies that will help you build successful relationships in school and elsewhere.

In this chapter you explore answers to the following questions:

Analytical

- Analyzing your eight multiple intelligences
- Investigating how you relate to others
- Evaluating the assumptions that underlie prejudice and stereotypes

Creative

- Creating new ways to develop your abilities
- Developing a new vision of yourself as a learner
- Creating new ideas about what diversity means

Practical

- How to choose and use your best study strategies
- How to adjust to an instructor's teaching style
- How to relate to others with cultural competence

Why Explore Who You Are as a Learner?

Have you ever thought about yourself as a learner? Most students, even those who do well in the areas traditionally valued by schools (verbal and mathematical skills), conclude that "this high (or low) GPA is who I am. I am intelligent (or not)." More often than not, decisions stretching throughout a lifetime are made based on that self-assessment.

Your Unique Intelligence Can Change and Develop

© Jaimie Duplass—Fotolia.com

Each person in the world is unique, with an individual blend of characteristics. Likewise, each person has a particular way in which his or her mind receives and processes information. Everyone is also born with particular levels of ability and potential in different areas. For example, some musicians can play anything they hear. Your natural abilities, plus effort and environmental influences, combine to create a recipe for the achievement level you can attain.

Picture a bag of a variety of rubber bands. Some are thick, some are thin; some are long, some are short. *But all of them can stretch*. A small rubber band, stretched out, can reach the length of a larger one that lies unstretched. In other words, with effort and focus, you can grow to some extent whatever raw material you

How can I maximize what I do well?

How can I make the most of my strengths in a course if the professor doesn't use teaching methods that I can relate to? For example, I'm an artist and I tend to connect with information visually. I tend to rely on written notes, maps, and diagrams to absorb information. When I have professors who only lecture, I find it very hard to listen and take notes at the same time—but I need the notes to look at later for studying. How can I deal with this situation?

Cheryl Whitley
Florida Community College
at Jacksonville

PRACTICAL ANSWERS

Use what you do well to adapt to what challenges you.

Darren Love
Midwestern University,
Phoenix, Arizona

I know firsthand that it takes time and some training to adapt to a different teaching style than you're used to. When I began college, I was mostly a visual learner, and I quickly learned that I had to either adapt to different styles or be left behind. I became more flexible with practice as I tried new study techniques. As the years passed, I discovered I could adjust to whatever format I encountered in the classroom, including lecture and group-based learning.

Try using techniques in an area of strength to compensate for an area of weakness. I know that you are a visual learner (strength) but most of your courses are lecture-based (weakness). Using visually focused techniques will help you adjust to lectures and ultimately integrate the two styles. First, ask your professor if you can videotape or audiotape the lectures so that you will always have the lecture material. Second, when you write your notes, fold your paper in half. On one side, write the notes in pencil or one color of pen; then, when you go home, complement the partial notes that you took earlier by consulting your text and writing text notes in pen (if you used pencil) or a different color of pen (if you used pen) on the other side of the paper. Third, use the audio or videotape of the lecture and convert the material to something that is more visual, such as charts, graphs, or a picture. Fourth, try writing your notes in shorthand, using your visual strength to convert words to symbols or pictures to represent the professor's words.

Now I am in grad school, where one course is often taught by several professors, each with a different style of lecturing. I am adapting once again, accenting my strengths in visual and interpersonal learning to manage the challenges I face in lecture-based classrooms. Over time, as you emphasize your strength, the confidence you build will help you face styles less natural to you.

have at the start. *To reach your individual potential is your most worthy goal, and the most you can ask of yourself.*

Studies of the brain, showing that humans of any age are able to build new neuropathways and thereby learn new ideas and skills, support Sternberg's theory that intelligence can change over time.[1] Set aside the notion that your intelligence has a "fixed" level as you continue through this chapter, through college, and into your life after college. Work instead to understand your strengths—to define the characteristics of your rubber band and stretch it to the limit.

Assessments Can Help You Learn About Yourself

POTENTIALS

Abilities that may be developed.

An assessment, as professor and psychologist Howard Gardner puts it, is "the obtaining of information about a person's skills and potentials . . . providing useful feedback to the person."[2] With the information you gain from the two assessments you will take in this chapter—*Multiple Pathways to Learning* and the *Personality Spectrum*—you will learn more about what your strengths and weaknesses are, leading you to the ability to maximize those strengths and compensate for those weaknesses as a successfully intelligent learner. (You will learn about these intelligences and other characteristics later in the chapter.)

INTELLIGENCE

As defined by Howard Gardner, an ability to solve problems or create products that are of value in a culture.

Understanding yourself as a learner will also help you to see and appreciate how people differ. In a study group or classroom, each person is taking in the material in a unique way. What you know about how others learn can help you improve communication and teamwork.

Self-knowledge is a key to personal power. With self-knowledge, you can work toward controlling how you respond to circumstances as you and your environment change, making adjustments that will help you cope and grow. Use these assessments to help you look at the present—and plan for the future—by asking questions: "Who am I right now?" "How does this compare with who I want to be?"

Compare the process of responding to the assessment questions to the experience of trying on new eyeglasses to correct blurred vision. The glasses will not create new paths and possibilities, but they will help you see more clearly the ones that exist today.

What Tools Can Help You Assess How You Learn and Interact with Others?

This chapter presents two assessments designed to help you get a closer look at your learning capacities and favored modes of interaction with others. The first—*Multiple Pathways to Learning*—focuses on eight areas of potential and is based on Howard Gardner's Multiple Intelligences theory. The second—the *Personality Spectrum*—is based on the Myers-Briggs Type Indicator® (MBTI) and helps you evaluate how you react to people and situations.

Following each assessment is information about the typical traits of each intelligence or personality spectrum dimension. As you will see from your scores, you have abilities in all areas, though some are more developed than others.

Assess your Multiple Intelligences with *Multiple Pathways to Learning*

In 1983, Howard Gardner changed the way people perceive intelligence and learning with his Multiple Intelligences theory. Like Robert Sternberg,

Gardner had developed the belief that the traditional view of intelligence—based on mathematical, logical, and verbal measurements comprising an "intelligence quotient" or IQ—did not comprehensively reflect the spectrum of human ability. Whereas Sternberg focused on the spectrum of actions that help people achieve important goals, Gardner honed in on the idea that humans possess a number of different areas of natural ability and potential:

> I believe that we should . . . look . . . at more naturalistic sources of information about how peoples around the world develop skills important to their way of life. Think, for example, of sailors in the South Seas, who find their way around hundreds, or even thousands, of islands by looking at the constellations of stars in the sky, feeling the way a boat passes over the water, and noticing a few scattered landmarks. A word for intelligence in a society of these sailors would probably refer to that kind of navigational ability.[3]

The Theory of Multiple Intelligences

Gardner's reading and research in biology, neuropsychology, and other disciplines led him to believe that there are eight unique "intelligences," or areas of ability. These include the areas traditionally associated with the term *intelligence*—logic and verbal skills—but go beyond, to encompass a wide range of potentials of the human brain. Note that these intelligences almost never function in isolation. Gardner emphasizes that, with few exceptions, "intelligences always work in concert," and adults will almost always use several of them for any significant role or task.[4]

Look at Key 3.1 for descriptions of each intelligence. To further illustrate the intelligences, the table lists examples of people who have unusually high levels of ability in each intelligence. Although few people will have the verbal-linguistic intelligence of William Shakespeare or the interpersonal intelligence of Oprah Winfrey, everyone has some level of ability in each intelligence. Your goal is to identify what your levels are and to work your strongest intelligences to your advantage.

Gardner defines *an intelligence* as "a biophysical potential to process information that can be activated in a cultural setting to solve problems or create products that are of value in a culture."[5] Restated more simply, an intelligence is an ability that is valued by a group of people for what it can produce. This definition takes the concept of intelligence beyond what a standard IQ test can measure. As Tibetan mountain natives prize the bodily-kinesthetic ability of a top-notch Himalayan mountain guide, so the Detroit auto manufacturing community appreciates the visual-spatial talents of a master car designer.

Your Own Eight Intelligences

You have your own personal "map" of abilities, which is a combination of what you are born with and what you work to develop. Gardner believes that all people possess some capacity in each of the eight

Each intelligence is linked to specific abilities.

INTELLIGENCE	DESCRIPTION	HIGH-ACHIEVING EXAMPLE
Verbal-Linguistic	Ability to communicate through language; listening, reading, writing, speaking	Playwright William Shakespeare
Logical-Mathematical	Ability to understand logical reasoning and problem solving; math, science, patterns, sequences	Microsoft founder Bill Gates
Bodily-Kinesthetic	Ability to use the physical body skillfully and to take in knowledge through bodily sensation; coordination, working with hands	Ice skating champion Michelle Kwan
Visual-Spatial	Ability to understand spatial relationships and to perceive and create images; visual art, graphic design, charts and maps	Architect Frank Gehry
Interpersonal	Ability to relate to others, noticing their moods, motivations, and feelings; social activity, cooperative learning, teamwork	Telejournalist Oprah Winfrey
Intrapersonal	Ability to understand one's own behavior and feelings; self-awareness, independence, time spent alone	The Dalai Lama
Musical	Ability to comprehend and create meaningful sound; sensitivity to music and musical patterns	Singer and musician Alicia Keys
Naturalist	Ability to identify, distinguish, categorize, and classify species or items, often incorporating high interest in elements of the natural environment	Conservationist Steve Irwin

intelligences, and that every person has developed some intelligences more fully than others. When you find a task or subject easy, you are probably using a more fully developed intelligence. When you have trouble, you may be using a less developed intelligence.[6] Furthermore, Gardner believes your levels of development in the eight intelligences can grow or recede throughout your life, depending on your efforts and experiences, reflecting how the brain grows with learning and slows without it.

The *Multiple Pathways to Learning* assessment helps you determine the levels to which your eight intelligences are developed. Key 3.2, immediately following the assessment, describes specific skills associated with the eight intelligences. Finally, the *Multiple Intelligence Strategies* grids in chapters 5 through 8 will demonstrate how to apply your knowledge to key college success skills and to specific areas of study.

ULTIPLE PATHWAYS TO LEARNING

ligence has a set of numbered statements.
each statement on its own. Then, on a scale from
) to 4 (highest), rate how closely it matches who
ght now and write that number on the line next
tement. Finally, total each set of six questions.

rarely	sometimes	usually	always
1	2	3	4

___ I enjoy physical activities.

___ I am uncomfortable sitting still.

___ I prefer to learn through doing.

___ When sitting, I move my legs or hands.

___ I enjoy working with my hands.

___ I like to pace when I'm thinking or studying.

___ TOTAL for BODILY–KINESTHETIC

1. ___ I enjoy telling stories.

2. ___ I like to write.

3. ___ I like to read.

4. ___ I express myself clearly.

5. ___ I am good at negotiating.

6. ___ I like to discuss topics that interest me.

___ TOTAL for VERBAL–LINGUISTIC

___ I use maps easily.

___ I draw pictures/diagrams when explaining ideas.

___ I can assemble items easily from diagrams.

___ I enjoy drawing or photography.

___ I do not like to read long paragraphs.

___ I prefer a drawn map over written directions.

___ TOTAL for VISUAL–SPATIAL

1. ___ I like math in school.

2. ___ I like science.

3. ___ I problem-solve well.

4. ___ I question how things work.

5. ___ I enjoy planning or designing something new.

6. ___ I am able to fix things.

___ TOTAL for LOGICAL–MATHEMATICAL

___ I listen to music.

___ I move my fingers or feet when I hear music.

___ I have good rhythm.

___ I like to sing along with music.

___ People have said I have musical talent.

___ I like to express my ideas through music.

___ TOTAL for MUSICAL

1. ___ I need quiet time to think.

2. ___ I think about issues before I want to talk.

3. ___ I am interested in self-improvement.

4. ___ I understand my thoughts and feelings.

5. ___ I know what I want out of life.

6. ___ I prefer to work on projects alone.

___ TOTAL for INTRAPERSONAL

___ I like doing a project with other people.

___ People come to me to help settle conflicts.

___ I like to spend time with friends.

___ I am good at understanding people.

___ I am good at making people feel comfortable.

___ I enjoy helping others.

___ TOTAL for INTERPERSONAL

1. ___ I like to think about how things, ideas, or people fit into categories.

2. ___ I enjoy studying plants, animals, or oceans.

3. ___ I tend to see how things relate to, or are distinct from, one another.

4. ___ I think about having a career in the natural sciences.

5. ___ As a child I often played with bugs and leaves.

6. ___ I like to investigate the natural world around me.

___ TOTAL for NATURALISTIC

Developed by Joyce Bishop, Ph.D., Golden West College, Huntington Beach, CA. Based on Howard Gardner, *of Mind: The Theory of Multiple Intelligences,* New York: HarperCollins, 1993.[8]

SCORING GRID FOR MULTIPLE PATHWAYS TO LEARI

For each intelligence, shade the box in the row that corresponds with the range where your score falls. For example, if you scored 17 in Bodily–Kinesthetic intelligence, you would shade the middle box in that row; if you scored a 13 in Visual–Spatial, you would shade the last box in that row. When you have shaded one box for each row, you will see a "map" of your range velopment at a glance.

A score of 20–24 indicates a high level o opment in that particular type of intelligence, a moderate level, and below 14 an underdev intelligence.

	20-24 (Highly Developed)	14–19 (Moderately Developed)	Below 1 (Underdevelop
Bodily–Kinesthetic			
Visual–Spatial			
Verbal–Linguistic			
Logical–Mathematical			
Musical			
Interpersonal			
Intrapersonal			
Naturalistic			

Particular abilities and skills are associated with each intelligence.

Verbal-Linguistic
- Analyzing own use of language
- Remembering terms easily
- Explaining, teaching, learning, using humor
- Understanding syntax and word meaning
- Using writing or speech to convince someone to do or believe something

Musical

- Sensing tonal qualities
- Creating/enjoying rhythms, melodies
- Being sensitive to sounds and rhythms
- Using an understanding of musical patterns to hear music
- Understanding the symbols and structure of music

Logical-Mathematical
- Recognizing abstract patterns
- Using facts to support an idea, and generating ideas based on evidence
- Discerning relationships and connections
- Performing complex calculations
- Reasoning scientifically (formulating and testing a hypothesis)

Visual-Spatial

- Perceiving and forming objects accurately
- Recognizing relationships between objects
- Representing something graphically
- Manipulating images
- Finding one's way in space

Bodily-Kinesthetic
- Strong mind–body connection
- Controlling and coordinating body movement
- Improving body functions
- Expanding body awareness to all senses
- Using the body to create products or express emotion

Intrapersonal
- Accessing one's internal emotions
- Understanding feelings and using them to guide behavior
- Evaluating own thinking
- Understanding self in relation to others
- Forming a comprehensive self-concept

Interpersonal

- Seeing things from others' perspectives
- Noticing moods, intentions, and temperaments of others
- Cooperating within a group
- Communicating verbally and nonverbally
- Creating and maintaining relationships

Naturalistic

- Ability to categorize something as a member of a group or species
- Ability to distinguish items in a group from one another
- Understanding of relationships among natural organisms
- Appreciation of the delicate balance in nature
- Deep comfort with, and respect for, the natural world

Source: Adapted from David Lazear, *Seven Pathways of Learning,* Tucson: Zephyr, 1994.

Assess Your Style of Interaction with the *Personality Spectrum*

The multiple intelligences assessment focuses on your potential in areas of ability. In contrast, personality assessments help you understand how you respond to the world around you, including people, work, and school. They also can help guide you as you explore majors and careers.

The concept of dividing human beings into four basic personality types goes as far back as Aristotle and Hippocrates, ancient Greek philosophers. Psychologist and philosopher Carl Jung, working in the early half of the 20th century, got more specific about personality typology. He defined the following:[7]

TYPOLOGY

A systematic classification or study of types.

- **An individual's preferred "world."** Jung said that *extroverts* tend to prefer the outside world of people and activities, while *introverts* tend to prefer the inner world of thoughts, feelings, and fantasies.

- **Different ways of dealing with the world, or "functions."** Jung said that we all use the same ones, but in different proportions. He laid out four: *sensing* (learning through what your senses take in), *thinking* (evaluating information rationally), *intuiting* (learning through an instinct that comes from many integrated sources of information), and *feeling* (evaluating information through emotional response).

Katharine Briggs and her daughter, Isabel Briggs Myers, developed an assessment based on Jung's typology. This Myers-Briggs Type Indicator®, or MBTI, is one of the most widely used personality inventories in the world. People completing the MBTI will find that they fall into one of 16 possible types (each a unique combination of the four dimensions). David Keirsey and Marilyn Bates combined the Myers-Briggs types into four temperaments, and developed a corresponding assessment called the Keirsey Sorter.

The *Personality Spectrum* assessment in this chapter is based on the Keirsey Sorter as well as on the MBTI. It adapts and simplifies the material into four personality types—Thinker, Organizer, Giver, and Adventurer—and was developed by Joyce Bishop, one of the authors of *Keys to Success*.

Like the assessments on which it is based, the *Personality Spectrum* assessment helps you identify the kinds of interactions that are most, and least, comfortable for you. As with multiple intelligences, personality results may change over time in reaction to new experiences, effort, and practice. Key 3.3, on page 79, shows skills that are characteristic of each personality type.

PERSONALITY SPECTRUM

1. Rank-order all four responses to each question [mo]st like you (4) to least like you (1) so that for each [...] you use the numbers 1, 2, 3, and 4 one time [...pla]ce numbers in the boxes next to the responses.

4	3	2	1
most like me	more like me	less like me	least like me

[...] instructors who

- [ ] tell me exactly what is expected of me.
- [ ] make learning active and exciting.
- [ ] maintain a safe and supportive classroom.
- [ ] challenge me to think at higher levels.

[...] best when the material is

- [ ] well organized.
- [ ] something I can do hands-on.
- [ ] about understanding and improving the human condition.
- [ ] intellectually challenging.

[...]gh priority in my life is to

- [ ] keep my commitments.
- [ ] experience as much of life as possible.
- [ ] make a difference in the lives of others.
- [ ] understand how things work.

[...]er people think of me as

- [ ] dependable and loyal.
- [ ] dynamic and creative.
- [ ] caring and honest.
- [ ] intelligent and inventive.

5. When I experience stress I would most likely

- a. [ ] do something to help me feel more in control of my life.
- b. [ ] do something physical and daring.
- c. [ ] talk with a friend.
- d. [ ] go off by myself and think about my situation.

6. I would probably not be close friends with someone who is

- a. [ ] irresponsible.
- b. [ ] unwilling to try new things.
- c. [ ] selfish and unkind to others.
- d. [ ] an illogical thinker.

7. My vacations could be described as

- a. [ ] traditional.
- b. [ ] adventuresome.
- c. [ ] pleasing to others.
- d. [ ] a new learning experience.

8. One word that best describes me is

- a. [ ] sensible.
- b. [ ] spontaneous.
- c. [ ] giving.
- d. [ ] analytical.

2. Add up the total points for each letter.

[...]L FOR   a. [ ] Organizer   b. [ ] Adventurer   c. [ ] Giver   d. [ ] Thinker

3. Plot these numbers on the brain diagram on page 78.

SCORING DIAGRAM FOR PERSONALITY SPECTR

Write your scores from page 77 in the four squares just outside the brain diagram—Thinker score at top left, Giver score at top right, Organizer score at bottom left, and Adventurer score at bottom right.

Each square has a line of numbers that go from the square to the center of the diagram. For each of your four scores, place a dot on the appropriate number in the that square. For example, if you scored 15 in the Give spectrum, you would place a dot between the 14 an the upper right-hand line of numbers. If you scored a Organizer spectrum, you would place a dot on the 26 lower left-hand line of numbers.

Connect the four dots to make a four-sided shape. If you like, shade the four sections inside the shape using four different colors.

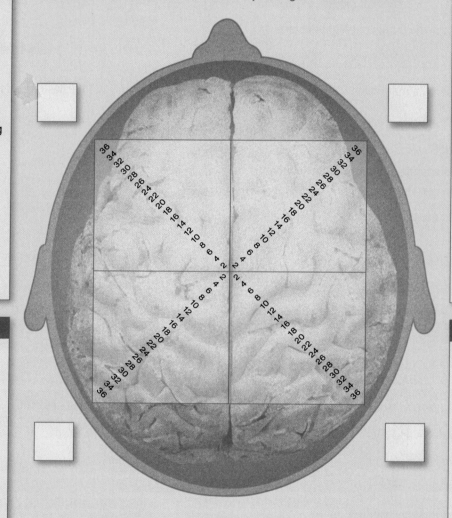

THINKER

- Technical
- Scientific
- Mathematical
- Dispassionate
- Rational
- Analytical
- Logical
- Problem-solving
- Theoretical
- Intellectual
- Objective
- Quantitative
- Explicit
- Realistic
- Literal
- Precise
- Formal

ORGANIZER

- Tactical
- Planning
- Detailed
- Practical
- Confident
- Predictable
- Controlled
- Dependable
- Systematic
- Sequential
- Structured
- Administrative
- Procedural
- Organized
- Conservative
- Safekeeping
- Disciplined

GIV

- Interp
- Em
- S
- S
- M
- Ro
- Peace
- T
- Ada
- Pass
- Harm
- Id
- Ta

ADVENT

- F
- O
- A
- S
- S
- Imp
- Meta
- Experi
- Div
- Fast-
- Simulta
- Comp
- Imagi
- Open-m
- Adventure

For the *Personality Spectrum*,
26–36 indicates a strong tendency in that dimension,
14–25 a moderate tendency,
and below 14 a minimal tendency.

Source for brain diagram: *Understanding Psychology*, 3rd ed. by Morris, © 1996.
Adapted by permission of Prentice-Hall, Inc., Upper Saddle River, NJ.

Particular abilities and skills are associated with each Personality Spectrum dimension.

Thinker

© Tracy Martinez—Fotolia.com

- Solving problems
- Developing models and systems
- Analytical and abstract thinking
- Exploring ideas and potentials
- Ingenuity
- Going beyond established boundaries
- Global thinking—seeking universal truth

Organizer

© mckryak—Fotolia.com

- Responsibility, reliability
- Operating successfully within social structures
- Sense of history, culture, and dignity
- Neatness and organization
- Loyalty
- Orientation to detail
- Comprehensive follow-through on tasks
- Efficiency
- Helping others

Giver

© James Steidl—Fotolia.com

- Honesty, authenticity
- Successful, close relationships
- Making a difference in the world
- Cultivating potential of self and others
- Negotiation; promoting peace
- Openness
- Helping others

Adventurer

© Howard Sandler—Fotolia.com

- High ability in a variety of fields
- Courage and daring
- Hands-on problem solving
- Living in the present
- Spontaneity and action
- Ability to negotiate
- Nontraditional style
- Flexibility
- Zest for life

Source: © 2001, Joyce Bishop, in *Keys to Success*, 3rd ed., Upper Saddle River, NJ: Pearson Prentice Hall, 2001.

How Can You Use Your Self-Knowledge?

The lecture format is most common in the college classroom. Students who find it challenging can make the most of a lecture-based course using strategies that suit their strenghts.

Now that you've completed your assessments, how can you apply what you learned about yourself to promote success? Generally, self-knowledge helps you make choices that maximize your strengths and manage your weaknesses. In completing the assessments, you have explored your levels of potential in eight abilities as well as how you tend to interact with others. This section of the chapter focuses on how you can use this new picture to choose—and most importantly, *use*—effective strategies inside the classroom, during study time, and in the workplace.

Classroom Benefits

Instructors have a range of teaching styles, reflecting their learning strengths and preferred styles of interaction. How you prefer to learn may work well with some instructors and be a mismatch with others. After several class meetings, you should be able to assess an instructor's teaching styles (see Key 3.4). Then you can use what you know about your most effective ways to learn to creatively get the most out of any instructor's teaching style.

Although presentation styles vary, the standard lecture is still the norm in most classrooms. For this reason, the traditional college classroom is generally a happy home for the verbal or logical learner and the Thinker and the Organizer. However, many students learn best when interacting with other students more than a traditional lecture allows. What can you do when your preferences don't match up with how your instructor teaches? Here are three suggestions:

- **Play to your strengths.** For example, a musical learner with an instructor who delivers material in a random way might record lecture highlights digitally and listen to them on an MP3 player as a study tool. Likewise, a Giver taking a straight lecture course with no student-to-student contact might be motivated by meeting with a study group to go over the details and fill in factual gaps.

- **Work to strengthen weaker areas.** While a visual learner is reviewing notes from a structured lecture course, he could use logical-mathematical strategies such as outlining notes or thinking about cause-and-effect relationships within the material. An Organizer, studying for a test from notes delivered by an instructor who used a random presentation, could find ways to organize the material (for example, by creating notes in a table format).

KEY 3.4 Instructors often prefer one or more teaching styles.

TEACHING STYLE	WHAT TO EXPECT IN CLASS
Lecture, verbal focus	Instructor speaks to the class for the entire period, with little class interaction. Lesson is taught primarily through words, either spoken or written on the board, overhead projector, handouts, or text.
Lecture with group discussion	Instructor presents material but encourages class discussion.
Small groups	Instructor presents material and then breaks class into small groups for discussion or project work.
Visual focus	Instructor uses visual elements such as PowerPoint slides, diagrams, photographs, drawings, transparencies, and videos.
Logical presentation	Instructor organizes material in a logical sequence, such as by steps, time, or importance.
Random presentation	Instructor tackles topics in no particular order, and may jump around a lot or digress.
Conceptual presentation	Instructor spends the majority of time on the big picture, focusing on abstract concepts and umbrella ideas.
Detailed presentation	Instructor spends the majority of time, after introducing ideas, on the details and facts that underlie them.
Experience-based presentation	Instructor uses demonstrations, experiments, props, and class activities to show key points.

- **Ask your instructor for additional help.** If you are having trouble with course work, take the initiative to communicate with your instructor through e-mail or during office hours. This is especially important in large lectures where you are anonymous unless you speak up. A visual learner, for example, might ask the instructor to recommend graphs, figures, or videos that illustrate the lecture.

No instructor can give every student in a diverse group of learners exactly what each one needs. The flexibility that helps you manage how you adjust to instructors' teaching styles is a tool for career and life success. Just as you can't hand-pick your instructors, you will rarely, if ever, be able to choose your work colleagues or their work styles. When there are many different instructors teaching sections of a course, ask other students about the instructors' teaching styles and how the courses are structured.

Maximize Your Classroom Experience

Consider first what you know about yourself as a learner. Then, reflect on your instructors' teaching styles this term. Analyze which instructors mesh well with how you learn, and which don't as much. Make notes here about the situation that you think is the most challenging.

Course: _____ Instructor style: _____

Your analysis of the problem: _____

_____

Next, brainstorm at least three ideas about actions you can take to improve the situation:

1. _____

2. _____

3. _____

Finally, choose one action and put it to practical use. Briefly note what happened: Were there improvements as a result? _____

_____

Study Benefits

First, when you can, use what you know about yourself to choose study techniques that capitalize on your strengths. For example, if you tend to learn successfully from a linear, logical presentation, you can look for order (for example, a *chronology*—information organized sequentially according to event dates—or a problem–solution structure) as you review notes. If you are strong in interpersonal intelligence, you can try to work in study groups whenever possible.

When you are faced with a task or topic that challenges your weaknesses, use strategies that may boost your ability in those areas. An Adventurer who does *not* respond well to linear information, for example, has two choices when faced with logical presentations: She can apply her strengths to the material—for example, she might find a hands-on approach— or she can focus on developing study skills that work well for Thinker-dominant learners.

 **KEY 3.5** Particular study techniques maximize each intelligence.

Verbal-Linguistic	• Reading text; highlighting selectively • Using a computer to retype and summarize notes • Outlining chapters • Teaching someone else • Reciting information or writing scripts/debates

Musical-Rhythmic

- Creating rhythms out of words
- Beating out rhythms with hand or stick while reciting concepts
- Writing songs or raps that help you learn concepts
- Writing out study material to fit into a wordless tune you have on a CD or MP3 player; chanting or singing the material to the tune as you listen
- Taking music breaks

Logical-Mathematical

- Organizing material logically; if it suits the topic, using a spreadsheet program
- Explaining material sequentially to someone
- Developing systems and finding patterns
- Writing outlines
- Analyzing and evaluating information

Visual-Spatial

- Developing graphic organizers for new material
- Drawing mind maps and think links
- Using a computer to develop charts and tables
- Using color in notes to organize
- Linking material in your mind with items or places that you can visualize (method of loci)

Bodily-Kinesthetic

- Moving while you learn; pacing and reciting
- Using tangible items as memory devices
- Rewriting or retyping notes to engage "muscle memory"
- Designing and playing games to learn material
- Acting out scripts of material

Intrapersonal

- Reflecting on personal meaning of information
- Visualizing information
- Keeping a journal
- Studying in quiet areas
- Imagining essays or experiments before beginning

Interpersonal

- Studying in a group
- As you study, discussing information over the phone or sending instant messages
- Using flash cards with others
- Teaching someone else the material
- Making time to discuss assignments and tests with your instructor

Naturalistic

- Breaking down information into categories
- Looking for ways that items fit or don't fit together
- Looking for relationships among ideas, events, facts
- Studying in a natural setting if it helps you to focus
- Forming study groups of people with similar interests

Source: Adapted from David Lazear, *Seven Pathways of Learning,* Tucson: Zephyr, 1994.

KEY 3.6 Particular study techniques maximize each Personality Spectrum dimension.

Thinker

© Tracy Martinez—Fotolia.com

- Finding time to reflect independently on new information
- Learning through problem solving
- Designing new ways of approaching issues
- Converting material into logical charts, flow diagrams, and outlines
- Trying to minimize repetitive tasks
- Looking for opportunities to work independently

Organizer

© mckryak—Fotolia.com

- Defining tasks in concrete terms so that you know what is required
- Looking for a well-structured study environment
- Requesting feedback from instructors and classmates via e-mail or phone
- Using a planner or PDA to schedule tasks and dates
- Organizing material by rewriting and summarizing class and/or text notes
- Using flash cards
- Highlighting materials and notes carefully

Giver

© James Steidl—Fotolia.com

- Studying with others in person, on the phone, or using instant messages
- Teaching material to others
- Seeking out tasks, groups, and subjects that involve helping people
- Expressing thoughts and feelings clearly and honestly
- Prioritizing your most important academic relationships

Adventurer

© Howard Sandler—Fotolia.com

- Looking for environments/courses that encourage nontraditional approaches
- Finding hands-on ways to learn
- Seeking instructors and students whom you find stimulating
- Using or developing games and puzzles to help memorize terms
- Fighting boredom by asking to do something extra or performing a task in a more active way

When you study with others, an understanding of diverse learning styles will help you assign tasks effectively and learn more comprehensively, as these suggestions show:

- An Interpersonal learner could take the lead in teaching material to others.
- An Organizer could coordinate the group schedule.
- A Naturalistic learner might organize facts into categories that solidify concepts.

Key 3.5 shows study strategies that suit each intelligence, and Key 3.6 shows study strategies that suit each Personality Spectrum dimension. Because you have some level of ability in each area, and because there will be times that you need to boost your ability in a weaker area, you may find useful suggestions under any of the headings. Try different techniques, analyze how effective they are, and use what works best for you.

Successful Intelligence Connections Online

Listen to author Sarah Kravits discuss analytical, creative, and practical ideas for how to choose your best setting for successful studying.

Go to the *Keys to Success* Companion Website at http://www.prenhall.com/carter to listen or download as a podcast.

Workplace Benefits

The self-knowledge you build throughout this chapter has practical application on the job and for career planning. A self-aware employee, or job candidate, can expect many benefits.

Better Performance and Teamwork

Knowing how you learn and interact with others will help you work more effectively. When you understand your strengths, you can find ways to use them on the job more readily. For tasks that require you to use less developed skills, you will be more able to find ways to compensate, such as seeking help. In addition, you will be better able to find ways to work with others effectively. For example, if you are a Giver you might enjoy helping new hires adjust to the people and environment. Or a team leader assigning tasks to an intrapersonal team member might offer the chance to take material home to think about before a meeting.

Better Career Planning

Exploring ways to use your strengths in school will help you make better choices about what internships, jobs, or careers will suit you. For instance, a love of math combined with strong interpersonal intelligence might guide you toward activities—such as math tutoring—that inform future career goals (teaching math, working with a research group in a lab).

For most college students, internships and majors are more immediate steps on the road to a career. A strength in one or more intelligences might lead you to particular internships and majors that may make sense for you. Key 3.7 shows some possibilities for majors and internships that link

This biology researcher engages her naturalistic intelligence and strength in the Thinker dimension on a daily basis as she studies the sensory organs of alligators and crocodiles.

KEY 3.7 Multiple intelligences may open doors to majors and internships.

Multiple intelligence	Consider majoring in . . .	Think about an internship at a . . .
Bodily-Kinesthetic	Massage or Physical Therapy Kinesiology Construction Engineering Sports Medicine Dance or Theater	Sports physician's office Physical or massage therapy center Construction company Dance studio or theater company Athletic club
Intrapersonal	Psychology Finance Computer Science Biology Philosophy	Accounting firm Biology lab Pharmaceutical company Publishing house Computer or Internet company
Interpersonal	Education Public Relations Nursing Business Hotel/Restaurant Management	Hotel or restaurant Social service agency Public relations firm Human Resources department Charter school
Naturalistic	Geology Zoology Atmospheric Sciences Agriculture Environmental Law	Museum National park Environmental law firm Zoo Geological research firm
Musical	Music Music Theory Voice Composition Performing Arts	Performance hall Radio station Record label or recording studio Children's music camp Orchestra or opera company
Logical-Mathematical	Math Physics Economics Banking/Finance Computer Science	Law firm Consulting firm Bank Information technology company Research lab
Verbal-Linguistic	Communications Marketing English/Literature Journalism Foreign Languages	Newspaper or magazine PR/marketing firm Ad agency Publishing house Network TV affiliate
Visual-Spatial	Architecture Visual Arts Multimedia Design Photography Art History	Photo or art studio Multimedia design firm Architecture firm Interior design firm Art gallery

to the eight intelligences. This list is by no means complete; rather, it represents only a fraction of the available opportunities. Use what you see here to inspire thought and spur investigation. See Key 8.8 on pages 276–277, in the section on careers in chapter 8, for ideas about how intelligences may link to particular careers.

Being sensitive to your unique way of learning will benefit you in ways beyond your education and career. A better understanding of your learning strengths and preferences and personality traits will help you identify, appreciate, and adapt to the diversity among people.

How Can You Develop Cultural Competence?

Interacting successfully with all kinds of people is the goal of *cultural competence*. As you learned in chapter 2, cultural competence refers to the ability to understand and appreciate differences among people and adjust your behavior in ways that enhance, rather than detract from, relationships and communication. According to the National Center for Cultural Competence, to develop cultural competence you must act upon the following five steps:[9]

1. Value diversity.
2. Identify and evaluate personal perceptions and attitudes.
3. Be aware of opportunities and challenges that occur when different cultures interact.

 **KEY 3.8**

Approaching diversity with an open mind builds relationships.

Your role	Situation	Closed-minded actions	Open-minded actions
Fellow student	For an assignment, you are paired with a student old enough to be your mother.	You assume the student will be clueless about the modern world. You think she might preach to you about how to do the assignment.	You get to know the student as an individual. You stay open to what you can learn from her experiences and knowledge.
Friend	You are invited to dinner at a friend's house. When he introduces you to his partner, you realize that he is gay.	You are turned off by the idea of two men in a relationship. You make an excuse to leave early. You avoid your friend after that.	You have dinner with the two men and make an effort to get to know more about them, individually and as a couple.
Employee	Your new boss is of a different racial and cultural background from yours.	You assume that you and your new boss don't have much in common. You think he will be distant and uninterested in you.	You rein in your stereotypes. You pay close attention to how your new boss communicates and leads. You adapt to his style and make an effort to get to know him better.

4. Build knowledge about other cultures.

5. Use what you learn to adapt to diverse cultures as you encounter them.

As you develop cultural competence, you heighten your ability to analyze how people relate to one another. Most important, you become better equipped to connect to others by bridging the gap between who you are and who they are.[10]

Value Diversity

Valuing diversity means having a basic respect for, and acceptance of, the differences among people. Every time you meet someone new, you have a choice about how to interact. You won't like everyone you meet, but if you value diversity, you will choose to treat people with tolerance and respect, avoiding assumptions about them and granting them the right to think, feel, and believe without being judged. Being open-minded in this way will help your relationships thrive, as shown in Key 3.8.

Identify and Evaluate Personal Perceptions and Attitudes

Whereas people may value the *concept* of diversity, attitudes and emotional responses may influence how they act when they confront the *reality* of diversity in their own lives. As a result, many people have prejudices that lead to damaging stereotypes.

Prejudice

PREJUDICE

A preconceived judgment or opinion formed without just grounds or sufficient knowledge.

Almost everyone has some level of **prejudice** resulting in the prejudging of others, usually on the basis of characteristics such as gender, race, sexual orientation, disability, or religion. People judge others without knowing anything about them because of factors like these:

- **Influence of family and culture.** Children learn attitudes, including intolerance, superiority, and hate, from their parents, peers, and community.

- **Fear of differences.** It is human to fear the unfamiliar and to make assumptions about it.

- **Experience.** One bad experience with a person of a particular race or religion may lead someone to condemn all people with the same background.

Stereotypes

STEREOTYPE

A standardized mental picture that represents an oversimplified opinion or uncritical judgment.

Prejudice is usually based on **stereotypes**—assumptions made, without proof or critical thinking, about the characteristics of a person or group of people. Stereotyping emerges from factors such as these:

- **Desire for patterns and logic.** People often try to make sense of the world by using the labels, categories, and generalizations that stereotypes provide.

- **Media influences.** The more people see stereotypical images—the airhead beautiful blonde, the jolly fat man—the easier it is to believe that stereotypes are universal.

KEY 3.9 Both positive and negative stereotypes mask uniqueness.

Positive stereotype	Negative stereotype
Women are nurturing.	Women are too emotional for business.
African Americans are great athletes.	African Americans struggle in school.
Hispanic Americans are family oriented.	Hispanic Americans have too many kids.
White people are successful in business.	White people are cold and power hungry.
Gay men have a great sense of style.	Gay men are sissies.
People with disabilities have strength of will.	People with disabilities are bitter.
Older people are wise.	Older people are set in their ways.
Asian Americans are good at math and science.	Asian Americans are poor leaders.

- **Laziness.** Labeling group members according to a characteristic they seem to have in common takes less energy than asking questions that illuminate the qualities of individuals.

Stereotypes derail personal connections and block effective communication, because pasting a label on a person makes it hard for you to see the real person underneath. Even stereotypes that seem positive may be untrue and may get in the way of perceiving uniqueness. Key 3.9 shows some positive and negative stereotypes.

Use your analytical abilities to question your own ideas and beliefs, weed out the narrowing influence of prejudice and stereotyping, and discover problems that need addressing. Giving honest answers to questions like the following is an essential step in the development of cultural competence:

- How do I react to differences?
- What prejudices or stereotypes come to mind when I see people, in real life or the media, who are a different color than I am? From a different culture? Making different choices?
- Where did my prejudices and stereotypes come from?
- Are these prejudices fair? Are these stereotypes accurate?
- What harm can having these prejudices and believing these stereotypes cause?

With the knowledge you build as you answer these questions, move on to the next stage: Looking carefully at what happens when people from different cultures interact.

Be Aware of Opportunities and Challenges That Occur When Cultures Interact

Interaction among people from different cultures can promote learning, build mutual respect, and broaden perspectives. However, as history has shown, such interaction can also produce problems caused by lack of understanding, prejudice, and stereotypical thinking. At their mildest, these problems create roadblocks that obstruct relationships and communication. At their worst, they set the stage for acts of discrimination and hate crimes.

Discrimination

Federal law says that you cannot be denied basic opportunities and rights because of your race, creed, color, age, gender, national or ethnic origin, religion, marital status, potential or actual pregnancy, or potential or actual illness or disability (unless the illness or disability prevents you from performing required tasks and unless accommodations are not possible). Despite these legal protections, discrimination is common and often appears on college campuses. Students may not want to work with students of other races. Members of campus clubs may reject prospective members because of religious differences. Outsiders may harass students attending gay and lesbian alliance meetings. Instructors may judge students according to their weight, accent, or body piercings.

DISCRIMINATION

Actions that deny people equal employment, educational, and housing opportunities, or treat people as second-class citizens.

Hate Crimes

When prejudice turns violent, it often manifests itself in *hate crimes*—crimes motivated by a hatred of a specific characteristic thought to be possessed by the victim—usually directed at people based on their race, ethnicity, religion, or sexual orientation. Because hate-crime statistics include only reported incidents, they tell just a part of the story—many more crimes likely go unreported by victims fearful of what might happen if they contact authorities.

Focusing on the positive aspect of intercultural interaction starts with awareness of the ideas and attitudes that lead to discrimination and hate crimes. With this awareness, you will be better prepared to push past negative possibilities and open your mind to positive ones.

Build Cultural Knowledge

The thinking response to discrimination and hate, and the next step in your path toward cultural competence, is to gather knowledge. You have a personal responsibility to learn about people who are different from you, including those you are likely to meet on campus.

What are some practical ways to begin?

- *Read* newspapers, books, magazines, and Web sites that expose you to different perspectives.
- *Ask questions* of all kinds of people, about themselves and their traditions.
- *Observe* how people behave, what they eat and wear, how they interact with others.
- *Travel internationally* to unfamiliar places where you can experience different ways of living.
- *Travel locally* to equally unfamiliar, but nearby, places that are home to a variety of people.
- *Build friendships* with fellow students or coworkers you would not ordinarily approach.

Building knowledge also means exploring yourself. Talk with family, read, seek experiences that educate you about your own cultural heritage. Then share what you know with others.

Adapt to Diverse Cultures

Here's where you take everything you have gathered—your value of diversity, your self-knowledge, your understanding of how cultures interact, your information about different cultures—and put it to work with practical actions. As you question, you can define actions and solutions that improve how you relate to others, and perhaps even change how people relate to one another on a larger scale. Choose actions that feel right to you, that cause no harm, and that may make a difference, however small.

Dr. Martin Luther King Jr. believed that careful thinking could change attitudes. As he put it:

> The tough-minded person always examines the facts before he reaches conclusions: in short, he postjudges. The tender-minded person reaches conclusions before he has examined the first fact; in short, he prejudges and is prejudiced. . . . There is little hope for us until we become tough minded enough to break loose from the shackles of prejudice, half-truths, and down-right ignorance.[11]

Let the following suggestions inspire your own creative ideas about what you can do to improve how you relate to others.

Look past external characteristics. If you meet a woman with a disability, get to know her. She may be an accounting major, a daughter, and a mother. She may love baseball, politics, and science fiction novels. These characteristics—not just her physical person—describe who she is.

Put yourself in other people's shoes. Attend a meeting about an issue that people in your community face but that is unfamiliar to you. Ask questions about what other people feel, especially if there's a conflict. Offer information and friendship to someone new who is adjusting to your school community.

Adjust to cultural differences. When you understand someone's way of being and put it into practice, you show respect and encourage communication. If a friend's family is formal at home, dress appropriately and behave formally when you visit. If an instructor maintains a lot of personal space, keep a respectful distance when you visit during office hours. If a study group member takes offense at a particular kind of language, avoid it when you meet.

Help others in need. When you see or uncover a problem, do what you can to help solve it. Newspaper columnist Sheryl McCarthy wrote about an African American who, in the midst of the 1992 Los Angeles riots, saw an Asian American man being beaten and helped him to safety: "When asked why he risked grievous harm to save an Asian man he didn't even know, the African-American man said, 'Because if I'm not there to help someone else, when the mob comes for me, will there be someone there to save me?'"[12]

Stand up against prejudice, discrimination, and hate. When you hear a prejudiced remark or notice discrimination taking place, ask yourself questions about how to encourage a move in the right direction. Then act. You may choose to make a comment, or to get help by approaching an authority such as an instructor or dean. Sound the alarm on hate crimes—let authorities know if you suspect that a crime is about to occur, join campus protests, support organizations that encourage tolerance.

Recognize that people everywhere have the same basic needs. Everyone loves, thinks, hurts, hopes, fears, and plans. When you are trying to find common ground with diverse people, remember that you are united first through your essential humanity.

Diversity also occurs in the way people communicate. Understanding who you are and how you learn, and how people differ from one another, will promote successful communication.

How Can You Communicate Effectively?

Spoken communication that is clear promotes success at school, at work, and in personal relationships. Successfully intelligent communicators analyze and adjust to communication styles, learn to give and receive criticism, analyze and make practical use of body language, and work through communication problems.

Adjust to Communication Styles

When you speak, your goal is for listeners to receive the message as you intended. Problems arise when one person has trouble "translating" a message coming from someone using a different communication style. Your knowledge of the Personality Spectrum dimensions will help you understand and analyze the ways diverse people communicate.

Identify Your Styles

Following are some communication styles that tend to be associated with the four dimensions in the Personality Spectrum. No one style is better than another. Successful communication depends on understanding your personal style and becoming attuned to the styles of others.

Thinker-dominant communicators focus on facts and logic. As speakers, they tend to rely on logical analysis to communicate ideas and prefer quantitative concepts to those that are conceptual or emotional. As listeners, they often do best with logical messages. Thinkers may also need time to process what they have heard before responding. Written messages—on paper or via e-mail—are often useful for these individuals because writing can allow for time to put ideas together logically.

Organizer-dominant communicators focus on structure and completeness. As speakers, they tend to deliver well-thought-out, structured messages that fit into an organized plan. As listeners, they often appreciate a well-organized message that defines practical tasks in concrete terms. As with Thinkers, a written format is often an effective form of communication to or from an Organizer.

Giver-dominant communicators focus on concern for others. As speakers, they tend to cultivate harmony, analyzing what will promote closeness in relationships. As listeners, they often appreciate messages that emphasize personal connection and address the emotional side of an issue. Whether speaking or listening, Givers often favor in-person talks over written messages.

Adventurer-dominant communicators focus on the present. As speakers, they focus on creative ideas, tending to convey a message as soon as the idea arises and then move on to the next activity. As listeners, they appreciate up-front, short, direct messages that don't get side-tracked. Like Givers, Adventurers tend to communicate and listen more effectively in person.

What is your style? Use this information as a jumping-off point for your self-exploration. Just as people tend to demonstrate characteristics from more than one Personality Spectrum dimension, communicators may demonstrate different styles.

When you share an interest with someone, you may find that communication flows and personal differences fade into the background. These students, both interested in television, work together to learn how to operate broadcasting equipment.

Put Your Knowledge of Communication Style to Use

Analyze your style by thinking about the communication styles associated with your dominant Personality Spectrum dimensions. Compare them to how you tend to communicate and how others seem to respond to you. Then, use creative and practical thinking skills to decide what works best for you as a communicator.

Speakers adjust to listeners. Listeners may interpret messages in ways you never intended. Think about practical solutions to this kind of problem as you read the following example involving a Giver-dominant instructor and a Thinker-dominant student (the listener):

Instructor: Your essay didn't communicate any sense of your personal voice.

Student: What do you mean? I spent hours writing it. I thought it was on the mark.

- **Without adjustment:** The instructor ignores the student's need for detail and continues to generalize. Comments like "You need to elaborate" "Try writing from the heart" or "You're not considering your audience" might confuse or discourage the student.

- **With adjustment:** Greater logic and detail will help. For example, the instructor might say, "You've supported your central idea clearly, but you didn't move beyond the facts into your interpretation of what they mean. Your essay reads like a research paper. The language doesn't sound like it is coming directly from you."

Listeners adjust to speakers. As a listener, improve understanding by being aware of stylistic differences and translating the message into one that makes sense to you. The following example of an Adventurer-dominant employee speaking to an Organizer-dominant supervisor shows how adjusting can pay off:

Employee: I'm upset about the e-mail you sent me. You never talked to me directly and you let the problem build into a crisis. I haven't had a chance to defend myself.

- **Without adjustment:** If the supervisor is annoyed by the employee's insistence on direct personal contact, he or she may become defensive: "I told you clearly what needs to be done. I don't know what else there is to discuss."

- **With adjustment:** In an effort to improve communication, the supervisor responds by encouraging the in-person exchange that is best for the employee: "Let's meet after lunch so you can explain to me how you believe we can improve the situation."

Although adjusting to communication styles helps you speak and listen more effectively, you also need to understand, and learn how to effectively give and receive, criticism.

Know How to Give and Receive Criticism

Criticism can be either *constructive* or *unconstructive*. Constructive criticism is a practical problem-solving strategy, involving goodwill suggestions for improving a situation. In contrast, unconstructive criticism focuses on what went wrong, doesn't offer alternatives that might help solve the problem, and is often delivered negatively, creating bad feelings.

CONSTRUCTIVE CRITICISM

Criticism that promotes improvement or development.

When offered constructively, criticism can help bring about important changes. Consider a case in which someone has continually been late to study group sessions. The group leader can comment in one of two ways. Which comment would encourage you to change your behavior?

- **Constructive.** The group leader talks privately with the student, saying, "I've noticed that you've been late a lot. We count on you, because our success depends on what each of us contributes. Is there a problem that is keeping you from being on time? Can we help?"

- **Unconstructive.** The leader watches the student arrive late and says, in front of everyone, "If you can't start getting here on time, there's really no point in your coming."

At school, instructors criticize classwork, papers, and exams. On the job, criticism may come from supervisors, coworkers, or customers. No matter the source, constructive comments can help you grow as a person. Be open to what you hear, and remember that most people want you to succeed.

Offering Constructive Criticism

When offering constructive criticism, use the following strategies to be effective:

- **Criticize the behavior rather than the person.** Avoid personal attacks. "You've been late to five group meetings" is much preferable to "You're lazy."
- **Define the problematic behavior specifically.** Try to focus on the facts, substantiating with specific examples and minimizing emotions. Avoid additional complaints—people can hear criticisms better if they are discussed one at a time.
- **Suggest new approaches and offer help.** Talk about ways of handling the situation. Work with the person to develop creative options. Help the person feel supported.
- **Use a positive approach and hopeful language.** Express the conviction that changes will occur and that the person can turn the situation around.

Receiving Criticism

When you are on criticism's receiving end, use the following techniques to handle it constructively:

- **Analyze the comments.** Listen carefully, then evaluate what you heard. What does it mean? What is the intent? Try to let unconstructive comments go without responding.
- **Request suggestions on how to change your behavior.** Ask, "How would you like me to handle this in the future?"
- **Summarize the criticism and your response to it.** Make sure everyone understands the situation.
- **Use a specific strategy.** Use problem-solving skills to analyze the problem, brainstorm ways to change, choose a strategy, and take action to make it happen.

One of the biggest barriers to successful communication is conflict, which can result in anger and even violence. With effort, you can successfully manage conflict and stay away from those who cannot.

Manage Conflict

Conflicts, both large and small, arise when there is a clash of ideas or interests. You may have small conflicts with a housemate over a door left unlocked. You may have major conflicts with your partner about finances or with an instructor about a failing grade. Conflict, as unpleasant as it can be, is a natural element in the dynamic of getting along with others. Prevent it when you can—and when you can't, use problem-solving strategies to resolve it.

Conflict-Prevention Strategies

The following two strategies can help you to prevent conflict from starting in the first place.

KEY 3.10 Assertiveness fosters successful communication.

AGGRESSIVE	ASSERTIVE	PASSIVE
Blaming, name-calling, and verbal insults: "You have created this mess!"	Expressing oneself and letting others do the same: "I have thoughts about this—first, what is your opinion?"	Feeling that one has no right to express anger: "No, I'm fine."
Escalating arguments: "You'll do it my way, no matter what it takes."	Using "I" statements to defuse arguments: "I am uncomfortable with that choice and want to discuss it."	Avoiding arguments: "Whatever you want to do is fine."
Being demanding: "Do this."	Asking and giving reasons: "Please consider doing it this way, and here's why . . ."	Being noncommittal: "You don't have to do this unless you really want to . . ."

Send "I" messages. "I" messages help you communicate your needs rather than attacking someone else. Creating these messages involves some simple rephrasing: "You didn't lock the door!" becomes "I felt uneasy when I came to work and the door was unlocked." Similarly, "You never called last night" becomes "I was worried when I didn't hear from you last night."

"I" statements soften the conflict by highlighting the effects that the other person's actions have on you, rather than focusing on the other person or the actions themselves. These statements help the receiver feel freer to respond, perhaps offering help and even acknowledging mistakes.

Be assertive. Most people tend to express themselves in one of three ways—aggressively, assertively, or passively. *Aggressive* communicators focus primarily on their own needs and can become impatient when needs are not satisfied. *Passive* communicators focus primarily on the needs of others and often deny themselves power, causing frustration. *Assertive* communicators are able to declare and affirm their opinions while respecting the rights of others to do the same. Assertive behavior strikes a balance between aggression and passivity and promotes the most productive communication. Key 3.10 contrasts the characteristics of these three.

What can aggressive and passive communicators do to move toward a more assertive style? Aggressive communicators might take time before speaking, use "I" statements, listen to others, and avoid giving orders. Passive communicators might acknowledge anger, express opinions, exercise the right to make requests, and know that their ideas and feelings are important.

Conflict Resolution

All too often, people deal with conflict through *avoidance* (a passive tactic that shuts down communication) or *escalation* (an aggressive tactic that often leads to fighting). Conflict resolution demands calm communication, motivation, and careful thinking. Use your thinking skills to apply the problem-solving approach you will learn in chapter 4.

Your ability to communicate and manage conflict has a major impact on your relationships with friends and family. Successful relationships are built on self-knowledge, good communication, and hard work.

Manage Communication Technology

Modern technology has revolutionized the way people communicate with one another. You can call or text on a mobile phone; you can send a note via e-mail or instant message, from a computer or a PDA such as a BlackBerry or Treo; you can communicate through Internet-based venues such as blogs and chat rooms; and you can learn about one another by frequenting social networking sites such as MySpace or Facebook.

Communication technologies have many advantages. You can communicate faster, more frequently, and with more people at one time than ever before. However, there are drawbacks. It's easy to misunderstand the tone or meaning of instant messages (IMs), e-mails, and text messages. Many of these communication methods are addictive—you might look up at the clock and realize you've spent hours of study time IM-ing your friends. In addition, revealing too much about yourself on social networking sites may come back to haunt you. Increasingly, employers are checking MySpace and Facebook for information about prospective job candidates.[13] Before posting words or images, remember that once this information is in cyberspace, you cannot pull it back.

The best way for you to create your ideal communication "recipe" is to analyze situations carefully, think creatively, and make practical decisions about how to move forward. How do you prefer to communicate with others? What are the effects? Use moderation, letting modern communication methods *enhance* in-person interaction rather than replace it.

Choose Communities That Enhance Your Life

Personal relationships often take place within *communities*, or groups that include people who share your interests—for example, sororities and fraternities, athletic clubs, and political groups. The presence of the Internet has added chat rooms, blogs, and newsgroups to the scope of social communities available to you. Some colleges even put their facebooks online and have school-sponsored online communities.

So much of what you accomplish in life is linked to your network of personal contacts. If you affiliate with communities that are involved in positive activities, you are more likely to surround yourself with responsible and character-rich people who may become your friends and colleagues. You may find among them your future spouse or partner, your best friend, a person who helps you land a job, your doctor, accountant, real estate agent, and so on. Finding and working with a community of people with similar interests can have positive effects in personal relationships and in workplace readiness.

If you find yourself drawn toward groups that encourage negative and even harmful behavior—such as gangs, organizations that haze pledges, or mean-spirited online communities—stop and think. Analyze why you are drawn to these groups. Resist the temptation to join in. If you are already involved and want out, stand up for yourself and be determined.

© Andres Rodriguez—Fotolia.com

Successful Intelligence Wrap-Up

Think back to chapter 1, and to Robert Sternberg's definition of successful intelligence—"the kind of intelligence used to achieve important goals." Knowing who you are and how you learn, and using that knowledge to communicate successfully with all kinds of people in a variety of situations, are keys to your successful pursuit of goals that are important to you. Here's how you have built skills in chapter 3:

Analytical

With the two self-assessments, you analyzed your levels of ability in the eight intelligences and examined how you relate to people and the world around you. In the *Maximize Your Classroom Experience* exercise, you examined how your instructors' teaching styles relate to how you learn. In the section about cultural competence, you gathered the tools you need to analyze your attitudes toward people, cultures, and values that differ from yours. You explored the ways in which you and others communicate and the effects of various styles.

Creative

As you read about the multiple intelligences and the personality spectrum, you may have developed new ideas about your abilities and talents and how you relate to others. In the *Maximize Your Classroom Experience* exercise, you brainstormed ideas about how to improve a situation where how you learn doesn't match up well with how an instructor teaches. You expanded your range of ideas for how to accept and support different people and cultures and how to communicate in ways that promote understanding.

Practical

In the *Maximize Your Classroom Experience* exercise, you put an action to practical use in trying to improve your experience in a classroom where you have trouble with the teaching style. Reading Keys 3.5 and 3.6 gave you practical study strategies relating to each intelligence and Personality Spectrum dimension. You considered practical strategies for avoiding prejudice, stereotyping, and discrimination, keeping in mind what experience has taught you in those areas.

Oruko lonro ni
(o-roo-ko lon-ro nee)

In the language of the Yoruba, an ethnic group living primarily in Nigeria and other West African countries, *oruko lonro ni* translates as "names affect behavior." This belief, common among the Yoruba people, refers to the idea that people live up to the names given to them by others or even chosen by themselves.[14] As Robert Sternberg learned when he found himself living up to the "lackluster" label given to him as an elementary school student, names and labels have enormous power.

As you think about how you learn and relate to others, use this idea to understand, and rise above, the confines of the names and labels that you give yourself and others or that others give to you. Find new and culturally competent ways to interact with those around you in ways that transcend labels. Know that you have potential for change.

". . . no two selves, no two consciousnesses, no two minds are exactly alike. Each of us is therefore situated to make a unique contribution to the world."

HOWARD GARDNER, PSYCHOLOGIST AND EDUCATOR

PERSONAL TRIUMPH CASE STUDY

KNOWING YOURSELF AS A LEARNER

DR. JOYCE BISHOP

PROFESSOR OF PSYCHOLOGY, GOLDEN WEST COLLEGE, HUNTINGTON BEACH, CALIFORNIA

Dr. Bishop, the creator of the assessments in this chapter, has a passion for learning that was inspired by her ordeal as a college student with a learning disability. As it did with her, knowing who you are as a learner can help you surmount the obstacles that come your way. Read the account; then answer the questions on page 101.

I have difficulty understanding words I hear, which made listening to lectures in college very hard. No one would know I had this difficulty because I learned how to compensate for it. In fact, I didn't know it myself until years after I graduated. It is a learning disability in the area of auditory discrimination.

College was confusing for me. I did well in some classes and felt totally lost in others. The hardest were the lecture-based classes. When I wasn't familiar with the information or the words, I couldn't make sense of what I was hearing.

If I read the material ahead of time, I could make visual pictures in my mind that would help me absorb the material. I could also look up words and research concepts I didn't understand. Then the lectures made more sense.

I read lips and facial expressions well, so I did well in small classes where I could consistently see the teacher's face. The disadvantage for me in small classes was that, because I heard voices around me as much as I heard the speaker, I had trouble blocking the extra noise. In an attempt to make lecture classes easier to understand, I would drag a tape recorder to class so that I could play back the lecture a number of times later. I found, however, that it didn't really help when I re-listened to the tapes. After that, I bargained with my classmates to borrow their notes in exchange for typing their term papers. Typing is bodily-kinesthetic and helped me to internalize what I was learning.

What helped me get by in college was that I am strong in logical-mathematical intelligence. School is primarily taught in the verbal-linguistic and logical-mathematical learning styles. I am also a strong visual learner. Science classes were easiest for me because they are more visual. I switched from sociology to biology my freshman year; it was easier for me to remember the visual biology material as opposed to the more verbal liberal arts classes. Without my commitment to my education and my will to succeed, I probably would not have graduated.

Twelve years after graduating, I pursued my master's in public health. Part of why I waited so long was that I needed to heal from the trauma of my own learning process. My graduate classes were much more hands-on, but there was still a great deal of reading. One day my eye doctor expressed concern about the stress my school work was causing my eyes and suggested that I get tested for a learning problem. He sent me to a center that usually tests small children for learning disabilities. The person giving the test said words and I was to spell out the words with blocks. I couldn't get some of the words right. I would consistently confuse or mistake words with close sounds. It was determined that I processed language on a fourth-grade level, a condition that has not changed in my adult life.

"How far did you go through school?" asked the therapist conducting the test.

"How far do you think I went?" I asked.

After thinking for a moment, she answered, "The tenth grade." I shared that I was just completing my master's degree. Her eyes got big and she said, "You work really hard in school, don't you?"

At that moment my head flooded with memories of report cards saying "Doesn't pay attention in class" and "Isn't working up to potential." I started to cry. An explanation for what had brought years of pain and struggle had finally come to the surface.

Now that I know what the problem is, I use strategies that allow me to deal with the way I learn. This is why I am so passionate about the power of knowing how you learn. We all have our strengths and weaknesses; the way we work to manage those weaknesses while maximizing our strengths makes all the difference.

Matthew Denman, the student artist who created this drawing, brings his unique eye to each subject he draws. Like Joyce, Matthew was diagnosed with a disability that affects his learning—autism. With the help of family and teachers, he discovered that he had an eye for structure, which has helped him in his academic career and beyond. Currently, he is attending Boulder Technical College. For more of Matthew's story, please visit www.prenhall.com/carter.

Building World-Class Skills

for College, Career, and Life Success

SUCCESSFUL INTELLIGENCE

Think, Create, Apply

Learn from the experiences of others. Look back to Joyce Bishop's Personal Triumph on page 100. After you've read her story, relate her experience to your own life by completing the following on a separate sheet of paper or on a computer file:

Step 1. Think it through: *Analyze your experience and compare it to Joyce's.* How do you feel "different" in the classroom? What is a consistent academic challenge for you, and how does this relate to Joyce's experience? How might this be explained by your knowledge of how you learn?

Step 2. Think out of the box: *Imagine ways of advising.* You are an advisor to a student identical to yourself. Be a harsh advisor—how would you criticize your performance as a student? Then be a wise advisor, focused on tapping into information about intelligences and the Personality Spectrum dimensions—how would you identify challenges and suggest ways to handle them?

Step 3. Make it happen: *Head off your own challenges with practical strategies.* You have named a consistent challenge—and you have imagined what you would say as your own advisor. Now identify steps that will help you face your challenge (choosing particular courses, meeting with an advisor or instructor who can give you ideas, approaching work in particular ways).

TEAMWORK

Create Solutions Together

Ideas about personality types. Divide into groups according to the four types of the *Personality Spectrum* assessment—Thinker-dominant students in one group, Organizer-dominant students in another, Giver-dominant students in a third, and Adventurer-dominant students in the fourth. If you have scored the same in more than one of these types, join whatever group is smaller. With your group, brainstorm the following lists for your type:

1. The strengths of this type
2. The struggles it brings
3. The stressors (things that cause stress) for this type
4. Career areas that tend to suit this type
5. Career areas that are a challenge for this type
6. People who clash with this type the most (often because they are strong in areas where this type needs to grow)

If there is time, each group can present this information to the entire class; this will boost understanding and acceptance of diverse ways of relating to information and people.

WRITING

Journal and Put Skills to Work

Record your thoughts on a separate piece of paper, in a journal, or on a computer file.

Journal entry: Personal diversity. Being able to respond to people as individuals requires that you become more aware of the diversity that is not always on the surface. Start by examining your own uniqueness. Write down, and expand upon if you wish, 10 words or phrases that describe you. The challenge: Keep references to your ethnicity or appearance (brunette, Cuban American, wheelchair-dependent, and so on) to a minimum, and fill the rest of the list with characteristics others can't see at a glance (laid-back, only child, 24 years old, drummer, marathoner, interpersonal learner, and so on).

Real-life writing: Improve communication. Few students make use of the wealth of ideas and experience that academic advisors can offer. Think of a question you have—regarding a specific course, major, or academic situation—that your advisor might help you answer. Craft an e-mail in appropriate language to your advisor, and send it. Then, to stretch your communication skills, rewrite the same e-mail twice more: once in a format you would send to an instructor, and once in a format appropriate for a friend. Send either or both of these if you think the response would be valuable to you.

PERSONAL PORTFOLIO

Prepare for Career Success

Complete the following on separate sheets of paper or electronically (if you can use a graphics program).

Self-portrait. Because self-knowledge helps you to make the best choices about your future, a self-portrait is an important step in your career exploration. Use this exercise to synthesize everything you have been exploring about yourself into one comprehensive self-portrait. Design your portrait in "think link" style, using words and visual shapes to describe your dominant multiple intelligences, Personality Spectrum dimensions, values, abilities and interests, personal characteristics, and anything else that you have discovered through self-exploration.

A *think link* is a visual construction of related ideas, similar to a map or web, which represents your thought process. Ideas are written inside geometric shapes, often boxes or circles, and related ideas and facts are attached to those ideas by lines that connect the shapes (see the note-taking section in chapter 6 for more about think links).

If you want to use the style shown in the example in Key 3.11, create a "web" of ideas coming off your central shape. Then, spreading out from each of those ideas (interests, values, and so forth), draw lines connecting

KEY 3.11

One example of a self-portrait.

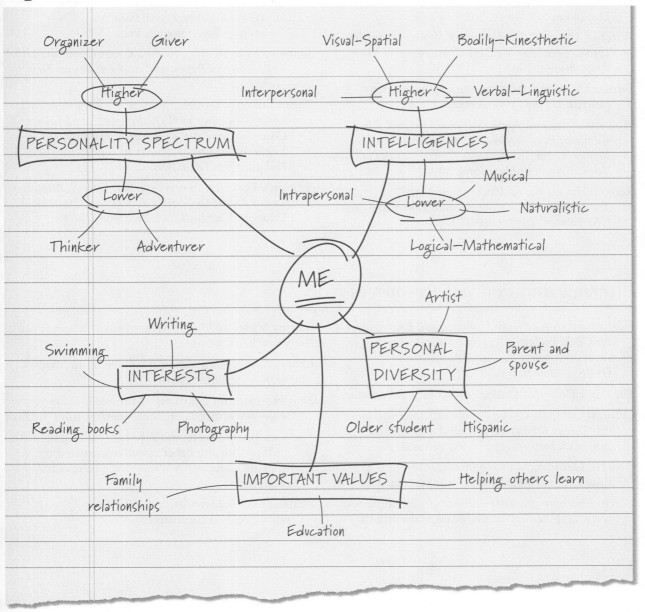

the thoughts that go along with that idea. Connected to "Interests," for example, might be "Singing," "Stock market," and "History."

You don't have to use the wheel image, however. You might design a treelike think link, a line of boxes with connecting thoughts, or some other format. Let your design reflect who you are, just as what you write does. You may want to look back at it at the end of the term to see how you have changed and grown from the self-image you have today.

Suggested Readings

Dublin, Thomas, ed. *Becoming American, Becoming Ethnic: College Students Explore Their Roots*. Philadelphia: Temple University Press, 1996.

Furlong, Gary. *The Conflict Resolution Toolbox*. Hoboken, NJ: Wiley, 2005.

Gardner, Howard. *Intelligence Reframed: Multiple Intelligences for the 21st Century*. New York: Basic Books, 2000.

Gardner, Howard. *Multiple Intelligences: New Horizons*. New York: Perseus Books, 2006.

Howard, Kim, and Annie Stevens. *Out and About Campus: Personal Accounts by Lesbian, Gay, Bisexual and Transgender College Students*. New York: Alyson Publications, 2000.

Keirsey, David. *Please Understand Me II: Temperament, Character, Intelligence*. Del Mar, CA: Prometheus Nemesis, 1998.

Levine, Mel. *A Mind at a Time*. New York: Simon & Schuster, 2003.

Pearman, Roger R., and Sarah C. Albritton. *I'm Not Crazy, I'm Just Not You: The Real Meaning of the 16 Personality Types*. Palo Alto, CA: Consulting Psychologists Press, 1997.

Qubein, Nido R. *How to Be a Great Communicator: In Person, on Paper, and at the Podium*. New York: Wiley, 1996.

Tatum, Beverly Daniel. *"Why Are All the Black Kids Sitting Together in the Cafeteria?" and Other Conversations About Race: A Psychologist Explains the Development of Racial Identity*. Philadelphia: Basic Books, 2003.

Watkins, Boyce D. *Everything You Ever Wanted to Know About College: A Guide for Minority Students*. Camillus, NJ: Blue Boy, 2004.

Internet and Podcast Resources

Association of American Colleges and Universities—AAC&U Podcasts (podcasts about on-campus diversity): **www.aacu.org/Podcast/DL06_podcasts.cfm**

The Black Collegian Online: **www.black-collegian.com**

Cultural Competency Web page (information from the Center for Effective Collaboration and Practice): **http://cecp.air.org/cultural**

Howard Gardner, Multiple Intelligences, and Education: **www.infed.org/thinkers/gardner.htm**

Internet Archive (podcast on multiple intelligences): **www.archive.org/details/dcampdaraabrams**

Keirsey Sorter and other Myers-Briggs information: **www.keirsey.com**

Latino USA (with podcasts available on the Web site): **www.latinousa.org**

New Horizons for Learning—Multiple Intelligences: **www.newhorizons.org/strategies/mi/front_mi.htm**

The Sociology of Race and Ethnicity (Web page with multiple links to other resources, created by Michael C. Kearl): **www.trinity.edu/mkearl/race.html**

Prentice Hall Student Success SuperSite: **www.prenhall.com/success**

Endnotes

1 One such study is K. Warner Schaie, "The Seattle Longitudinal Studies of Adult Intelligence," in *Essential Papers on the Psychology of Aging,* M. Powell Lawton and Timothy A. Salthouse, eds., New York: New York University Press, 1998, pp. 263–271. Also available online (www.memory-key .com/Seniors/longitudinal_study.htm).

2 Howard Gardner, *Multiple Intelligence: New Horizons,* New York: Basic Books, 2006, p. 180.

3 Howard Gardner, *Multiple Intelligences: The Theory in Practice,* New York: HarperCollins, 1993, pp. 5–49.

4 Gardner, *Multiple Intelligence: New Horizons,* p. 8.

5 Howard Gardner, *Intelligence Reframed,* New York: Basic Books, 1999, pp. 33–34.

6 Gardner, *Multiple Intelligences: The Theory in Practice,* p. 7.

7 C. George Boeree, "Personality Theories: Carl Jung," 2006 (http://webspace.ship.edu/cgboer/ jung.html).

8 Developed by Joyce Bishop, Ph.D., Golden West College, Huntington Beach, CA. Based on Howard Gardner, *Frames of Mind: The Theory of Multiple Intelligences,* New York: HarperCollins, 1993.

9 "Conceptual Frameworks/Models, Guiding Values and Principles," National Center for Cultural Competence, 2002 (www11.georgetown.edu/ research/gucchd/nccc/foundations/ frameworks.html).

10 Information in the sections on the five stages of building competency is based on Mark A. King, Anthony Sims, and David Osher, "How Is Cultural Competence Integrated in Education?" n.d., Center for Effective Collaboration and Practice (http://cecp.air.org/cultural/ Q_integrated.htm).

11 Martin Luther King Jr., from his sermon "A Tough Mind and a Tender Heart," *Strength in Love,* Philadelphia: Fortress Press, 1986, p. 14.

12 Sheryl McCarthy, *Why Are the Heroes Always White?* Kansas City, MO: Andrews McMeel, 1995, p. 137.

13 Betsy Israel, "The Overconnecteds," *New York Times* Education Life, November 5, 2006, p. 20.

14 Christopher J. Moore, *In Other Words: A Language Lover's Guide to the Most Intriguing Words Around the World,* New York: Walker, 2004, p. 78.

Prepare with a Study Plan and Schedule

Because some instructors may schedule exams early and often in the term, begin now to develop strategies for test success. The material in this segment is designed to help you organize yourself and manage time efficiently as you prepare for exams. When you reach chapter 7, "Test Taking: Showing What You Know," you will study test taking in depth, including test preparation, test anxiety, general test-taking strategies, strategies for handling different types of test questions, and learning from test mistakes.

Decide on a Study Plan

Start your test preparation by deciding what you will study. Go through your notes, texts, related primary sources, and handouts, and set aside materials you don't need. Then prioritize the remaining materials. Your goal is to focus on information that is most likely to be on the exam. Use the test-preparation tips on pages 220–225 in chapter 7 and the material on studying your text in chapter 5 to boost your effectiveness as you prepare.

Create a Study Schedule and Checklist

Next, use the time-management and goal-setting skills from chapter 2 to prepare a schedule. Consider all of the relevant factors—your study materials, the number of days until the test, and the time you can study each day. If you establish your schedule ahead of time and write it in a planner, you are more likely to follow it.

A comprehensive checklist like the one on the facing page will help you organize and stay on track as you prepare. Use a checklist to assign specific tasks to particular study times and sessions. That way, not only do you know when you have time to study, but you also have defined goals for each study session.

Decide How Well These Techniques Work for You

Now put these studying and scheduling techniques into action by using them every time you prepare for an exam. Make extra copies of the checklist so that they're ready to fill out as soon as an exam is announced.

Prepare for a Test

Complete the following checklist for each exam to define your study goals, get organized, and stay on track:

Course: _____   Instructor: _____

Date, time, and place of test: _____

Type of test (Is it a midterm or a minor quiz?): _____

What instructor said about the test, including types of test questions, test length, and how much the test counts toward your final grade:

_____

_____

Topics to be covered on the test, in order of importance (information should also come from your instructor):

1. _____

2. _____

3. _____

4. _____

5. _____

Study schedule, including materials you plan to study (texts, class notes, homework problems, and so forth) and dates you plan to complete each:

Material	**Completion Date**
1. _____	_____
2. _____	_____
3. _____	_____
4. _____	_____
5. _____	_____

Materials you are expected to bring to the test (textbook, sourcebook, calculator, etc.):

_____

_____

_____

Special study arrangements (such as planning study group meeting, asking the instructor for special help, getting outside tutoring):

_____

_____

_____

Life-management issues (such as rearranging work hours):

_____

_____

_____

Source: Adapted from Ron Fry, *"Ace" Any Test,* 3rd ed., Franklin Lakes, NJ: Career Press, 1996, pp. 123–124.

After you use these strategies one or more times, answer the following questions:

- How did this approach help you organize your time before an exam?

  _____

  _____

  _____

  _____

- How did this approach help you organize your study material so that you remembered to cover every topic?

  _____

  _____

  _____

  _____

- Can you think of ways to change the checklist to improve your test-prep efficiency? If you can, list the ways here and incorporate them into the checklist.

  _____

  _____

  _____

  _____

PART
II

Developing Skills for School and Life

CRITICAL, CREATIVE, AND PRACTICAL THINKING

Solving Problems and Making Decisions

> *"Successfully intelligent people define problems correctly and thereby solve those problems that really confront them, rather than extraneous ones. . . . [They] carefully formulate strategies for problem solving. In particular, they focus on long-range planning rather than rushing in and then later having to rethink their strategies."*

ROBERT STERNBERG

To serve you successfully, your education must do more than fill your head with facts and figures: It must also give you the tools to work through problems and decisions. These tools take the form of analytical, creative, and practical thinking skills and are at the heart of *successful intelligence*.

This chapter will help you build your ability to analyze information, come up with creative ideas, and put a practical plan into action. As you build these skills, you will become a better problem solver and decision maker, moving ever more effectively toward your goals.

In this chapter you explore answers to the following questions:

Analytical	Creative	Practical
• Evaluating fact, opinion, assumptions, and perspectives • Analyzing whether examples support ideas • Evaluating potential and actual solutions and choices	• Brainstorming • Taking risks and promoting a creative environment • Developing potential solutions and choices	• How to identify problems and decisions • How to use a plan to work through problems and decisions • How to adapt to your environment and learn from experience

What Does It Mean to Think with Successful Intelligence?

Some tasks primarily engage one thinking skill at a time. You might use analytical thinking (also known as *critical thinking*) to complete a quiz, creative thinking to write a poem, or practical thinking to get errands done on a busy day. However, when you need to solve a problem or make a decision, combining your analytical, creative, and practical thinking skills gives you the greatest chance of moving forward successfully.[1] These three skills give you myriad ways to connect to material in school and out (see Key 4.1).

Successfully Intelligent Thinking Means Asking and Answering Questions

What is thinking? According to experts, it is what happens when you ask questions and move toward the answers.[2] "To think through or rethink anything," says Dr. Richard Paul, director of research at the Center for Critical Thinking, "one must ask questions that stimulate our thought. Questions define tasks, express problems, and delineate issues. . . . Only students who have questions are really thinking and learning."[3]

As you answer questions, you transform raw data into information that you can use to achieve goals. A *Wall Street Journal* article titled "The Best Innovations Are Those That Come from Smart Questions" relays the story of a cell biology student, William Hunter, whose professor told him that "the difference between good science and great science is the quality of the

How can I succeed in college if I don't test well?

My grades were good in high school, and I was also involved in extracurricular activities such as the freshman mentor program and tae kwon do (I am a black belt and instructor). My family and my teachers always told me that I will do well in college.

But I am not so sure. I have a hard time with multiple-choice tests and I did not do well on the SAT and ACT. I worry that maybe I am just not smart enough, even though I can express myself well in essays and conversation. How can I do better on these tests, and how can I make the most of what I already do well?

Parisa Malekzadeh
University of Arizona
Major: Undeclared

Benjamin E. Victorica,
MD Professor Emeritus,
Pediatric Cardiology
University of Florida

Strive to improve your skills, and know that your other strengths will lead you to success.

To accomplish goals, one must remain focused on the objectives and maintain perseverance. You have already demonstrated that you can focus and persevere by your academic performance and level of expertise in tae kwon do. These qualities will prove more important to your success than test scores.

I had a similar experience with multiple-choice testing. At the time of my medical education in Argentina, all my tests were oral. In order to continue my postgraduate education in this country, I had to pass the ECFMG examination, which is almost entirely multiple-choice. Since I knew the medical material, I learned how to properly answer multiple-choice questions by reviewing and taking sample tests. The majority of my wrong answers occurred because I was quickly glancing at the questions instead of reading carefully. With more focus, I passed the test and was able to continue my training.

My success as a physician has come from combining analytical work (analyzing the key signs and symptoms of a condition and correlating them to clinical and laboratory findings) with creativity (thinking through situations comprehensively) and practical ability (discussing the diagnosis with the patient, applying the appropriate treatment, and monitoring the results). Work hard to improve testing and analytical skills, but value and build your practical and creative skills just as much, knowing that the combination will help you reach your goals.

questions posed."[4] Now a physician, Dr. Hunter asks questions about new ways to use drugs. His questions have led to the promotion of a revolutionary product—a drug-coated mesh used to strengthen vessels in limbs that are threatened by late-stage arterial disease. Through seeking answers to probing questions, Dr. Hunter reached a significant goal.[5]

You use questions in order to analyze ("How bad is my money situation?"), come up with creative ideas ("How can I earn more money?"), and apply practical solutions ("Who do I talk to about getting a job on campus?"). Later in the chapter, in the sections on analytical, creative, and

KEY 4.1 Successful intelligence helps you achieve goals in any discipline.

DISCIPLINE	ANALYTICAL THINKING	CREATIVE THINKING	PRACTICAL THINKING
Behavioral Science	Comparing one theory of child development with another	Devising a new theory of child development	Applying child development theories to help parents and teachers understand and deal with children more effectively
Literature	Examining the development of the main character in a novel	Writing alternative endings to the novel	Using the experience of the main character to better understand and manage one's own life situations
History	Considering similarities and differences between World War I and World War II	Imagining yourself as a German citizen dealing with economic depression after WWI	Seeing what WWI and WWII lessons can be applied to current Middle East conflicts
Sports	Taking a close look at the opposing team's strategy on the soccer field	Coming up with innovative ways to move the ball downfield	Using tactics to hide your strategy from an opposing team—or a competing company

Source: Adapted from Robert J. Sternberg, *Successful Intelligence,* New York: Plume, 1996, p. 149.

practical thinking, you will find examples of the kinds of questions that drive each skill.

Like any aspect of thinking, questioning is usually not a straightforward process. Sometimes the answer doesn't come right away. Often the answer leads to more—and more specific—questions. Patience is key in your exploration as you search for results.

Successfully Intelligent Thinking Requires Purpose and Drive

In order to ask useful questions, you need to know *why* you are questioning. A general question can be your starting point for defining your purpose: "What am I trying to accomplish, and why?" As you continue your thought process, you will find more specific purposes that help you generate questions along the way.

Knowing your purpose helps you with one of the most important tools you need in order to activate your thinking powers: The *drive* to think. "Critical-thinking skills are different from critical-thinking dispositions, or a willingness to deploy these skills," says cognitive psychologist D. Alan Bensley of Frostburg State University in Maryland. In other words, having the skills isn't enough—you also have to want to use them. Skilled thinkers not motivated to use their thinking skills are likely to make decisions in ways similar to those who don't have the skills to deploy.[6]

114   KEYS TO SUCCESS

The bottom line is that the three skills, or aspects, of successful intelligence are useful to you only if you activate them. As Sternberg says, "It is more important to know when and how to use these aspects of successful intelligence than just to have them."[7] If you know and understand your purpose, you are more likely to be willing to use your skills.

Begin by exploring the analytical thinking skills that you'll need to solve problems and make decisions effectively.

How Can You Improve Your Analytical Thinking Skills?

Analytical thinking is the process of gathering information, analyzing it in different ways, and evaluating it for the purposes of gaining understanding, solving a problem, or making a decision. The first step in analytical thinking is to define your purpose by asking what you want to analyze, and why. Then you gather the necessary information, analyze and clarify the ideas, and evaluate what you've found. Throughout the process, you will formulate new questions that may take you in unforeseen directions or even change your purpose.

Gather Information

Information is the raw material for thinking. Choosing what to gather requires analyzing how much information you need, how much time to spend gathering it, and whether it is relevant. Say, for instance, that you have to write a paper on one aspect of the media (TV, radio, Internet) and its influence on a particular group. If you gathered every available resource on the topic, the course would be over long before you got to the writing stage.

Here's how you might use analysis to effectively gather information for that paper:

You will rarely use just one aspect of successful intelligence at a time. This instructor and student are gathering data (analytical intelligence) as they work hands-on with terrapins in a bayside marsh (practical intelligence).

- Reviewing the assignment, you learn that the paper should be approximately 10 pages and describe at least three significant points of influence.

- At the library and online, you find thousands of articles on the topic. After an hour, you decide to focus your paper on how the Internet influences young teens (ages 13–15).

- You get an overview from six comprehensive articles that lead you to three in-depth sources.

In this way you achieve a subgoal—a selection of useful materials—on the way to your larger goal of writing a well-crafted paper.

Analyze and Clarify Information

Once you've gathered the information, the next step is to analyze it to determine whether the information is reliable and useful in helping you answer your questions.

Break Information into Parts

When analyzing information, you break information into parts and examine the parts so that you can see how they relate to each other and to information you already know. The following strategies help you break down information into pieces and set aside what is unclear, unrelated, or unimportant, resulting in a deeper and more reliable understanding:

Separate the ideas. If you are reading about how teens aged 13–15 use the Internet, you might discuss method of access, popular Web sites, and how they interact via instant message or blogs.

Compare and contrast. Look at how things are similar to, or different from, each other. You might explore how different young teen subgroups (boys versus girls, for example) have different purposes for setting up pages on sites such as Facebook or MySpace.

Examine cause and effect. Look at the possible reasons why something happened (possible causes) and its consequences (effects, both positive and negative). You might examine the effect that Internet use has on how young teens spend their time outside of school.

© David Davis—Fotolia.com

An important caution: Analyze carefully to seek out *true causes*—some apparent causes may not be actual causes (often called *false causes*). For example, changes in this group since the Internet became popular may have been the result of a number of different factors, including increased or decreased parental and school pressure and the impact of other media such as film and television.

Look for themes, patterns, and categories. Note connections that form as you look at how bits of information relate to one another. For example, you might see patterns of Internet use that link young teens from particular cultures or areas of the country together into categories.

Once the ideas are broken down, you can examine whether examples support ideas, separate fact from opinion, consider perspective, and investigate hidden assumptions.

Examine Whether Examples Support Ideas

When you encounter an idea or claim, examine how it is supported with examples or *evidence* (facts, expert opinion, research findings, personal experience, and so on). How useful an idea is to your work may depend on whether, or how well, it is backed up with solid evidence or made concrete with examples. Be critical of the information you gather; don't take it at face value.

For example, a blog written by a 12-year-old may make statements about what kids do on the Internet. The word of one person, who may or may not be telling the truth, is not adequate support. On the other hand, a study of kids' technology use by the Department of Commerce under the provisions of the Children's Internet Protection Act may be more reliable. Whenever you see an (argument) in written materials, you use questioning to judge the quality of the evidence, whether it supports the central idea, and whether examples and ideas connect logically.

Finding credible, reliable information with which to answer questions and come up with ideas enables you to separate fact from opinion.

ARGUMENT

A set of connected ideas, supported by examples, made by a writer to prove or disprove a point.

Distinguish Fact from Opinion

A *statement of fact* is information presented as objectively real and verifiable ("The Internet is a research tool"). In contrast, a *statement of opinion* is a belief, conclusion, or judgment that is inherently difficult, and sometimes impossible, to verify ("The Internet is always the best and most reliable research tool"). When you critically evaluate materials that you read, looking carefully at whether an argument is based on fact or opinion will help you determine how reliable it is. Key 4.2 defines important characteristics of fact and opinion.

Even though facts may seem more solid, you can also make use of opinions if you determine that they are backed up with facts. However, it is important to examine opinions for their underlying perspectives and assumptions.

KEY 4.2

Examine how fact and opinion differ.

Facts include statements that . . .	Opinions include statements that . . .
. . . *deal with actual people, places, objects, or events.* Example: "In 2002, the European Union introduced the physical coins and banknotes of a new currency—the euro—that was designed to be used by its member nations."	. . . *show evaluation.* Any statement of value indicates an opinion. Words such as *bad, good, pointless,* and *beneficial* indicate value judgments. Example: "The use of the euro has been beneficial to all the states of the European Union."
. . . *use concrete words or measurable statistics.* Example: "The charity event raised $50,862."	. . . *use abstract words.* Hard-to-define words like *misery* or *success* usually indicate a personal opinion. Example: "The charity event was a smashing success."
. . . *describe current events in exact terms.* Example: "Mr. Barrett's course has 378 students enrolled this semester."	. . . *predict future events.* Statements about future occurrences are often opinions. Example: "Mr. Barrett's course is going to set a new enrollment record this year."
. . . *avoid emotional words and focus on the verifiable.* Example: "Citing dissatisfaction with the instruction, 7 out of the 25 students in that class withdrew in September."	. . . *use emotional words.* Emotions are unverifiable. Words such as *delightful* or *miserable* express an opinion. Example: "That class is a miserable experience."
. . . *avoid absolutes.* Example: "Some students need to have a job while in school."	. . .*use absolutes.* Absolute *qualifiers,* such as *all, none, never,* and *always,* often express an opinion. Example: "All students need to have a job while in school."

Source: Adapted from Ben E. Johnson, *Stirring Up Thinking,* New York: Houghton Mifflin, 1998, pp. 268–270.

Examine Perspectives and Assumptions

PERSPECTIVE

A characteristic way of thinking about people, situations, events, and ideas.

ASSUMPTION

A judgment, generalization, or bias influenced by experience and values.

BIAS

A preference or inclination, especially one that prevents evenhanded judgment.

A **perspective** can be broad, such as a generally optimistic or pessimistic view of life. Or it can be more focused, such as an attitude about whether students should commute or live on campus.

Perspectives are associated with **assumptions.** For example, the perspective that there are many successful ways to handle the issue of media exposure leads to assumptions such as "Parents can control children's exposure to the Internet" and "Children can access the Internet without being exposed to inappropriate content." Having a particular experience with children and the Internet can build or reinforce a perspective.

Assumptions often hide within questions and statements, blocking you from considering information in different ways. Take this classic puzzler as an example: "Which came first, the chicken or the egg?" Thinking about this question, most people assume that the egg is a chicken egg. If you think past that assumption and come up with a new idea—such as, the egg is a dinosaur egg—then the obvious answer is that the egg came first!

Examining perspectives and assumptions enables you to judge whether material is reliable and free of **bias,** what particular perspective and intent the author may have, and what assumptions underlie the material. It also helps you identify whether your own perspectives and assumptions are clouding your judgment.

Perspectives and assumptions in information. Perspectives and assumptions permeate nearly everything you read. Being able to separate them from the facts will help you identify bias and evaluate information effectively. For example, the conclusions in two articles on Internet advertising may differ if one appears on the Web site of a company that advertises on the Internet and one appears in a publication that wants the Internet to be an advertising-free zone. Another example: A historical Revolutionary War document that originated in the colonies may assume that the rebellion against the British was entirely justified and leave out information to the contrary.

Personal perspectives and assumptions. Your perspective affects how accurately you view information. A student who thinks that the death penalty is wrong, for example, may have a hard time analyzing arguments that defend it, or when researching may focus on materials that support his perspective. Try to set aside perspectives and assumptions when you analyze information. "Anticipate your reactions and prejudices and then consciously resist their influence," says Colby Glass, professor of information research and philosophy at Palo Alto College.[8]

There's an added benefit to opening yourself to new perspectives: It will give you more information to work with as you encounter life's problems. Come to the classroom ready to hear and read new ideas, think about their merits, and make informed decisions about what you believe. Says Sternberg: "We need to . . . see issues from a variety of viewpoints and, especially, to see how other people and other cultures view issues and problems facing the world."[9]

Evaluate Information

You've gathered and analyzed your information. You examined its components, its evidence, its validity, its perspective, and any underlying assumptions. Now, based on an examination of evidence and careful analysis, you *evaluate* whether an idea or piece of information is important or unimportant, applicable or trivial, strong or weak, and why. You then set aside what is not useful and use the rest to form an opinion, possible solution, or decision.

In preparing your paper on young teens and the Internet, for example, you gathered pertinent information, came up with an idea you wanted to write about, researched information and materials, and analyzed how your research applied to your position. You then drafted your paper, presenting what you learned in an organized, persuasive way.

See Key 4.3 for some questions you can ask to build and use analytical thinking skills.

 KEY 4.3

Ask questions like these in order to analyze.

To gather information, ask:	• What kinds of information do I need to meet my goal? • What information is available? Where and when can I get to it? • Of the sources I found, which ones will best help me achieve my goal?
To analyze, ask:	• What are the parts of this information? • What is similar to this information? What is different? • What are the reasons for this? Why did this happen? • What ideas, themes, or conclusions emerge from this material? • How would you categorize this information?
To see if evidence or examples support an idea, ask:	• Does the evidence make sense? • How do the examples support the idea/claim? • Are there examples that might disprove the idea/claim?
To distinguish fact from opinion, ask:	• Do the words in this information signal fact or opinion? • What is the source of this information? Is the source reliable? • If this is an opinion, is it supported by facts?
To examine perspectives and assumptions, ask:	• What perspectives might the author have, and what may be emphasized or deemphasized as a result? • What assumptions might lie behind this statement or material? • How could I prove, or disprove, an assumption? • How might my perspective affect the way I see this material?
To evaluate, ask:	• What information will support what I'm trying to prove or accomplish? • Is this information true or false, and why? • How important is this information?

Source: Adapted from "Questions That Probe Reasons and Evidence" (www-ed.fnal.gov/trc/tutorial/taxonomy.html), based on Richard Paul, *Critical Thinking: How to Prepare Students for a Rapidly Changing World,* Santa Rosa, CA: Center for Critical Thinking, 1993; and from Barbara Fowler, "Bloom's Taxonomy and Critical Thinking," 1996, Longview Community College (http://mcckc.edu/longview/ctac/blooms.htm).

Analyze a Statement

Consider this statement; then analyze it by answering the questions that follow.

"The Internet is the best place to find information about any topic."

Is this statement fact or opinion? Why?

_____

_____

What examples can you think of that support or negate this statement?

_____

_____

What perspectives are guiding this statement?

_____

_____

What assumptions underlie the statement? Pose a problem: What negative effects might result from accepting these assumptions and therefore agreeing with the statement?

_____

_____

As a result of your critical thinking, what is your evaluation of this statement?

_____

_____

Pursuing your goals, in school and in the workplace, requires not just analyzing information but also thinking creatively about how to use what you've learned from your analysis.

How Can You Improve Your Creative Thinking Skills?

What is creativity?

- Some researchers define *creativity* as combining existing elements in an innovative way to create a new purpose or result (using a weak adhesive to mark pages in a book, a 3M scientist created Post-it Notes).

- Others see creativity as the ability to generate new ideas from looking at how things are related (noting what ladybugs eat inspired organic farmers to bring them in to consume crop-destroying aphids).[10]

- Still others, including Sternberg, define it as the ability to make unusual connections—to view information in quirky ways that bring about unique results.

To think creatively is to generate new ideas that may bring change. Here's an example of how creativity can work in the classroom: Working with study group partners, Smith College junior Meghan E. Taugher devised a solar-powered battery for a laptop for their class on electrical circuits:

> We took the professor's laptop, put all the parts together, and sat outside watching it with a little device to see how much power it was saving. When it fully charged the battery, it was one of those times I felt that what I was learning was true, because I was putting it to use in real life.[11]

Meghan's experience led her to generate an idea of a new major and career—engineering.

Even though some people seem to have more or better ideas than others, creative thinking is a skill that can be developed. Creativity expert Roger von Oech highlights mental flexibility. "Like race-car drivers who shift in and out of different gears depending on where they are on the course," he says, you can enhance creativity by learning to "shift in and out of different types of thinking depending on the needs of the situation at hand."[12]

The following actions will help you make those shifts and build your ability to think creatively. Because ideas often pop up randomly, get in the habit of writing them down as they arise. Keep a pen and paper by your bed, your PDA in your pocket, a notepad in your car, or a tape recorder in your backpack so that you can grab ideas before they fade.

Brainstorm

Brainstorming is also referred to as *divergent thinking*: You start with a question and then let your mind diverge—go in many different directions—in search of solutions. Brainstorming is *deliberate* creative thinking. When you brainstorm, try to generate ideas without thinking about how useful they are; evaluate their quality later. Brainstorming works well in groups because group members can become inspired by, and make creative use of, one another's ideas.[13]

One way to inspire ideas when brainstorming is to think of similar situations—in other words, to make *analogies* (comparisons based on a resemblance of things otherwise unlike). For example, Velcro is a product of analogy: When imagining how two pieces of fabric could stick to each other, the inventor thought of the similar situation of a burr sticking to clothing.

When you are brainstorming ideas, don't get hooked on finding the one right answer. Questions may have many "right answers"—or many answers

BRAINSTORMING

Letting your mind free-associate to come up with different ideas or answers.

that have degrees of usefulness. The more possibilities you generate, the better your chance of finding the best one. Also, don't stop the process when you think you have the best answer—keep going until you are out of steam. You never know what may come up in those last gasps of creative energy.[14]

Take a New and Different Look

If no one ever questioned established opinion, people would still think the sun revolved around the earth. Here are some ways to change how you look at a situation or problem:

Challenge assumptions. In the late 1960s, conventional wisdom said that school provided education and television provided entertainment. Jim Henson, a pioneer in children's television, asked, "Why can't we use TV to educate young children?" From that question, the characters of Sesame Street, and eventually a host of other educational programs, were born.

Shift your perspective. Try on new perspectives by asking others for their views, reading about new ways to approach situations, or deliberately going with the opposite of your first instinct.[15] Then use those perspectives to inspire creativity. For a political science course, for example, craft a position paper for a senatorial candidate. For a fun example of how looking at something in a new way can unearth a totally different idea, look at the perception puzzles in Key 4.4.

Ask "what if" questions. Set up hypothetical environments in which new ideas can grow—for example, "What if I had unlimited money or time?" The founders of Seeds of Peace, faced with generations of conflict in the Middle East, asked: What if Israeli and Palestinian teens met at a summer camp in Maine so that the next generation has greater understanding and

 **KEY 4.4** Use perception puzzles to experience a shift in perspective.

There are two possibilities for each image. What do you see? (See page 143 for answers.)

Source of middle puzzle: "Sara Nadar" illustration from *Mind Sights* by Roger Shepard. Copyright © 1990 by Roger Shepard. Reprinted by permission of Henry Holt and Company, LLC.

respect? And what if follow-up programs and reunions are set up to cement friendships so that relationships change the politics of the Middle East? Based on the ideas that came up, they created an organization that helps teenagers from the Middle East develop leadership and communication skills.

Set the Stage for Creativity

Use these strategies to give yourself the best possible chance at generating creative ideas:

Choose, or create, environments that free your mind. Find places that energize you. Play music that moves you. Seek out people who inspire you.[16]

Be curious. Try something new and different: Take a course outside of your major, listen to a new genre of music, read a book on an unfamiliar topic. Try something you don't think you would like in order to see if you had misjudged your reaction. Seeking out new experiences will broaden your knowledge, giving you more raw materials with which to build creative ideas.[17]

Give yourself time to "sit" with a question. American society values speed, so much so that we equate being "quick" with being smart.[18] In fact, however, creative ideas often come when you give your brain permission to "leave the job" for a while.[19] Take breaks when figuring out a problem—get some exercise, nap, talk with a friend, work on something else, do something fun.

Take Risks

Creative breakthroughs can come from sensible risk taking.

Fly in the face of convention. Entrepreneur Michael Dell turned tradition on its ear when he took a "tell me what you want and I will build it for you" approach to computer marketing instead of a "build it and they will buy it" approach. The possibility of failure did not stop him from risking money, time, energy, and reputation to achieve a truly unique and creative goal.

Let mistakes be okay. Open yourself to the learning that comes from not being afraid to mess up. When a pharmaceutical company failed to develop a particular treatment for multiple sclerosis, the CEO said, "You have to celebrate the failures. If you send the message that the only road to career success is experiments that work, people won't ask risky questions, or get any dramatically new answers."[20]

As with analytical thinking, asking questions powers creative thinking. See Key 4.5 for examples of the kinds of questions you can ask to get your creative juices flowing.

Creativity connects analytical and practical thinking. When you generate ideas, solutions, or choices, you need to think analytically to evaluate their quality. Then, you need to think practically about how to make the best solution or choice happen.

KEY 4.5 Ask questions like these in order to jump-start creative thinking.

To brainstorm, ask:	• What do I want to accomplish? • What are the craziest ideas I can think of? • What are 10 ways that I can reach my goal? • What ideas have worked before, and how can I apply them?
To shift your perspective, ask:	• How has this always been done—and what would be a different way? • How can I approach this task or situation from a new angle? • How would someone else do this or view this? • What if . . . ?
To set the stage for creativity, ask:	• Where, and with whom, do I feel relaxed and inspired? • What music helps me think out of the box? • When in the day or night am I most likely to experience a flow of creative ideas? • What do I think would be new and interesting to try, to see, to read?
To take risks, ask:	• What is the conventional way of doing this? What would be a totally different way? • What would be a risky approach to this problem or question? • What is the worst that can happen if I take this risk? What is the best? • What have I learned from this mistake?

How Can You Improve Your Practical Thinking Skills?

You've analyzed a situation. You've brainstormed ideas. Now, with your practical skill, you make things happen and learn from your actions.

Practical thinking does incorporate "common sense" or "street smarts" but has a broader reach. When you take practical action, you figure out how to adapt to your environment, or shape or change your environment to adapt to you, in order to pursue important goals. Think again about the successfully intelligent boy in the story in chapter 1: He quickly sized up his environment (bear and slower boy) and adapted (got ready to run) in order to pursue his goal (to escape becoming the bear's dinner).

Here is another example: Your goal is to pass your required freshman composition course. You are a visual learner. To achieve your goal, you can use the instructor's PowerPoints or other visual media to enhance your learning (adapt to your environment) or enroll in an Internet course that is primarily visual (change your environment to adapt to you)—or both.

Why Practical Thinking Is Important

Although the traditional classroom tends to focus on analytical thinking, real-world problems and decisions require you to move beyond analysis

Activate Your Creative Powers

get creative!

First, think about the past month; then, list three creative acts you performed.

1. In order to study, I _____

2. In my personal life, I _____

3. At work or in the classroom, I _____

Now think of a problem or situation that is on your mind. Brainstorm one new idea for how to deal with it.

_____

_____

Write down a second idea—but focus on the risk-taking aspect of creativity. What would be a risky way to handle the situation? How do you hope it would pay off?

_____

_____

Finally, sit with the question—then write down one more idea *only* after you have been away from this page for at least 24 hours.

_____

_____

Keep these in mind. You may want to use one soon!

alone. Your success in a sociology class, for example, usually is not just a product of your academic work—it may depend in part on adapting to your instructor's style or personality as well. Similarly, the way you solve a personal financial dilemma has a more significant impact on your life than how you work through a problem in an accounting course.

Furthermore, academic knowledge on its own isn't enough to bring you success in the workplace. You need to be able to actively apply what you know to problems and decisions that come up periodically. For example, while students majoring in elementary education may successfully quote child development facts on an exam, it won't mean much to their career success unless they can adapt to the classroom by evaluating and addressing real children's needs. Successfully solving real-world problems demands a practical approach.[21]

The accomplishments of David Hosei, a finance and entrepreneurship major at Indiana University, show how practical thinking helps you bridge the gap between being a successful student and achieving real-world success. Pursuing a goal to help others, Hosei formed HELP (Help Educate Lots of People), a nonprofit organization, to teach peers about money management. In addition, he organizes an annual fund-raiser—the IU Battle of the Bands—to raise money for Jill's House, a refuge for families seeking cancer treatments at a local medical center.[22] Achieving any important goal requires you to put practical skill into play.

Through Experience You Acquire Emotional and Social Intelligence

You gain much of your ability to think practically from personal experience, rather than from formal lessons.[23] What you learn from experience answers "how" questions—how to talk, how to behave, how to proceed.[24] For example, after completing several papers for a course, you may learn what your instructor expects and deliver it. Following a couple of conflicts with a partner, you may learn how to avoid sore spots when the conversation heats up. See Key 4.6 for ways in which this kind of knowledge can be shown in "if-then" statements.

Experience teaches you how to "navigate" personal emotions and social interactions. The emotional and social intelligence you gain as a result of life experiences are essential tools for achieving personal and professional goals.

- *Emotional intelligence.* As you learned in chapter 1, *emotional intelligence* is defined by psychologist Daniel Goleman as the ability to

 KEY 4.6 **Here is one way to map out what you learn from experience.**

Goal: You want to talk to the soccer coach about your status on the team.

IF the team has had a good practice and IF you've played well during the scrimmage and IF the coach isn't rushing off somewhere, THEN grab a moment with him right after practice ends.

perceive, assess, and manage one's own emotions and understand the emotions of others. This ability helps you to notice what emotions arise in others in reaction to what you say or do, make choices about how to respond to those emotions, and assess what results from your choices. This sequence results in a greater ability to choose appropriate practical actions in future situations.

- *Social intelligence.* The concept of *social intelligence*, also introduced in chapter 1, involves understanding social interactions and using that understanding to maximize your relationships. If you pay attention to how things work in social situations at school, at home, and at work, experience can provide continual practical lessons about which actions to take.

Social intelligence skills, such as sensing what others feel and making a desired impression through what you say verbally and nonverbally, will help you make the most out of your interactions with instructors.

Look closely at what happens among the social players as well as within your emotional landscape, and consider what will promote success. Say, for example, that you receive a disappointing grade on a paper, and you are angry about it. An emotionally and socially intelligent response involves these practical actions:

- Cooling off before you schedule a meeting with the instructor
- Calmly making your point at the meeting
- Listening carefully to what your instructor says in response
- Politely requesting what is possible (a rewrite, for example)

With this course of action, you maximize the likelihood that your instructor will be receptive and helpful (social intelligence), and you maximize your ability to manage your own emotions and use them effectively to work toward your goal (emotional intelligence).

Practical Thinking Means Action

Action is an extension of practical thinking. Basic student success strategies that promote action—staying motivated, making the most of your strengths, learning from failure, managing time, taking the initiative to seek help from instructors and advisors, and believing in yourself—will keep you moving toward your goals.[25]

The key to making practical knowledge work is to use what you discover, assuring that you will not have to learn the same lessons over and over again. As Sternberg says, "What matters most is not how much experience you have had but rather how much you have profited from it—in other words, how well you apply what you have learned."[26]

See Key 4.7 for some questions you can ask in order to apply practical thinking to your problems and decisions.

KEY 4.7 Ask questions like these to activate practical thinking.

To learn from experience, ask:	• What worked well, or not so well, about my approach? My timing? My tone? My wording? • What did others like or not like about what I did? • What did I learn from that experience, conversation, event? • How would I change things if I had to do it over again? • What do I know I would do again?
To apply what you learn, ask:	• What have I learned that would work here? • What have I seen others do, or heard about from them, that would be helpful here? • What does this situation have in common with past situations I've been involved in? • What has worked in similar situations in the past?
To boost your ability to take action, ask:	• How can I get motivated and remove limitations? • How can I, in this situation, make the most of what I do well? • If I fail, what can I learn from it? • What steps will get me to my goal, and what trade-offs are involved? • How can I manage my time more effectively?

get practical!

Take a Practical Approach to Building Successful Intelligence Skills

Use the wheel on the facing page to get a big-picture look at how you perceive your skills in all three aspects of successful intelligence. In the appropriate sections of the circle, write your self-assessment scores from *Get Analytical* (page 12), *Get Creative* (page 19), and *Get Practical* (page 25) in chapter 1. Then, in each of the three areas of the wheel, draw a curved line approximately at the level of the number of your score and fill in the wedge below that line. Look at what the wheel says about how balanced you perceive your three aspects of successful intelligence to be. If it were a real wheel, would it roll?

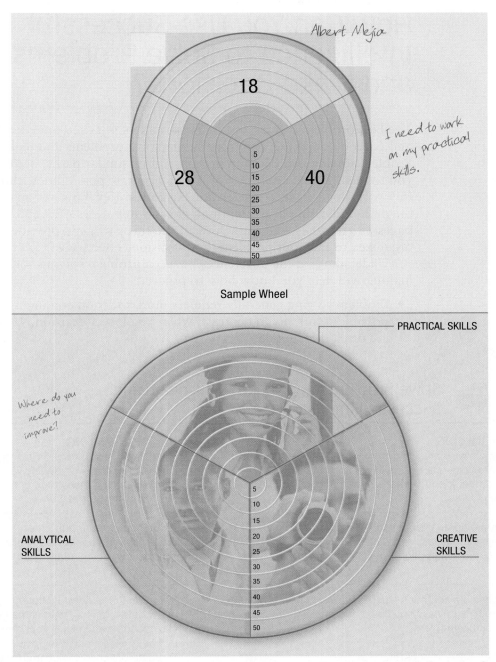

Albert Mejia

18

28

40

I need to work on my practical skills.

Sample Wheel

PRACTICAL SKILLS

Where do you need to improve?

ANALYTICAL SKILLS

CREATIVE SKILLS

Source: Based on "The Wheel of Life" model developed by the Coaches Training Institute. © Co-Active Space 2000.

Based on looking at your wheel, in which area do you most want to build strength?

_____

Write down two practical actions you can take that will improve your skills in that area. For example, someone who wants to be more creative could take a course focused on creativity; someone who wants to be more practical could work on paying attention to social cues; someone who wants to be more analytical could decide to analyze one newspaper article every week.

_____

_____

How Can You Use Successful Intelligence to Solve Problems and Make Decisions?

The best problem solvers and decision makers put their analytical, creative, and practical thinking skills together to solve problems and make decisions. Problem solving and decision making follow similar paths, both requiring you to identify and analyze a situation, generate possibilities, choose one, follow through on it, and evaluate its success. Key 4.8 gives an overview of the path, indicating how you think at each step. Keys 4.10 and 4.11 on pages 133 and 134 will show how to use this path, and provide a visual organizer, to map out problems and decisions effectively.

Understanding the differences between problem solving and decision making will help you know how to proceed:

- Problem solving generally requires more focus on coming up with possible solutions. In contrast, when you face a decision, your choices are often determined.

KEY 4.8 Solve problems and make decisions using successful intelligence.

PROBLEM SOLVING	THINKING SKILL	DECISION MAKING
Define the problem—recognize that something needs to change, identify what's happening, look for true causes.	STEP 1 DEFINE	Define the decision—identify your goal (your need) and then construct a decision that will help you get it.
Analyze the problem—gather information, break it down into pieces, verify facts, look at perspectives and assumptions, evaluate information.	STEP 2 ANALYZE	Examine needs and motives—consider the layers of needs carefully, and be honest about what you really want.
Generate possible solutions—use creative strategies to think of ways you could address the causes of this problem.	STEP 3 CREATE	Name and/or generate different options—use creative questions to come up with choices that would fulfill your needs.
Evaluate solutions—look carefully at potential pros and cons of each, and choose what seems best.	STEP 4 ANALYZE (EVALUATE)	Evaluate options—look carefully at potential pros and cons of each, and choose what seems best.
Put the solution to work—persevere, focus on results, and believe in yourself as you go for your goal.	STEP 5 TAKE PRACTICAL ACTION	Act on your decision—go down the path and use practical strategies to stay on target.
Evaluate how well the solution worked—look at the effects of what you did.	STEP 6 ANALYZE (REEVALUATE)	Evaluate the success of your decision—look at whether it accomplished what you had hoped.
In the future, apply what you've learned—use this solution, or a better one, when a similar situation comes up again.	STEP 7 TAKE PRACTICAL ACTION	In the future, apply what you've learned—make this choice, or a better one, when a similar decision comes up again.

- A problem exists when a situation has negative effects, and problem solving aims to remove or counteract those effects. In contrast, decision making aims to fulfill a need.

See Key 4.9 for some examples. Remember, too, that whereas all problem solving involves decision making, only some decision making requires you to solve a problem.

Solving a Problem

Use these strategies as you move through the problem-solving process outlined in Key 4.8.

Use probing questions to define problems. Focus on causes. If you are not happy in a class, for example, you could ask questions like these:

- What do I think about when I feel unhappy?
- Do my feelings involve my instructor? My classmates? School in general?
- Is the subject matter difficult? The volume of work too much?

Chances are that how you answer one or more of these questions may lead to a clear definition—and ultimately to the right solution.

Analyze carefully. Gather information for a comprehensive examination. Consider how the problem is similar to, or different from, other problems. Clarify facts. Note your own perspective, and ask others for theirs. Make sure your assumptions are not clouding your analysis.

Generate possible solutions based on causes, not effects. Addressing a cause provides a lasting solution, whereas "fixing" an effect cannot. Say, for example, that your shoulder hurts when you use your computer. Getting a friend to massage it is a helpful but temporary solution, because the pain returns whenever you go back to work. Changing the height of your keyboard and mouse is a better idea, because it eliminates the cause of your pain.

 KEY 4.9

Examine how problems and decisions differ.

Situation	You have a problem if . . .	You need to make a decision if . . .
Planning summer activities	Your low GPA means you need to attend summer school—and you've already accepted a summer job.	You've been accepted into two summer abroad internship programs.
Declaring a major	It's time to declare, but you don't have all the prerequisites for the major you want.	There are three majors that appeal to you and you qualify for them all.
Handling communications with instructors	You are having trouble following the lecture style of a particular instructor.	Your psychology survey course has seven sections taught by different instructors; you have to choose one.

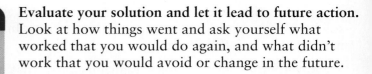
Evaluate your solution and let it lead to future action. Look at how things went and ask yourself what worked that you would do again, and what didn't work that you would avoid or change in the future.

What happens if you don't work through a problem comprehensively? Take, for example, a student having an issue with an instructor. The student may get into an argument with the instructor, stop showing up to class, or take a quick-and-dirty approach to assignments. All of these choices have negative consequences. Now look at how the student might work through this problem using analytical, creative, and practical thinking skills. Key 4.10 shows how his effort can pay off.

Making a Decision

As you use the steps in Key 4.8 to make a decision, remember these strategies:

Look at the given options—then try to think of more. Some decisions have a given set of options. For example, your school may allow you to major, double major, or major and minor. However, you may be able to brainstorm with an advisor to come up with more options, such as an interdisciplinary major. As with problem solving, consider similar situations you've been in or heard about, what decisions were made, and what resulted from those decisions.

Think about how your decision affects others. What you choose might have an impact on friends, family, and others around you. Your conclusions about that impact may affect what decision you ultimately make.

Gather perspectives. Talk with others who have made similar decisions. There are more ways of doing things than one brain can possibly imagine on its own.

Look at the long-term effects. As with problem solving, a final evaluation is crucial. For important decisions, do a short-term evaluation and another evaluation after a period of time. Examine whether your decision has sent you down a path that has continued to bring positive effects or whether you should rethink your choice.

Consider all of the factors. Psychologists who study decision making realize that many random factors influence the choices people make. For example, you may choose a major, not because you love the subject, but because you think your parents will approve of it. The goal is to make well-considered decisions despite factors that may derail your thinking.

What happens when you make important decisions too quickly? Consider the student trying to decide whether to transfer schools. If she makes her decision based on a reason that ultimately is not the most important one for her (for example, a boyfriend or close friends go to the other school), she may regret her choice later. Key 4.11 shows how she worked through the analytical, creative, and practical parts of the process.

Working through a problem relating to an instructor.

DEFINE PROBLEM HERE:	ANALYZE THE PROBLEM
I don't like my Freshman Composition instructor	We have different views and personality types— I don't feel respected or heard. I'm not interested in being there and my grades are suffering from my lack of motivation.

Use boxes below to list possible solutions:

POTENTIAL POSITIVE EFFECTS	SOLUTION #1	POTENTIAL NEGATIVE EFFECTS
List for each solution: Don't have to deal with that instructor Less stress	Drop the course	*List for each solution:* Grade gets entered on my transcript I'll have to take the course eventually; it's required for my major
Getting credit for the course Feeling like I've honored a commitment	SOLUTION #2 Put up with it until the end of the semester	Stress every time I'm there Lowered motivation Probably not such a good final grade
A chance to express myself Could get good advice An opportunity to ask direct questions of the instructor	SOLUTION #3 Schedule meetings with advisor and instructor	Have to face instructor one-on-one Might just make things worse

Now choose the solution you think is best—circle it and make it happen.

ACTUAL POSITIVE EFFECTS	PRACTICAL ACTION	ACTUAL NEGATIVE EFFECTS
List for chosen solution: Got some helpful advice from advisor Talking in person with the instructor actually promoted a fairly honest discussion I won't have to take the course again	I scheduled and attended meetings with both advisor and instructor, and opted to stick with the course.	*List for chosen solution:* The discussion was difficult and sometimes tense I still don't know how much learning I'll retain from this course

FINAL EVALUATION: Was it a good or bad solution?

The solution has improved things. I'll finish the course, and even though the instructor and I aren't the best of friends, we have a mutual understanding now. I feel more respected and more willing to put my time into the course.

Source: Based on heuristic created by Frank T. Lyman Jr. and George Eley, 1985.

Making a decision about whether to transfer schools.

DEFINE THE DECISION	EXAMINE NEEDS AND MOTIVES
Whether or not to transfer schools	I attend a small private college. My father has changed jobs and can no longer afford my tuition. My goal is to become a physical therapist, so I need a school with a full physical therapy program. My family needs to cut costs. I need to transfer credits.

Use boxes below to list possible choices:

POTENTIAL POSITIVE EFFECTS	CHOICE #1	POTENTIAL NEGATIVE EFFECTS
List for each solution:	Continue at the current college	*List for each solution:*
No need to adjust to a new place or new people		Need to finance most of my tuition and costs on my own
Ability to continue course work as planned		Difficult to find time for a job
		Might not qualify for aid
	CHOICE #2	
Opportunity to connect with some high school friends	Transfer to a state college	Need to earn some money or get financial aid
Cheaper tuition and room costs		Physical therapy program is small and not very strong
Credits will transfer		
	CHOICE #3	
Many physical therapy courses available	Transfer to the community college	No personal contacts there that I know of
School is close so I could live at home and save room costs		Less independence if I live at home
Reasonable tuition; credits will transfer		No bachelor's degree available

Now choose the one you think is best—circle it and make it happen.

ACTUAL POSITIVE EFFECTS	PRACTICAL ACTION	ACTUAL NEGATIVE EFFECTS
List for chosen solution:	Go to community college for two years; then transfer to a four-year school to get a B.A. and complete physical therapy course work.	*List for chosen solution:*
Money saved		Loss of some independence
Opportunity to spend time on studies rather than on working to earn tuition money		Less contact with friends
Availability of classes I need		

FINAL EVALUATION: Was it a good or bad choice?
I'm satisfied with the decision. It can be hard being at home at times, but my parents are adjusting to my independence and I'm trying to respect their concerns. With fewer social distractions, I'm really getting my work done. Plus the financial aspect of the decision is ideal.

Source: Based on heuristic created by Frank T. Lyman Jr. and George Eley, 1985.

Keeping Your Balance

No one has equal strengths in analytical, creative, and practical thinking. Successfully intelligent thinkers are able to analyze their abilities, come up with creative ideas about how to maximize their strengths and build their weaknesses, and put them to use with practical action. Staying as balanced as possible requires that you do the following:

- Use what you've learned in this chapter and the rest of the text to maximize your analytical, creative, and practical abilities.

- Reflect on what you do well, and focus on strengthening weaker skills.

- Combine all three thinking skills to accomplish your goals, knowing when and how to apply your analytical, creative, and practical abilities.

- Believe in your skills as a thinker.

"Successfully intelligent people," says Sternberg, "defy negative expectations, even when these expectations arise from low scores on IQ or similar tests. They do not let other people's assessments stop them from achieving their goals. They find their path and then pursue it, realizing that there will be obstacles along the way and that surmounting these obstacles is part of the challenge."[27] Let the obstacles come, as they will for everyone, in all aspects of life. You can face and overcome them with the power of your successfully intelligent thinking.

Successful Intelligence Wrap-Up

With the power of successful intelligence, you can identify your most significant goals, devise ways to pursue them, and most importantly, take concrete actions to attain them. In addition, you can move beyond a fixed view of your intelligence. Here's how you have built skills in chapter 4:

Analytical

You explored the steps and parts of analytical thinking in the section on analytical thinking skills, including crucial topics such as fact vs. opinion, perspective, and how examples support an idea. In the *Get Analytical* exercise, you honed your skills by analyzing a statement. At the end of the chapter, you considered how to use your analytical skills to evaluate potential ideas and choices in the problem-solving and decision-making processes.

Creative

You developed a detailed understanding of creative thinking as you read the section on creative thinking skills. You learned of some creativity-boosting strategies and probably thought of more. In the *Get Creative* exercise, you brainstormed creative acts as well as new ideas about how to deal with a problem. In the section on problem solving and decision making, you explored ways to brainstorm solutions and choices.

Practical

You broadened your concept of practical thinking as you read the section on practical thinking skills, including developing more specific ideas of how to apply your emotional and social intelligence. In the *Get Practical* exercise, you built a picture of how you see your successful intelligence and generated practical ideas about how to improve. When reading about problem solving and decision making, you explored practical ways to put solutions and choices to work.

kunnskaping
(kun-skahp-ping)

This Norwegian word is a creative combination of *kunnskap* (meaning "knowledge") and *verdiskaping* (meaning "value creation"). It translates loosely as "knowledging," which can be read as developing knowledge and meaning that are of use in school and work.[28] In the global marketplace described by Thomas Friedman (see chapter 1), knowledge as a tool and product is more important than ever before.

Think of this concept as you use your analytical, creative, and practical thinking skills to solve problems, make decisions, innovate, and question. Successful intelligence enables you to put knowledge to work as you strive toward your goals. It also empowers you to be creative, in much the same way that some clever Norwegian was when he or she coined *kunnskaping* and made it part of the language.

"I am enough of an artist to draw freely upon my imagination. Imagination is more important than knowledge. Knowledge is limited. Imagination encircles the world."

ALBERT EINSTEIN, MATHEMATICIAN AND SCIENTIST

Building World-Class Skills
for College, Career, and Life Success

SUCCESSFUL INTELLIGENCE

Think, Create, Apply

Make an important decision. Put the decision-making process to work on something that matters to you. You will apply your analytical, creative, and practical thinking skills. Use a separate sheet of paper for steps 2, 3, and 5.

Step 1. Analyze: *Define the decision.* Write an important long-term goal that you have, and define the decision that will help you fulfill it. Example: "My goal is to become a nurse. My decision: What to specialize in."

Step 2. Analyze: *Examine needs and concerns.* What are your needs, and how do your values come into play? What is most needed in the health market, and how can you fulfill that need? What roadblocks might be involved? List everything you come up with. For example, the prospective nurse might list needs like these: "I need to feel that I'm helping people. I intend to help with the shortage of perinatal or geriatric nurses. I need to make a good living."

Step 3. Be creative: *Generate options.* Ask questions to imagine what's possible. Where might you work? What might be the schedule and pace? Who might work with you? What would you see, smell, and hear on your job? What would you do every day? List, too, all of the options you know of. The prospective nurse, for example, might list perinatal surgery, neonatal intensive care unit, geriatric nursing in a hospital or in a retirement community, and so forth.

Step 4. Analyze: *Evaluate options.* Think about how well your options will fulfill your needs. For two of your options, write potential positive and negative effects (pros and cons) of each.

Option 1:

_____

Potential pros:

_____

Potential cons:

Option 2:

Potential pros:

Potential cons:

Step 5. Get practical: *Imagine acting on your decision.* Describe one practical course of action, based on your thinking so far, that you might follow. List the specific steps you would take. For example, the prospective nurse might list actions that help him determine what type of nursing suits him best, such as interning, summer jobs, academic goals, and talking to working nurses.

An additional practical action is to go where the job is and talk to people. The prospective nurse might go to a hospital, a clinic, and a health center at a retirement community. Get a feel for what the job is like day-to-day so that can be part of your decision.

TEAMWORK

Create Solutions Together

Powerful group problem solving. On a 3-by-5 card or a plain sheet of paper, each student in the class writes a school-related problem—this could be a fear, a challenge,  a sticky situation, or a roadblock. Students hand these in without names. The instructor writes the list on the board.

Divide into groups of two to four. Each group chooses one problem to work on (try not to have two groups working on the same problem). Use the problem-solving flowchart (Key 4.12) on page 139 to fill in your work.

Analyze: *Define and examine the problem.* As a group, look at the negative effects and state your problem specifically. Write down the causes and examine them to see what's happening. Gather information from all group members, verify facts, and go beyond assumptions.

Create: *Generate possible solutions.* From the most likely causes of the problem, derive possible solutions. Record all the ideas that group members offer. After 10 minutes or so, each group member should choose one possible solution to evaluate independently.

Analyze: *Evaluate each solution.* In thinking independently through the assigned solution, each group member should (1) weigh the positive and negative effects, (2) consider similar problems, and (3) describe how the solution affects the causes of the problem. Will your solution work?

Get practical: *Choose a solution.* Group members then come together, share observations and recommendations, and then take a vote: Which solution is the best? You may have a tie or may want to combine two different solutions. Try to find the solution that works for most of the group. Then, together, come up with a plan for how you would put your solution to work.

Work through a problem using this flowchart.

DEFINE PROBLEM HERE: | **ANALYZE THE PROBLEM**

Use boxes below to list possible solutions:

| POTENTIAL POSITIVE EFFECTS | SOLUTION #1 | POTENTIAL NEGATIVE EFFECTS |

List for each solution: | | *List for each solution:*

SOLUTION #2

SOLUTION #3

Now choose the solution you think is best—circle it and make it happen.

| ACTUAL POSITIVE EFFECTS | PRACTICAL ACTION | ACTUAL NEGATIVE EFFECTS |

List for chosen solution: | | *List for chosen solution:*

FINAL EVALUATION: Was it a good or bad solution?

Source: Based on heuristic created by Frank T. Lyman Jr. and George Eley, 1985.

WRITING

Journal and Put Skills to Work

Record your thoughts on a separate piece of paper, in a journal, or on a computer file.

Journal entry: Make a wiser choice. Think about a decision you made that you wish you had handled differently. Describe the decision and its consequences. Then, describe what you would do if you could approach the decision again, applying your analytical, creative, and practical skills to reach a more effective outcome.

Real-life writing: Address a problem. Think about a problem that you are currently experiencing in school—it could be difficulty with a course, a scheduling nightmare, or perhaps a conflict with a classmate. Write a letter—to an advisor, instructor, friend, medical professional, or anyone else who may logically help—that would solicit input on your problem. Be specific about what you want and how the person to whom you are writing can help you. After you finish, you may want to consider sending your letter via mail or e-mail. Carefully assess the potential effects that your letter may have—and if you determine that it is likely to help more than harm, send it only after having someone you trust review it for you.

PERSONAL PORTFOLIO

Prepare for Career Success

Generating ideas for internships. Pursuing internships is part of a comprehensive career decision-making process. It's a practical way to get experience, learn what you like and don't like, and make valuable connections. Even if you intern in a career area that you don't ultimately pursue, you build skills that are useful in any career.

First, use personal contacts to gather information about career fields. List three people here:

People whom I want to interview about their fields/professions, and why:

1. _____   *Field:* _____

Because: _____

2. _____   *Field:* _____

Because: _____

3. _____   *Field:* _____

Because: _____

_____

_____

Talk to the people you have listed, and take notes.

Next, look up each of these fields in the *Occupational Outlook Handbook* published by the U.S. Department of Labor (available at the library, or online at http://stats.bls.gov/oco/home.htm). To get a better idea of whether you would want to intern in these fields, read OOH categories for each—such as Nature of the Work, Training, Working Conditions, Advancement, Job Outlook, Earnings, and so on. Take notes and compare the fields based on what you've learned.

Finally, consult someone in your school's career office about local companies that offer internships. Get specific information about internship job descriptions, timing (during the term, summer), and whether there is any pay involved.

Analyze what you have learned from your reading, your interviews, and the career office information. Write here in what field or fields you would like to intern and why, and describe what practical action you plan to take to secure an internship within the next two years:

_____

_____

_____

_____

_____

Suggested Readings

Cameron, Julia, with Mark Bryan. *The Artist's Way: A Spiritual Path to Higher Creativity,* 10th ed. New York: Putnam, 2002.

deBono, Edward. *Lateral Thinking: Creativity Step by Step.* New York: Perennial Library, 1990.

Goleman, Daniel. *Emotional Intelligence: Why It Can Matter More Than IQ, 10th Anniversary Edition.* New York: Bantam Books, 2006.

Goleman, Daniel. *Social Intelligence: The New Science of Social Relationships.* New York: Bantam Books, 2006.

Moscovich, Ivan. *1000 Playthinks.* New York: Workman, 2001.

Noone, Donald J. *Creative Problem Solving.* New York: Barron's, 1998.

SARK. *Make Your Creative Dreams Real: A Plan for Procrastinators, Perfectionists, Busy People, and People Who Would Rather Sleep All Day.* New York: Fireside, 2004.

von Oech, Roger. *A Kick in the Seat of the Pants.* New York: Harper & Row, 1986.

von Oech, Roger. *A Whack on the Side of the Head.* New York: Warner Books, 1998.

Internet and Podcast Resources

Creativity at Work (resources for workplace creativity): **www.creativityatwork.com**

Creativity for Life (tips and strategies for creativity): **www.creativityforlife.com**

Free Management Library—Problem Solving: **www.managementhelp.org/prsn_prd/prob_slv.htm**

"Get Creative" podcast from Podcast Alley, on the topic of problem solving and creativity: **www.podcastalley.com/search.php?searchterm=problem+solving**

"LSAT Logic in Everyday Life" podcasts on thinking, from the *Princeton Review:* **www.princetonreview.com/podcasts/lsat.asp**

Mind Tools—Decision Making Techniques:
www.mindtools.com/pages/main/newMN_TED.htm

Roger von Oech's Creative Think Web site:
www.creativethink.com

Prentice Hall Student Success Supersite:
www.prenhall.com/success

Endnotes

[1] Matt Thomas, "What Is Higher-Order Thinking and Critical/Creative/Constructive Thinking?" n.d., Center for Studies in Higher-Order Literacy (http://a-s.clayton.edu/tparks/What%20is%20Higher%20Order%20Thinking.doc).

[2] Vincent Ruggiero, *The Art of Thinking*, 2001, quoted in "Critical Thinking," Oregon State University (http://success.oregonstate.edu/criticalthinking.html).

[3] From "The Role of Socratic Questioning in Thinking, Teaching, and Learning," n.d., The Critical Thinking Community, Foundation for Critical Thinking (www.criticalthinking.org/page.cfm?PageID=522&CategoryID=71), based on Richard W. Paul, Douglas Martin, and Ken Adamson, *Critical Thinking Handbook: High School*, 1989, Foundation for Critical Thinking.

[4] "The Best Innovations Are Those That Come from Smart Questions," *Wall Street Journal*, April 12, 2004, p. B1.

[5] Angiotech Pharmaceuticals, "Angiotech Submits Application for European Regulatory Approval for Its Vascular Wrap Product," news release, November 16, 2006 (www.angiotech.com/news/press-releases/?id=709).

[6] Sharon Begley, "Critical Thinking: Part Skill, Part Mindset and Totally Up to You," *Wall Street Journal*, October 20, 2006, p. B1.

[7] Robert J. Sternberg, *Successful Intelligence*, New York: Plume, 1996, p. 128.

[8] Colby Glass, "Strategies for Critical Thinking," March 1999 (www.criticalthink.info/Phil1301/ctstrategies.htm).

[9] Sternberg, *Successful Intelligence*, p. 49.

[10] Charles Cave, "Definitions of Creativity," August 1999 (http://members.optusnet.com.au/~charles57/Creative/Basics/definitions.htm).

[11] Elizabeth F. Farrell, "Engineering a Warmer Welcome for Female Students: The Discipline Tries to Stress Its Social Relevance, an Important Factor for Many Women," *Chronicle of Higher Education*, February 22, 2002 (http://chronicle.com/weekly/v48/i24/24a03101.htm).

[12] Roger von Oech, *A Kick in the Seat of the Pants*, New York: Harper & Row, 1986, pp. 5–21.

[13] Dennis Coon, *Introduction to Psychology: Exploration and Application*, 6th ed., St. Paul: West, 1992, p. 295.

[14] Roger von Oech, *A Whack on the Side of the Head*, New York: Warner Books, 1990, pp. 11–168.

[15] J. R. Hayes, *Cognitive Psychology: Thinking and Creating*, Homewood, IL: Dorsey, 1978.

[16] Sternberg, *Successful Intelligence*, p. 219.

[17] Adapted from T. Z. Tardif and R. J. Sternberg, "What Do We Know About Creativity?" in *The Nature of Creativity*, R. J. Sternberg, ed., London: Cambridge University Press, 1988.

[18] Sternberg, *Successful Intelligence*, p. 212

[19] Hayes, *Cognitive Psychology*.

[20] "The Best Innovations," p. B1.

[21] Sternberg, *Successful Intelligence*, pp. 229–230.

[22] "Amazing Student, David Hosei—Entrepreneur with a Heart," 2003 Indiana University (http://excellence.indiana.edu/hosei; no longer available).

[23] Sternberg, *Succesful Intelligence*, p. 236.

[24]Robert J. Sternberg and Elena L. Grigorenko, "Practical Intelligence and the Principal," Yale University: Publication Series No. 2, 2001, p. 5.

[25]Sternberg, *Successful Intelligence*, pp. 251–269.

[26]Ibid., p. 241.

[27]Ibid., p. 128.

[28]Christopher J. Moore, *In Other Words: A Language Lover's Guide to the Most Intriguing Words Around the World*, New York: Walker, 2004, p. 61.

Answers to perception puzzles on page 122

First puzzle: A duck or a rabbit

Second puzzle: A face or a musician

Third puzzle: Lines or the letter E

"Successful intelligence is most effective when it balances all three of its analytical, creative, and practical aspects. It is more important to know when and how to use these aspects of successful intelligence than just to have them."

ROBERT J. STERNBERG

Your ability to read—and to understand, analyze, and use what you read—is the cornerstone of college learning. Taking a step-by-step approach to reading linked to analytical, creative, and practical thinking techniques will help you master content, whether you are getting ahead of the game with a stack of summer reading or staying up late studying for finals. This chapter introduces strategies to increase your efficiency and depth of understanding so that every hour you spend reading will be more valuable.

In this chapter you explore answers to the following questions:

- What will improve your reading comprehension? 146
- How can SQ3R help you master content? 157
- How can you respond critically to what you read? 166
- How do you customize your text with highlighting and notes? 167
- Successful Intelligence Wrap-Up 173

Analytical

- Identifying steps to improve comprehension
- Mastering SQ3R
- Building vocabulary by mastering roots, prefixes, and suffixes
- Critically evaluating reading passages

Creative

- Creating an environment that encourages concentration
- Adapting SQ3R to your unique studying needs
- Using colors and notations to highlight text and take text notes

Practical

- How to study word parts to build vocabulary
- How to make SQ3R a personal tool
- How to put highlighting and note-taking systems into action

What Will Improve Your Reading Comprehension?

Reading is an analytical process that requires you, the reader, to make meaning from written words. You do this by connecting what you know to what you read. Your understanding is affected by your familiarity with a subject, your cultural background and life experiences, and the way you interpret words and phrases.

Because these factors are different for every person, your reading experiences are uniquely your own. If, for example, your family owns a hardware store where you worked during summers, you will read a retailing chapter in a business text from the perspective of your work in the store. While you are comparing text concepts to your family's business practices, your classmates may be reading for basic ideas and vocabulary.

Improving your reading comprehension is especially important in college because assignments are generally longer, more difficult, and require a lot of independent work. In addition, what you learn from introductory-level texts is the foundation for your understanding in advanced courses. When you struggle through and master concepts that you considered impossible the first time you read them, you'll be proud of your ability to overcome obstacles instead of giving up. This pride will motivate you every time you read.

How can I improve my reading and studying despite my learning disabilities?

In elementary school I needed extra help with reading. By high school, I was having a hard time keeping up, and a test showed I had dyslexia. Study assistance helped, but I attended high school for an extra year to improve my record.

I learn best by hearing, seeing, and doing all at once. If I just hear something, it doesn't sink in. I keep hanging in there though. Eventually, when I have a career, I would like to help others. I can see myself being on the lookout for early signs of disabilities like mine. What suggestions do you have that will help me cope with my learning disabilities?

Darrin Estepp
Ohio State University,
Columbus, Ohio

PRACTICAL ANSWERS

Morgan Paar
Graduate Student,
Academy of Art College
San Francisco, California

One thing I learned in college is that there is more than one way to succeed, even when I had trouble keeping up with the reading.

First, I attended every single class without exception. Second, if I got behind in my note taking (and I often did), I would borrow a friend's notes and rewrite mine, combining the two versions. Third, I made friends with my teachers, and they would help me during their office hours.

One incident showed me that anything is possible. A friend worked for a newspaper and asked me to write a story. I laughed—I said I could barely spell my name, never mind write an article. I labored through it; my friend loved the writing (despite my "creative grammar"), and it appeared as a two-part story in the travel section. I have since had 17 articles published.

It never gets easy—but one route to success is to do something you love. I write travel stories because I love traveling and sharing stories. I am now a filmmaker, and I am studying film in graduate school so I can someday teach it. Darrin, you already know the skills you need to achieve your goals, though maybe they are deep in your subconscious mind. I was 27 years old before I knew what I really wanted to do. Just keep following your passions, never give up, figure out what you need to do to achieve your goals, and know that there is more than one path to your destination.

Set Your Expectations

On any given day, you may be faced with reading assignments like this:

- A 10-page textbook chapter on the history of South African apartheid (world history)
- An original research study on the relationship between sleep deprivation and the development of memory problems (psychology)
- The first three chapters in John Steinbeck's classic novel, *The Grapes of Wrath* (American literature)
- A technical manual on the design of computer antivirus programs (computer science, software design)

SUCCESSFUL INTELLIGENCE

get creative!

See the Movie—Read the Book

Movies from *Gone With the Wind* to *The Devil Wears Prada* are based on popular books. The Mid-Continent Public Library (www.mcpl.lib.mo.us/readers/movies/year.cfm) compiles a yearly list of movies made from books. Search this list, choose a movie you would like to see (or see again), and then watch it on video. List the name of the movie here:

____

On a separate sheet or computer file, jot down your thoughts about the plot and characters and describe your reaction. Hold on to these thoughts for later.

During a school break, when you have time to read for pleasure, *read the book* on which the movie is based and write a similar page of reflections.

Then compare what you thought of the movie version to what you thought of the book. List three major differences here:

1. ______________________________
2. ______________________________
3. ______________________________

Describe what you gained from reading the book that you *did not* get from watching the movie.

____

____

Based on this experience, are you likely to make the movie–book connection again? Why or why not?

____

____

How might you use another work as a starting point for your own creative effort?

____

____

____

This material is rigorous by anyone's standards. You can help yourself handle it by setting higher expectations—*know at the start that you will read more than you ever did in high school*—and by challenging yourself to handle more complex ideas.

To get through it all—and master what you read—you need a systematic approach that taps into your analytic and practical thinking skills. Without one, you may face problems similar to those of a student at a large northeastern university, who explains:

> I did not get off to a great start because I had never really learned to study this enormous amount of material in a systematic way. I tended to do one subject for a big span of time and then neglect it for a week. Then I moved on to another subject, and forgot about that for a week. So there was no continuity within each course. That had a lot to do with it. Finally I figured it out. This year, I'm pushing myself to spend a little bit of time every day on each subject.[1]

Take an Active Approach to Difficult Texts

Because college texts are generally written to challenge the intellect, even those that are well written may be tough going, especially when you encounter new concepts and terms. This is often the case when assignments are from *primary sources*—original documents, including academic journal articles and scientific studies—rather than from *secondary sources*—other writers' interpretations of these documents.

The following strategies will help you take an active, positive approach to reading difficult material:

Think positively. Instead of telling yourself that you cannot understand, think positively. Tell yourself: *I can learn this material. I am a good reader. I can succeed.*

Have an open mind. Be careful not to prejudge assignments as impossible or boring or a waste of time and energy before you begin.

Look for order and meaning in seemingly chaotic reading materials. Use SQ3R and the critical reading strategies introduced later in this chapter to discover patterns and connections.

Don't expect to master material on the first pass. Instead, create a multistep plan: On your first reading, your goal is to gain an overview of key concepts and interrelationships. On subsequent readings, you grasp ideas and relate them to what you already know. By your last reading, you master concepts and details and can apply the material to problems.

Know that some texts require extra work and concentration. If new material doesn't click, scan background material—including the text you used last term—for information that will help you understand. Set a goal to make your way through the material, whatever it takes. *If you want to learn, you will.*

Define unclear concepts and words. Use your practical intelligence as you consult resources—instructors, study group partners, tutors, and reference materials—for help. Build a library of texts in your major and minor areas of study and refer to them when needed, and bookmark helpful Web sites.

Ask yourself questions. Put on your analytical thinking cap as you engage in an internal question-and-answer session before reading a chapter. Look at the chapter headings and think about what the material means and why it is being presented in this way. Write down your thoughts. Then read the chapter summary to see if your questions are answered. (Questioning is at the heart of the SQ3R study system that you will learn later in this chapter.)

Be honest with yourself. Ask yourself: Do I understand what I just read? Are ideas and supporting evidence clear? Am I able to explain the material to someone else?

Choose the Right Setting

Find the right place and time to focus on your reading:

Select the right company (or no company at all). If you prefer to read alone, find an out-of-the-way spot at the library. Even if you don't mind activity nearby, try to minimize distractions.

Select the right location. Many students study at a desk or in a comfortable chair. Still others like to spread out papers on the floor. Be careful about studying in bed—some students tend to fall asleep.

Select a time when you are alert and focused. Eventually, you will associate certain times with focused reading. Pay attention to your natural body rhythms and study when your energy is high. While night owls are productive when everyone else is sleeping, morning people have a hard time working during late-night sessions. Knowing yourself is a key to emotional intelligence.

Students with young children face the additional challenge of keeping their family busy while they work. Key 5.1 explores some ways that parents or others caring for children can maximize their study efforts.

Learn to Concentrate

CONCENTRATION

The act of applying all your mental energy and focus to your academic work.

When you focus your attention on one thing and one thing only, you are engaged in the act of concentration. Following are active learning methods for remaining focused as you study. Many involve tapping your emotional and social intelligence.

Be intensely involved. Tell yourself that what you are doing is important and needs your full attention—no matter what is going on around you. It might help to place a purpose statement at the top of your desk. For example: "I'm concentrating on the U.S. Constitution because it is the basis for our laws and because it will be on Friday's exam."

Banish extraneous thoughts onto paper. Don't let unrelated thoughts block your efforts. When such thoughts come up, write them down and deal with them later. Keeping a monthly calendar of classes, appointments, and events will help you stay organized.

Deal with internal distractions. Internal distractions—for example, personal worries or even hunger—can get in the way of work. Taking a break to deal with what's bothering you (a sign of emotional intelligence) will make you more efficient. Physical exercise may relax and focus you; studying while listening to music may relieve stress; and a snack break will reduce hunger.

KEY 5.1

Use these techniques to manage children while studying.

KEEP THEM UP-TO-DATE ON YOUR SCHEDULE

Let them know when you have a big test or project due and when you are under less pressure, and what they can expect of you in each case.

EXPLAIN WHAT YOUR EDUCATION ENTAILS

Tell them how it will improve your life and theirs. This applies, of course, to older children who can understand the situation and compare it with their own schooling.

FIND HELP

Ask a relative or friend to watch your children or arrange for a child to visit a friend. Consider trading baby-sitting hours with another parent, hiring a sitter to come to your home, or using a day care center.

KEEP THEM ACTIVE WHILE YOU STUDY

Give them games, books, or toys. If there are special activities that you like to limit, such as watching videos or TV, save them for your study time.

STUDY ON THE PHONE

You might be able to have a study session with a fellow student over the phone while your child is sleeping or playing quietly.

OFFSET STUDY TIME WITH FAMILY TIME AND REWARDS

Children may let you get your work done if they have something to look forward to, such as a movie night or a trip for ice cream.

SPECIAL NOTES FOR INFANTS

Study at night if your baby goes to sleep early, or in the morning if your baby sleeps late.

Study during nap times if you aren't too tired yourself.

Lay your notes out and recite information to the baby. The baby will appreciate the attention, and you will get work done.

Put baby in a safe and fun place while you study, such as a playpen, motorized swing, or jumping seat.

Compartmentalize your life. Social invitations may be easier to resist if you have a policy of separating study time from play time. Tell yourself: "I will be able to go out with my friends on Saturday because I'm finishing this assignment on Friday so I won't have to work over the weekend."

Analyze your environment to see if it helps or hurts concentration. Think about your last study session. How long did you *try to* concentrate and how long did you *actually* concentrate? If you spent more than 10% of

Different people respond better to some reading environments than to others. This student chose to live in a substance-free dormitory and prefers to study in her room.

your time blocking out distractions (people, things going on around you), try another location.

Don't let technology distract you. Don't Web-surf, e-mail, instant-message, or download songs onto your iPod while you are trying to read. Get into the habit of turning off your cell phone, and check voice mail and text messages only after you finish your work.

Structure your study session so you know the time you will spend and the material you will study. No one can concentrate for unlimited periods, so set realistic goals and a specific plan for dividing your time. Tell yourself: "I'm going to answer these 15 questions and then eat lunch with my friends for 45 minutes."

Plan a reward. Make sure you have something to look forward to, because you deserve it!

The strongest motivation to concentrate comes from within—not from the fear of failing a test or disappointing a teacher. When you see the connection between what you study and your short- and long-term goals, you will be better able to focus, to remember, to learn, and to apply.

Become Emotionally Involved

You are more likely to remember material that evokes an emotional response than material that does not affect you, as student success expert Eric Jensen explains:

> The stronger you feel about something you read the more likely you are to remember it and make sense out of it. The good thing about this is that it works both ways; hating something or disagreeing with something works just as well as liking something or strongly agreeing with it.[2]

This is easy to do with controversial material, but how do you surround normally "dry" text chapters with emotions? These suggestions might help:

- Stop and think about your reaction to ideas, to the author's point of view and writing style, to chapter features and text design, and even to the chapter order.

- Discuss specific points with classmates, and have a heated discussion when you disagree. This will also help you understand the material.

- Think through the implications of a concept when it is applied in the real world.

Define Your Reading Purpose

When you define your purpose, you ask yourself *why* you are reading particular material. One way to do this is by completing this sentence: "In reading this material, I intend to define/learn/answer/achieve . . ." *Write down your goal before you begin and look at it whenever you lose focus or get bogged down in details.* With a clear purpose, you can decide how much time and effort to expend on various assignments. This is particularly important in college where you may be overwhelmed by assignments unless you prioritize. Later in this chapter, you will find suggestions for prioritizing the readings on your plate.

Purpose Determines Reading Strategy

Following are four reading purposes. You may have one or more for any "reading event."

- *Purpose 1: Read for understanding.* Here you read to comprehend concepts and details. Details help explain or support general concepts, and concepts provide a framework for details.

- *Purpose 2: Read to evaluate analytically.* Analytical evaluation requires that you approach material with an open mind as you examine causes and effects, evaluate ideas, and ask questions that test arguments and assumptions. Analytical reading brings a level of understanding that goes beyond basic information recall (see pages 166–167 for more on this topic).

- *Purpose 3: Read for practical application.* Here you gather usable information to apply to a specific goal. When you read an instruction booklet for new software or a lab manual for chemistry, your goal is to learn how to do or use something. Reading and action usually go hand in hand.

- *Purpose 4: Read for pleasure.* Some materials you read for entertainment, such as *Sports Illustrated* magazine or a mystery or romance novel.

Use your class syllabus to help define your purpose for each assignment. If, for example, you know that the topic of inflation will be discussed in your next economics class, read the assigned chapter, targeting what your instructor will expect you to know and do with the material. He may expect you to master definitions, economic models, causes and consequences, government intervention strategies, and historical examples—and be able to apply your knowledge to economic problems. In this case, depending on what your instructor expects, you may have three reading purposes—understanding, critical evaluation, and practical application. If you are confused about your purpose, e-mail your instructor for clarification. He is likely to be impressed with your motivation to stay on top of your assignments.

Spend Enough Time

You'll need more than good intentions to finish assignments on schedule. You'll have to put in hours of work every day. One formula for success is this: *For every hour you spend in the classroom each week, spend at least two hours preparing for the class.* For example, if you are carrying a course load of 15 credit hours, you should spend 30 hours a week studying outside of class. Students who fall far short of this goal are likely to have trouble keeping up. Check your syllabus for the dates reading assignments are due, and give yourself enough time to complete them. (The syllabus on page 14 specifies reading assignments and due dates.)

Use Special Strategies with Math and Science Texts

Math and science readings present unique challenges to many students. Try some of the following analytical, creative, and practical thinking techniques to succeed:

- *Interact with the material critically as you go.* Math and science texts are problem-and-solution based. Keep a pad nearby to solve problems and take notes. Draw sketches to help visualize material. Try not to move on until you understand the example and how it relates to the central ideas. Write down questions for your instructor or classmates.

- *Note formulas.* Make sure you understand the principle behind every formula—why it works—before memorizing it.

- *Use memory techniques.* Science textbooks are packed with specialized vocabulary. To learn these new words, use mnemonic devices, flash cards, and rehearsing aloud or silently (for more on memory techniques, see chapter 6). Selective highlighting and summarizing your readings in table format will also help.

Develop Strategies to Manage Learning Disabilities

Students with reading-related learning disabilities may need to engage their practical thinking skills and emotional and social intelligence to manage reading assignments. Roxanne Ruzic of the Center for Applied Special Technology explored the strategies used by two LD students at an urban college in the Northeast:

- Danielle received an A in her Art History survey course, in part because she chose some courses with heavy reading requirements and some with light requirements. This allowed her to complete all her assignments on time. In addition, she frequently sought instructors' advice about what they wanted her to learn from assigned texts and used tutors whenever she needed extra help.

- Chloe received an A in her Introduction to Psychology course, in part because she met twice weekly with a tutor who helped her prioritize reading assignments and keep on top of her work. She also learned to tailor the amount of time she spent on different text sections to the importance of the material on upcoming tests. Finally, when she felt comfortable with text concepts, she read them quickly or skipped them entirely, but when she had trouble with the material, she did extra reading or sought help.[3]

If you have a learning disability, think of these students as you investigate the services your college offers through reading centers and tutoring programs. Remember: *The ability to succeed is often linked to the willingness to ask for help.* (See chapter 1 for more on learning disabilities and support services.)

Expand Your Vocabulary

As reading materials become more complex, your vocabulary influences how much you comprehend—and how readily you do it. Use the following techniques to learn unfamiliar words as you encounter them.

Analyze Word Parts

If you understand part of a word, you often can figure out the entire word. This is true because many English words combine Greek and Latin prefixes, roots, and suffixes. *Prefixes* are word parts that are added to the beginning of a root. The root is the central part or basis of a word around which prefixes and/or suffixes are added to produce different words. *Suffixes* are added to the end of the root.

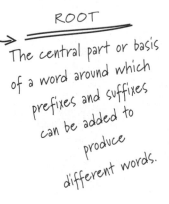

ROOT

The central part or basis of a word around which prefixes and suffixes can be added to produce different words.

Key 5.2 contains just a few of the prefixes, roots, and suffixes you will encounter as you read. Taking the time to memorize these verbal building blocks will help you grow your vocabulary. (Keep in mind that although prefixes, roots, and suffixes are reliable tools, they do not always apply to words with complex origins.)

Use a Dictionary

When reading a textbook, the first "dictionary" to search is the end-of-book glossary that explains technical words and concepts. Those definitions are usually limited to the meanings used in the text.

Standard dictionaries provide broader information such as word origin, pronunciation, part of speech, synonyms, antonyms, and multiple meanings. Buy a standard dictionary, keep it nearby, and consult it to learn unfamiliar words. You may even want to invest in an electronic handheld dictionary or, if you prefer an online version, investigate Web sites like Dictionary.com (http://dictionary.reference.com). The following suggestions will help you make the most of your dictionary:

Read every meaning, not just the first. Think critically about which meaning suits the context of the word in question, and choose the one that makes the most sense to you.

Say the word out loud—then write it down to make sure you can spell it. Check your pronunciation against the dictionary symbols as you say each word, or listen to the pronunciation on a handheld electronic or online dictionary. (Merriam-Webster Online, at http://merriamwebster.com, has a pronunciation feature.) Speaking and writing new words will boost recall.

Restate the definition in your own words. When you can do this with ease, you know that you understand the meaning and are not merely parroting a dictionary definition.

Try to use the word in conversation in the next 24 hours. Not only does this demonstrate that you know how the word is used, but it also aids memorization.

Learn Specialized Vocabulary

As you learn a subject, you will encounter specialized, unfamiliar vocabulary (see Key 5.3 for examples from four college texts). Even if you

Build your vocabulary with common prefixes, roots, and suffixes.

PREFIX	PRIMARY MEANING	EXAMPLE
a-, ab-	from	abstain, avert
ad-, af-, at-	to	adhere, affix, attain
con-, cor-, com-	with, together	convene, correlate, compare
di-	apart	divert, divorce
il-	not	illegal, illegible
ir-	not	irresponsible
post-	after	postpone, postpartum
pro-	before	prologue
sub-, sup-	under	subordinate, suppose
ROOT	**PRIMARY MEANING**	**EXAMPLE**
-logue	to speak	dialogue
-com	fill	incomplete
-strict	bind	restriction
-cept	take	receptacle
-chron	time	synchronize
-ann	year	biannual
-sper	hope	desperate
-clam	cry out	proclamation
-voc	speak, talk	convocation
SUFFIX	**PRIMARY MEANING**	**EXAMPLE**
-able	able	recyclable
-arium	place for	aquarium, solarium
-cule	very small	molecule
-ist	one who	pianist
-meter	measure	thermometer
-ness	state of	carelessness
-sis	condition of	hypnosis
-y	inclined to	sleepy

feel like you are diving into a foreign language, know that continual exposure will lead to mastery.

Apply a basic vocabulary-building approach to learn these terms. Understand words in the context of the chapter; then turn to the glossary for a review, record definitions in your notes, create vocabulary flash cards, use terms in your own sentences, and more. Instead of rushing through unfamiliar words, look them up, ask other students about them, and relate them to what you already know.

KEY 5.3 Every text includes specialized vocabulary.

BIOLOGY TEXT	CRIMINAL JUSTICE TEXT	PSYCHOLOGY TEXT	BUSINESS TEXT
actin	biometrics	experimental method	double-entry accounting
chaparral	detainee	great person theory	leverage
exoskeleton	habitual offender	homeostasis	relationship marketing
gravitropism	RICO statute	trichromats	strategic alliance
prophase	writ of habeas corpus	vestibular senses	Uniform Commercial Code (UCC)

Your instructors will test you on your ability to define and use course-specific vocabulary, so make sure you understand terms well enough to define them correctly on short-answer tests and to use them on essay exams.

Use Memory Aids to Ensure Recall

Most students find that their most important vocabulary-building tool is the simple but very practical flash card. Your efforts will pay off if you study several cards a day and push yourself to use your new words in conversation and writing. Memorization tools, including mnemonic devices and flash cards, are discussed in chapter 6.

How Can SQ3R Help You Master Content?

SQ3R stands for *Survey, Question, Read, Recite,* and *Review*. Developed more than 60 years ago by Francis Robinson, the technique is still used today because it works.[4]

As you move through the stages of SQ3R, you will skim and scan your text. Skimming refers to the rapid reading of such chapter elements as section introductions and conclusions, boldfaced or italicized terms, pictures and charts, and summaries. The goal of skimming is a quick construction of the main ideas. In contrast, scanning involves a careful search for specific information. You might use scanning during the SQ3R review phase to locate particular facts.

Approach SQ3R as a *flexible framework* on which to build your study method. When you bring your personal learning styles and study preferences to the system, it will work better than if you follow it rigidly. For example, you and another classmate may focus on elements in a different order when you survey, write different types of questions, or favor different sets of

SKIMMING
Rapid, superficial reading of material to determine central ideas and main elements.

SCANNING
Reading material in an investigative way to search for specific information.

review strategies. Explore different strategies, evaluate what works, and then make the system your own. (Note that SQ3R is not appropriate for literature.)

Survey

Surveying, the first stage in SQ3R, is the process of previewing, or pre-reading, a book before you study it. Compare it to looking at a map before starting a road trip; determining the route and stops along the way in advance will save time and trouble while you travel.

Most textbooks include elements that provide a big-picture overview of the main ideas and themes. You need the big picture to make sense of the thousands of information nuggets contained in the text and to learn the order of topics and the amount of space allotted to each.

Front Matter

Skim the *table of contents* for the chapter titles, the main chapter topics, and the order in which they will be covered, as well as special features. Then skim the *preface,* which is a note from the author that tells you what the book will cover and its point of view. For example, the preface for the American history text *Out of Many* states that it highlights "the experiences of diverse communities of Americans in the unfolding story of our country."[5] This tells you that cultural diversity is a central theme.

Chapter Elements

Generally, every chapter includes structural elements that highlight important content:

- Chapter title, which establishes the topic and often the author's perspective
- Chapter introduction, outline, list of objectives, or list of key topics
- First, second, and third level headings
- Information in the margins including definitions, quotes, questions, and exercises
- Tables, charts, photographs, and captions that express important concepts
- Side-bar boxed features that are connected to text-wide themes
- Particular styles or arrangements of type (**boldface,** *italics,* <u>underlining,</u> larger fonts, bullet points, boxed text) that call attention to vocabulary or concepts
- An end-of-chapter summary that reviews chapter content
- Review questions and exercises that help you analyze and master content

In Key 5.4, a typical page from the college textbook *Psychology: An Introduction* by Charles G. Morris and Albert A. Maisto, how many elements do you recognize? How do these elements help you grasp the subject even before reading it?[6]

Various survey elements are included on this text page.

Classical (or Pavlovian) conditioning The type of learning in which a response naturally elicited by one stimulus comes to be elicited by a different, formerly neutral stimulus.

Unconditioned stimulus (US) A stimulus that invariably causes an organism to respond in a specific way.

Unconditioned response (UR) A response that takes place in an organism whenever an unconditioned stimulus occurs.

Conditioned stimulus (CS) An originally neutral stimulus that is paired with an unconditioned stimulus and eventually produces the desired response in an organism when presented alone.

Conditioned response (CR) After conditioning, the response an organism produces when only a conditioned stimulus is presented.

you are experiencing insight. When you imitate the steps of professional dancers you saw last night on television, you are demonstrating observational learning. Like conditioning, cognitive learning is one of our survival strategies. Through cognitive processes, we learn which events are safe and which are dangerous without having to experience those events directly. Cognitive learning also gives us access to the wisdom of people who lived hundreds of years ago, and it will give people living hundreds of years from now some insight into our experiences and way of life.

Our discussion begins with *classical conditioning*. This simple kind of learning serves as a convenient starting point for examining what learning is and how it can be observed.

Classical Conditioning

How did Pavlov's discovery of classical conditioning help to shed light on learning?

Ivan Pavlov (1849–1936), a Russian physiologist who was studying digestive processes, discovered classical conditioning almost by accident. Because animals salivate when food is placed in their mouths, Pavlov inserted tubes into the salivary glands of dogs to measure how much saliva they produced when they were given food. He noticed, however, that the dogs salivated before the food was in their mouths: The mere sight of food made them drool. In fact, they even drooled at the sound of the experimenter's footsteps. This aroused Pavlov's curiosity. What was making the dogs salivate even before they had the food in their mouths? How had they learned to salivate in response to the sound of the experimenter's approach?

To answer these questions, Pavlov set out to teach the dogs to salivate when food was not present. He devised an experiment in which he sounded a bell just before the food was brought into the room. A ringing bell does not usually make a dog's mouth water but, after hearing the bell many times just before getting fed, Pavlov's dogs began to salivate as soon as the bell rang. It was as if they had learned that the bell signaled the appearance of food, and their mouths watered on cue even if no food followed. The dogs had been conditioned to salivate in response to a new stimulus—the bell—that would not normally have prompted that response (Pavlov, 1927). Figure 5–1, shows one of Pavlov's procedures in which the bell has been replaced by a touch to the dog's leg just before food is given.

Elements of Classical Conditioning

Generally speaking, **classical (or Pavlovian) conditioning** involves pairing an *involuntary* response (for example, salivation) that is usually evoked by one stimulus with a different, formerly neutral stimulus (such as a bell or a touch on the leg). Pavlov's experiment illustrates the four basic elements of classical conditioning. The first is an **unconditioned stimulus (US)**, such as food, which invariably prompts a certain reaction—salivation, in this case. That reaction—the **unconditioned response (UR)**—is the second element and always results from the unconditioned stimulus: Whenever the dog is given food (US), its mouth waters (UR). The third element is the neutral stimulus—the ringing bell—which is called the **conditioned stimulus (CS).** At first, the conditioned stimulus is said to be "neutral" with respect to the desired response (salivation), because dogs do not salivate at the sound of a bell unless they have been conditioned to react in this way by repeatedly presenting the CS and US together. Frequent pairing of the CS and US produces the fourth element in the classical conditioning process: the **conditioned response (CR).** The conditioned response is the behavior that the animal has learned in response to the conditioned stimulus. Usually, the unconditioned response and the conditioned

Back Matter

Some texts include a *glossary* that defines text terms, an *index* to help you locate topics, and a *bibliography* that lists additional readings.

SUCCESSFUL ANALYTICAL INTELLIGENCE

Survey a Text

Practice will improve your surveying skills. So start now with this text or another you are currently using.

- Skim the front matter, including the table of contents and preface. What does this material tell you about the theme? About the book's approach and point of view?

  _____

  _____

  _____

- Are there unexpected topics listed in the table of contents? Are there topics you expected to see that are missing?

  _____

  _____

- Now look at a typical chapter. List the devices that organize the structure and content of the material.

  _____

  _____

- After skimming the chapter, what do you know about the material? What elements helped you skim quickly?

  _____

  _____

- Finally, skim the back matter. What elements can you identify?

  _____

  _____

- How do you plan to use each of the elements you identified in your text survey when you begin studying?

  _____

  _____

Question

Your next step is to *ask questions* about your assignment. This process leads you to discover knowledge on your own, which is the essence of critical thinking (see chapter 4). As you pose questions and discover the answers in your text, you teach yourself the material.

Step 1: Ask Yourself What You Know About the Topic

Before you begin reading, summarize in writing what you already know about the topic, if anything. As you perform this task, you delve into your knowledge base, preparing yourself to apply what you know to new material.

Thinking about your current knowledge is especially important in your major, where the concepts you learn in one course prepare you for subsequent courses. For example, while your first business course may introduce the broad concept of marketing research, an upper-level marketing course may explore how marketing research analyzes consumer behavior according to age, education, income and economic status, and attitudes. Learning this advanced material depends on understanding the basics.

Step 2: Write Questions Linked to Chapter Headings

Next, examine the chapter headings and, on a separate page or in the text margins, write questions linked to them. For an assignment without headings, divide the material into logical sections, and then develop questions based on what you think is the main idea of each section.

Key 5.5 shows how this works. The column on the left contains primary- and secondary-level headings from a section of *Out of Many*. The column on the right rephrases these headings in question form.

 KEY 5.5

Create questions from headings.

HEADING	QUESTION
The Meaning of Freedom	What did freedom mean for both slaves and citizens in the United States?
Moving About	Where did African Americans go after they were freed from slavery?
The African American Family	How did freedom change the structure of the African American family?
African American Churches and Schools	What effect did freedom have on the formation of African American churches and schools?
Land and Labor after Slavery	How was land farmed and maintained after slaves were freed?
The Origins of African American Politics	How did the end of slavery bring about the beginning of African American political life?

There is no "correct" set of questions. Given the same headings, you could create different questions. Your goal is to engage the material as you begin to think critically about it.

Use Bloom's Taxonomy to Formulate Questions

Educational psychologist Benjamin Bloom developed Bloom's taxonomy because he believed that not all questions are created equal and that the greatest learning results from rigorous inquiry.[7] While some questions ask for a simple recall, said Bloom, others ask for higher levels of thinking. Key 5.6 shows the six levels of questions identified by Bloom: knowledge, understanding, application, analysis, synthesis, and evaluation. It also identifies verbs that are associated with each level. As you read, using these verbs to formulate specific questions will help you learn. Recognizing these verbs on essay tests will help you answer effectively.

 KEY 5.6 **Use Bloom's taxonomy to formulate questions at different cognitive levels.**

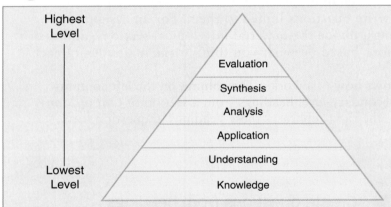

Verbs That Indicate Each Level

1. *Knowledge:* average, define, duplicate, label, list, memorize, name, order, recognize, relate, recall, repeat, reproduce, state.
2. *Understanding:* classify, describe, discuss, explain, express, identity, indicate, locate, recognize, report, restate, review, select, translate.
3. *Application:* apply, choose, demonstrate, dramatize, employ, illustrate, interpret, operate, practice, schedule, sketch, solve, use, write.
4. *Analysis:* analyze, appraise, calculate, categorize, compare, contrast, criticize, differentiate, discriminate, distinguish, examine, experiment, question, test.
5. *Synthesis:* arrange, assemble, collect, compose, construct, create, design, develop, formulate, manage, organize, plan, prepare, propose, set up, write.
6. *Evaluation:* appraise, argue, assess, attach, choose, compare, defend, estimate, judge, predict, rate, score, select, support, value, evaluate.

Read

Your text survey and questions give you a starting point for *reading*, the first R in SQ3R. Retaining what you read requires an active approach, as follows:

- *Focus on the key points of your survey.* Pay special attention to points raised in headings, in italics and boldface type, in chapter objectives, and in the summary.

- *Focus on your Q-stage questions.* Read the material with the purpose of answering each question. Write down or highlight ideas and examples that relate to your questions.

- *Mark up your text and take text notes.* Write notes in the margins or on separate paper, circle critical ideas, or highlight key points to focus on what's important. These cues will help you study for exams. Text-marking and note-taking techniques will be examined later in the chapter.

- *Create text tabs.* Place plastic index tabs or adhesive notes at the start of different chapters so you can flip back and forth with ease.

Find the Main Idea

Understanding what you read depends on your ability to recognize *main ideas* and link other ideas to them. Here are places you are likely to find these core ideas:

- In a topic sentence at the beginning of the paragraph, stating the topic of the paragraph and what about that topic the author wants to communicate, followed by support

- At the end of the paragraph, following supporting details that lead up to it

- Buried in the middle of the paragraph, sandwiched between supporting details

- In a compilation of ideas from various sentences, each of which contains a critical element, leaving it up to you to piece together these elements to find the main idea

When the main idea of a passage is unclear, use a three-step approach to decide what it is:[8]

1. *Search for the topic of the paragraph.* The topic of the paragraph is not the same as the main idea. Rather, it is the broad subject being discussed—for example, Apple CEO Steve Jobs, hate crimes on campus, or binge drinking on campus.

2. *Identify the aspect of the topic that is the paragraph's focus.* If the general topic is Steve Jobs, the author may focus on any of thousands of aspects of that topic, such as his cofounding of Apple Computer in 1976, his role in the Pixar computer animation company, or his role in the development of the iPod portable music player.

3. *Find what the author wants you to know about that specific aspect; this is the main idea.* The main idea of a paragraph dealing with Jobs's role in the development of the iPod may be this:

    > In his role as CEO of Apple, Steve Jobs oversaw the creation of the iPod portable music player, which changed the way the world listens to and purchases music.

Prioritize Your Reading Assignments

Ask yourself what is important and what you have to remember. According to Adam Robinson, cofounder of the *Princeton Review,* successful students can tell the difference between information worthy of study, information they should know in a general way, and information they should ignore. Says Robinson: "The only way you can effectively absorb the relevant information is to ignore the irrelevant information. . . . Trying to digest and understand all the information in a textbook is . . . an excellent way to become quickly and hopelessly confused."[9]

The following questions will help you determine if text material is important enough to study in depth:

- Is the material stressed in headings, charts, tables, captions, key terms, and definitions? In mid-chapter and end-of-chapter exercises? In the chapter introduction and summary? (Surveying before reading will help you answer these questions.)

- Is the material a definition, a crucial concept, an example, an explanation of a variety or type, a critical relationship or comparison?

- Does it spark questions and reactions as you read?

- Does it surprise or confuse you?

- Did your instructor stress the material in class? Does your assignment ask you to focus on something specific?

When trying to figure out what to study and what to skim, ask yourself whether your instructor would expect you to know the material. If you are unsure and if the topic is not on your syllabus, e-mail your instructor and ask for clarification.

Recite

Once you finish reading a topic, stop and answer the questions you raised in the Q stage of SQ3R. *Even if you have already done this during the reading phase, do it again now—with the purpose of learning and committing the material to memory.*

You may decide to *recite* each answer aloud, silently speak the answers to yourself, "teach" the answers to another person, or write your ideas and answers in note form. Whatever recitation method you choose, make sure you know how ideas connect to one another and to the general concept being discussed.

Writing is the most effective way to learn new material. Using your own words to explain new concepts gives you immediate feedback: When you can do it effectively, you know the material. When you can't, you still need to work with the text or a study partner. Whatever you do, don't get discouraged. Just go back and search for what you missed.

Writing comprehensive responses at this stage can save time later. As you respond to your Q-stage questions, you can compare what you write to the text and make adjustments. Your responses then become a study tool for review.

Keep your learning styles in mind when you explore different strategies (see chapter 3). For example, an intrapersonal learner may prefer writing, while an interpersonal learner may choose to recite answers aloud to a classmate. A logical-mathematical learner may benefit from organizing material into detailed outlines or charts, while a musical learner might want to chant information aloud to a rhythm.

When do you stop to recite? Waiting for the end of a chapter is too late; stopping at the end of a paragraph is too soon. The best plan is to recite at the end of each text section, right before a new text heading. Repeat the question-read-recite cycle until you complete the chapter.

If you find yourself fumbling for thoughts, you have not mastered the ideas. Reread the section that's giving you trouble until you know it cold.

Review

Reviewing, both immediately and periodically in the days and weeks after you read, will help you learn and memorize material. If you close the book after reading it once, chances are that you will forget almost everything—which is why students who read material for the first time right before a test often do poorly. *Reviewing is your key to learning.*

Reviewing the same material over time will also help you identify knowledge gaps. It's natural to forget material between study sessions, especially if it's confusing or complex. When you come back after a break, you can focus on your deficits.

Here are some reviewing techniques. Try them all, and use the ones that work best:

- Reread your notes. Then summarize them from memory.

- Review and summarize in writing the text sections you highlighted or bracketed. Try to condense the material so that you can focus on key ideas.

- Answer the end-of-chapter review, discussion, and application questions.

- Reread the preface, headings, tables, and summary.

- Recite important concepts to yourself, or record and play them back on a tape player.

- Listen to audio recordings of your text and other reading materials on your MP3 player.

- Make flash cards with a word or concept on one side and a definition, examples, or other related information on the other. Test yourself.

- Quiz yourself, using the questions you raised in the Q stage. If you can't answer a question, scan the text for the answer.

- Discuss the concepts with a classmate or in a study group. Use each other's Q-stage questions to help one another learn.

- Finally, ask your instructor for help with difficult material. Define exactly what you want to discuss and then schedule a meeting during office hours or e-mail your questions.

Reviewing material with a classmate nearby can give you the opportunity to discuss and clarify ideas together.

Use SQ3R to become an active reader and learn new concepts.

STAGE OF SQ3R	DESCRIPTION
Survey	Pre-reading a book before studying it—involves skimming and scanning as you examine the front matter, chapter elements, and back matter for clues about text content and organization.
Question	Developing questions linked to chapter headings and to what you already know about the topic. Questioning engages your critical thinking skills.
Read	Reading the material to answer the questions formulated in the Q stage and find main ideas. You can take notes as you read or highlight key ideas and information in your text.
Recite	Recitation involves answering—perhaps for a second time—your Q-stage questions. You may decide to recite the answers aloud or silently to yourself, teach them to a study partner, or record them in writing.
Review	Using various techniques to learn the material before an exam. Become actively involved with the material through summarizing notes, answering study questions, writing outlines or think links, reciting concepts, using flash cards, thinking critically, and so on.

All this effort takes time, but the potential payoff is huge if you're motivated to work hard. Although at times it may be tempting to photocopy a classmate's text notes instead of reading and taking your own notes, you will learn only if you do the work yourself.

Refreshing your knowledge is easier and faster than learning the first time. Make a review schedule—for example, every three days—and stick to it until you're sure of your knowledge. Use different reviewing techniques as you work toward mastery.

Key 5.7 summarizes how SQ3R turns you into an active reader.

How Can You Respond Critically to What You Read?

Think of the reading process as an archaeological dig. The first step is to excavate a site and uncover the artifacts. The second step is to investigate your findings, evaluate meaning, and derive knowledge from your discoveries. Critical reading is comparable to this crucial second step.

Critical reading, like critical thinking, taps your analytical intelligence (see chapter 4). Instead of simply *accepting* what you read, seek *understanding* by questioning material as you move from idea to idea. The best critical readers question every statement for accuracy, relevance, and logic.

Use Knowledge of Fact and Opinion to Evaluate Arguments

Critical readers evaluate arguments to determine whether they are accurate and logical. In this context, the word *argument* refers to a persuasive case—a set of connected ideas supported by examples—that a writer makes to prove or disprove a point.

It's easy—and common—to accept or reject an argument outright, according to whether it fits with your point of view. If you ask questions, however, you can determine the argument's validity and understand it in greater depth. Evaluating an argument involves looking at these factors:

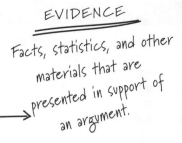

EVIDENCE

Facts, statistics, and other materials that are presented in support of an argument.

- The quality of the (evidence)
- Whether the evidence fits the concept
- The logical connections

When quality evidence combines with tight logic, the argument is solid.

What is the quality of the evidence? Ask the following questions to evaluate the evidence:

- What is the source?
- Is the source reliable and free of bias?
- Who wrote this and with what intent?
- What assumptions underlie this material?
- Is the argument based on opinion?
- How does the evidence compare with evidence from other sources?

How well does the evidence support the idea? Ask these questions to determine whether the evidence fits the concept:

- Is there enough evidence to support the central idea?
- Do examples and ideas logically connect to one another?
- Is the evidence convincing? Do the examples build a strong case?
- What different and perhaps opposing arguments seem just as valid?

Approach every argument with healthy skepticism. Have an open mind in order to assess whether you are convinced or have serious questions.

In addition to the foregoing critical reading strategies, transforming your textbook into a valuable work tool through highlighting and notes will help you make the most of study time as you set the stage for review.

How Do You Customize Your Text with Highlighting and Notes?

Textbooks are designed and written with students in mind, but they are not customized to meet your unique reading and studying needs. It is up to you

to do that for yourself through text highlighting and notes. Your goal is to transform your texts into very personal study tools.

How to Highlight a Text

Highlighting involves the use of special markers or regular pens or pencils to flag important passages. When used correctly, highlighting is an essential study technique. The following techniques will help you make highlighting a learning tool:

- *Develop a highlighting system and stick to it.* For example, use your creative intelligence to decide if you will use different colored markers for different elements, brackets for long passages, or pencil underlining. Make a key that identifies each notation.

- *Consider using a regular pencil or pen instead of a highlighter pen.* The copy will be cleaner and look less like a coloring book than a textbook.

- *Read an entire paragraph before you begin to highlight, and don't start until you have a sense of what is important.* Only then put pencil or highlighter to paper as you pick out key terms, phrases, and ideas.

- *Avoid overmarking.* A phrase or two in any paragraph is usually enough. Enclose long passages with brackets rather than marking every line. Avoid underlining entire sentences, when possible. The less color the better.

- *Highlight supporting evidence.* Mark examples that explain important ideas.

Although these techniques will help you highlight effectively, they won't help you learn the material and, ironically, they may actually obstruct learning as you diligently add color to the page. Experts agree that you will not learn what you highlight unless you *interact* with the material through surveying, questioning, reciting, and review. Without this interaction, all you are doing is marking your book.

How to Take Text Notes

When you combine highlighting with marginal notes or text flags, you remind yourself what a particular passage is about and why you consider it important. This combination customizes your text, which helps you study for exams. Going a step further by taking a full set of text notes is an excellent way to commit material to memory.

As you will also see in chapter 6, note taking on texts and in class is critical because material is cumulative—that is, what you learn today builds on what you learned yesterday and the day before since the beginning of the term.

Taking Marginal Notes

Here are some tips for taking marginal notes right on the pages of your text:

- Use pencil so you can erase comments or questions that are answered as you read.

- Write your Q questions from SQ3R in the margins right next to text headings.

- Mark critical sections with marginal notations such as "def." for definition, "e.g." for helpful example, or "concept" for an important concept.

- Write notes at the bottom of the page connecting the text to what you learned in class or in research. You can also attach adhesive notes with your comments.

Key 5.8 shows how to underline effectively and take marginal notes in an introduction to business textbook that introduces the concept of target marketing and market segmentation.

Your customized text will be uniquely yours; no one else will highlight or take text notes as you do because no one else has your knowledge, learning style, or study techniques. Because text customization is so important to learning, you may find it hard to use previously owned texts that are heavily highlighted or filled with marginal notations. Even if the prior owner was a good student, he or she is not you—and that fact alone will affect your ability to master content.

Creating Full-Text Summaries

Taking a full set of notes on assigned readings helps you learn as you summarize main ideas in your own words. Taking notes makes you an active participant as you think about how material fits into what you already know and how to capture key points.

To construct a summary, focus on the main ideas and examples that support them. Don't include your own ideas or evaluations at this point. Your summary should simply condense the material, making it easier to focus on concepts and interrelationships when you review.

Here are suggestions for creating effective full-text summaries:

- Try to use your own words, because repeating the author's words may mean parroting concepts you do not understand. When studying a technical subject with precise definitions, you may have little choice but to use text wording.

- Try to make your notes simple, clear, and brief. Include what you need to understand about the topic, while eliminating less important details.

- Consider outlining the text so you can see how ideas relate to one another.

- Before you write, identify the main idea of a passage.

- Once that idea ends and another begins, begin taking notes from memory, using your own words. Go back into the text, as needed, to cull information that you didn't get on first reading.

- Take notes on tables, charts, photographs, and captions; these visual presentations may contain information presented nowhere else in the text.

- Use shorthand symbols to write quickly (see chapter 6).

- Create notes in visual form:
  - Construct your own charts, tables, and diagrams to depict written concepts.

Underlining and taking marginal notes help you master content.

How does target marketing and market segmentation help companies sell product?

TARGET MARKETING AND MARKET SEGMENTATION

Marketers have long known that products cannot be all things to all people. Buyers have different tastes, goals, lifestyles, and so on. The emergence of the marketing concept and the recognition of consumer needs and wants led marketers to think in terms of **target markets**—groups of people with similar wants and needs. Selecting target markets is usually the first step in the marketing strategy.

~~Target marketing requires~~ **market segmentation** ~~div~~iding a market into categories of customer types or "segments." Once they have identified segments, companies may adopt a variety of strategies. Some ~~firms market products to more than one~~ ~~segment. General Motors~~ (*www.gm.com*), for ~~example, offers compact cars,~~ vans, ~~trucks, luxury cars, and sports~~ cars with various features and at various price levels. GM's strategy is to provide an automobile for nearly every segment of the market.

In contrast, some businesses offer a narrower range of products, each aimed toward a specific s~~egment. Note that segmentation is a strategy for analy~~zing consumers, not products. The process of fixing, adapting, and communicating the nature of the product itself is called *product positioning.*

Definitions ↙

target market
Gro~~up~~ of ~~people~~ that has similar ~~wa~~ ~~Chap~~ ds and that can be ~~ow~~ interest in the sa~~me~~

← GM eg

market segmentation
Pr~~oc~~ess of dividing a market into c~~ustomer~~ ~~Market~~stomer types have

GM makes cars for diff. market segments

How do companies identify market segments?

Identifying Market Segments

By definition, members of a market segment must share some common traits that affect their purch~~asing decisions. In identifying~~ segments, researchers look at several different influ~~ences on consumer~~ behavior. Three of the most important are *geographic, demographic,* and *psychographic variables.*

Geographic Variables *What effect does geography have on segmentation strategies?* Many buying decisions are affected by the places people call home. The heavy rainfall in Washington State, for instance, means that people there buy more umbrellas than people in the Sun Belt. Urban residents don't need agricultural equipment, and sailboats sell better along the coasts than on the Great Plains. **Geographic variables** are the geographical units, from countries to neighborhoods, that may be considered in a segmentation strategy.

These patterns affect decisions about marketing mixes for a huge range of products. For ~~example, consider a plan to market down-filled parkas in rural Minnesota.~~ Dem~~and~~ will be high and price competition intense. Local newspaper ads may be

Buying decisions influenced by where people live

geographic variables
Geo~~graphical~~ units that may be c~~onsidered~~ ~~by developing a~~ ~~affect~~ strategy diffe

— good eg — selling parkas in Minnesota

Thought
Geographical variables change with the seasons

Source: Business Essentials, 5th ed., by Ebert/Griffin, © 2005. Reprinted by permission of Pearson/Prentice Hall, Upper Saddle River, NJ.

- ○ Devise a color-coding system to indicate level of importance of different ideas, and then mark up your notes with these colors.
- ○ Devise symbols and numbers and use them consistently to indicate the level of importance of different ideas. Write these in different-colored pens.

Mark Up a Page to Learn a Page

Below, the text material in Key 5.8 continues. Put your own pencil to paper as you highlight concepts and take marginal notes. Compare your efforts to those of your classmates to see how each of you approached the task and what you can learn from their methods.

---

effective, and the best retail location may be one that is easily reached from several small towns.

Although the marketability of some products is geographically sensitive, others enjoy nearly universal acceptance. Coke, for example, gets more than 70 percent of its sales from international markets. It is the market leader in Great Britain, China, Germany, Japan, Brazil, and Spain. Pepsi's international sales are about 15 percent of Coke's. In fact, Coke's chief competitor in most countries is some local soft drink, not Pepsi, which earns 78 percent of its income at home.

demographic variables
Characteristics of populations that may be considered in dev̶e̶l̶ **298** segmentation strategy

Demographic Variables Demographic variables describe populations by identifying such traits as age, income, gender, ethnic background, marital status, race, religion, and social class. For example, several general consumption characteristics can be attributed to certain age groups (18–25, 26–35, 36–45, and so on). A marketer can, thus, divide markets into age groups. Table 10.1 lists some possible demographic breakdowns. Depending on the marketer's purpose, a segment can be a single classification (*aged 20–34*) or a combination of categories (*aged 20–34, married with children, earning* $25,000–$34,999). Foreign competitors, for example, are gaining market share in U.S. auto sales by appealing to young buyers (under age 30) with limited incomes (under $30,000). Whereas companies such as Hyundai (*www.hyundai.net*), Kia (*www.kia.com*), and Daewoo (*www.daewoous.com*) are winning entry-level customers with high quality and generous warranties, Volkswagen (*www.vw.com*) targets under-35 buyers with its entertainment-styled VW Jetta.[4]

psychographic variables
Consumer characteristics, such as lifestyles, opinions, intere̶s̶t̶s̶ a̶n̶d̶ attitudes, that may be con̶s̶i̶d̶e̶r̶e̶d̶ i̶n̶ developing a segmentation̶ s̶t̶r̶a̶t̶e̶g̶y̶

Psychographic Variables Markets can also be segmented according to such **psychographic variables** as lifestyles, interests, and attitudes. Take, for example, Burberry (*www.burberry.com*), whose raincoats have been a symbol of British tradition since 1856. Burberry has repositioned itself as a global luxury brand, like Gucci (*www.gucci.com*) and Louis Vuitton (*www.vuitton.com*). The strategy, which recently resulted in a 31-percent sales increase, calls for attracting a different type of customer—the top-of-the-line, fashion-conscious individual—who shops at such stores as Neiman Marcus and Bergdorf Goodman.[5]

Psychographics are particularly important to marketers because, unlike demographics and geographics, they can be changed by marketing efforts. For example, Polish companies have overcome consumer resistance by promoting the safety and desirability of using credit rather than depending solely on cash. One product of changing attitudes is a booming economy and the emergence of a robust middle class.

TABLE 10.1
Demographic Variables

Age	Under 5, 5–11, 12–19, 20–34, 35–49, 50–64, 65+
Education	Grade school or less, some high school, graduated high school, some college, college degree, advanced degree
Family life cycle	Young single, young married without children, young married with children, older married with children under 18, older married without children under 18, older single, other
Family size	1, 2–3, 4–5, 6+
Income	Under $9,000, $9,000–$14,999, $15,000–$24,999, $25,000–$34,999, $35,000–$45,000, over $45,000
Nationality	African, American, Asian, British, Eastern European, French, German, Irish, Italian, Latin American, Middle Eastern, Scandinavian
Race	Native American, Asian, Black, White
Religion	Buddhist, Catholic, Hindu, Jewish, Muslim, Protestant
Sex	Male, female

MULTIPLE INTELLIGENCE STRATEGIES

FOR READING

APPLY DIFFERENT INTELLIGENCES TO CONCEPTS IN SOCIOLOGY.

INTELLIGENCE	USE MI STRATEGIES *to become a better reader*	APPLY MI READING STRATEGIES *to learn about social groups for your introduction to sociology course*
Verbal-Linguistic	• Use the steps in SQ3R, focusing especially on writing Q-stage questions, summaries, and so on. • Make marginal text notes as you read.	• Summarize in writing the technical differences among social groups, categories, and crowds.*
Logical-Mathematical	• Logically connect what you are reading with what you already know. Consider similarities, differences, and cause-and-effect relationships. • Draw charts showing relationships and analyze trends.	• Create a table comparing and contrasting the characteristics of primary and secondary social groups.
Bodily-Kinesthetic	• Use text highlighting to take a hands-on approach to reading. • Take a hands-on approach to learning experiments by trying to re-create them yourself.	• Create an experiment that might turn a crowd of strangers into a social group joined together by a common problem.
Visual-Spatial	• Make charts, diagrams, or think links illustrating difficult ideas you encounter as you read. • Take note of photos, tables, and other visual aids in the text.	• Create a visual aid showing four primary mechanisms through which people with shared experiences, loyalties, and interests meet—for example, through school and business—and how initial contacts may lead to deep social group relationships.
Interpersonal	• Discuss reading material and clarify concepts in a study group. • Talk to people who know about the topic you are studying.	• Interview people who shared a difficult experience with a crowd of strangers—for example, people stuck in an elevator or train for an extended period—about how relationships changed as focus turned to a common problem.
Intrapersonal	• Apply concepts to your own life; think about how you would manage. • Try to understand your personal strengths and weaknesses to lead a study group on the reading material.	• After reading about the nature of primary groups, think about the nature of your personal family relationships and the degree to which family members are your key support system.
Musical	• Recite text concepts to rhythms or write a song to depict them. • Explore relevant musical links to the material.	• Listen to a rock concert that was performed in front of a live crowd. Then listen to the same music recorded in a studio. Think about performance differences that might link to the presence or absence of a crowd.
Naturalistic	• Tap into your ability to notice similarities and differences in objects and concepts by organizing reading materials into relevant groupings.	• Over the next few weeks, ask some close friends if you can have dinner with them and their families. After the visits, try to identify characteristics that all the families share. Create a chart to report your findings.

*For information on social groups, see John J. Macionis, *Sociology,* 11th ed., Upper Saddle River, NJ: Prentice Hall, 2007.

Successful Intelligence Wrap-Up

Reading and studying are the tools you will use over and over again to acquire information in your personal and community life and career. After college, you will be figuring out almost everything on your own—your 401(k) retirement plan, a new office-wide computer system, or even the fine print in a cell phone contract. Your reading success may depend on your ability to use successful intelligence. Here's how you have built skills in chapter 5:

Analytical

You explored an analytical approach to reading comprehension, taking a close look at reading environment, reading purpose, and vocabulary. In the *Get Analytical* exercise, you used surveying skills to analyze the front matter and one chapter of a textbook. Within the section on critical reading, you examined how to consider fact and opinion, how arguments are supported, and perspectives in your approach to reading materials.

Creative

In the *Get Creative* exercise, you generated ideas from reading a book and then seeing a movie made from the same story. Reading about concentration may have inspired ideas about how to create a reading environment that suits you best. When exploring the SQ3R reading method, you may have adopted different ideas about how to implement it into a blend that is uniquely your own.

Practical

You discovered practical actions that can build your knowledge of roots, prefixes, and suffixes. You explored how emotional involvement can deepen your reading experience. You saw examples of how to put the practical steps of the SQ3R reading system into action. In the *Get Practical* exercise, you applied your knowledge of how to highlight and mark up text to a specific textbook page, solidifying your understanding of what strategies work best for you.

yokomeshi
(*yo-ko-meh-shi*)

Reading your college textbooks may feel at times like what this Japanese word literally means: "eating a meal sideways" (*meshi* means "boiled rice" and *yoko* means "horizontal"). The Japanese use this word to describe how difficult it is to learn a foreign language, since Japanese characters are vertical while most other world languages are horizontal. When the Japanese use this word to describe a difficult intellectual task, they force themselves to laugh at the image, which decompresses the stress.

If you feel overwhelmed by the new concepts and specialized vocabulary in your readings, just think of the challenge of eating a meal sideways. Then take heart in the certainty that you are not alone in trying to figure out what things mean. You will succeed by taking as many deep breaths as you need, by keeping your sense of humor, and by committing yourself to using the strategies suggested in this chapter to meet new reading challenges.[10]

"Somewhere, something incredible is waiting to be known."

CARL SAGAN, ASTRONOMER

Building World-Class Skills
for College, Career, and Life Success

SUCCESSFUL INTELLIGENCE
Think, Create, Apply

Studying a text page. The following page is from the chapter "Groups and Organizations" in the sixth edition of John J. Macionis's *Sociology*.[11] Apply SQ3R as you read the excerpt. Using what you learned in this chapter about study techniques, complete the questions that follow (some questions ask you to mark the page itself).

Step 1. Think it through: *Gather information and analyze it.* Skim the excerpt. Identify the headings on the page and the relationships among them. Mark primary-level headings with a #1, secondary headings with a #2, and tertiary (third-level) headings with a #3. Then analyze:

Which heading serves as an umbrella for the rest?

_____

What do the headings tell you about the content of the page?

_____

What are three concepts that seem important to remember?

    1. _____

    2. _____

    3. _____

Step 2. Think out of the box: *Create useful study questions.* Based on the three concepts you pulled out, write three study questions that you can review with an instructor, a teaching assistant, or a fellow student:

    1. _____

    2. _____

    3. _____

Step 3. Make it happen: *Read and remember.* Read the excerpt, putting SQ3R to work. Using a marker, highlight key phrases and sentences. Write

SOCIAL GROUPS

Virtually everyone moves through life with a sense of belonging; this is the experience of group life. A **social group** refers to *two or more people who identify and interact with one another.* Human beings continually come together to form couples, families, circles of friends, neighborhoods, churches, businesses, clubs, and numerous large organizations. Whatever the form, groups encompass people with shared experiences, loyalties, and interests. In short, while maintaining their individuality, the members of social groups also think of themselves as a special "we."

Groups, Categories, and Crowds

People often use the term "group" imprecisely. We now distinguish the group from the similar concepts of category and crowd.

Category. A *category* refers to people who have some status in common. Women, single fathers, military recruits, homeowners, and Roman Catholics are all examples of categories.

Why are categories not considered groups? Simply because, while the individuals involved are aware that they are not the only ones to hold that particular status, the vast majority are strangers to one another.

Crowd. A *crowd* refers to a temporary cluster of individuals who may or may not interact at all. Students sitting in a lecture hall do engage one another and share some common identity as college classmates; thus, such a crowd might be called a loosely formed group. By contrast, riders hurtling along on a subway train or

bathers enjoying a summer day at the beach pay little attention to one another and amount to an anonymous aggregate of people. In general, then, crowds are too transitory and impersonal to qualify as social groups.

The right circumstances, however, could turn a crowd into a group. People riding in a subway train that crashes under the city streets generally become keenly aware of their common plight and begin to help one another. Sometimes such extraordinary experiences become the basis for lasting relationships.

Primary and Secondary Groups

Acquaintances commonly greet one another with a smile and the simple phrase, "Hi! How are you?" The response is usually a well scripted, "Just fine, thanks, how about you?" This answer, of course, is often more formal than truthful. In most cases, providing a detailed account of how you are *really* doing would prompt the other person to beat a hasty and awkward exit.

Sociologists classify social groups by measuring them against two ideal types based on members' genuine level of personal concern. This variation is the key to distinguishing *primary* from *secondary* groups.

According to Charles Horton Cooley (1864–1929), a **primary group** is a *small social group whose members share personal and enduring relationships.* Bound together by primary relationships, individuals in primary groups typically spend a great deal of time together, engage in a wide range of common activities, and feel that they know one another well. Although not without periodic conflict, members of primary groups display sincere concern for each other's welfare. The family is every society's most important primary group.

Cooley characterized these personal and tightly integrated groups as *primary* because they are among the first groups we experience in life. In addition, the family and early play groups also hold primary importance in the socialization process, shaping attitudes, behavior, and social identity.

Source: Sociology, 6th ed., by John J. Macionis, © 1997. Reprinted by permission of Pearson Education, Inc., Upper Saddle River, NJ.

short marginal notes to help you review the material later. After reading this page thoroughly, write a short summary paragraph:

_____

_____

_____

Step 4. Tap your multiple intelligences: *Use MI strategies to improve your reading.* The Multiple Intelligence Strategies table in this chapter (see page 172) encourages you to use different reading strategies to study the topic of social groups. Identify the strategies that work best for you and incorporate them into your studying routine.

TEAMWORK
Create Solutions Together

Organizing a study group. Organize a study group with three or four members of your class. At the group's first meeting do the following:

- **Set a specific goal**—to prepare for an upcoming test, for example—and create a weekly schedule. Write everything down and give everyone a copy.

- **Talk about the specific ways you will work together.** Discuss which of the following methods you want to try in the group: pooling your notes; teaching each other difficult concepts; making up, administering, and grading quizzes for each other; creating study flash cards; using SQ3R to review required readings. Set specific guidelines for how group members will be held accountable.

As an initial group exercise, try the following:

- **Review the study questions that you wrote for the *Sociology* excerpt in the previous exercise.** Each person should select one question to focus on while reading (no two people should have the same question). Group members should then reread the excerpt individually, thinking about their questions as they read and answering them in writing.

- **When you finish reading critically, gather as a group.** Each person should take a turn presenting the question, the response or answer that was derived through critical reading, and other thoughts. Other members may then add to the discussion. Continue until everyone presents a concept.

Over several weeks, evaluate the different methods as a group, singling out those that were most helpful. Then incorporate them into your ongoing study sessions.

WRITING
Journal and Put Skills to Work

Record your thoughts on a separate piece of paper, in a journal, or on a computer file.

Journal entry: Reading challenges. Which of the courses you are currently taking presents your most difficult reading challenge? What makes the reading tough—the type of material, the length of the assignments, the level of difficulty? Describe techniques you learned in this chapter that you will use to meet your reading challenge. Describe why you think they will help.

Real-life writing: Asking for help. Self-help plans often involve reaching out to others. Draft an e-mail to your instructor that describes the difficulties you are facing in the course you wrote about in the journal entry and that details the specific help you need in order to move to the next step.

To accomplish your goal while also coming across as a respectful, diligent student, make sure that your message is clear and accurate; that your grammar, spelling, and punctuation are correct; and that your tone is appropriate. (See Quick Start to College at the front of the book for guidelines for communicating with instructors.) Whether or not you send the e-mail is up to you. In either case, writing it will help you move forward in your reading improvement plan.

PERSONAL PORTFOLIO
Prepare for Career Success

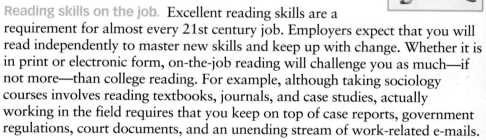

Complete the following in your electronic portfolio or on separate paper.

Reading skills on the job. Excellent reading skills are a requirement for almost every 21st century job. Employers expect that you will read independently to master new skills and keep up with change. Whether it is in print or electronic form, on-the-job reading will challenge you as much—if not more—than college reading. For example, although taking sociology courses involves reading textbooks, journals, and case studies, actually working in the field requires that you keep on top of case reports, government regulations, court documents, and an unending stream of work-related e-mails.

Prepare yourself for what's ahead by honestly assessing your practical skills *right now*. Use the following list to rate your ability on a scale of 1 to 10, with 10 being the highest:

- Ability to concentrate, no matter the distractions
- Ability to use emotional triggers to learn and remember material
- Ability to define your reading purpose and use it to guide your focus and pace
- Ability to use specific vocabulary-building techniques to improve comprehension
- Ability to use every aspect of SQ3R to master content
- Ability to skim and scan
- Ability to use analytical thinking skills when reading
- Ability to use highlighting and notes to help you master content

For the two skill areas in which you rated yourself lowest, think about how you can improve. Make a problem-solving plan for each (you may want to use a flowchart like the one on page 139). Check your progress in one month and at the end of the term. Finally, write down the ways in which you anticipate using the reading skills you learned in this chapter in your chosen career.

Suggested Readings

Armstrong, William H., and M. Willard Lampe II. *Barron's Pocket Guide to Study Tips: How to Study Effectively and Get Better Grades*. New York: Barron's, 2004.

Chesla, Elizabeth. *Reading Comprehension Success: In 20 Minutes a Day*, 2nd ed. Florence, KY: Thomson Delmar Learning, 2002.

Cutler, Wade E. *Triple Your Reading Speed*, 4th ed. New York: Pocket Books, 2003.

Labunski, Richard E. *The Educated Student: Getting the Most Out of Your College Years*. Versailles, KY: Marley and Beck, 2003.

Luckie, William R., Wood Smethurst, and Sarah Beth Huntley. *Study Power Workbook: Exercises in Study Skills to Improve Your Learning and Your Grades*. Cambridge, MA: Brookline Books, 1999.

Olsen, Amy E. *Active Vocabulary: General and Academic Words*, 3rd ed. New York: Longman, 2006.

Silver, Theodore. *The Princeton Review Study Smart: Hands-On, Nuts and Bolts Techniques for Earning Higher Grades*. New York: Villard Books, 1996.

Internet and Podcast Resources

Academictips.org (study tips and links): **www.academictips.org**

College Tutor Study Guide: **www.amelox.com/study.htm**

HowToStudy.com (study advice with valuable links): **www.howtostudy.com**

Improve Your Study Skills (tips from SoYouWanna.com): **www.soyouwanna.com/site/syws/studyskills/studyskills.html**

Lesson Tutor—Good Study Habits: **www.lessontutor.com/studygeneralhome.html**

Merriam-Webster's Word of the Day (free word of the day in audio form available on the Internet or as podcasts): **www.merriam-webster.com/cgi-bin/mwwod.pl**

Princeton Review Vocab Minute (free vocabulary-building podcasts using songs to help you remember): **RobinR@Review.com**

Study Guides and Strategies: **www.studygs.net**

Taking College Courses: **www.math.usf.edu/~mccolm/Aclasses.html**

Prentice Hall Student Success SuperSite: **www.prenhall.com/success**

Endnotes

[1] Richard J. Light, *Making the Most of College: Students Speak Their Minds,* Cambridge, MA: Harvard University Press, 2001, pp. 23–24. Copyright © 2001 by Richard J. Light. Reprinted by permission of the publisher.

[2] Eric Jensen, *Student Success Secrets*, 5th ed., New York: Barron's, 2003, p. 88.

[3] Roxanne Ruzic, "Lessons for Everyone: How Students with Reading-Related Learning Disabilities Survive and Excel in College Courses with Heavy Reading Requirements," paper presented at the Annual Meeting of the American Educational Research Association, Seattle, April 13, 2001 (http://iod.unh.edu/EE/articles/lessons_for_everyone.html).

[4] Francis P. Robinson, *Effective Behavior,* New York: Harper & Row, 1941.

[5] John Mack Faragher, Mari Jo Buhle, Daniel Czitrom, and Susan H. Armitage, *Out of Many: A History of the American People*, 3rd ed., Upper Saddle River, NJ: Prentice Hall, p. xxxvii.

[6] Charles G. Morris and Albert A. Maisto, *Psychology: An Introduction,* 12th ed., Upper Saddle River, NJ: Pearson/Prentice Hall, 2005, p. 186.

[7] Benjamin S. Bloom, *Taxonomy of Educational Objectives, Handbook I: The Cognitive Domain,* New York: McKay, 1956.

[8] Ophelia H. Hancock, *Reading Skills for College Students,* 5th ed., Upper Saddle River, NJ: Prentice Hall, 2001, pp. 54–59.

[9] Adam Robinson, *What Smart Students Know,* New York: Three Rivers Press, 1993, p. 82.

[10] Christopher J. Moore, *In Other Words: A Language Lover's Guide to the Most Intriguing Words Around the World,* New York: Walker, 2004, p. 87.

[11] John J. Macionis, *Sociology,* 6th ed., Upper Saddle River, NJ: Prentice Hall, 1997, p. 174.

LISTENING, NOTE TAKING, AND MEMORY

Taking In, Recording, and Remembering Information

6

"Successfully intelligent people find their path and then pursue it, realizing that there will be obstacles along the way and that surmounting these obstacles is part of their challenge."

ROBERT J. STERNBERG

College exposes you daily to all kinds of information—and your job as a student is to take it in, write it down, and keep what is important. This chapter shows you how to accomplish this by building your skills in the area of listening (taking in information), note-taking (recording what's important), and memory (remembering information). Each process engages your analytical, creative, and practical abilities and helps you build knowledge you can use.

In this chapter you explore answers to the following questions:

Analytical	Creative	Practical
• Understanding the listening process and the challenge of good listening • Evaluating the importance of class notes and different note-taking systems • Analyzing the nature of memory and why memory strategies work	• Constructing active listening strategies that help you learn • Personalizing note-taking systems and strategies • Thinking of and using mnemonic devices to boost recall	• How to overcome distractions to listen actively • How to use note-taking systems and shorthand and craft a master note set • How to use mnemonics to learn

How Can You Become a Better Listener?

LISTENING

A process that involves sensing, interpreting, evaluating, and reacting to spoken messages.

The act of hearing is not the same as the act of listening. *Hearing* refers to sensing spoken messages from their source. Listening involves a complex process of communication. Successful listening occurs when the listener understands the speaker's intended message. In school and at work, poor listening may cause communication breakdowns, while skilled listening promotes success. The good news is that listening is a teachable—and learnable—skill that engages analytical and practical abilities.

Know the Stages of Listening

Listening is made up of four stages that build on one another: sensing, interpreting, evaluating, and reacting. These stages take the message from the speaker to the listener and back to the speaker (see Key 6.1), as follows:

- During the *sensation* stage (also known as *hearing*) your ears pick up sound waves and transmit them to the brain. For example, you are sitting in class and hear your instructor say, "The only opportunity to make up last week's test is Tuesday at 5 p.m."

- In the *interpretation* stage, you attach meaning to a message: You understand what is said and link it to what you already know. You relate this message to your knowledge of the test, whether you need to make it up, and what you are doing on Tuesday at 5:00.

REAL QUESTIONS

How can I improve my memory?

When I took a memory test in a psychology class, I discovered that my classmates and I are better at remembering a full definition to a word rather than reading the definition and remembering the word. We would have thought that it would be easier to recall a word than an entire definition, but that was not the case.

Sometimes I find memorization work difficult, even though I know I have the ability. For instance, I know I have the material written down in my notes, down to the exact page, but then on the test, I sometimes can't remember the answers.

I try to incorporate mnemonic devices as I study, but that doesn't always work. I know that rereading and repetition reinforce learning, but it's hard to devote enough time to retaining information for five classes. I've just been accepted to law school, and I'm concerned because law requires learning technical terms. Can you suggest ways for me to improve my memory?

Shyama Parikh
DePaul University
Chicago, Illinois

PRACTICAL ANSWERS

Stephen Beck
or, Learn-to-Learn Company
Winston-Salem,
North Carolina

Understanding material will help you memorize and retain information.

Understanding what you study and grasping the way material is organized are crucial memory tools. The definitions exercise you took in your psychology class illustrates that you are more likely to remember a sentence of 30 words than a list of 15 random words because the sentence has meaning for you. Similarly, if a system of categorizing biology terms makes sense, you are more likely to understand and remember the terms. Mentally placing information in logical categories enhances recall, as do mnemonic devices.

Take the time to scope out the organization of a text or chapter before you start reading. Read the table of contents, preface, and chapter section and subsection titles. Look at chapter objectives and summaries. This overview will help you form meaningful connections and will set the stage for learning the details.

As you study, be an active participant by continually asking yourself whether information makes sense. If it doesn't, try to figure out why you're stuck—what strand of understanding is missing. To reinforce reading comprehension, pause at good stopping points and take notes from memory. Your notes are proof that you can recall and understand the material. How do you know if you have memorized a list? Write it down to find out exactly what you do and do not know.

This active pause-reflect-and-write technique is critical for learning new material.

• In the *evaluation* stage, you evaluate the message as it relates to your needs and values. If the message goes against your values or does not fulfill your needs, you may reject it, stop listening, or argue in your mind with the speaker. In this example, if you need to make up the test but have to work Tuesday at 5:00, you may evaluate the message in an unfavorable way.

The listening process moves messages along a listening loop.

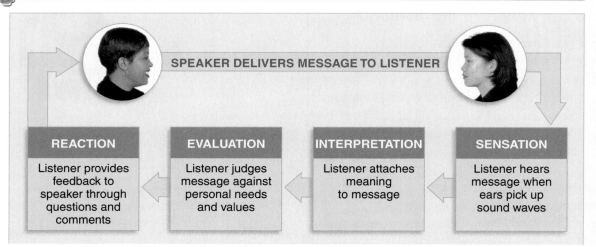

SPEAKER DELIVERS MESSAGE TO LISTENER

REACTION	EVALUATION	INTERPRETATION	SENSATION
Listener provides feedback to speaker through questions and comments	Listener judges message against personal needs and values	Listener attaches meaning to message	Listener hears message when ears pick up sound waves

- The final stage of listening is a *reaction* to the message in the form of direct feedback. In a classroom, direct feedback often comes in the form of questions and comments. Your reaction, in this case, may be to ask the instructor if she can schedule another test time.

You will become a better listener by learning to recognize and manage listening challenges and becoming actively involved with the material.

Manage Listening Challenges

Classic studies have shown that immediately after listening, students are likely to recall only half of what was said. This low retention rate is due, in part, to the following listening challenges.[1]

Divided Attention and Distractions

Internal and external distractions often divide your attention. *Internal distractions* include anything from hunger to headache to personal worries. Something the speaker says may also trigger a recollection that may cause your mind to drift. In contrast, *external distractions* include factors outside yourself, such as noise and excessive heat or cold. They also involve sending and receiving text messages on your cell phone, instant-messaging friends, or surfing the Internet on your laptop.

Use practical strategies that tap your emotional and social intelligence to reduce distractions as they arise: Try your best to put your worries aside during class; sit near the front of the room; move away from chatting classmates; ban technology for social uses during class; get enough sleep to stay alert; and eat enough to avoid hunger.

Listening Lapses

Your instructors are responsible for communicating information, but they cannot make you listen. That responsibility is in your hands. If you decide that a subject is too difficult or uninteresting, you may tune out and miss the foundation for what comes next. You may also fall into the trap of focusing on specific points and shutting out the rest of the message. If you experience a listening lapse, try to refocus quickly instead of worrying about what you missed. After class, look at a classmate's notes to fill in the gaps.

Preventing listening lapses starts with having the right attitude. Remind yourself that what your instructors say is valuable and that they often present material in class that is not in the text. If you work to take in the whole message, you will be able to read over your notes later, combine your class and text notes, and think critically about what is important.

The Rush to Judgment

It is common for people to stop listening when they hear something they don't like. Their focus turns to their personal reactions and away from the message. Students who disagree during a lecture often spend valuable class time thinking about their reaction.

Judgments also involve reactions to the speakers themselves. If you do not like your instructors or have preconceived notions about their ideas or background, you may dismiss their message. Anyone whose words have ever been ignored because of race, ethnicity, gender, physical characteristics, or disability understands how prejudice interferes with listening. Although it is human nature to stop listening at times in reaction to a speaker or message, this tendency can get in the way of your education. Use your analytical intelligence to overcome the tendency to rush to judgment. It will make you more socially and emotionally competent.

Partial Hearing Loss and Learning Disabilities

If you have a hearing loss, seek out special services, including tutoring and equipment, that can help you listen in class. For example, listening to a taped lecture at a higher-than-normal volume can help you hear things you missed. Ask your instructors if digitalized recordings are available, which you can download onto your computer or MP3 player. Meeting with your instructor outside of class to clarify your notes may also help, as will sitting near the front of the room.

Other disabilities, such as attention deficit disorder (ADD) or a problem with processing spoken language, can add to listening difficulties. People with these problems may have trouble paying attention or understanding what they hear. If you have a disability that creates a listening challenge, seek help through the services available at your college.

Active listening means being in class and connecting with the material by taking notes and asking questions. These students benefit from a visual aid as they take notes in an anatomy class.

Become an Active Listener

On the surface, listening seems like a passive activity: You sit back as someone else speaks. In reality, effective listening is an active process that involves the following factors:

Be There

Being an active listener requires that you show up on time—preferably a few minutes before class begins. Instructors often make important announcements in the first few minutes and may also summarize the last lecture.

Set Purposes for Listening

Before every class, use your analytical intelligence to establish what you want to achieve, such as understanding difficult concepts or mastering a task. Many instructors start a lecture with a statement of purpose, so listen carefully to their introductory words. Then write them at the top of your notes to help you focus.

Accomplishing your purpose requires that you read assignments before class and review your notes from the previous class. This preparation will set the stage for you to follow the lecture and will help you tell the difference between important and unimportant material. Without it, you may find yourself scrambling to take down every word.

Making your purpose for listening *personal* will motivate you to listen closely. As you prepare for class, ask yourself how the material relates to your academic goals. With the mind-set that what you hear will help *you,* you will be more able to make listening a top priority in class.

Focus on Understanding

Rather than taking notes on everything, record information only when you can say to yourself, "I get it!" If you miss important material, leave holes in your notes and return later. Your instructor may repeat the point you missed, or another comment may help you piece it together.

Ask Questions

Active listeners ask analytical questions to clarify their understanding and to associate new ideas with what they already know. Questions like "What is this part of?" or "How is it similar to yesterday's topic?" signal active involvement. Get into the habit of jotting down your questions and coming back to them during a discussion period so they don't interfere with listening.

VERBAL SIGNPOSTS Spoken words or phrases that call attention to information that follows.

Pay Attention to Verbal Signposts

Instructors' choice of words may tell you what they consider important and help you predict test questions. For example, an idea described as "new and exciting" or "classic" is more likely to be on a test than one described as "interesting." Verbal signposts—words or phrases that call attention to what comes next—help organize information, connect ideas, and indicate what is important and what is not (see Key 6.2). Use your practical intelligence to pay attention to these signals and to become more socially attuned.

KEY 6.2   Pay attention to verbal signposts.

SIGNALS POINTING TO KEY CONCEPTS	SIGNALS OF SUPPORT
A key point to remember . . .	A perfect example . . .
Point 1, point 2, etc. . . .	Specifically . . .
The impact of this was . . .	For instance . . .
The critical stages in the process are . . .	Similarly . . .

SIGNALS POINTING TO DIFFERENCES	SIGNALS THAT SUMMARIZE
On the contrary . . .	From this you have learned . . .
On the other hand . . .	In conclusion . . .
In contrast . . .	As a result . . .
However . . .	Finally . . .

Expect the Unexpected

Active listening requires opening your mind to diverse points of view and to the heated classroom debates that may result. When the literature students in the following example listened actively, where the discussion led surprised them:

> The professor said she had attended a symposium where the author Ward Just said: "In my books, I always make sure readers know by about page 35 how each of the key characters earns their living. I just think this is critical to help each reader put all the characters in my writing in a context."
>
> My instructor then assigned two books for us to read. One was by Ward Just, and it was organized exactly as promised. The other was by a different writer, who . . . obviously couldn't care less whether readers ever learned how characters earned their living. Each of us was asked to come prepared to either agree or disagree with Mr. Just's idea. . . . It was clear the professor was hoping for some disagreement.
>
> Well, she got it. Three of us took the same position as Mr. Just. The other five strongly disagreed. And about a half-hour into the discussion, which was as spirited as we had all semester, one of the women said she couldn't help noticing that the three who shared Mr. Just's view just happened to be the three men in the class, while the five who disagreed happened to be the five women. "Does that imply anything?" she wondered. Which, as you can easily imagine, quickly led to an even more spirited discussion about how gender of both author and reader might influence the way we think about the structure of writing.[2]

Effective listening skills are the basis for effective note taking—an essential and powerful study tool.

Successful Intelligence Connections Online

Listen to author Sarah Kravits describe how to use analytical, creative, and practical intelligence to improve your listening skills.

Go to the *Keys to Success* Companion Website at www.prenhall.com/carter to listen or download as a podcast.

GET ANALYTICAL!

Discover Yourself as a Listener

Complete the following as you focus on your personal listening habits:

- Analyze how present you are as a listener. Are you easily distracted, or can you focus well? Do you prefer to listen or do you tend to talk?

  _____

  _____

- When you are listening, what tends to distract you?

  _____

  _____

- What happens to your listening skills when you become confused?

  _____

  _____

- How do you react when you strongly disagree with something your instructor says—when you are convinced that you are "right" and your instructor is "wrong"?

  _____

  _____

- Thinking about your answers and about your listening challenges, list two strategies from the chapter that will help you improve your listening skills:

  1. _____

  2. _____

How Can You Make the Most of Class Notes?

Taking notes makes you an active class participant—even when you don't say a word—and provides you with study materials. What's on the line is nothing short of your academic success.

Class notes have two primary purposes: to serve as a record of what happened in class and to use for studying, alone and in combination

with your text notes. Because it is virtually impossible to take notes on everything you hear, note taking encourages you to use your analytical intelligence to critically evaluate what is worth remembering.

Note-Taking Systems

The most common note-taking systems are outlines, the Cornell system, and think links. Choose the system that you find most comfortable and that works best with course content. Be willing to change systems in different sitations.

Take Notes in Outline Form

Outlines use a standard structure to show how ideas interrelate. *Formal outlines* indicate idea dominance and subordination with Roman numerals, uppercase and lowercase letters, and numbers. In contrast, *informal outlines* show the same associations but replace the formality with a system of consistent indenting and dashes (see Key 6.3). Many students find informal outlines easier for in-class note taking. Key 6.4 shows how the structure of an informal outline helps a student take notes on the topic of tropical rain forests. The Multiple Intelligence Strategies table in this chapter (see page 191) is designed to help harness different learning approaches for an earth science course. Specifically, the table will suggest different note-taking strategies you can use when you study the topic of tropical rain forests.

From time to time, an instructor may give you a guide, usually in outline form, to help you take notes in class. This outline, known as

KEY 6.3 Outlines show levels of importance as they link details to main ideas.

FORMAL OUTLINE	INFORMAL OUTLINE
TOPIC	TOPIC
I. First Main Idea	First Main Idea
A. Major supporting fact	—Major supporting fact
B. Major supporting fact	—Major supporting fact
1. First reason or example	—First reason or example
2. Second reason or example	—Second reason or example
a. First supporting fact	—First supporting fact
b. Second supporting fact	—Second supporting fact
II. Second Main Idea	Second Main Idea
A. Major supporting fact	—Major supporting fact
1. First reason or example	—First reason or example
2. Second reason or example	—Second reason or example
B. Major supporting fact	—Major supporting fact

An informal outline is excellent for taking class notes.

Tropical Rain Forests[3]
—What are tropical rain forests?
—Areas in South America and Africa, along the equator
—Average temperatures between 25° and 30° C (77°–86° F)
—Average annual rainfalls range between 250 to 400 centimeters (100 to 160 inches)
—Conditions combine to create the Earth's richest, most biodiverse ecosystem.
—A biodiverse ecosystem has a great number of organisms co-existing within a defined area.
—Examples of rain forest biodiversity
—2½ acres in the Amazon rain forest has 283 species of trees
—A 3-square-mile section of a Peruvian rain forest has more than 1,300 butterfly species and 600 bird species.
—Compare this biodiversity to what is found in the entire U.S.
—only 400 butterfly species and 700 bird species
—How are humans changing the rain forest?
—Humans have already destroyed about 40% of all rain forests.
—They are cutting down trees for lumber or clearing the land for ranching or agriculture.
—Biologist Edwin O. Wilson estimates that this destruction may lead to the extinction of 27,000 species.
—Rain forest removal is also linked to the increase in atmospheric carbon dioxide, which worsens the greenhouse effect.
—The greenhouse effect refers to process in which gases such as carbon dioxide trap the sun's energy in the Earth's atmosphere as heat, resulting in global warming.
—Recognition of the crisis is growing as are conservation efforts.

guided notes, may be on the board, on an overhead projector, or on a hand-out that you receive at the beginning of class. Because guided notes are usually general and sketchy, they require that you fill in the details.

Use the Cornell System

The *Cornell note-taking system*, also known as the *T-note system,* consists of three sections on ordinary notepaper:[4]

- Section 1, the largest section, is on the right. Record your notes here in whatever form you choose. Skip lines between topics so you can clearly see where a section begins and ends.

- Section 2, to the left of your notes, is the *cue column.* Leave it blank while you read or listen, and then fill it in later as you review. You might insert key words or comments that highlight ideas, clarify meaning, add examples, link ideas, or draw diagrams. Many students use this column to raise questions, which they answer when they study.

- Section 3, at the bottom of the page, is known as the *summary area.* Here you reduce your notes to critical points, a process that will help you learn the material. Use this section to provide an overview of what the notes say.

MULTIPLE INTELLIGENCE STRATEGIES

FOR NOTE TAKING

APPLY DIFFERENT INTELLIGENCES TO TAKING NOTES IN EARTH SCIENCE.

INTELLIGENCE	USE MI STRATEGIES *to become a better note taker*	APPLY MI NOTE-TAKING STRATEGIES *to the topic of tropical rain forests for an earth science course*
Verbal-Linguistic	• Rewrite your class notes in an alternate note-taking style to see connections more clearly. • Combine class and text notes to get a complete picture.	• Rewrite and summarize your reading and lecture notes to understand the characteristics of tropical rain forests.*
Logical-Mathematical	• When combining notes into a master set, integrate the material into a logical sequence. • Create tables that show relationships.	• Create a table comparing and contrasting the different species found in a typical rain forest.
Bodily-Kinesthetic	• Think of your notes as a crafts project that enables you to see "knowledge layers." Use colored pens to texture your notes. • Study with your notes spread in sequence around you so that you can see knowledge building from left to right.	• Fill a tube with 160 inches of water (that's $13\frac{1}{3}$ feet!) to give you a physical sense of the annual rainfall in a rain forest. Or fill a bathtub with 10 inches of water and multiply by 16 to imagine rainfall totals. How would you react to living with so much rain? Take notes on your reaction.
Visual-Spatial	• Take notes using colored markers or pens. • Rewrite lecture notes in think link format, focusing on the most important points.	• As part of your notes, create a chart that covers the types of vegetation that grow in a rain forest. Use a different colored marker for each plant species.
Interpersonal	• Try to schedule a study group right after a lecture to discuss class notes. • Review class notes with a study buddy. Compare notes to see what the other missed.	• Interview someone you know who has visited a rain forest about what she saw, or interview a natural scientist at a museum about this environment. Use a different note-taking system for each person.
Intrapersonal	• Schedule some quiet time soon after a lecture to review and think about your notes. • As you review your notes, decide whether you grasp the material or need help.	• Think about the conflict between economic modernization and the preservation of rain forests in underdeveloped areas. Include your thoughts in your notes.
Musical	• To improve recall, recite concepts in your notes to rhythms. • Write a song that includes material from your class and text notes. Use the refrain to emphasize what is important.	• Use the Internet to find songs about the biodiversity of rain forests written by indigenous peoples who live in or near them. Then, use the song to remember key concepts. Take notes on what you find.
Naturalistic	• As you create a master note set, notice similarities and differences in concepts by organizing material into natural groupings.	• If possible, visit a museum of natural history with exhibits of rain forests. Try to see common characteristics that make vegetation and species thrive in this environment. Take notes on your observations.

* For information on tropical rain forests, see Frederick Lutgens, Edward Tarbuck, and Dennis Tasa, *Foundations of Earth Science*, 5th ed., Upper Saddle River, NJ: Prentice Hall, 2008.

Create this note-taking structure before class begins. Picture an upside-down letter T as you follow these directions:

- Start with a sheet of $8\frac{1}{2}$-by-11-inch lined paper. Label it with the date and lecture title.

- To create the cue column, draw a vertical line about $2\frac{1}{2}$ inches from the left side of the paper. End the line about 2 inches from the bottom of the sheet.

- To create the summary area, start at the point where the vertical line ends (about 2 inches from the bottom of the page) and draw a horizontal line that spans the entire paper.

Key 6.5 shows how the Cornell system is used in a business course.

Create a Think Link

A *think link*, also known as a *mind map* or *word web*, is a visual form of note taking that encourages flexible thinking. When you draw a think link, you use shapes and lines to link ideas with supporting details and examples. The visual design makes the connections easy to see, and shapes and pictures extend the material beyond words.

To create a think link, start by circling or boxing your topic in the middle of the paper. Next, draw a line from the topic and write the name of one major idea at the end of the line. Circle that idea. Then, jot down specific facts related to the idea, linking them to the idea with lines. Continue the process, connecting thoughts to one another with circles, lines, and words. Key 6.6, a think link on the sociological concept of stratification, follows this structure, just one of many possible designs.

Other examples of think link designs include stair steps showing connected ideas that build toward a conclusion, and a tree with trunk and roots as central concepts and branches as examples. Key 6.1 on page 184 shows another type of think link.

A think link may be difficult to construct in class, especially if your instructor talks quickly. If this is the case, transform your notes into think link format later when you review.

Use Other Visual Strategies

Other strategies that help organize information are especially useful to visual learners, although they may be too involved to complete during class. Use them when taking text notes or combining class and text notes for review. These strategies include the following:

- *Time lines.* Use a time line to organize information into chronological order. Draw a vertical or horizontal line on the page and connect each item to the line, in order, noting the dates and basic event descriptions.

- *Tables.* Use the columns and rows of a table to organize information as you condense and summarize your class and text notes.

- *Hierarchy charts.* Charts showing an information hierarchy can help you visualize how pieces fit together. For example, you can use a hierarchy chart to show levels within a government bureaucracy or levels of scientific classification of animals and plants.

The Cornell system has space for notes, comments, and a summary.

October 3, 200x, p. 1

UNDERSTANDING EMPLOYEE MOTIVATION

Why do some workers have a better attitude toward their work than others?

Purpose of motivational theories
—To explain role of human relations in motivating employee performance
—Theories translate into how managers actually treat workers

Some managers view workers as lazy; others view them as motivated and productive.

2 specific theories
—Human resources model, developed by Douglas McGregor, shows that managers have radically different beliefs about motivation.
—Theory X holds that people are naturally irresponsible and uncooperative
—Theory Y holds that people are naturally responsible and self-motivated

Maslow's Hierarchy

self-actualization needs (challenging job)
esteem needs (job title)
social needs (friends at work)
security needs (health plan)
physiological needs (pay)

—Maslow's Hierarchy of Needs says that people have needs in 5 different areas, which they attempt to satisfy in their work.
—Physiological need: need for survival, including food and shelter
—Security need: need for stability and protection
—Social need: need for friendship and companionship
—Esteem need: need for status and recognition
—Self-actualization need: need for self-fulfillment
Needs at lower levels must be met before a person tries to satisfy needs at higher levels.
—Developed by psychologist Abraham Maslow

Two motivational theories try to explain worker motivation. The human resources model includes Theory X and Theory Y. Maslow's Hierarchy of Needs suggests that people have needs in 5 different areas: physiological, security, social, esteem, and self-actualization.

Note Taking Is a Three-Step Process

Taking good class notes requires practice—practice preparing, practice doing, and practice reviewing. Involved are a number of analytical and practical strategies.

Prepare

Showing up for class on time with pad and pen in hand is only the beginning.

Use a think link to connect ideas visually.

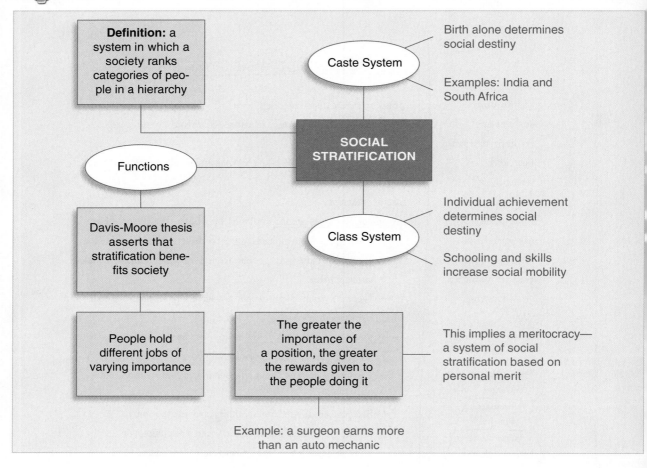

Definition: a system in which a society ranks categories of people in a hierarchy

Caste System

Birth alone determines social destiny

Examples: India and South Africa

SOCIAL STRATIFICATION

Functions

Davis-Moore thesis asserts that stratification benefits society

Class System

Individual achievement determines social destiny

Schooling and skills increase social mobility

People hold different jobs of varying importance

The greater the importance of a position, the greater the rewards given to the people doing it

This implies a meritocracy—a system of social stratification based on personal merit

Example: a surgeon earns more than an auto mechanic

Preview your reading material. *More than anything else you can do, reading assigned materials before class will give you the background to take effective notes.* Check your class syllabi daily to see when assignments are due, and then plan your reading time with these deadlines in mind. (The syllabus on page 14 shows when specific reading assignments are due.)

Review what you know. Taking 15 minutes before class to review your notes from the previous class and your reading assignment notes for that day will enable you to follow the lecture from the start. Without this preparation, you may find yourself flipping back in your notebook instead of listening to new information.

Gather your supplies. Use a separate notebook for each course, and start a new page for each class. If you use a three-ring binder, punch holes in handouts and insert them right after your notes for that day. If you use a laptop, open the file containing your class notes right away.

Location, location, location. Find a comfortable seat that is away from friends to minimize distractions. Be ready to write as soon as the instructor begins speaking.

Choose the best note-taking system. Use your emotional and social intelligence to select a system that will work best in each class. Take these factors into account when making your choices:

- *The instructor's style* (which will be clear after a few classes). In the same term, you may have one instructor who is organized and speaks slowly, another who jumps around and talks rapidly, and a third who digresses in response to questions. Be flexible enough to adapt your note taking to each situation.

- *The course material.* You may decide that an informal outline works best for a highly structured lecture and that a think link is right for a looser presentation. Try one note-taking system for several classes, then adjust if necessary.

- *Your learning style.* Choose strategies that make the most of your strengths and compensate for weaknesses. A visual-spatial learner might prefer think links or the Cornell system; a thinker type might be comfortable with outlines; an interpersonal learner might use the Cornell system and fill in the cue column in a study group. You might even find that one system is best in class and another in review sessions.

Gather support. In each class, set up a support system with one or two students so you can look at their notes after an absence.

Record Information Effectively During Class

The following practical suggestions will help you record what is important in a format that you can review later:

- Date and identify each page. When you take several pages of notes, add an identifying letter or number to the date to keep track of page order: 11/27A, 11/27B, for example, or 11/27—1 of 2, 11/27—2 of 2. Indicate the lecture topic at the top so you can gather all your notes on that topic.

- If your instructor jumps from topic to topic during a single class, it may help to start a new page for each new topic.

- Record whatever your instructor emphasizes by paying attention to verbal and nonverbal cues (see Key 6.7).

- Write down all key terms and definitions.

- Try to capture explanations of difficult concepts by noting relevant examples, applications, and links to other material.

- Write down every question your instructor raises, since these questions may be on a test.

- Be organized, but not fussy. Remember that you can always improve your notes later.

- Write quickly but legibly, using shorthand and short phrases instead of full sentences.

get practical!

Face a Note-Taking Challenge

In the spaces below, record how you will prepare to take notes in your most challenging course.

- Course name and date of class:

  _____

- List all the reading assignments you have to finish before your next class:

  _____

  _____

- Where will you sit in class to focus your attention and minimize distractions?

  _____

- Which note-taking system is best suited for the class and why?

  _____

  _____

- Write the phone numbers or e-mail addresses of two students whose notes you can look at if you miss a class:

  _____

  _____

- Leave blank spaces between points to make it easy see where one topic ends and another begins. (This suggestion does not apply if you are using a think link.)
- Draw pictures and diagrams to illustrate ideas.
- A consistent system will help you find information with minimal stresss. Use the same system to show importance—such as indenting, spacing, or underlining—on each page.
- If you have trouble understanding a concept, record as much as you can; then, leave space for an explanation, and flag the margin with a large question mark. After class, try to clarify your questions in the text or ask a classmate or your instructor for help.
- Consider that your class notes are part, but not all, of what you need to learn. As you will see later in this chapter, you will learn best when you combine your text and class notes into a comprehensive master set.

Instructors signal important material in a variety of ways.

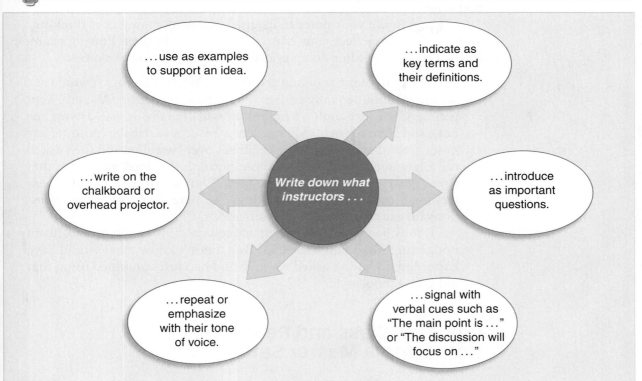

...use as examples to support an idea.

...indicate as key terms and their definitions.

...write on the chalkboard or overhead projector.

Write down what instructors . . .

...introduce as important questions.

...repeat or emphasize with their tone of voice.

...signal with verbal cues such as "The main point is . . ." or "The discussion will focus on . . ."

Take notes during class discussions. During discussion periods, one student may say something, then another, and finally the instructor may summarize or link the comments to make a point. Getting the most out of class discussions and recording critical points engages your ability to "read" others, which is the basis for social intelligence. Here are suggestions for recording what you need to know during these discussions:

- Listen carefully to everyone. Jot down relevant points and ignore points that seem tangential. If you're not sure, ask the instructor whether a student's statement is important.

- Listen for idea threads that weave through comments.

- Listen for ideas the instructor picks up on and for encouraging comments to students, such as "You make a great point," "I like your idea," and so on.

- Take notes when the instructor rephrases and clarifies a student's point.

- Try using a think link since discussions often take the form of brainstorming sessions. A think link will help you connect ideas that come at you from different perspectives.

Review and Revise

By their very nature, class notes require revision. They may be incomplete in some places, confusing in others, and illegible in still others. That is why it is critical that you review and revise your notes as soon as possible after class. This will enable you to fill in gaps while the material is fresh, to clarify sloppy handwriting, or to raise questions. Reviewing and revising your class notes prepares you for the vital step of combining class and text notes.

When you use your notes to inspire successfully intelligent thinking, your grades may reflect your efforts. The student in the following example learned this lesson after doing poorly on some tests. He explains:

> All four of us in my rooming group are taking economics. I would say we are all about equally smart. . . . Yet they are getting A's and I kept getting C's. I just couldn't figure out why. Finally, it was driving me nuts, so I went for help. My resident advisor asked if she could see my notes from that class. She looked them over carefully, and then asked me a few questions based on those notes. She helped me realize that I was great on "giving back the facts," but not so good at all at extending those facts to new situations. Yet here at college, all the questions on exams are about new situations. . . .
>
> It took someone here to help me refocus how I study. . . . I still am not getting A's, but at least solid B+'s. I don't know what would have happened if I hadn't asked for help and had just continued using that old high school style.[5]

Combine Class and Reading Notes into a Master Set

Studying from either text or class notes alone is not enough, because your instructor may present material in class that is not in your text or may gloss over topics that your text covers in depth. The process of combining class and text notes enables you to see patterns and relationships among ideas, find examples for difficult concepts, and much more.

Follow these steps to combine your class and text notes into a master note set:

MASTER NOTE SET
The complete, integrated note set that contains both class and text notes.

Step 1: Act quickly. Combine your class and reading notes into a logical, comprehensive presentation while the material is fresh in your mind.

Step 2: Focus on what's important by condensing to the essence. Now, reduce your combined notes so they contain only key terms and concepts. (You are likely to find repetition in your notes, which will make it easy to reduce the material.) Tightening and summarizing forces you to critically evaluate which ideas are most important and to rewrite your notes with only this material. As you begin to study, move back and forth between the full set and the reduced set. Key 6.8 shows a comprehensive outline and a reduced key term outline of the same material.

Step 3: Recite what you know. As you approach exam time, use the terms in your bare-bones notes as cues for reciting what you know about a topic. Many students assume that they know concepts simply because they understand what they read. What they are actually demonstrating is a passive understanding that doesn't necessarily mean that they can re-create the material on an exam or apply it to problems. Make the process more active by reciting out loud during study sessions, writing your responses on paper, making flash cards, or working with a partner.

Reducing a full set of notes into key term notes will help you master content.

MASTER SET OF CLASS AND TEXT NOTES

Different Views of Freedom and Equality in the American Democracy

I. U.S. democracy based on 5 core values: freedom and equality, order and stability, majority rule, protection of minority rights, and participation.

    A. U.S. would be a "perfect democracy" if it always upheld these values.

    B. U.S. is less than perfect; so it is called an "approaching democracy."

II. Freedom and Equality

    A. Historian Isaiah Berlin defines freedom as either positive or negative.

        1. Positive freedoms allow us to exercise rights under the Constitution, including right to vote.

        2. Negative freedoms safeguard us from government actions that restrict certain rights, such as the right to assemble. The 1st Amendment restricts government action by declaring that "Congress shall make no law . . ."

    B. The value of equality suggests that all people be treated equally, regardless of circumstance. Different views on what equality means and the implications for society.

        1. Equality of opportunity implies that everyone has the same chance to develop inborn talents.

            a. But life's circumstances—affected by factors like race and income—differ. This means that people start at different points and have different results. E.g., a poor, inner-city student will be less prepared for college than an affluent, suburban student.

            b. It is impossible to equalize opportunity for all Americans.

        2. Equality of result seeks to eliminate all forms of inequality, including economic differences, through wealth redistribution.

    C. Freedom and equality are in conflict, say text authors Berman and Murphy: "If your view of freedom is freedom from government intervention, then equality of any kind will be difficult to achieve. If government stays out of all citizen affairs, some people will become extremely wealthy, others will fall through the cracks, and economic inequality will multiply. On the other hand, if you wish to promote equality of result, then you will have to restrict some people's freedoms—the freedom to earn and retain an unlimited amount of money, for example."[6]

KEY TERM OUTLINE OF THE SAME MATERIAL

Different Views of Freedom and Equality in the American Democracy

I. America's 5 core values: freedom and equality, order and stability, majority rule, protection of minority rights, and participation.

    a. "Perfect democracy"

    b. "Approaching democracy"

II. Value #1—Freedom and equality

    a. Positive Freedoms and Negative Freedoms

    b. Different views of equality: equality of opportunity versus equality of result

    c. Conflict between freedom and equality centers on differing views of government's role

Step 4: Use critical thinking. Now toss around ideas in the following ways as you reflect on your combined notes—both the comprehensive and reduced sets:

- Brainstorm examples from other sources that illustrate central ideas. Write down new ideas or questions that come up as you review.

- Think of ideas from your readings or from class that support or clarify your notes.

- Consider what in your class notes differed from your reading notes and why.

- Apply concepts to problems at the end of text chapters, to problems posed in class, or to real-world situations.

Reviewing notes with a classmate improves your memory and comprehension of the material. These students look over notes together between classes.

Step 5: Review and review again. To ensure learning and prepare for exams, review your key word summary and critical thinking questions until you know every topic.

Try to vary your review methods, focusing on active involvement. Recite the material to yourself, have a Q&A session with a study partner, take a practice test. Another helpful technique is to summarize your notes in writing from memory after you review them. This will tell you whether you'll be able to recall the information on a test. You may even want to summarize as you read, then summarize from memory, and compare the two summaries.

How Can You Take Notes Faster?

Personal (shorthand) is a practical intelligence strategy that enables you to write faster. Because you are the only intended reader, you can misspell and abbreviate words in ways that only you understand. A risk of using shorthand is that you might forget what your writing means. To avoid this problem, review your notes shortly after class and spell out words that could be misinterpreted.

SHORTHAND

A system of rapid handwriting that employs symbols, abbreviations, and shortened words to represent words and phrases.

Another risk is forgetting to remove shorthand from work you hand in. This can happen when you use the same system for class notes as you do when talking to friends online. For example, when students take notes in text message "language," they may be so accustomed to omitting capitalization and punctuation, using acronyms, and replacing long words with incorrect contractions that they may forget to correct their final work.

The following suggestions will help you master shorthand. Many will be familiar and, in fact, you may already use them to speed up your e-mail and text and instant messaging.

1. Use standard abbreviations in place of complete words:

w/	with	cf	compare, in comparison to
w/o	without	ff	following
→	means; resulting in	Q	question
←	as a result of	p.	page
↑	increasing	*	most importantly
↓	decreasing	<	less than
∴	therefore	>	more than
∵ or b/c	because	=	equals
≈	approximately	%	percent
+ or &	and	△	change
−	minus; negative	2	to; two; too
NO. or #	number	vs	versus; against
i.e.	that is,	e.g.	for example
etc.	and so forth	c/o	care of
ng	no good	lb	pound

2. Shorten words by removing vowels from the middle of words:

   prps   =   purpose
   lwyr   =   lawyer
   cmptr   =   computer

3. Substitute word beginnings for entire words:

   assoc   =   associate; association
   info   =   information
   subj   =   subject

4. Form plurals by adding *s* to shortened words:

   prblms =   problems
   envlps =   envelopes
   prntrs =   printers

5. Make up your own symbols and use them consistently:

   b/4   =   before
   4tn   =   fortune
   2thake =   toothache

6. Use standard or informal abbreviations for proper nouns such as places, people, companies, scientific substances, events, and so on:

   DC   =   Washington, D.C.
   H_2O =   water
   Moz.   =   Wolfgang Amadeus Mozart

7. If you know that a word or phrase will be repeated, write it once, and then establish an abbreviation for the rest of your notes. For example, the first time your political science instructor mentions the *Iraq Study Group*, the 2006 bipartisan commission that issued recommendations to the president on the Iraq War, write the name in full. After that, use the initials *ISG*.

8. Write only what is essential. Include only the information nuggets you want to remember, even if your instructor says much more. Do this by paring down your writing. Say, for example, your instructor had this to say on the subject of hate crimes:

> After the terrorist attacks on September 11, 2001, law enforcement officials noted a dramatic shift in the nature of hate crimes. For the first time, replacing crimes motivated by race as the leading type of hate crime were crimes that targeted religious and ethnic groups and particularly Muslims. [7]

Your notes, which include some shorthand, might look something like this:

—After 9/11 HCs ▲ & focus targeted religious and ethnic groups, esp. Muslims.
—Reduction of HC based on race.

How Can You Improve Your Memory?

Your accounting instructor is giving a test tomorrow on key taxation concepts. You feel confident because you spent hours last week memorizing your notes. Unfortunately, as you start the test, you can't answer half the questions, even though you studied the material. This is not surprising, because most forgetting occurs within minutes after memorization.

If forgetting is so common, why do some people have better memories than others? Some may have an inborn talent for remembering. More often, though, they succeed because they take an active approach and master techniques to improve recall.

How Your Brain Remembers: Short-Term and Long-Term Memory

Memories are stored in three different "storage banks" in your brain. The first, called *sensory memory*, is an exact copy of what you see and hear and lasts for a second or less. Certain information is then selected from sensory memory and moved into short-term memory, a temporary information storehouse that maintains data for no more than 10 to 20 seconds. You are consciously aware of material in short-term memory. Unimportant information is quickly dumped. Important information is transferred to long-term memory—the mind's more permanent storehouse.

Targeting long-term memory will solidify learning the most. "Short-term—or working—memory is useful when we want to remember a phone number until we can dial or an e-mail address until we can type it into the computer," says biologist James Zull. "We use short-term memory for these

SHORT-TERM MEMORY
The brain's temporary information storehouse in which information remains for only a few seconds.

LONG-TERM MEMORY
The brain's permanent information storehouse from which information can be retrieved.

momentary challenges, all the time, every day, but it is limited in capacity, tenacity, and time."[8] Zull explains that short-term memory holds only small amounts of information for brief periods and is unstable—a distraction can easily bump out information. As you learn new material, your goal is to anchor information in long-term memory.

Memory Strategies Improve Recall

The following strategies will help improve your ability to remember what you learn.

Have Purpose, Intention, and Emotional Connection

Why can you remember the lyrics to dozens of popular songs but not the functions of the pancreas? Perhaps this is because you *want* to remember the lyrics or you have an emotional tie to them. To achieve the same results at school, try to create the purpose and will to remember. This is often linked to being emotionally involved with the material.

For example, as a student in a city-planning course, it may be easier for you to remember the complex rules surrounding housing subsidies if you think about families who benefit from these programs. If someone you know lives in a city housing project, the personal connection will probably make recall even easier.

Understand What You Memorize

If you are having trouble remembering something new, think about how the new idea fits into what you already know. A simple example: If you can't remember the meaning of the word *antebellum*, try to identify the word's root, prefix, or suffix. Knowing that the root *bellum* means "war" and the prefix *ante* means "before" will help you remember that *antebellum* means "before the war." If you take the additional step of searching the Internet for the term, you'll discover that the elegant plantation homes in the classic movie *Gone with the Wind* were built before the Civil War and are considered *antebellum architecture*.

This basic, practical principle applies to everything you study. Identify logical connections, and use these connections to aid learning. In a plant biology course, memorize plant families; in a history course, memorize events by linking them in a cause-and-effect chain.

Use Critical Thinking

Critical thinking encourages you to associate new information with what you already know. Imagine that you have to remember information about the signing of the Treaty of Versailles, the agreement that ended World War I. You might use critical thinking—combined with some quick Internet research—in the following ways:

- Recall everything that you know about the topic.

- Think about how this event is similar to other events in history.

- Consider what is different and unique about this treaty in comparison with other treaties.

- Explore the causes that led up to this event, and look at the event's effects.
- From the general idea of treaties that ended wars, explore other examples of such treaties.

Critical exploration of this kind will make it easier for you to remember specific facts and overarching concepts.

Recite, Rehearse, and Write

When you *recite* material, you repeat key concepts aloud, in your own words, to aid memorization. *Rehearsing* is similar to reciting but is done silently. *Writing* is reciting on paper. All three processes are practical tools that actively involve you in learning and remembering material. You will get the greatest benefit if you separate your learning into the following steps:

- As you read, focus on the points you want to remember. These are usually found in the topic sentences of paragraphs. Then recite, rehearse, or write down the ideas.
- Convert each main idea into a key word, phrase, or visual image—something that is easy to recall and that will set off a chain of memories that will bring you back to the original information. Write each key word or phrase on an index card.
- One by one, look at the key words on your cards and recite, rehearse, or write all the associated information you can recall. Check your recall against your original material.

These steps are part of the process for consolidating and summarizing your lecture and text notes as you study.

Reciting, rehearsing, and writing involve more than rereading material and parroting words out loud, in your head, or on paper. Because rereading does not necessarily require any involvement, you can reread without learning. However, you cannot help but think and learn as you convert text concepts into key points and rewrite important points as key words and phrases.

Limit and Organize the Items You Are Processing

This involves three key activities:

- *Separate main points from unimportant details.* Highlight only the key points in your texts, and write notes in the margins about central ideas (see Key 5.8 on page 170.)
- *Divide material into manageable sections.* Generally, when material is short and easy to understand, studying it from start to finish improves recall. Divide longer material into logical sections, master each section, put all the sections together, and then test your memory of all the material.
- *Use organizational tools.* Rely on an outline or another organizational tool to connect ideas. These tools will show logical connections and expose gaps in understanding.

Study During Short, Frequent Sessions

Research has shown that you can improve your chances of remembering material by learning it more than once. Spread your study sessions over time: A pattern of short sessions—say three 20-minute study sessions, followed by brief periods of rest—is more effective than continual studying with little or no rest. With this in mind, try studying during breaks in your schedule, and even consider using these time slots to study with classmates.

Sleep can actually aid memory because it reduces interference from new information. Because you can't always go to sleep immediately after studying for an exam, try postponing the study of other subjects until your exam is over. When studying for several tests at once, avoid studying two similar subjects back to back. Your memory is likely to be more accurate when you study history right after biology rather than chemistry after biology.

Practice the Middle

When you are trying to learn something, you usually study some material first, attack other material in the middle of the session, and approach still other topics at the end. The weak link is likely to be the material you study midway. It pays to give this material special attention in the form of extra practice.

Use Flash Cards

Flash cards are a great visual memory tool. They give you short, repeated review sessions that provide immediate feedback, and they are portable, which gives you the flexibility to use them wherever you go. Use the front of a 3-by-5-inch index card to write a word, idea, or phrase you want to learn. Use the back for a definition, explanation, and other key facts. Key 6.9 shows two flash cards used to study for a pychology exam.

Here are some suggestions for making the most of your flash cards:

- *Use the cards as a self-test.* As you go through them, divide them into two piles—the material you know and the material you are learning.

KEY 6.9

Flash cards help you memorize important facts.

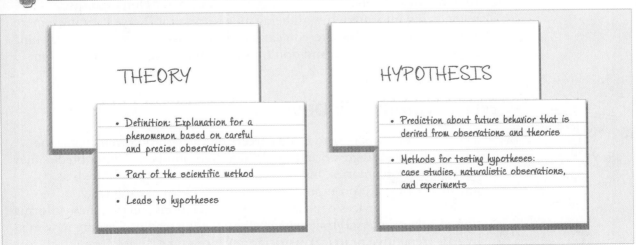

THEORY

- Definition: Explanation for a phenomenon based on careful and precise observations
- Part of the scientific method
- Leads to hypotheses

HYPOTHESIS

- Prediction about future behavior that is derived from observations and theories
- Methods for testing hypotheses: case studies, naturalistic observations, and experiments

- *Carry the cards with you and review them frequently.* You'll learn the most if you start using your flash cards early in the course, well ahead of exam time.

- *Shuffle the cards and learn the information in various orders.* This will help you avoid putting too much focus on some information and not enough on other.

- *Test yourself in both directions.* First, look at the terms and provide the definitions or explanations. Then turn the cards over and reverse the process.

- *Reduce the stack as you learn.* Eliminate cards when you are certain of your knowledge. Watching the pile get smaller is a reward that reinforces your motivation. As test time approaches, put all the cards together again for a final review.

Use a Tape Recorder and MP3 Player

Questions on tape can work like audio flash cards. One method is to record short-answer study questions, leaving 10 to 15 seconds between questions for you to answer out loud. Recording the correct answer after the pause will give you immediate feedback. For example, part of a recording for a writing class might say, "Three elements that require analysis before writing are . . . (10–15 second pause) . . . topic, audience, and purpose."

Pearson Education, the publisher of this and many of the other textbooks you will be using in college, developed VangoNotes to help you learn material through your MP3 player. Plug in your earphones to listen to chapter summaries and answer audio tests while walking between classes or shopping for food. Lindleigh Whetstone, a student at Tidewater Community College in Virginia, uses her iPod to learn Spanish when she is doing her laundry. "I get a lot more listening in than I did before," she says. She estimates that her listening/study time has grown from 30 minutes a week to about five hours a week.[9]

Use the Information

In the days after you learn something new, use your analytical intelligence to use what you learned. Think about other contexts in which the information applies and link it to new problems. Then test your knowledge to make sure the material is in long-term memory. "Don't confuse recognizing information with being able to recall it," says learning expert Adam Robinson. "Be sure you can recall the information without looking at your notes for clues. And don't move on until you have created some sort of sense-memory hook for calling it back up when you need it."[10]

Use Mnemonic Devices

MNEMONIC DEVICES
Memory techniques that use vivid associations to link new information with information you already know.

There are performers who build careers on the ability to remember the names of 100 strangers or repeat 30 ten-digit numbers. Undoubtedly, they have superior memories, but they also rely on techniques known as mnemonic devices (pronounced neh-*mahn*-ick) for assistance.

Mnemonic devices depend on vivid associations (relating new information to other material) that engage emotions. Instead of learning new facts by *rote* (repetitive practice), associations give you a "hook" on which to hang these facts for later retrieval. They are formed with the help of your creative intelligence.

There are different kinds of mnemonic devices, including visual images and associations and acronyms. Study how these devices work, then apply them to your own challenges. These devices take time and effort to create, and you'll need motivation to remember them. Because of this, it is smart to use mnemonic devices only when you really need them—for instance, to distinguish confusing concepts that consistently trip you up or to recall items in order.

Create Visual Images and Associations

To remember that the Spanish artist Picasso painted *The Three Women*, you might imagine the women in a circle dancing to a Spanish song with a pig and a donkey (pig-asso). The most effective images involve bright colors, three dimensions, action scenes, inanimate objects with human traits, and humor. The more outlandish the image, the better.

Use Visual Images to Remember Items in a List

Using the *mental walk* strategy, imagine yourself storing new ideas in familiar locations. Say, for example, that for your biology course you have to remember the major endocrine glands, starting in the brain and working downward through the body. To do this, think of your route to the library. You pass the campus theater, the science center, the bookstore, the cafeteria, the athletic center, and the social science building before reaching your destination. At each spot along the way, you "place" the concept you want to learn. You then link the concept with a similar-sounding word that brings to mind a vivid image (see Key 6.10):

- At the campus theater, you imagine bumping into actor Brad <u>Pitt</u>, who is holding <u>two</u> cell phones and has a <u>terr</u>ible cold (pituitary gland).
- At the science center, you visualize Mr. Universe with bulging <u>thighs</u>. When you are introduced, you learn that his name is <u>Roy</u> (thyroid gland).
- At the campus bookstore, you envision a second Mr. Universe with his <u>thighs</u> covered in <u>mus</u>tard (thymus gland).
- In the cafeteria, you see an <u>ad</u> for <u>Dean Al</u> for president (adrenal gland).
- At the athletic center, you visualize a student throwing a ball into a <u>pan</u> and <u>creatures</u> applauding from the bleachers (pancreas).
- At the social science building, you imagine receiving a standing <u>ovation</u> (ovaries).
- And at the library, you visualize sitting at a table taking a <u>test</u> that is <u>easy</u> (testes).

Create Acronyms

An (acronym) is a word formed from the first letters of a series of words created in order to help you remember the series. In history class, you can remember the Allies during World War II—Britain, America, and Russia— with the acronym *BAR*. This is an example of a *word acronym*, because the first letters of the items you want to remember spell a word. Keep in mind that the word or words spelled don't necessarily have to be real words.

> ACRONYM
> A word formed from the first letters of a series of words, created to help you recall the series.

A mental walk mnemonic helps you remember items in a list.

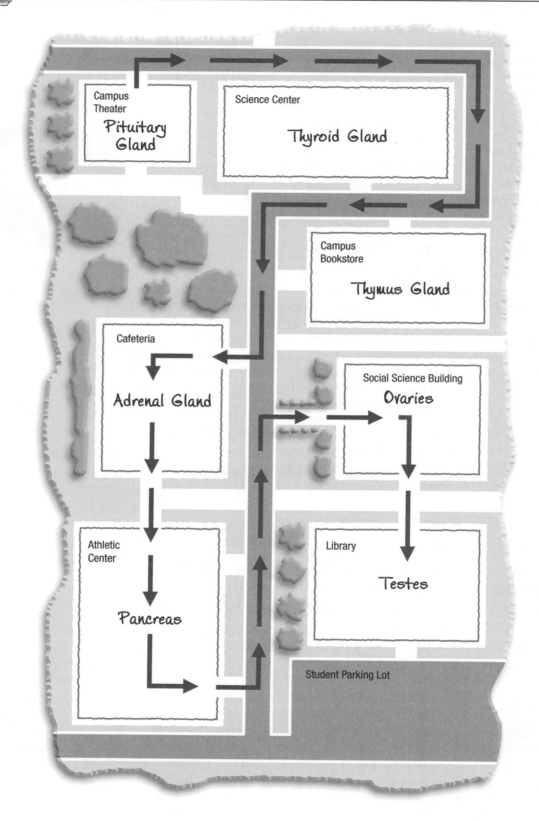

Other acronyms take the form of an entire sentence in which the first letter of each word in the sentence stands for the first letter of the memorized term. This is called a *list order acronym*. For example, music students use the phrase *Every Good Boy Does Fine* to remember the notes that correspond to the lines on the treble clef (E, G, B, D, and F).

You can create your own acronyms. For example, to remember the names of the first six U.S. presidents—Washington, Adams, Jefferson, Madison, Monroe, and Adams—you notice that the first letters of their last names read *W A J M M A*. To remember them, first you might insert an *e* after the *J* and create a short nonsense word: *wajemma*. Then, to make sure you don't forget the nonsense word, picture the six presidents sitting in a row and wearing pajamas.

Use Songs or Rhymes

Some of the classic mnemonic devices are rhyming poems that tend to stick in your mind. One you may have heard is the rule about the order of *i* and *e* in spelling.

> I before E, except after C, or when sounded like "A" as in "neighbor" and "weigh." Four exceptions if you please: either, neither, seizure, seize.

Use your creativity to make up your own poems or songs, linking familiar tunes or rhymes with information you want to remember. Thinking back to the "wajemma" example, imagine that you want to remember the presidents' first names as well. You might set these names—George, John, Thomas, James, James, and John—to the tune of "Happy Birthday." Or, to extend the history theme, you might use the first musical phrase of "The Star-Spangled Banner."

Haverford College physics professor Walter Smith hosts a Web site—www.physicssongs.org—dedicated to helping students enjoy physics and learn essential concepts by putting them to music. Here, for example, is "The Gauss's Law Song," written by Professor Smith and Marian McKenzie and sung to the tune of "East Side, West Side."

> *Inside, outside, count the lines to tell—*
>
> *If the charge is inside, there will be net flux as well.*
>
> *If the charge is outside, be careful and you'll see*
>
> *The goings in and goings out are equal perfectly.*
>
> *If you wish to know the field precise,*
>
> *And the charge is symmetric,*
>
> *you will find this law is nice—*
>
> *Q upon a constant—eps'lon naught they say—*
>
> *Equals closed surface integral of E dot n dA.*

© 2001 Walter Fox Smith [11]

Professor Smith's students credit musical mnemonics for helping them retain complex equations. Some students, like Katie Baratz, have been inspired to write their own songs. For her final class project she paired lyrics entitled "In My Mind, I've Got Physics Equations" with the James Taylor tune "Carolina in My Mind."[12]

Craft Your Own Mnemonic

Create a mnemonic to help you remember some facts.

- Identify a group of connected facts that you have to memorize—for example, for political science, the names of every presidential candidate after World War II; for literature, the names of all the characters in Shakespeare's *Romeo and Juliet*. Write your choice here:

  _____

  _____

  _____

  _____

- Now create your own mnemonic to remember the grouping using any of the devices in this chapter. Write the mnemonic here and on additional paper if necessary.

  _____

  _____

  _____

  _____

  _____

  _____

  _____

  _____

Improving your memory requires energy, time, and work. It also helps to master SQ3R, the textbook study technique that was introduced in chapter 5. By going through the steps in SQ3R and using the specific memory techniques described in this chapter, you will be able to learn more in less time—and remember what you learn long after exams are over. These techniques will be equally valuable when you start a career.

Successful Intelligence Wrap-Up

Achieving competence in listening, note taking, and memorizing requires more than just analytical ability. When you use all three components of successful intelligence to find your own way to listen and take in information, record information that you will need in the future, and remember what you learn, you set yourself up for future academic success. Here's how you have built skills in chapter 6:

Analytical

Within the material about listening, you examined the listening process and the challenges you face each step along the way, getting more specific in your analysis of your own listening skills with the *Get Analytical* exercise. You explored note-taking systems, considering what systems may work best for your particular classroom and study situations. Near the end of the chapter, you examined the nature of memory and the importance of memory challenges.

Creative

Investigating different note-taking systems may have inspired new ideas about how to approach note taking in your courses. With what you learned about note taking, you are prepared to create self-styled methods that suit your personal preferences, the material you are working with, and your instructor's style. After you explored how mnemonic devices work, completing the *Get Creative* exercise gave you experience in crafting your own original mnemonic device.

Practical

You compiled practical tools for listening actively in class, getting a sense of how to manage listening challenges. You explored how to use different note-taking systems in different situations, applying your knowledge to a specific note-taking challenge in the *Get Practical* exercise. You added practical techniques in personal shorthand and creating a master set of notes to your skills. You broadened your understanding of the ways in which experience solidifies memory.

Lagom
(lag-ohm)

In Swedish, the word *lagom* refers to the place between extremes, the spot that is neither too much nor too little, but just right. Many Swedish people aspire to this place in everything they do. They tend to seek stability yet remain open to what is new and different.

Think of the quest for *lagom* as you challenge yourself to improve your listening, note-taking, and memory skills. With *lagom* as your guide, you will appreciate that your goal is not perfection in any of these skills, but rather the ability to hear as much as you can, to take appropriate notes that will be the foundation for your studying, and to develop just the right number of memory strategies that will help you remember what is valuable. You can never hope to take in, record, and memorize every word that your instructor speaks—and that's okay. You are aiming for "just right."[13]

"Happiness does not come from doing easy work but from the afterglow of satisfaction that comes after the achievement of a difficult task that demanded our best."

THEODORE I. RUBIN, PSYCHIATRIST AND AUTHOR

*ion. Perseverance. Drive. Determination. Words
dequate to describe Victoria Gough's journey
melessness to college success—a journey fueled
ower, native intelligence, support from family,
herself, and practical learning methods. Read
unt, then use separate paper or a computer file
er the questions on page 214.*

I grew up homeless in southern Illinois. I've lived in sheds, boxcars, and salvage yards—with my parents and without them. Sometimes I wouldn't eat for three days in a row. I attended school on and off starting in third grade, but never ck after eighth. I never set foot inside a high It may be hard to believe that people grow poor and isolated in the United States, but

a short while I lived with my dad. When he re- s, my brothers and sister and I left. My mom we would have to go to a state home. When I she convinced me to marry at 13, which I did. ree children in five years. I was able to let my ve with me. We got odd jobs cleaning houses le and working at restaurants. We rented a vhich was the nicest place I'd ever lived. Mean- dreamed of going to school and longed to live se and go to a grocery store. I took a giant step that goal when I got my high school equiva- egree in 1993.

994 I married again. My husband and I live near e Community College, and he encouraged me . I entered the admissions office shaking like a e administrators helped me register for reme- ses to start with. In class I said as little as pos- idn't know where to write my name on a paper to buy books at a bookstore. The first time I how to turn on a computer I cried. first instructor told me I should drop out before 't get my money back. I went back to my

admission counselor, who put me in a different class with a wonderful instructor. I ate up the material. When I started getting 100% correct on my papers, I thought maybe the teachers considered me a sympathy case. When I received a letter telling me I made the national honor roll, I thought they made a mistake. Slowly, I'm starting to realize how capable I really am. My long-term goal is to be involved in some type of research in the medical field.

I study from six to eight hours every day, because I have so much catching up to do. Recently, an instructor nominated me for the Outstanding Achievement award on our campus. She said she never had a student sit through as many classes as I do. If the instructor lets me, I sit through the class twice. The first time I listen, and the second time I take notes.

I see students on my campus who quit school, and I have friends who say, "This is too hard." I think they're giving up too easily. If I don't understand something in class, I'll raise my hand. Sometimes I'll hear students in the back of the class say, "Someone make her shut up." It hurts my feelings a little, but I feel sadder for them than for myself. They don't seem to realize what a treasure education is. If I keep going, I'll be able to get my associate's degree in general studies the same time my granddaughter graduates from high school. What a great celebration that will be!

My personal mission is to help my other family members to break free of their grim existence and to expose the marginalized in our society to the outside world. No one in my family has ever graduated from high school, and I'm the first to enroll in college. All my children graduated from high school and went on to college. My son has a Ph.D., is a professor of sociology and criminology, and has written a book. I get goose bumps thinking about how far I've come and all the possibilities ahead of me. Learning is one of the greatest joys of my life.

anon, the student artist who created this drawing, emigrated from Haiti at 8 years old. Two years later his mother died, and like Victoria he had normous adjustments to face, dealing with his loss as well as with a new y, a new language, and family financial pressures. He had shown artistic t an early age, and through encouragement from a mentor as well as his etermination, he was ultimately accepted to the prestigious Rhode Island l of Design where he is currently studying. For more of Elie's story, please visit www.prenhall.com/carter.

Building World-Class Skills

for College, Career, and Life Success

SUCCESSFUL INTELLIGENCE

Think, Create, Apply

Learn from the experiences of others. Look back at Victoria Gough's Personal Triumph on page 213. Read her story, and then relate her experience to your own life by completing the following:

Think it through: *Analyze your own motivation.* How motivated are you to achieve your academic goals? What challenges have you overcome to get where you are today? From your memory of reaching important goals, what strategies will you use to make sure you complete your education? How does reading about Victoria affect your commitment to overcome obstacles in your life?

Think out of the box: *Let others inspire ideas.* Choose two people whom you respect. Put your listening skills to work: Spend a few minutes talking with each of them about the major obstacles they overcame to achieve success. Ask them for advice that will help ensure that you will stay in school and get a degree. From what you hear, begin brainstorming ideas about how to overcome obstacles that may stand in the way of graduation. Take notes throughout this listening process.

Make it happen: *Put a practical plan together.* Map out your action steps. Create a mnemonic device that will help you remember your plan. Envision your success as you put your plan into action.

TEAMWORK

Create Solutions Together

Create a note-taking team. In your most demanding course, form a study group with two classmates. Ask everyone to gather together a week's worth of class notes

so that you can review and compare the different versions. Focus on the following:

- Legibility (Can everyone read what is written?)
- Completeness (Did you all record the same information? If not, why not?)
- Organizational effectiveness (Does everyone get an idea of how ideas flow?)
- Value of the notes as a study aid (Will this help everyone remember the material?)

What did you learn? Use your insights to improve your personal note-taking skills.

WRITING

Journal and Put Skills to Work

Record your thoughts on a separate piece of paper, in a journal, or on a computer file.

Journal entry: How people retain information. How do you react to the following statement?

> We retain 10% of what we read, 20% of what we hear, 30% of what we see, 50% of what we hear and see, 70% of what we say, and 90% of what we say and do.

How can you use this insight to improve your ability to retain information? What will you do differently as a result of this insight?

Real-life writing: Combining class and text notes. Create a master set of notes for one course that combines one week's classes and reading assignments. Your goal is to summarize and connect all the important information covered during the period.

PERSONAL PORTFOLIO

Prepare for Career Success

Learning more about career success. Put your listening and note-taking skills to work as you investigate what brings success in the workplace. Choose a career area that interests you, and then interview two people in that area—one from an academic setting (such as an instructor or an academic advisor) and one from the working world (a person who is doing a job that interests you). Choose a setting where you can listen well and take effective notes.

Ask your interview subjects what they feel is the recipe for success in their career. You might ask specifically about curriculum (what courses are required for this area, and what courses are beneficial but not required), other preparation such as extracurricular activities and internships, qualities such as leadership and commitment, day-to-day attitudes, and anything else you are wondering about. Ask them also about the role that listening, note-taking, and memory skills play in career success. For example, if you are interviewing an account manager at an advertising agency, he might tell you that the ability to listen well, take accurate notes, and recall critical concepts is essential at client meetings. Practicing and perfecting these skills while listening to your instructors will help you in your career.

When you complete your interviews, create a report that lays out the "recipe for success." Keep in mind the skills and attitudes you wish to develop as you choose next term's courses and activities.

Suggested Readings

Burley-Allen, Madelyn. *Listening: The Forgotten Skill: A Self-Teaching Guide*. New York: Wiley, 1995.

DePorter, Bobbi, and Mike Hernacki. *Quantum Notes: Whole-Brain Approaches to Note-Taking*. Chicago: Learning Forum, 2000.

Dunkel, Patricia A., Frank Pialorsi, and Joane Kozyrez. *Advanced Listening Comprehension: Developing Aural and Note-Taking Skills,* 3rd ed. Boston: Heinle & Heinle, 2004.

Higbee, Kenneth L. *Your Memory: How It Works and How to Improve It*. New York: Marlowe, 2001.

Lebauer, R. Susan. *Learn to Listen, Listen to Learn: Academic Listening and Note-Taking*. Upper Saddle River, NJ: Prentice Hall, 2000.

Levin, Leonard. *Easy Script Express: Unique Speed Writing Methods to Take Fast Notes and Dictation*. Chicago: Legend, 2000.

Lorayne, Harry. *Super Memory—Super Student: How to Raise Your Grades in 30 Days*. Boston: Little, Brown, 1990.

Lorayne, Harry. *The Memory Book: The Classic Guide to Improving Your Memory at Work, at School, and at Play*. New York: Ballantine Books, 1996.

Roberts, Billy. *Working Memory: Improving Your Memory for the Workplace*. London: Bridge Trade, 1999.

Roberts, Billy. *Educate Your Memory: Improvement Techniques for Students of All Ages*. London: Allison & Busby, 2000.

Zull, James. *The Art of Changing the Brain: Enriching the Practice of Teaching by Exploring the Biology of Learning*. Sterling, VA: Stylus, 2002.

Internet and Podcast Resources

Coping.org—Tools for Coping with Life's Stressors—Improving Listening Skills: www.coping.org/dialogue/listen.htm

Dyslexia at College—Taking Notes (tips on taking notes from books and at lectures): www.dyslexia-college.com/notes.html

ForgetKnot (a source for mnemonic devices): http://members.tripod.com/~ForgetKnot

Kishwaukee College Learning Skills Center (helpful advice on listening skills): www.kish.cc.il.us/learning_skills_center/study_skills_help/good_listening.shtml

Merriam-Webster's Word of the Day (free word of the day in audio form available on the Internet or as podcasts): www.merriam-webster.com/cgi-bin/mwwod.pl

Princeton Review Vocab Minute (free vocabulary-building podcasts using songs to help you remember): RobinR@Review.com

Prentice Hall Student Success Supersite: www.prenhall.com/success

Endnotes

[1]Ralph G. Nichols, "Do We Know How to Listen? Practical Helps in a Modern Age," *Speech Teacher*, March 1961, pp. 118–124.

[2]Richard J. Light, *Making the Most of College: Students Speak Their Minds*, Cambridge, MA: Harvard University Press, 2001, pp. 48–49. Copyright © 2001 by Richard J. Light. Reprinted by permission of the publisher.

[3]Teresa Audesirk, Gerald Audesirk, and Bruce E. Byers, *Life on Earth*, 2nd ed., Upper Saddle River, NJ: Prentice Hall, 2000, pp. 660–662.

[4]System developed by Cornell professor Walter Pauk. See Walter Pauk, *How to Study in College*, 7th ed., Boston: Houghton Mifflin, 2001, pp. 236–241.

[5]Light, *Making the Most of College*, p. 38.

[6]Based on Larry Berman and Bruce Allen Murphy, *Approaching Democracy: Portfolio Edition*, Upper Saddle River, NJ: Pearson/Prentice Hall, 2005, pp. 6–8.

[7]Information from Frank Schmalleger, *Criminal Justice Today*, 8th ed., Upper Saddle River, NJ: Prentice Hall, 2005, p. 71.

[8]James Zull, *The Art of Changing the Brain: Enriching Teaching by Exploring the Biology of Learning*, Sterling, VA: Stylus, 2002.

[9]Cited in Madlen Read, "Growing Number of Students Use MP3 Players as a Study Tool," *Napa Valley Register*, February 7, 2007 (www.napavalleyregister.com/articles/2007/02/07/business/local/doc45c9e13a31a47296818650.txt).

[10]Adam Robinson, *What Smart Students Know: Maximum Grades, Optimum Learning, Minimum Time*, New York: Three Rivers Press, 1993, p. 118.

[11]"The Gauss's Law Song," © 2001 Walter Fox Smith, Haverford College (www.haverford.edu/physics-astro/songs/Gauss).

[12]Christopher Conkey "It's All Relative: Songs to Make Physics Easier," *Wall Street Journal*, March 17, 2005, p. B1.

[13]Christopher J. Moore, *In Other Words: A Language Lover's Guide to the Most Intriguing Words Around the World*, New York: Walker, 2004, p. 45.

TEST TAKING

Showing What You Know

7

"Successfully intelligent people seek to perform in ways that not only are competent but distinguish them from ordinary performers. They realize that the gap between competence and excellence may be small but the greatest rewards, both internal and external, are for excellence."

ROBERT J. STERNBERG

When you successfully show what you know on tests, you achieve educational goals and develop confidence. Exams also help you gauge your progress so that, when needed, you can ramp up your efforts. Most importantly, smart test preparation results in real learning that you take from course to course and into your career and life. As you will see in this chapter, test taking is about preparation, persistence, and strategy—all of which tap into your analytical, creative, and practical abilities. It is also about conquering fears, focusing on details, and learning from mistakes.

In this chapter you explore answers to the following questions:

- How can preparation improve test performance? 220
- How can you work through test anxiety? 225
- What general strategies can help you succeed on tests? 227
- How can you master different types of test questions? 231
- How can you learn from test mistakes? 241
- *Successful Intelligence Wrap-Up 244*

Analytical

- Matching test-preparation strategies with personal needs
- Identifying the nature of test anxiety
- Analyzing how to answer objective and subjective test questions
- Identifying patterns that cause you to make test errors

Creative

- Constructing a new perspective of tests as helpful evaluative tools
- Developing a pretest to assess material mastery before an exam
- Creating an effective study schedule and regimen

Practical

- How to attack objective test questions
- How to write a test essay
- How to evaluate and learn from test mistakes

How Can Preparation Improve Test Performance?

You prepare for exams every day of the term. By attending class, staying on top of assignments, completing readings and projects, and participating in class discussions, you are actively learning and retaining what you need to know in order to do well on exams. This knowledge is the most important test-preparation tool you have.

The following additional measures will help you prepare as exams approach because they put your analytical, creative, and practical thinking skills into action.

Identify Test Type and Material Covered

Before you begin studying, be practical as you find out as much as you can about the test, including the following:

- *Topics that will be covered:* Will the test cover everything since the term began, or will it be more limited?

REAL QUESTIONS

How can I combat test anxiety?

I am a Yu'pik Eskimo from a village on the Yukon River. Before attending college, I worked for six years as a clerk at the Native Corporation, a gas station and general store. When the manager passed away, the business offered to make me a manager. Even though I knew how to do the work, I didn't feel I was ready, so I decided to go to school for more training.

I felt like I was a success at work, but I don't feel successful as a student. College life is different from what I am accustomed to. The hardest part has been taking tests. I study hard, but then when the test begins, my mind goes blank. Sometimes I feel like quitting, but I also think that I will have more choices if I stick with it. How can I conquer my test anxiety?

Peter Changsak
Sheldon-Jackson College
Sitka, Alaska

PRACTICAL ANSWERS

Tonjua Williams, M.Ed.
Associate Provost,
Health Programs
St. Petersburg College

Preparation and a positive attitude will help you cope with test pressure.

Many students experience test anxiety, especially when they are new to college. Often, anxiety is a result of feeling uncomfortable in unfamiliar waters. That's why the first test in a class can be nerve-racking. Preparation is the best way to deal with nerves:

- Attend class regularly.
- Pay attention and take good notes.
- Join a study group.
- Spend two hours studying outside of class for every hour you spend in class and start studying early.
- Communicate with your instructor to make sure you understand course expectations; use your syllabus as a guide.
- Before the exam, get plenty of rest and eat a light breakfast or snack.

To calm yourself right before the exam, try the following:

- Close your eyes, take a deep breath, then review the test.
- Start with questions you are comfortable answering.
- Look for clues that will help you answer more difficult questions.

After the exam review what you did right and wrong to pinpoint areas you need to work on.

Test anxiety, believe it or not, can encourage you to rise to the occasion. The stress of an upcoming test can help you work hard so you are fully prepared. It is important to think of exams as opportunities to show off your knowledge. Changing your attitude and looking forward to the chance to demonstrate what you know will help you do your best work.

- *Material you will be tested on:* Will the test cover only what you learned in class and in the text, or will it also include outside readings? Will you be given material to work with—for example, will you be asked to analyze a poem?

- *Types of questions:* Will the questions be objective (multiple-choice, true/false, sentence-completion), subjective (essay), or a combination?

- *How the test will be graded:* Will partial credit be given for short-answer questions? Do you need to show problem-solving steps to get full credit? Are certain sections worth more than others?

Your instructors may answer many of these questions. They may tell you the question format and the topics that will be covered. They may also drop hints about possible questions, either directly ("I might ask a question on . . .") or more subtly ("One of my favorite theories is . . . "). Use your social intelligence to pick up as many clues as you can.

As you begin thinking about the test, remember that *not all tests are created equal*—a quiz is not as important as a midterm or final, although accumulated grades on small quizzes add up and can make a difference in your final grade. Plan and prioritize your study time and energy according to the value of the quiz or test. Your syllabus will tell you when quizzes and tests are scheduled throughout the term (see page 14 for a sample syllabus).

Here are other practical strategies for predicting what may be on a test. To prepare effectively, combine these with the strategies you learned throughout *Keys to Success:*

Use SQ3R to identify what's important. Often, the questions you ask yourself as you read assigned materials will be part of the test. Textbook study questions are also good candidates.

Listen for clues at review sessions. Many instructors offer review sessions before midterms and finals in order to answer last-minute questions. Bring your questions to these sessions and listen to the questions others ask. They may cover material you thought you knew, but actually need to review or learn more about.

Make an appointment to see your instructor. Spending a few minutes talking about the test one-on-one may clarify misunderstandings and help you focus on what to study.

Talk to people who already took the course and look at comments on teacher evaluation Web sites. Try to get a sense of test difficulty, whether tests focus primarily on assigned readings or class notes, what materials are usually covered, and the types of questions that are asked. If you learn that the instructor emphasizes specific facts, for example, use flash cards to drill. If she emphasizes a global overview, focus on big-picture concepts. Use your social intelligence to make others want to share information about their experiences.

Examine old tests, if the instructor makes them available. You may find old tests in class, online, or on reserve in the library. Old tests will help you answer questions like these:

- Do tests focus on examples and details, general ideas and themes, or a combination?
- Are the questions straightforward, or confusing and sometimes tricky?
- Will you be asked to apply principles to new situations and problems?

After taking the first exam in a course, you will have a better idea of what to expect.

Create a Study Schedule and Checklist

Use the guidelines presented in the *Get Focused!* end-of-part section on page 106 to create a study plan and schedule. Make copies of the checklist on page 107 and complete it for every exam. It is an invaluable tool for organizing your pre-exam studying.

Studying for final exams, which usually take place the last week of the term, is a major commitment that requires careful time management. Your college may schedule study days (also called a "reading period") between the end of classes and the beginning of finals. Lasting from a day or two to several weeks, these days give you uninterrupted hours to prepare for exams and finish papers.

End-of-year studying often requires flexibility. For example, instead of working at the library during this period, some students at the University of Texas at Austin are often seen at Barton Springs, a spring-fed pool near campus. Anna Leeker and Jillian Adams chose this site to study biology because of the beautiful surroundings—and also because they had little choice. "We heard that the libraries are packed, and that students are waiting in line for tables," said Jillian. Both realize that they have to work to maintain their focus, no matter where they study.[1]

Prepare Through Careful Review

A thorough review, using analytical and practical strategies like the following, will give you the best shot at remembering material:

Use SQ3R. This reading method provides an excellent structure for reviewing your reading materials (see pages 157–166).

Actively review your combined class and text notes. One of the best ways to review for an exam is to combine and condense your text and class notes (see chapter 6). Work with this combined note set to prepare for exams as follows:

- *As exam time nears, go through your key terms and concepts outline and recite everything you know about a topic.* Reading your notes is not enough. Learning takes place only if you express content in your own words and apply it to problems.

- *Use critical thinking to become actively involved.* Think about examples and ideas from outside readings and experiences that illustrate concepts, and ideas and opinions that take another point of view. Use what you know to solve problems.

- *Continue to actively review until you demonstrate a solid knowledge of every topic.* Involve yourself with the material by taking a practice test, doing a Q&A with a study partner, and answering your SQ3R questions in writing one more time. Don't stop until you are sure you can apply concepts to new material.

Take a Pretest

Use end-of-chapter text questions to create your own pretest. If your course doesn't have an assigned text, develop questions from your notes and assigned outside readings. Old homework problems will also help target areas that need work. Choose questions that are likely to be covered, then answer them under test-like conditions—in a quiet place, with no books or notes (unless the exam is open book), and with a clock to tell you when to quit.

The same test-preparation skills you learn in college will help you do well on standardized tests for graduate school. Sharon Smith describes how students in her preparatory program used practice tests and other techniques to help boost their scores on the Medical College Admission Test (MCAT). They "started with un-timed practices in order to work on accuracy, and timed practices were incorporated as the term progressed. Everyone tried to finish the tests/passages in the allotted time, and, at the end of each practice session, go over answer choices to understand why they are correct or incorrect." During the spring term they were "given mock exams, and it was important to treat the mock MCAT as if it were the real exam. This gave the best assessment of performance on test day."[2]

get creative!

Write Your Own Test

Check your syllabi for the courses you are taking now, and find the test that is coming up first. Use the tips in this chapter to predict the material that will be covered on this test, the types of questions that will be asked (multiple-choice, essay, and so forth), and the nature of the questions (a broad overview of the material or specific details).

Then be creative. Your goal is to write questions that your instructor is likely to ask—interesting questions that tap what you have learned and make you think about the material in different ways. Go through the following steps:

1. Write the questions you come up with on a separate sheet of paper.

2. Use what you created as a pretest. Set up test-like conditions—a quiet, timed environment—and see how you do.

3. Evaluate your pretest answers against your notes and the text. How did you do?

_____

_____

4. Finally, after you take the actual exam, evaluate whether you think this exercise improved your performance. Would you use this technique again? Why or why not?

_____

_____

Prepare Physically

Most tests ask you to work at your best under pressure, so try to get a good night's sleep before the exam. Sleep improves your ability to remember what you studied before you went to bed.

Eating a light, well-balanced meal that is high in protein (eggs, milk, yogurt, meat, fish, nuts, or peanut butter) will keep you full longer than carbohydrates (breads, candy, or pastries). When time is short, don't skip breakfast—grab a quick meal such as a few tablespoons of peanut butter, a banana, or a high-protein granola bar.

Make the Most of Last-Minute Cramming

Cramming—studying intensively and around the clock right before an exam—often results in information going into your head and popping right back out when the exam is over. *If learning is your goal, cramming will not help you reach it.* The reality, however, is that you are likely to cram for tests, especially midterms and finals, from time to time in your college career. Use these hints to make the most of this study time:

- *Focus on crucial concepts.* Summarize the most important points and try to resist reviewing notes or texts page by page.

- *Create a last-minute study sheet to review right before the test.* Write down key facts, definitions, and formulas on a single sheet of paper or on flash cards. If you prefer visual notes, use think links to map out ideas and supporting examples.

- *Arrive early.* Review your study aids until you are asked to clear your desk.

After your exam, evaluate how cramming affected your performance. Did it help, or did it load your mind with disconnected details? Did it increase or decrease your anxiety when the test began? Then evaluate how cramming affected your recall. Within a few days, you will probably remember very little—a reality that will work against you in advanced courses that build on this knowledge and in careers that require it. Think ahead about how you can start studying earlier to prepare for your next exam.

How Can You Work Through Test Anxiety?

Some students experience incapacitating stress, known as test anxiety, before and during exams, especially midterms and finals. Test anxiety can cause sweating, nausea, dizziness, headaches, and fatigue. It can reduce your ability to concentrate, make you feel overwhelmed, and cause you to "blank out" during the exam. As a result, test anxiety often results in lower grades that do not reflect what you really know. The following strategies, which tap your emotional intelligence, will help you control reactions that may get in the way of your performance.

TEST ANXIETY
A bad case of nerves that can make it hard to think or remember during an exam.

Prepare and Have a Positive Attitude

Being on top of your work from the beginning of the term is the greatest stess reliever. Similarly, creating and following a detailed study plan will build knowledge and a sense of control, as will finding out what to expect on the exam. The following strategies will help you build a positive attitude:

- *See tests as opportunities to learn.* Instead of thinking of tests as contests that you either "win" or "lose," think of them as signposts along the way to mastering material.

- *Understand that tests measure performance, not personal value.* Grades don't reflect your ability to succeed or your self-worth. Whether you get an A or an F, you are the same person.

- *Believe that instructors are on your side.* Your instructors want you to do well, even when they give challenging tests—so contact them if you need help.

- *Seek study partners who challenge you.* Find study partners who inspire you to do your best. Try to avoid people who are also anxious because you may pick up their fears and negativity. (See chapter 1 for more on study groups.)

- *Get tutored.* Many schools offer tutoring help at no charge. Find out what's available and then sign up for sessions.

- *Practice relaxation.* When you feel test anxiety mounting, breathe deeply and slowly, close your eyes, and visualize positive mental images such as getting a good grade. Try to ease muscle tension—stretch your neck, tighten and then release your muscles.

- *Shut out negative vibrations.* If you arrive at the testing room early for a last-minute review, pick a seat far away from others who are nervously discussing the test.

- *Practice positive self-talk.* Tell yourself that you can do well and that it is normal to feel anxious, particularly before an important exam.

- *Remind yourself of your goals.* Connecting the test to your long-term goals will help you calm down as you focus on what's important.

Math exams are a special problem for many students. Dealing with the anxieties associated with these exams will be examined in the *Get Focused!* end-of-part section on pages 295–298 where you will find stress-management, studying, and exam-taking techniques.

Finally, a good attitude involves expecting different test-taking challenges from those you experienced in high school. College exams may ask you to critically analyze and apply material in ways that you never did before. For example, your history instructor may ask you to place a primary source in its historical context. Prepare for these challenges as you study by continually asking critical-thinking questions.

Test Anxiety and the Returning Student

If you're returning to school after years away, you may wonder how well you will handle exams. To deal with these feelings, focus on what you have learned through life experience, including the ability to handle work and family pressures. Without even knowing it, you may have developed the time-management, planning, organizational, and communication skills needed for college success.

In addition, your life experiences will give real meaning to abstract classroom ideas. For example, workplace relationships may help you understand social psychology concepts, and refinancing your home mortgage may help you grasp a key concept in economics—how the actions of the Federal Reserve Bank influence interest rate swings.

Studying for a test with children underfoot is a reality for many students who are also parents. This student manages his 3-year-old while pursuing a degree from home.

Parents who have to juggle child care with study time can find the challenge especially difficult before a test. Here are some suggestions that might help:

- *Find help.* Join a babysitting cooperative, switch off with a neighbor, post a sign for a part-time babysitter at the local high school.

- *Plan activities.* With younger children, have a supply of games, books, and videos. Give young artists a box of markers and unlimited paper. Then tell them to draw scenes of their family, their home, their friends—all in brilliant color.

- *Explain the time frame.* Tell school-aged children your study schedule and test date. Then promise them a reward for cooperating.

What General Strategies Can Help You Succeed on Tests?

Even though every test is different, there are general strategies that will help you handle almost all tests, including short-answer and essay exams.

Choose the Right Seat

Your goal is to choose a seat that will put you in the right frame of mind and minimize distractions. Find a seat near a window, next to a wall, or in the front row so you can look into the distance. Know yourself: For many students, it's smart to avoid sitting near friends.

Write Down Key Facts

Before you even look at the test, write down key information, including formulas, rules, and definitions, that you don't want to forget. (Use the back of the question sheet so your instructor knows that you made these notes after the test began.)

Begin with an Overview

Although exam time is precious, spend a few minutes at the start gathering information about the questions—how many there are in each section, what types, and their point values. Use this information to schedule your time. For example, if a two-hour test is divided into two sections of equal value—an essay section with four questions and a short-answer section with 60 questions—you might spend an hour on the essays (15 minutes per question) and an hour on the short-answer section (one minute per question).

Take level of difficulty into account as you parcel out your time. For example, if you think you can get through the short-answer questions in 45 minutes and sense that the writing section will take longer, you can budget an hour and a quarter for the essays.

Read Test Directions

Reading test directions carefully can save you trouble. For example, although a history test of 100 true/false questions and one essay may look straightforward, the directions may tell you to answer 80 of the 100 questions or that the essay is optional. If the directions indicate that you are penalized for incorrect answers—meaning that you lose points instead of simply not gaining points—avoid guessing unless you're fairly certain.

When you read directions, you may learn that some questions or sections are weighted more heavily than others. For example, the short-answer questions may be worth 30 points, whereas the essays are worth 70. In this case, it's smart to spend more time on the essays.

Mark Up the Questions

QUALIFIERS

Words and phrases that can alter the meaning of a test question and that require careful attention.

Mark up instructions and key words to avoid careless errors. Circle qualifiers such as *always, never, all, none, sometimes,* and *every*; verbs that communicate specific instructions; and concepts that are tricky or need special attention.

Take Special Care on Machine-Scored Tests

Use the right pencil (usually a #2) on machine-scored tests, and mark your answer in the correct space, filling it completely. (Use a ruler or your pencil as a straightedge to focus on the correct line for each question.) Periodically, check the answer number against the question number to make sure they match. If you mark the answer to question 4 in the space for question 5, not only will your response to question 4 be wrong, but also your responses to all subsequent questions will be off by a line. When you plan to return to a question and leave a space blank, put a small dot next to the number on the answer sheet. Neatness counts on these tests because the computer may misread stray pencil marks or partially erased answers.

Work from Easy to Hard

Begin with the easiest questions and answer them as quickly as you can without sacrificing accuracy. This will boost your confidence and leave more time for questions that require greater focus and effort. Mark tough questions as you reach them, and return to them after answering the questions you know.

Watch the Clock

Some students are so concerned about time that they rush through the test and have time left over. If this happens to you, spend the remaining time checking your work instead of leaving early. If, on the other hand, midway through the test you realize that you are falling behind, try to evaluate the best use of the remaining time. Being flexible will help you handle the crunch.

Take a Strategic Approach to Questions You Cannot Answer

Even if you are well prepared, you may be faced with questions you do not understand or cannot answer. What do you do in this situation?

- If your instructor is proctoring the exam, ask for clarification. Sometimes a simple rewording will make you realize that you really know the material.

- If this doesn't work, skip the question and come back to it later. Letting your subconscious mind work on the question sometimes makes a difference.

- Use what you do know about the topic to build logical connections that may lead you to the answer. Take a calculated risk by using your analytical intelligence.

- Try to remember where the material was covered in your notes and text. Creating this kind of visual picture may jog your memory about content as well.

- Start writing—even if you think you're going in the wrong direction and not answering the question that was asked. The act of writing about related material may help you recall the targeted information. You may want to do this kind of "freewriting" on a spare scrap of paper, think about what you've written, and then write your final answer on the test paper or booklet. Put yourself out there.

- If you think of an answer right before the bell, write on the paper that you only have minutes left, so you are answering in outline form. While most instructors will deduct points for this approach, they may also give partial credit because you showed that you know the material.

Master the Art of Intelligent Guessing

When you are unsure of an answer on an objective test, you can leave it blank or guess. As long as you are not penalized for incorrect answers, guessing may help you. When you use what you know to figure out what you don't know, you have a reasonable chance of guessing right.

When you check your work at the end of the test, decide whether you would make the same guesses again. Because your first instincts are usually best, chances are that you will leave your answers alone. However, you may notice something that changes your mind—a qualifier that affects meaning, for example—or you may recall information that you couldn't remember the first time around.

Be Prepared for Open-Book Exams

From time to time, you may encounter an *open-book* exam—an exam during which you have permission to access a particular set of materials, often including textbooks and readings. It's tempting to think that this type of exam will be a breeze—but don't be fooled. Put your preparation into high gear for any open-book exam, as many of them tend to be *harder* than a regular exam because of the fact that you can refer to your books.

The exam strategies you've been reading about—watch the clock, answer easy questions first, and so on—all apply to any open-book exam. Testtakingtips.com offers these additional specific tips:

- Be as familiar with the materials as you can, so you don't spend precious exam time wading through pages looking for a key fact.

- Know exactly what materials you are permitted to use, and bring everything on the list.

- If permitted, mark or flag important information in your materials for use as you proceed through the exam and/or write key points or formulas on a separate sheet.

- Don't rely too heavily on quoting your materials to support your key points. Prioritize your own voice.

Maintain Academic Integrity

Cheating as a strategy to pass a test or get a better grade robs you of the opportunity to learn, which, ultimately, is your loss. Cheating also jeopardizes your future if you are caught. You may be seriously reprimanded—or even expelled—if you violate your school's code of academic integrity. Remember too that cheating in school may damage your ability to get a job.

In recent years, cheating has become high-tech, with students using their cell phones, MP3 players, personal digital assistants (PDAs), graphing calculators, and Internet-connected laptops to share information through text messaging or to search the Internet. Because this type of cheating can be difficult to discover when exams are administered in large lecture halls, some instructors ban all electronic devices from the room.

How Can You Master Different Types of Test Questions?

Every type of test question has a different way of finding out how much you know about a subject. For (objective questions,)you choose or write a short answer, often making a selection from a limited number of choices. Multiple-choice, fill-in-the-blank, matching, and true/false questions fall into this category. (Subjective questions)demand the same information recall as objective questions, but they also require you to plan, organize, draft, and refine a response. All essay questions are subjective.

Key 7.1 shows samples of real test questions from Western civilization, geometry, Spanish, and biology college texts published by Pearson Education. Included are multiple-choice, true/false, fill-in-the-blank, matching, essay questions, and exercises. Problems and applications are also included for geometry. Analyzing the types, formats, and complexity of these questions will help you gauge what to expect when you take your exams.

As you review the questions on geometry in Key 7.1, look also at the Multiple Intelligence Strategies for Test Preparation on page 233. Harness the strategies that fit your learning strengths to prepare for geometry exams.

OBJECTIVE QUESTIONS
Short-answer questions that test your ability to recall, compare, and contrast information and to choose the right answer from a limited number of choices.

SUBJECTIVE QUESTIONS
Essay questions that require written responses that tap your personal knowledge and perspective.

 **KEY 7.1**   Real test questions from real college texts.

From chapter 29, "The End of Imperialism," in *Western Civilization: A Social and Cultural History,* 2nd edition.[3]

▥ **MULTIPLE-CHOICE QUESTION**
India's first leader after independence was:
A. Gandhi   B. Bose   C. Nehru   D. Sukharno   *(answer: C)*

▥ **FILL-IN-THE-BLANK QUESTION**
East Pakistan became the country of _____ in 1971.
A. Burma   B. East India   C. Sukharno   D. Bangladesh   *(answer: D)*

▥ **TRUE/FALSE QUESTION**
The United States initially supported Vietnamese independence.   T   F   *(answer: false)*

▥ **ESSAY QUESTION**
Answer one of the following:
1. What led to Irish independence? What conflicts continued to exist after independence?
2. How did Gandhi work to rid India of British control? What methods did he use?

From chapter 2, "Geometric Shapes and Measurement," in *College Geometry: A Problem-Solving Approach with Applications,* 2nd edition.[4]

▥ **EXERCISES/PROBLEMS**
• All squares are kites, but not all kites are squares. What additional conditions must be satisfied for a kite to be a square?
(answer: Equiangular—all right angles)

• In the following figure, find one example of the following angles.
a. supplementary   b. complementary   c. right   d. adjacent   e. acute   f. obtuse

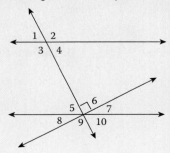

(Key 7.1 continues on next page)

(Geometry answers)

a. ∠1 and ∠2, ∠3 and ∠4, ∠1 and ∠3, ∠2 and ∠4, ∠6 and ∠9
b. ∠7 and ∠10, ∠5 and ∠8, ∠5 and ∠7, ∠8 and ∠10
c. ∠9 or ∠6
d. ∠1 and ∠2, ∠2 and ∠4, ∠4 and ∠3, ∠3 and ∠1, ∠5 and ∠6, ∠6 and ∠7, ∠7 and ∠10, ∠10 and ∠9, ∠9 and ∠8, ∠8 and ∠5
e. ∠1, ∠4, ∠7, ∠10, ∠8, ∠5
f. ∠2, ∠3

■ APPLICATIONS

- The bed of a gravel truck has the shape shown next where the lateral faces are rectangles. Describes the shape as completely as possible.

(answer: right trapezoidal prism)

■ TRUE/FALSE

- A circle is the set of all points in a plane that are the same distance from a fixed point.   T   F
- A parallelogram with four congruent sides is a rhombus.   T   F   *(answers: T, T)*

From *Mosaicos: Spanish as a World Language,* 3rd edition.[5]

■ MATCHING QUESTIONS

You are learning new words and your teacher asks you to think of an object similar to or related to the words he says. His words are listed below. Next to each word, write a related word from the list below.

| el reloj | el cuaderno | el pupitre | una computadora |
| el televisor | la tiza | el lápiz | la mochila |

1. el escritorio _____   4. la pizarra _____
2. el bolígrafo _____   5. el libro _____
3. la videocasetera _____

(answers: 1. el pupitre; 2. el lápiz;
3. el televisor; 4. la tiza; 5. el cuaderno)

■ ESSAY QUESTION

Your mother always worries about you and wants to know what you are doing with your time in Granada. Write a short letter to her describing your experience in Spain. In your letter, you should address the following points:

1. What classes you take   4. What you do with your time (mention three activities)
2. When and where you study   5. Where you go during your free time (mention two places)
3. How long you study every day

From chapter 13, "DNA Structure and Replication," in *Biology: A Guide to the Natural World,* 2nd edition.[6]

■ MULTIPLE-CHOICE QUESTION

What units are bonded together to make a strand of DNA?

A. chromatids   B. cells   C. enzymes   D. nucleotides   E. proteins   *(answer: D)*

■ TRUE/FALSE QUESTION

Errors never occur in DNA replication, because the DNA polymerases edit out mistakes.   T   F   *(answer: false)*

■ FILL-IN-THE-BLANK QUESTION

In a normal DNA molecule, adenine always pairs with _____ and cytosine always
pairs with _____.   *(answers: thymine; guanine)*

■ MATCHING QUESTIONS

Match the scientists and the approximate time frame (decades of their work) with their achievements.

Column 1	Column 2
_____ 1. Modeled the molecular structure of DNA	_____ A. George Beadle and Edward Tatum, 1930s and 1940s
_____ 2. Generated X-ray crystallography images of DNA	_____ B. James Watson and Francis Crick, 1950s
_____ 3. Correlated the production of one enzyme with one gene	_____ C. Rosalind Franklin and Maurice Wilkins, 1950s

(answers: 1–B; 2–C; 3–A)

MULTIPLE INTELLIGENCE STRATEGIES

FOR TEST PREPARATION

APPLY DIFFERENT INTELLIGENCES TO PREPARING FOR A GEOMETRY EXAM.

INTELLIGENCE	USE MI STRATEGIES *to improve test preparation*	APPLY MI TEST-PREP STRATEGIES *to study for a test on geometric shapes and measurement**
Verbal-Linguistic	• Write test questions your instructor might ask. Answer the questions and then try rewriting them in a different format (essay, true/false, and so on). • Underline important words in review or practice questions.	• Underline important vocabulary words in the chapter. Then make a set of flash cards, with the word on one side and the definition on the other. Test yourself.
Logical-Mathematical	• Logically connect what you are studying with what you know. Consider similarities, differences, and cause-and-effect relationships. • Draw charts that show relationships and analyze trends.	• Create a table that highlights the similarities and differences among polygons, circles, and three-dimensional shapes. Use columns to note qualities such as number of sides, number of angles, measurement of angles, formulas that apply consistently, and special features (for example, in a rectangle, all angles are right angles).
Bodily-Kinesthetic	• Use text highlighting to take a hands-on approach to studying. • Create a sculpture, model, or skit to depict a tough concept that will be on the test.	• Use pencils, popsicle sticks, pipe cleaners, containers, or other materials to create the shapes on which you will be tested.
Visual-Spatial	• Make charts, diagrams, or think links illustrating concepts. • Make drawings related to possible test topics.	• Draw illustrations that represent all of the postulates (statements assumed to be true) in the chapter.
Interpersonal	• Form a study group to prepare for your test. • In your group, come up with possible test questions. Then use the questions to test each other's knowledge.	• With a study partner, work through the exercise set on polygons and circles. Try either working through problems together or having partners "teach" problems to each other.
Intrapersonal	• Apply concepts to your own life; think about how you would manage. • Brainstorm test questions and then take the sample "test" you developed.	• Reread the "Geometry Around Us" material in your text to reinforce your understanding of how geometry functions in the real world. Write two additional ideas about how geometry relates to your world.
Musical	• Recite text concepts to rhythms or write a song to depict them. • Explore relevant musical links to reading material.	• Write a song that helps you remember the types of triangles and their definitions.
Naturalistic	• Try to notice similarities and differences in objects and concepts by organizing your study materials into relevant groupings.	• Create a table or visual organizer that arranges all of the types of two- and three-dimensional shapes into logical groupings.

* For information on geometric shapes and measurement, see Gary L. Musser, Lynn E. Trimpe, and Vikki R. Maurer, *College Geometry: A Problem-Solving Approach with Applications,* 2nd ed., Upper Saddle River, NJ: Pearson/Prentice Hall, 2008.

Note that some suggestions are repeated in the following sections, in order to reinforce the importance of these suggestions and their application to different types of test questions.

Multiple-Choice Questions

Multiple-choice questions are the most popular type of question on standardized tests. Examples of these questions are on page 235. The following analytical and practical strategies will help you answer them:

Read the directions carefully. Directions tell you precisely what to do. For example, whereas most test items ask for a single correct answer, some give you the option of marking several choices that are correct.

Read each question thoroughly and try to think of the answer before looking at the choices. Then read the choices and make your selection. When the answer you thought of matches one of the choices, it is most likely correct. Do not second-guess!

Underline key words and phrases. If the question is complicated, try to break it down into small sections that are easy to understand.

Make sure you read every word of every answer. Instructors have been known to include answers that are right, except for a single word. Focus especially on qualifying words such as *always, never, tend to, most, often*, and *frequently*. Look also for negatives in a question ("Which of the following is *not* . . . ").

Once you read every word, take the question on face value. Don't spend time "reading between the lines" to figure out what the instructor is *really* asking.

If you don't know the answer, eliminate answers that you know or suspect are wrong. If you can leave yourself with two possible answers, you will have a 50-50 chance of making the right choice. To narrow down, ask these questions about each of the choices:

- *Is the choice accurate on its own terms?* If there's an error in the choice—for example, a term that is incorrectly defined—the answer is wrong.

- *Is the choice relevant?* An answer may be accurate, but unrelated to the question.

- *Are there any qualifiers?* Absolute qualifiers like *always, never, all, none,* or *every* often signal an exception that makes a choice incorrect. For example, the statement "Normal children *always* begin talking before the age of 2" is untrue (most normal children begin talking before age 2, but some start later). Analysis has shown that choices containing conservative qualifiers like *often, most, rarely,* or *may sometimes be* are often correct.

- *Do the choices give clues?* Does a puzzling word remind you of a word you know? Do any parts of an unfamiliar word—its prefix, suffix, or root—ring a bell?

When questions are linked to a reading passage, read the questions first. This will help you focus on the information you need to answer the questions.

True/False Questions

Read true/false questions carefully to evaluate what they are asking. If you're stumped, guess (unless you're penalized for wrong answers). Some examples of true/false questions are on page 235.

Look for qualifiers in true/false questions—such as *all, only,* and *always* (the absolutes that often make a statement false) and *generally, often, usually,* and *sometimes* (the conservatives that often make a statement true)—that can make a true statement false and vice versa. For example, "The grammar rule 'I before E except after C' is *always* true" is false, whereas "The grammar rule 'I before E except after C' is *usually* true" is true. The qualifier makes the difference.

Be sure to read *every* word of a true/false question to avoid jumping to an incorrect conclusion. Common problems in reading too quickly include missing negatives (*not, no*) that would change your response and deciding on an answer before reading the complete statement.

Matching Questions

Matching questions ask you to match the terms in one list with the terms in another list, according to the directions. For example, the directions may tell you to match a communicable disease with the microorganism that usually causes it. The following strategies will help you handle these questions.

Make sure you understand the directions. The directions tell you whether each answer can be used only once (common practice) or more than once.

Work from the column with the longest entries. The column on the left usually contains terms to be defined or questions to be answered, while the column on the right has longer definitions or answers. Reading the items on the right only once will save time as you work to match them with the shorter phrases on the left.

Start with the matches you know. On your first run-through, mark these matches with a penciled line. When you can use an answer only once, you may have to make changes if you reconsider a choice.

Finally, tackle the matches you're not sure of. On your next run-through, focus on the more difficult matches. If one or more phrases seem to have no correct answer and you can use answers only once, consider the possibility that one of your sure-thing answers is wrong.

Fill-in-the-Blank Questions

Fill-in-the-blank questions, also known as sentence-completion questions, ask you to supply one or more words or phrases to complete the sentence. Some examples are below. The following strategies will help.

Here are examples of fill-in-the-blank questions you might encounter in an introductory astronomy course[9] (correct answers follow questions):

1. A _____ is a collection of hundreds of billions of stars. *(galaxy)*

2. Rotation is the term used to describe the motion of a body around some _____. *(axis)*

3. The solar day is measured relative to the sun; the sidereal day is measured relative to the _____. *(stars)*

4. On December 21, known as the _____ _____, the sun is at its _____ _____.
   (winter solstice; southernmost point)

Be logical. Insert your answer; then reread the sentence to be sure it is factually and grammatically correct. Consider thinking of the right answer *before* looking at the choices, then finding the choice that most closely matches.

Note the length and number of the blanks. These are clues but not absolute guideposts. If two blanks appear together, the instructor is probably looking for a two-word answer. If a blank is longer than usual, the correct response may require additional space. However, if you are certain of an answer that doesn't seem to fit the blanks, trust your knowledge.

If there is more than one blank and the blanks are widely separated, treat each one separately. Answer each as if it were a separate sentence-completion question.

Think outside the box. If you can think of more than one correct answer, consider putting them both down. Your instructor may be impressed by your assertiveness and creativity.

If you are uncertain, guess. Have faith that after hours of studying, your guess is not completely random.

Essay Questions

Essay questions ask you to express your knowledge and views in a less structured way than short-answer questions. With freedom of thought and expression comes the challenge to organize your ideas and write well under time pressure.

Essay questions require you to budget some planning time when you think through how you will spend the time allotted for the test. This student works through an essay question on a final exam.

The following steps will help improve your responses to essay questions. The process is basically a less extensive version of a general writing process—you plan, draft, revise, and edit your response. The primary differences here are that you are writing under time pressure and that you are working from memory.

1. Start by reading the questions. Decide which to tackle (if there's a choice). Use critical thinking to identify exactly what the question is asking.

2. Map out your time. Use the techniques you learned earlier in this chapter to schedule your time, remembering that things don't always go as planned. Try to remain flexible if an answer takes longer than expected.

3. Focus on action verbs. Verbs, like those in Key 7.2 on the next page, tell you what to do to answer the question. Underline them and use them to guide your writing.

4. Plan. Think carefully about what the question is asking and what you know about the topic. On a piece of scrap paper, create an informal outline or a think link to map your ideas and supporting evidence. Then develop a thesis statement that defines your content and point of view. If necessary—and if you have the time—reorganize your planning notes into an exact writing road map.

The biggest mistake students make in answering essay questions is to skip the planning stage and start writing without thinking through their answers. Not only does planning result in a better essay, it also reduces stress. Instead of scrambling for ideas as you write, you are carrying out an organized plan.

To answer question three in the box of sample essay questions below, one student created the planning outline shown in Key 7.3. Notice how abbreviations and shorthand help the student write quickly (see chapter 6 for shorthand notes strategies).

Here are some examples of essay questions you might encounter in an interpersonal communication course. In each case, notice the action verbs from Key 7.2.

1. Summarize the role of the self-concept as a key to interpersonal relationships and communication.

2. Explain how internal and external noise affects the ability to listen effectively.

3. Describe three ways that body language affects interpersonal communication.

KEY 7.2   Focus on action verbs on essay tests.

ANALYZE—Break into parts and discuss each part separately.

COMPARE—Explain similarities and differences.

CONTRAST—Distinguish between items being compared by focusing on differences.

CRITICIZE—Evaluate the issue, focusing on its problems or deficiencies.

DEFINE—State the essential quality or meaning.

DESCRIBE—Paint a complete picture; provide the details of a story or the main characteristics of a situation.

DIAGRAM—Present a drawing, chart, or other visual.

DISCUSS—Examine completely, using evidence and often presenting both sides of an issue.

ELABORATE ON—Start with information presented in the question, and then add new material.

ENUMERATE/LIST/IDENTIFY—Specify items in the form of a list.

EVALUATE—Give your opinion about the value or worth of something, usually by weighing positive and negative effects, and justify your conclusion.

EXPLAIN—Make the meaning of something clear, often by discussing causes and consequences.

ILLUSTRATE—Supply examples.

INTERPRET—Explain your personal views and judgments.

JUSTIFY—Discuss the reasons for your conclusions or for the question's premise.

OUTLINE—Organize and present main and subordinate points.

PROVE—Use evidence and logic to show that something is true.

REFUTE—Use evidence and logic to show that something is not true or how you disagree with it.

RELATE—Connect items mentioned in the question, showing, for example, how one item influenced the other.

REVIEW—Provide an overview of ideas and establish their merits and features.

STATE—Explain clearly, simply, and concisely.

SUMMARIZE—Give the important ideas in brief, without comments.

TRACE—Present a history of the way something developed, often by showing cause and effect.

5. Draft. Your first draft on an exam is usually the one you hand in. If you plan effectively, you should have enough material to construct a suitable answer. Use the following guidelines as you draft your answer:

- Spend the bulk of your time developing your thesis and supporting evidence and logic. Most instructors do not expect fully developed introductions or conclusions.

Write to the Verb

Focusing on the action verbs in essay test instructions can mean the difference between giving instructors what they want and answering off the mark. Try this exercise.

- Start by choosing a topic you learned about in this text—for example, the concept of successful intelligence or different barriers to listening. Write your topic here:

  _____

  _____

- Put yourself in the role of instructor. Write an essay question on this topic, using one of the action verbs in Key 7.2 to frame the question. For example, "List the three aspects of successful intelligence," or "Analyze the classroom-based challenges associated with internal barriers to listening." Write your question here:

  _____

  _____

- Now choose three other action verbs from Key 7.2. Use each one to rewrite your original question:

  1. _____
  2. _____
  3. _____

- Finally, analyze how each new verb changes the focus of the essay:

  1. _____

  _____

  2. _____

  _____

  3. _____

  _____

- Start by stating your thesis, and then get right to the evidence that backs it up.
- Pay close attention to how you organize your ideas and how well you support them with evidence. Try to structure your essay so that each paragraph presents an idea that supports the thesis.

KEY 7.3   Create an informal outline during essay tests.

Roles of BL in IC
1. To contradict or reinforce words
   — e.g., friend says "I'm fine"
2. To add shades of meaning
   — saying the same sentence in 3 diff. ways
3. To make lasting 1st impression
   — impact of nv cues and voice tone greater than words
   — we assume things abt person based on posture, eye contact, etc.

- Use clear language and tight logic to link ideas to your thesis and to create transitions between paragraphs.
- Look back at your outline periodically to make sure you cover everything.
- Wrap it up with a short, to-the-point conclusion.

Pay attention to the test directions when drafting your answer. Your essay may need to be of a certain length, for example, or may need to take a certain form (for example, a particular format such as a business letter). Finally, write on only one side of the page so that the grader can easily read your response.

6. Revise. Take a few moments to evaluate your word choice, paragraph structure, and style. Although you may not have the time or opportunity to rewrite your entire answer, you can certainly improve it with minor deletions or additions in the margin. If you find a problem in your work—an idea without support, for example, or some unnecessary information—add the new material in the margins and cross out what you don't need. When adding material, you can indicate with an arrow where it fits or note that inserts can be found on separate pages. If you have more than one insert, label each to avoid confusion (Insert #1, Insert #2). Be neat as you make changes.

As you check over your essay, ask yourself these questions:

- Have I answered the question?
- Does my essay begin with a clear thesis statement, and does each paragraph start with a strong topic sentence that supports the thesis?

- Have I provided the support necessary in the form of examples, statistics, and relevant facts to prove my argument?
- Is my logic sound and convincing?
- Have I covered all the points in my original outline?
- Is my conclusion an effective wrap-up?
- Does every sentence effectively communicate my point?

7. Edit. Check for mistakes in grammar, spelling, punctuation, and usage. No matter your topic, correct language leaves a positive impression and reduces problems that may lower your grade.

Key 7.4 shows the student's completed response to the essay question on body language, including the word changes and inserts she made while revising the draft.

Neatness is crucial. No matter how good your ideas are, if your instructor can't read them your grade will suffer. If your handwriting is a problem, try printing or skipping every other line, and be sure to write on only one side of the page. Students with illegible handwriting might ask to take the test on a computer.

The purpose of a test is to see how much you know, not merely to get a grade. Embrace this attitude to learn from your mistakes.

How Can You Learn from Test Mistakes?

In life—and on exams—people learn most from their mistakes. With exam in hand, use the following strategies to reduce the likelihood of making the same errors again. (If your instructor posts grades but does not hand exams back, ask to see your paper.)

Try to identify patterns in your mistakes. Ask yourself global questions that may help you identify correctable patterns:

- *Can you identify your biggest problems?* Did you get nervous, misread the question, fail to study enough, study incorrectly, focus on memorizing material instead of on understanding and applying it?
- *Did your instructor's comments clarify what you failed to do?* Did your answer lack specificity? Did you fail to support your thesis with concrete examples? Was your analysis weak?
- *Were you surprised by the questions?* For example, did you expect them all to be from the lecture notes and text instead of from your notes, text, and supplemental readings?
- *Did you make careless errors?* Did you misread the question or directions, blacken the wrong box on the answer sheet, skip a question, write illegibly?

QUESTION: Describe three ways that body language affects interpersonal communication.

Body language plays an important role in interpersonal communication and helps shape the impression you make~~,~~ *, especially when you meet someone for the first time* Two of the most important functions of body language are to contradict and reinforce verbal statements. When body language contradicts verbal language, the message ~~conveyed~~ *delivered* by the body is dominant. For example, if a friend tells you that she is feeling "fine," but her posture is slumped, *her eye contact minimal,* and her facial expression troubled, you have every reason to wonder whether she is telling the truth. If the same friend tells you that she is feeling fine and is smiling, walking with a bounce in her step, and has direct eye contact, her body language is ~~telling the truth.~~ *accurately reflecting and reinforcing her words.*

The nonverbal cues that make up body language also have the power to add shades of meaning. Consider this statement: "This is the best idea I've heard all day." If you were to say this three different ways—in a loud voice while standing up; quietly while sitting with arms and legs crossed and looking away; and while ~~maintening~~ *maintaining* eye contact and taking the receiver's hand—you might send three different messages.

Finally, the impact of nonverbal cues can be greatest when you meet someone for the first time. *Although first impressions emerge from a combination of nonverbal cues, tone of voice, and choice of words, nonverbal elements (cues and tone) usually come across first and strongest.* When you meet someone, you tend to make assumptions based on nonverbal behavior such as posture, eye contact, gestures, and speed and style of movement.

In summary, nonverbal communication plays a ~~crusial~~ *crucial* role in interpersonal relationships. It has the power to send an accurate message that may ~~destroy~~ *belie* the speaker's words, offer shades of meaning, and set the tone of a first meeting.

- *Did you make conceptual or factual errors?* Did you misunderstand a concept? Did you fail to master facts or concepts? Did you skip part of the text or miss classes in which ideas were covered?

Honest answers will help you change the way you study for the next exam.

Rework the questions you got wrong. Based on instructor feedback, try to rewrite an essay, recalculate a math problem from the original question, or redo questions following a reading selection. If you discover a pattern of careless errors, redouble your efforts to be more careful, and save time to double-check your work from now on.

After reviewing your mistakes, fill in your knowledge gaps. If you made mistakes because you didn't understand important concepts, develop a plan to learn the material.

Talk to your instructor. Focus on specific mistakes on objective questions or a weak essay. The fact that you care enough to review your errors will leave a positive, lasting impression. If you are not sure why you were marked down on an essay, ask what you could have done better. If you feel that an essay was unfairly graded, ask for a rereading. When you use your social intelligence and approach your instructor in a nondefensive way, you are likely to receive help.

Rethink the way you studied. Make changes to avoid repeating your errors. Use the varied techniques in *Keys to Success* to study more effectively so that you can show yourself and your instructors what you are capable of

Learn from Your Mistakes

get practical!

Look at an exam on which your performance fell short. If possible, choose one that contains different types of objective and subjective questions. With the test and the answer sheet in hand, use your analytical thinking skills to answer the following questions and learn from your mistakes:

- Identify the types of questions on which you got the most correct answers (for example, matching, essay, multiple-choice):

  _____

- Identify the types of questions on which you made the greatest number of errors:

  _____

- Analyze your errors to identify patterns—for example, did you misread test instructions or ignore qualifiers that changed meaning? What did you find?

  _____

  _____

- Finally, list two practical steps you are prepared to take during your next exam to avoid the same problems:

  Action 1: _____

  Action 2: _____

doing. The earlier in the term you make positive adjustments the better, so make a special effort to analyze and learn from early test mistakes.

If you fail a test, don't throw it away. Use it to review troublesome material, especially if you will be tested on it again. You might also want to keep it as a reminder that you can improve if you have the will to succeed. When you compare a failure to later successes, you'll see how far you've come.

Successful Intelligence Wrap-Up

Tests ask you to show what you know to someone who will judge your performance. However, far more important than the information a test gives to an instructor is the information it gives to you, the test taker. Tests can be your road map to subject mastery, showing you what you have learned, what you are still learning, and what stumps you. Here's how you have built skills in chapter 7:

Analytical

You examined test-preparation techniques with an eye toward what works best for you. You investigated specific ways to maximize your chances of answering objective and subjective test questions correctly. In the *Get Analytical* exercise, you wrote a series of original essay questions, analyzing the effect that different action verbs had on what the questions were asking. You considered the potential positive effects from a careful analysis of test mistakes.

Creative

With the *Get Creative* exercise, you produced your own pretest that will help you assess if you have mastered crucial material. In reading about test anxiety, you encountered a different perspective of tests as opportunities to learn rather than contests that you win or lose. The scheduling and study techniques may have inspired you to create a personal study schedule and regimen that help you make the most of your time.

Practical

You gathered specific test-preparation techniques. You learned specific ways to calm test anxiety and to attack objective test questions. You expanded your knowledge of how to use planning tools, such as a key word outline, to help you write test essays. You deepened your understanding of how examining test mistakes helps you learn from experience. In the *Get Practical* exercise, you explored your mistakes on a particular test and identified steps you will take to avoid the same mistakes in the future.

hart ducha
(hahrt doo-cha)

In Polish, *hart ducha* literally means "strength of spirit" or "strength of will" to overcome life's challenges. In college, instructors challenge you on tests to demonstrate what you know and what you can do. Both before and during each test, your success depends on your *hart ducha*. With strength of will, you can commit to spending hours learning, reviewing, thinking about, and memorizing course material instead of cramming at the last minute. Think carefully about your approach because it determines far more than your exam grade. It determines what you will get out of your education.

There are no shortcuts to test success. Only old-fashioned hard work, driven by a powerful strength of will, will enable you to reach your academic potential.[10]

"The Five P's of Success: Prior preparation prevents poor performance."

JAMES A. BAKER III, FORMER SECRETARY OF STATE
AND WHITE HOUSE CHIEF OF STAFF

SUCCESSFUL INTELLIGENCE

Think, Create, Apply

Prepare effectively for tests. Take a careful look at your performance on and preparation for a recent test.

Step 1. Think it through: *Analyze how you did.* Were you pleased or disappointed with your performance and grade? Why?

_____

_____

Thinking about your performance, look at the problems listed below. Circle those that you feel were a factor in this exam. Fill in the empty spaces with problems not listed.

- Incomplete preparation
- Fatigue
- Feeling rushed during the test
- Shaky understanding of concepts
- Poor guessing techniques
- Feeling confused about directions
- Test anxiety
- Poor essay organization or writing
- _____
- _____
- _____

Now for each problem you identified, think about why you made mistakes.

Step 2. Think out of the box: *Be creative about test-preparation strategies.* If you had absolutely no restrictions on time or access to materials, how would you have prepared for this test to improve your performance? Describe briefly what your plan would be and how it would minimize the problems you encountered.

_____

_____

Now think back to your actual test preparation. What techniques did you use and how much time did you spend?

_____

_____

How does what you would do under ideal circumstances differ from what you actually did?

_____

_____

Step 3. Make it happen: *Improve preparation for the next exam.* Think about the practical actions you will take the next time you face a similar test. Write your answers here.

Actions I took this time, but do not intend to take next time:

_____

_____

Actions I did not take this time, but intend to take next time:

_____

_____

TEAMWORK

Create Solutions Together

Test study group. Form a study group with two or three other students. When your instructor announces the next exam, ask each study group member to record everything he or she does to prepare for the exam, including things like these:

- Learning what to expect on the test (topics and material that will be covered, types of questions that will be asked)

- Examining old tests

- Creating and following a study schedule and checklist

- Using SQ3R to review material

- Taking a pretest

- Getting a good night's sleep

- Doing last-minute cramming

- Mastering general test-taking strategies

- Mastering strategies for handling specific types of test questions

After the exam, come together to compare preparation strategies. What important differences can you identify in the routines followed by group members? How did learning styles play a role in those differences? How do you suspect that different routines affected test performance and outcome? On a separate piece of paper or on a computer file, for your own reference, write down what you learned from the test-preparation habits of your study mates that may help you as you prepare for upcoming exams.

WRITING

Journal and Put Skills to Work

Record your thoughts on a separate piece of paper, in a journal, or on a computer file.

Journal entry: Test anxiety. Do you experience test anxiety? Describe how tests generally make you feel (you might include an example of a specific test situation and what happened). Identify your specific test-taking fears, and brainstorm ideas for how to overcome fears and self-defeating behaviors.

Real-life writing: Ask your instructor for feedback on a test. Nearly all students have been in the position of believing that the response they wrote on an essay exam was marked down unfairly. The next time this happens to you—when you have no idea why you lost points or disagree with the instructor's assessment of your work—draft a respectful e-mail to your instructor explaining your position and asking for a meeting to discuss the essay. (See e-mail etiquette guidelines in Quick Start to College.) Use clear logic to defend your work and refer back to what you learned in class and in the text. It is important to address specifically any comments or criticisms the instructor made on the test paper. Before sending the e-mail, analyze your argument: Did you make your case effectively, or was the instructor correct? When you have the meeting, the work you did on the e-mail will prepare you to defend your position.

PERSONAL PORTFOLIO

Prepare for Career Success

Complete the following in your electronic portfolio or on separate paper.

Compiling a résumé. What you have accomplished in various work and school situations will be important for you to emphasize on a résumé when you apply for jobs. Your roles at work, in school, at home, and in the community help you gain knowledge and experience.

To start, use two sheets of paper or a computer to brainstorm. On one electronic page or sheet of paper, list your education and skills information. On another, list job experience. For each job, record job title, the dates of employment, and the tasks you performed (if the job had no particular title, come up with one yourself). Be as detailed as possible—it's best to write down everything you remember. When you compile your résumé, you will make this material more concise. Keep this list and update it periodically as you gain experience and accomplishments.

Using the information you have gathered and Key 7.5 as your guide, draft a résumé. Remember that there are many ways to construct a résumé; consult other resources for different styles. You may want to reformat your résumé according to a style that your career counselor or instructor recommends. Also, if you already have a specific career focus, that career area may favor a particular style of résumé. Ask questions to be sure.

Keep this résumé draft in hard copy and on a computer hard drive or disk. When you need to submit a résumé with a job application, update the draft and print it out on high-quality paper.

Set yourself apart with an attractive, clear résumé.

Désirée Williams

237 Custer Street, San Francisco, CA 94101 • 650/555-5252 (w) or 415/555-7865 (h)
• fax: 707/555-2735 • e-mail: desiree@zzz.com

EDUCATION

2005 to present   San Francisco State University, San Francisco, CA

Pursuing a B.A. in the Spanish BCLAD (Bilingual, Cross-Cultural Language Acquisition Development) Education and Multiple Subject Credential Program. Expected graduation: June 2008.

PROFESSIONAL EMPLOYMENT

10/06 to present   **Research Assistant, Knowledge Media Lab**

Developing ways for teachers to exhibit their inquiry into their practice of teaching in an online, collaborative, multimedia environment.

5/05 to present   **Webmaster/Web Designer**

Work in various capacities at QuakeNet, an Internet Service Provider and Web Commerce Specialist in San Mateo, CA. Designed several sites for the University of California, Berkeley, Graduate School of Education, as well as private clients such as A Body of Work and Yoga Forever.

9/05 to 6/06   **Literacy Coordinator**

Coordinated, advised, and created literacy curriculum for an America Reads literacy project at Prescott School in West Oakland. Worked with non-reader 4th graders on writing and publishing, incorporating digital photography, Internet resources, and graphic design.

8/05   **Bilingual Educational Consultant**

Consulted for Children's Television Workshop, field-testing bilingual materials. With a research team, designed bilingual educational materials for an ecotourism project run by an indigenous rain forest community in Ecuador.

1/05 to 6/06   **Technology Consultant**

Worked with 24 Hours in Cyberspace, an online worldwide photojournalism event. Coordinated participation of schools, translated documents, and facilitated public relations.

SKILLS

Languages: Fluent in Spanish.
Proficient in Italian and Shona (majority language of Zimbabwe).

Computer: Programming ability in HTML, Javascript, Pascal, and Lisp. Multimedia design expertise in Adobe Photoshop, Netobjects Fusion, Adobe Premiere, Macromedia Flash, and many other visual design programs.

Personal: Perform professionally in Mary Schmary, a women's a cappella quartet. Have climbed Mt. Kilimanjaro.

Here are some general tips for writing a résumé.

- Always put your name and contact information at the top. Make it stand out.
- State an objective if it is appropriate—for instance, if your focus is specific or you are designing this résumé for a particular interview or career area.
- List your postsecondary education, starting from the latest and working backward. This may include summer school, night school, seminars, and accreditations.
- List jobs in reverse chronological order (most recent job first). Include all types of work experience (full-time, part-time, volunteer, internship, and so on).
- When you describe your work experience, use action verbs and focus on what you have accomplished, rather than on the description of assigned tasks.
- List references on a separate sheet. You may want to put "References upon request" at the bottom of your résumé.
- Use formatting (larger font sizes, different fonts, italics, bold, and so on) and indents selectively to help the important information stand out.
- Get several people to look at your résumé before you send it out. Other readers will have ideas that you haven't thought of and may find errors that you have missed.

Suggested Readings

Browning, William G. *Cliffs Memory Power for Exams*. Lincoln, NE: Cliffs Notes, 1990.

Frank, Steven. *Test Taking Secrets: Study Better, Test Smarter, and Get Great Grades*. Holbrook, MA: Adams Media, 1998.

Fry, Ron. *"Ace" Any Test*, 5th ed. Florence, KY: Thomson Delmar Learning, 2004.

Hamilton, Dawn. *Passing Exams: A Guide for Maximum Success and Minimum Stress*. New York: Continuum International, 2003.

Kesselman-Turkel, Judy, and Franklynn Peterson. *Test Taking Strategies*. Madison: University of Wisconsin Press, 2004.

Luckie, William R., and Wood Smethurst. *Study Power: Study Skills to Improve Your Learning and Your Grades*. Cambridge, MA: Brookline Books, 1997.

Meyers, Judith N. *Secrets of Taking Any Test: Learn the Techniques Successful Test-Takers Know*. New York: Learning Express, July 2000.

Internet and Podcast Resources

Palm Beach Community College (list of sites offering information on test-taking skills): **www.pbcc.edu/x6838.xml**

TestTakingTips.com (tips to improve your test-taking and study skills): **www.testtakingtips.com**

University of North Dakota—Study Strategies Homepage: **www.d.umn.edu/student/loon/acad/strat**

Prentice Hall Student Success SuperSite: **www.prenhall.com/success**

Endnotes

[1]From Ben Gose, "Notes from Academe: Living It Up on the Dead Days," *Chronicle of Higher Education,* June 7, 2002 (http://chronicle.com/weekly/v48/i39/39a04801.htm).

[2]From "Students Speak," MEDPREP: Medical/Dental Education Preparatory Program, Southern Illinois University School of Medicine (www.siumed.edu/medprep/studentsspeak.html).

[3]Western civilization test items from Margaret L. King, *Western Civilization: A Social and Cultural History*, 2nd ed., Upper Saddle River, NJ: Pearson Education, 2003. Questions from *Instructor's Manual and Test Item File* by Dolores Davison Peterson. Used with permission.

[4]Geometry exercises from Gary L. Musser, Lynn E. Trimpe, and Vikki R. Maurer, *College Geometry: A Problem-Solving Approach with Applications,* 2nd ed., Upper Saddle River, NJ: Pearson/Prentice Hall, 2008, pp. 99–101. Used with permission.

[5]Spanish test items from Matilde Olivella de Castells, Elizabeth Guzmán, Paloma Lupuerta, and Carmen García, *Mosaicos: Spanish as a World Language,* 3rd ed., Upper Saddle River, NJ: Prentice Hall, 2002. Questions from *Testing Program* by Mark Harpring. Used with permission.

[6]Biology test items from David Krogh, *Biology: A Guide to the Natural World,* 2nd ed., Upper Saddle River, NJ: Prentice Hall, 2002. Questions from *Test Item File* edited by Dan Wivagg. Used with permission.

[7]From Gary W. Piggrem and Charles G. Morris, *Test Item File* for *Understanding Psychology,* 3rd ed., 1996. Reprinted by permission of Pearson Education, Inc., Upper Saddle River, NJ.

[8]Ibid.

[9]From Eric Chaisson and Steve McMillan, *Astronomy Today,* 3rd ed., 1999. Reprinted by permission of Pearson Education, Inc., Upper Saddle River, NJ.

[10]Christopher J. Moore, *In Other Words: A Language Lover's Guide to the Most Intriguing Words Around the World,* New York: Walker, 2004, p. 45.

WELLNESS, MONEY, AND CAREERS

Building a Successful Future

"Successfully intelligent people are flexible in adapting to the roles they need to fulfill. They recognize that they will have to change the way they work to fit the task and situation at hand, and then they analyze what these changes will have to be and make them."

ROBERT STERNBERG

As you come to the end of your work in this course, you have built a wealth of knowledge. You are facing important decisions about which direction you want to go in school—and perhaps considering where the choices you make now will lead you.

This chapter will help you build life skills that can fuel your future success—maintaining wellness, managing your money, and preparing for a career. You will also revisit the 20 important tools that will help you transfer the power of successful intelligence into your post-college life and guide you toward your dreams.

In this chapter you explore answers to the following questions:

- How can focusing on health help you manage stress? 254
- How can you make effective decisions about substances and sex? 262
- How can you manage money effectively? 269
- How can you prepare for career success? 273
- How can you continue to activate your successful intelligence? 282
- *Successful Intelligence Wrap-Up 285*

Chapter 8's
Successful Intelligence Skills

Analytical

- Analyzing the effects of alcohol, tobacco, and drug use
- Analyzing your money-related attitudes and goals
- Examining your development of the 20 self-activators

Creative

- Creating more beneficial eating, exercise, and sleep habits
- Creating new ways to connect how you learn to career areas
- Brainstorming ways to search for a job on the Internet

Practical

- How to seek support for stress and health issues
- How to make effective decisions about substances and sex
- How to use a monthly budget

How Can Focusing on Health Help You Manage Stress?

As you learned in chapter 2, *stress* refers to the physical or mental strain that occurs when your body reacts to pressure. Stress doesn't come just from negative events. When psychologists T. H. Holmes and R. H. Rahe measured the intensity of people's reaction to specific changes and the levels of stress related to them, they found that people experience both positive and negative events as stressors (see their Social Readjustment Rating Scale in Key 8.1).

At their worst, stress reactions can make you physically ill. However, stress can also supply the heightened readiness you need to do well on tests, finish assignments on time, prepare for a class presentation, or befriend new people. Your goal is to find a manageable balance. Key 8.2, based on research conducted by Robert M. Yerkes and John E. Dodson, shows that stress can be helpful or harmful, depending on how much you experience.

Being as physically and mentally healthy as possible is a crucial stress-management tool. Although no one is able to make healthy choices all the time, you can pledge to do your best. Focus on your physical health through what you eat, how you exercise, and how much you sleep. Focus on your mental health by recognizing mental health problems, whether related to stress or other causes, and understanding ways to get help.

knowledge will help me succeed in a changing world?

hool, we are required to focus on an area of interest starting in the second
r of sophomore year. At this point I'm planning on studying acting, with an
pursue an acting career after I graduate. However, I want to take time in
o explore other areas. Art history and religion both interest me, although I don't
w I would translate those interests into a career. Outside of the specific training
e in acting, how will what I'm doing in college serve me in a career?

Rachel Faison
Bard College, Annandale-
on-Hudson, New York

PRACTICAL ANSWERS

Carol Carter
ent and Founder,
LifeBound, LLC
Denver, Colorado

Internship experience and exploring your passions will help you achieve success.

If you learn to use your mind to the fullest, you will prepare yourself well for any profession you decide to pursue. The key right now is to develop several skillsets to complement your academic learning so that you will be versatile.

First, work at least two internships before you graduate. You will learn volumes from experiencing the culture and politics in different workplaces and by proving your instincts and skills in the real-world environment. This experience will also help you discover what you like and dislike. Many students select fields that sound good or pay a lot without discovering what succeeding in that field really entails.

Second, build your leadership skills. What organization can you join? What leadership role can you play? How will that organization be different and better because you have been a part of it? Stretch yourself. Sometimes when we move into areas that scare us, we grow the most.

Finally, think carefully about what you love (and don't love) doing. Ask probing questions about your values. What makes you feel purposeful, creative, joyful, and valued? What makes you want to wake up every morning? You may not come up with answers right away, but committing yourself to the process of asking the questions and "holding" the questions will allow you to dig genuinely and deeply for the way that you can make your mark in the world of work.

Food and Eating Habits

Making intelligent choices about what you eat can lead to more energy, better general health, and an improved quality of life. However, this is easier said than done, for two reasons in particular. One is that the *food environment* in which most people live—characterized by an overabundance of unhealthful food choices combined with the fact that the cheapest choices are often not the best—does not support people's efforts to choose well.[1]

The second reason is that college life can make it tough to eat right. Students spend hours sitting in class or studying and tend to eat on the

KEY 8.1

Use the Holmes-Rahe scale to find your "stress score."

To find your current "stress score," add the values of the events that you experienced in the past year. The higher the number, the greater the stress. Scoring over 300 points puts you at high risk for developing a stress-related health problem. A score between 150 and 299 reduces your risk by 30%, and a score under 150 means that you have only a small chance of a problem.

EVENT	VALUE	EVENT	VALUE
Death of spouse or partner	100	Son or daughter leaving home	29
Divorce	73	Trouble with in-laws	29
Marital separation	65	Outstanding personal achievement	28
Jail term	63	Spouse begins or stops work	26
Personal injury	53	Starting or finishing school	26
Marriage	50	Change in living conditions	25
Fired from work	47	Revision of personal habits	24
Marital reconciliation	45	Trouble with boss	23
Retirement	45	Change in work hours, conditions	20
Changes in family member's health	44	Change in residence	20
Pregnancy	40	Change in schools	20
Sex difficulties	39	Change in recreational habits	19
Addition to family	39	Change in religious activities	19
Business readjustment	39	Change in social activities	18
Change in financial status	38	Mortgage or loan under $10,000	17
Death of a close friend	37	Change in sleeping habits	16
Change to different line of work	36	Change in # of family gatherings	15
Change in # of marital arguments	35	Change in eating habits	15
Mortgage or loan over $10,000	31	Vacation	13
Foreclosure of mortgage or loan	30	Christmas season	12
Change in work responsibilities	29	Minor violation of the law	11

Source: Reprinted from *Journal of Psychosomatic Research, 11*(2), T. H. Holmes and R. H. Rahe, "The Social Readjustment Rating Scale," 1967, with permission from Elsevier.

run, build social events around food, and eat as a reaction to stress. Many new students find that the "freshman 15"—referring to 15 pounds that people say freshmen tend to gain in the first year of school—is an unpleasant reality.

Stress levels can help or hinder performance.

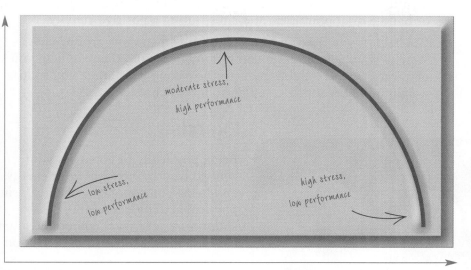

Performance or efficiency

moderate stress,
high performance

low stress,
low performance

high stress,
low performance

Stress or anxiety

Source: From *Your Maximum Mind* by Herbert Benson M.D., copyright © 1987 by Random House, Inc. Used by permission of Times Books, a division of Random House, Inc.

The two key ideas for healthy eating are *balance* (varying your diet) and *moderation* (eating reasonable amounts). It can be tough, however, to eat in a balanced and moderate way when unbalanced and overly generous food choices are consistently available to you. To incorporate these concepts into your day-to-day life, break them down into practical actions like the following:

- **Target your ideal weight.** Look for this information on Internet sites such as the Centers for Disease Control, which has a calculator for body mass index, or BMI, at www.cdc.gov/nccdphp/dnpa/bmi/index.htm.

  > BODY MASS INDEX (BMI)
  >
  > A number calculated from your weight and height, which provides a reliable indicator of body fatness.

- **Vary what you eat.** Focus especially on getting a variety of vegetables and fruits into your daily diet (take a look at the new "food pyramid" at www.mypyramid.gov).

- **Limit fat and cholesterol.** Watch the fat and cholesterol content of your food choices. When you can, minimize your intake of fried foods and foods that contain *trans fats*.

- **Cut down on sugar and alcohol.** Try to limit foods that contain mostly empty calories, like candy and sugar soda. Be aware that many alcoholic beverages are surprisingly calorie-heavy, especially if they are made with sweet mixers.

- **Reduce portion size.** A "serving" of cooked pasta is about one-half cup, for example, and cheese about 1.2 ounces. When you eat out, take home what you don't finish, or ask for a half portion.

- **Identify "emotional triggers" for your eating.** If you eat to relieve stress or handle disappointment, try substituting a positive activity.

- **Get help.** If you need to lose weight, find a support group, such as Weight Watchers or an on-campus organization, that can help you stay on target. Set reasonable goals for how long it will take you to lose weight and how much you plan to lose each week.

Exercise

Being physically fit enhances your general health, increases your energy, and helps you cope with stress. During physical activity, the brain releases *endorphins*, chemical compounds that have a positive and calming effect on the body.

College athletes use daily exercise as a stress reliever. "If I didn't have swimming, a place to release my academic stress, I don't think I'd be as effective in the classroom or studying at night," says Larisa Kindell, a senior and co-captain of Wesleyan University's swimming team. She credits her athletic routine with helping her build discipline and motivation.[2] Always check with a physician before beginning an exercise program.

There are many ways to get exercise in college. Some students, like these, participate in sports teams, sports clubs, or intramurals for the social experience as well as the workout.

Types of Exercise

There are three general categories of exercises. The type you choose depends on your exercise goals, available equipment, your time and fitness level, and other factors.

- *Cardiovascular training* strengthens your heart and lung capacity. Examples include running, swimming, in-line skating, aerobic dancing, and biking.

- *Strength training* strengthens different muscle groups. Examples include using weight machines and free weights and doing push-ups and abdominal crunches.

- *Flexibility training* increases muscle flexibility. Examples include stretching and yoga.

Busy students often have trouble getting to the gym, even when there is a fully equipped athletic center on campus. Even in the busiest weeks, you can stay on the move by walking to classes and meetings, using the stairs in buildings, or using home exercise equipment.

Sleep

College students, overwhelmed with responsibilities, often feel that they have no choice but to prioritize schoolwork over sleep. Although research indicates that students need eight to nine hours of sleep a night to function well, studies show that students average only six to seven hours—and often get much less.[3] Inadequate sleep hinders your ability to concentrate, raises stress levels, and makes you more susceptible to illness. It can also increase your risk of auto accidents. According to Dr. Tracy Kuo at the Stanford Sleep Disorders Clinic, "A sleepy driver is just as dangerous as a drunk driver."[4]

For the sake of your health and your GPA, find a way to get the sleep you need. Sleep expert Gregg D. Jacobs has the following practical suggestions for improving sleep habits:[5]

- Reduce consumption of alcohol and caffeine.
- Exercise regularly.
- Take naps.
- Be consistent with wake times and bed times.
- Complete tasks an hour or so before sleep.
- Establish a comfortable sleeping environment.

Sleep is crucial for both stress reduction and normal development. The *Multiple Intelligence Strategies* grid on page 260 presents different strategies for managing the stress of writing a final paper in a human development course, many of which involve time management tools that will help a student avoid writing the whole paper during a last-minute all-nighter.

It is not enough to have a healthy body alone, however. Your well-being also depends on a healthy mind.

Recognize Mental Health Problems

Staying positive about who you are, making hopeful plans for the future, and building resilience to cope with setbacks will all help you target positive mental health. However, some people experience emotional disorders that make it more difficult than usual to cope with life's stressful situations. If you recognize yourself in any of the following descriptions, take practical steps to improve your health. Most student health centers and campus counseling centers provide medical and psychological help or referrals for students with emotional disorders.

Depression. A *depressive disorder* is an illness that requires a medical evaluation and is treatable. Symptoms include constant sadness or anxiety, loss of interest in activities that you normally like, eating too much or too little, and low self-esteem. Depression can have a genetic, psychological, physiological, or environmental cause, or a combination. In extreme cases, depression can lead to suicide.

Anorexia nervosa. People with anorexia nervosa restrict their eating and become dangerously underweight. They may also engage in overexercising, vomiting, and abuse of diuretics and laxatives. Anorexia-induced starvation may cause loss of menstrual periods in women and impotence in men.

MULTIPLE INTELLIGENCE STRATEGIES

FOR STRESS MANAGEMENT

APPLY DIFFERENT INTELLIGENCES TO REDUCE THE STRESS OF WRITING A FINAL PAPER IN HUMAN DEVELOPMENT.

INTELLIGENCE	USE MI STRATEGIES *to manage stress*	APPLY MI STRESS-MANAGEMENT STRATEGIES *to handle a final paper on the stages of physical development in infancy**
Verbal-Linguistic	• Keep a journal of what situations, people, or events cause stress. • Write letters or e-mail friends about your problems.	• Early in the writing process, summarize in writing the different reflex reactions common in normal newborns.
Logical-Mathematical	• Think through problems using a problem-solving process, and devise a detailed plan. • Analyze the negative and positive effects that may result from a stressful situation.	• Analyze the functions of each of the six different states of being in infants: crying, waking activity, alert activity, drowsiness, irregular sleep, and regular sleep.
Bodily-Kinesthetic	• Choose a physical activity that helps you release tension—running, yoga, team sports—and do it regularly. • Plan physical activities during free time—go for a hike, take a bike ride, go dancing with friends.	• When you need a break from writing or research, re-create the classic experiment to test infants' depth perception, known as the "visual cliff."
Visual-Spatial	• Enjoy things that appeal to you visually—visit an exhibit, see an art film, shoot photos with your camera. • Use a visual organizer to plan out a solution to a stressful problem.	• Create a visual aid comparing the development of a full-term infant with that of a premature infant.
Interpersonal	• Talk with people who care about you and are supportive. • Shift your focus by being a good listener to others who need to talk about their stresses.	• Interview the parents of a premature infant to learn about the special challenges the family faced during the first year.
Intrapersonal	• Schedule down time when you can think through what is causing stress. • Allow yourself five minutes a day of meditation where you visualize a positive way in which you want a stressful situation to resolve.	• Separate your scheduled working times over a period of weeks so that you have time to contemplate individual development topics in between sessions.
Musical	• Listen to music that relaxes, inspires, and/or energizes you. • Write a song about what is bothering you.	• Listen to lullabies from different countries. Compare and contrast melody and rhythm. Link observations to what you know about infants' auditory systems.
Naturalistic	• See if the things that cause you stress fall into categories that can give you helpful ideas about how to handle situations. • If nature is calming for you, interact with it—spend time outdoors, watch nature-focused TV, read books or articles on nature or science.	• Visit the newborns at your local hospital during visiting hours. Search for common characteristics—for example, reflex responses and state of wakefulness or sleep. Create a chart to report your findings.

* For information on the newborn, see Robert S. Feldman, *Child Development*, 4th ed., Upper Saddle River, NJ: Prentice Hall, 2007.

Take Steps Toward Better Health

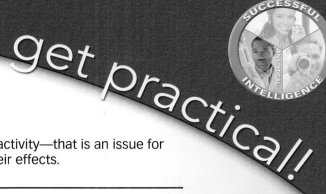

Name a topic—eating, drinking, sleeping, sexual activity—that is an issue for you. Identify behaviors and attitudes and note their effects.

Issue: _____

Behavior: _____

Attitude: _____

Effects: _____

Choose two actions to take—one to improve your attitude and one to improve your behavior—that you think would have the most positive effect for you. Commit to these actions with specific plans.

Attitude improvement plan: _____

Behavior improvement plan: _____

Finally, find a resource at your school that can support your effort to improve your health. Write the name, location, hours, phone number, and any other pertinent information:

Resource: _____

How it can help: _____

Pertinent information: _____

Other effects of anorexia nervosa include hair loss, loss of cognitive functioning, organ and bone damage, heart damage, and death.

Bulimia nervosa. People with bulimia engage in "binge episodes," which involve eating excessive amounts of foods and feeling out of control. Following the binge, the person feels remorseful and attempts to purge the calories through self-induced vomiting, laxative abuse, excessive exercise, or fasting. Negative effects of bulimia can include tooth enamel erosion, damage to the esophagus and digestive tract, and electrolyte imbalance, which can lead to heart failure.

Binge eating disorder. People with binge eating disorder eat large amounts of food and feel out of control, similar to those with bulimia, but they do not purge after a binge episode. They also tend to eat unusually fast, eat in secret, eat until they feel uncomfortably full, and feel ashamed of their eating behavior. Binge eaters may suffer from health problems associated with obesity.

Situations involving substances or sex are sources of stress for many college students. Use the following information and your successful intelligence to make decisions that are right for you.

How Can You Make Effective Decisions About Substances and Sex?

You are responsible for the choices you make regarding alcohol, tobacco, drugs, and sexual practices. As you read the information in this section, think about the effects of your actions on yourself and others, and continually look for ways to make positive, life-affirming choices.

Alcohol

Alcohol is a depressant that slows vital body functions and is the most frequently abused drug on campus. Even a few drinks affect thinking and muscle coordination. Heavy drinking can damage the liver, the digestive system, and brain cells and can impair the central nervous system. Prolonged use also leads to addiction, making it seem impossible to quit. In addition, alcohol contributes to the deaths of 100,000 people every year through both alcohol-related illnesses and accidents involving drunk drivers.[6]

> **ADDICTION**
> *The compulsive need for a habit-forming substance.*

Of all alcohol consumption, binge drinking is associated with the greatest problems and is consistently an issue on college campuses. Here are statistics from recent surveys:

> **BINGE DRINKING**
> *Having five or more drinks (for men) or four or more (for women) at one sitting.*

- Of respondents 18–25 years of age, 42% reported binge drinking in the month before the National Survey on Drug Use and Health (NSDUH). Of respondents 26–34 years of age, 33% reported binge drinking in the month before the survey.[7]

- In one survey, 8 of 10 students who do not binge-drink reported experiencing "secondhand effects" of others' binge drinking, including vandalism, sexual assault or unwanted sexual advances, or interrupted sleep or study.[8]

- Students who binge-drink are more likely to miss classes or work, perform poorly in class and on academic projects, experience physical problems (memory loss, headache, stomach issues), become depressed, and engage in unplanned or unsafe sexual activity.[9]

From what Darra Clark, a freshman at a large university in the Southwest, has seen, it is not possible to be a successful student if you drink too much. You can't do well in school and have friends if you "get drunk and stoned out of your gourd every night," she explains. "I think that the whole drinking scene is probably the thing I've found most appalling about college (our student handbook specifically outlaws beer funnels, for example). The problem, of course, is that drinking becomes a really hard behavior to regulate. . . . Drinking and drugs have done some awful things to some of the kids I've seen around here."[10]

Tobacco

The NSDUH found that nearly 30.6% of full-time college students reported smoking at least once in the month before they were surveyed, and 42.7%

of students attending less than full-time had smoked at least once within the previous month.[11]

When people smoke they inhale nicotine, a highly addictive drug found in all tobacco products. Nicotine's immediate effects may include an increase in blood pressure and heart rate, sweating, and throat irritation. Long-term effects may include high blood pressure, bronchitis and emphysema, stomach ulcers, and heart disease. Pregnant women who smoke increase their risk of having infants with low birth weight, premature births, or stillbirths. Furthermore, inhaling tobacco smoke damages the cells that line the air sacs of the lungs, potentially leading to lung cancer or mouth, throat, and other cancers (lung cancer causes more deaths in the United States than any other type of cancer).[12]

If you smoke regularly, you can quit by being motivated, persevering, and seeking help. The positive effects of quitting—increased life expectancy, lung capacity, and energy, as well as significant financial savings—may inspire any smoker to consider making a lifestyle change. Weigh your options and make a responsible choice.

Drugs

The NSDUH reports that more than 37% of college students surveyed had used illicit drugs in the year prior to the survey.[13] College students may use drugs to relieve stress, to be accepted by peers, or just to try something new.

In most cases, the negative consequences of drug use outweigh any temporary high. Drug use violates federal, state, and local laws, and you may be arrested, tried, and imprisoned for possessing even a small amount of drugs. You can jeopardize your reputation, your student status, and your ability to get a job if you are caught using drugs or if drug use impairs your performance. Finally, long-term drug use can damage your body and mind. Key 8.3 has comprehensive information about the most commonly used illicit drugs.

You are responsible for analyzing the potential consequences of what you introduce into your body. Ask questions like the following: Why do I want to do this? Am I taking drugs to escape from other problems? What positive and negative effects might my behavior have? Why do others want me to take drugs, and what do I really think of these people? How would my drug use affect the people in my life? The more carefully you analyze your situation, the more likely you will be to make choices that are in your own best interest.

Facing Addiction

People with addictions have lost control. If you think you may be addicted, take the initiative to seek help. Because substances often cause physical and chemical changes and psychological dependence, habits are tough to break and quitting may involve a painful withdrawal. Asking for help isn't an admission of failure but a courageous move to reclaim your life. The following resources can help you generate options and develop practical plans for recovery:

- **Counseling and medical care.** You can find help from school-based, private, government-sponsored, or workplace-sponsored resources. Ask

KEY 8.3   Drugs have potent effects on the user.

DRUG	DRUG CATEGORY	USERS MAY FEEL ...	POTENTIAL PHYSICAL EFFECTS, SHORT-TERM AND LONG-TERM	DANGER OF DEPENDENCE
Cocaine (also called *coke, blow, snow*) and **crack cocaine** (also called *crack* or *rock*)	Stimulant	Alert, stimulated, excited, energetic, confident	Nervousness, mood swings, sexual problems, stroke or convulsions, psychoses, paranoia, coma at large doses	Strong
Alcohol	Depressant	Sedated, relaxed, loose	Impaired brain function, impaired reflexes and judgment, cirrhosis, impaired blood production, greater risk of cancer, heart attack, and stroke	Strong with regular, heavy use
Marijuana and **hashish** (also called *pot, weed, herb*)	Cannabinol	Euphoric, mellow, little sensation of time, paranoid	Impaired judgment and coordination, bronchitis and asthma, lung and throat cancers, anxiety, lack of energy and motivation, hormone and fertility problems	Moderate
Heroin (also called *smack, dope, horse*) and **codeine**	Opiate	Warm, relaxed, without pain, without anxiety	Infection of organs, inflammation of the heart, convulsions, abscesses, risk of needle-transmitted diseases such as hepatitis and HIV	Strong, with heavy use
Lysergic acid diethylamide (LSD) (also called *acid, blotter, trips*)	Hallucinogen	Heightened sensual perception, hallucinations, distortions of sight and sound, little sense of time	Impaired brain function, paranoia, agitation and confusion, flashbacks	Insubstantial
Hallucinogenic mushrooms (psilocybin mushrooms or *amanita muscaria*) (also called *shrooms, magic mushrooms*)	Hallucinogen	Strong emotions, hallucinations, distortions of sight and sound, "out of body" experience	Paranoia, agitation, poisoning	Insubstantial
Glue, aerosols (also called *whippets, poppers, rush*)	Inhalants	Giddy, light-headed, dizzy, excited	Damage to brain, liver, lungs, and kidneys, suffocation, heart failure	Insubstantial

DRUG	DRUG CATEGORY	USERS MAY FEEL ...	POTENTIAL PHYSICAL EFFECTS, SHORT-TERM AND LONG-TERM	DANGER OF DEPENDENCE
Ecstasy (also called *X, XTC, vitamin E*)	Stimulant	Heightened sensual perception, relaxed, clear, fearless	Fatigue, anxiety, depression, heart arrhythmia, hyperthermia from lack of fluid intake during use	Insubstantial
Ephedrine (also called *chi powder, zest*)	Stimulant	Energetic	Anxiety, elevated blood pressure, heart palpitations, memory loss, stroke, psychosis, insomnia	Strong
Gamma hydroxyl butyrate (GHB) (also called *G, liquid ecstasy, goop*)	Depressant	Uninhibited, relaxed, euphoric	Anxiety, vertigo, increased heart rate, delirium, agitation	Strong
Ketamine (also called *K, Special K, vitamin K*)	Anesthetic	Dreamy, floating, having an "out of body" sensation, numb	Neuroses, disruptions in consciousness, reduced ability to move	Strong
OxyContin (also called *Oxy, OC, legal heroin*)	Analgesic (containing opiate)	Relaxed, detached, without pain or anxiety	Overdose death can result when users ingest or inhale crushed time-release pills, or take them in conjunction with alcohol or narcotics	Moderate, with long-term use
Anabolic steroids (also called *roids, juice, hype*)	Steroid	Increased muscle strength and physical performance, energetic	Stunted growth, mood swings, male-pattern baldness, breast development (in men) or body hair development (in women), liver damage, insomnia, aggression, irritability	Insubstantial
Methamphet-amine (also called *meth, speed, crank*)	Stimulant	Euphoric, confident, alert, energetic	Seizures, heart attack, strokes, vein damage (if injected), sleeplessness, hallucinations, high blood pressure, paranoia, psychoses, depression, anxiety, loss of appetite	Strong, especially if taken by smoking

Source: "Drug Facts," 2007, SafetyFirst, Drug Policy Alliance (www.safety1st.org/index.php?option=com_content&task=view&id=20&Itemid=37).

your school's counseling or health center, your personal physician, or a local hospital for a referral.

- **Detoxification ("detox") centers.** If you have a severe addiction, you may need a controlled environment where you can separate yourself completely from drugs or alcohol.

- **Support groups.** Alcoholics Anonymous (AA) is the premier support group for alcoholics. AA has led to other support groups for addicts, such as Narcotics Anonymous (NA). Many schools have AA, NA, or other group sessions on campus.

Another important aspect of both physical and mental health involves being comfortable with your sexuality and making wise sexual decisions. Choosing birth control and avoiding sexually transmitted infections have short- and long-term consequences for the rest of your life.

Sexual Decision Making

What sexuality means to you and the role it plays in your life are your own business. However, the physical act of sex goes beyond the private realm. Individual sexual conduct can result in an unexpected pregnancy and in contracting or passing on a sexually transmitted infection (STI). These consequences affect everyone involved in the sexual act and, often, their families as well.

Your self-respect depends on making choices that maintain health and safety—yours as well as those of the person with whom you are involved. Analyze sexual issues carefully, weighing the positive and negative effects of your choices.

Birth Control

Using birth control is a choice, and it is not for everyone. Evaluate the pros and cons of each option for yourself and your partner. Consider cost, ease of use, reliability, comfort, and protection against STIs. Communicate with your partner, and together make a choice that is comfortable for both of you. For more information, check your library, the Internet, or a bookstore; talk to your doctor; or ask a counselor at the student health center. Key 8.4 describes established methods, with effectiveness percentages and STI prevention based on proper and regular use.

Sexually Transmitted Infections

STIs spread through sexual contact (intercourse or other sexual activity that involves contact with the genitals). All are highly contagious. The only birth control methods that offer protection are the male and female condoms (latex or polyurethane only), which prevent skin-to-skin contact. Most STIs can also spread to infants of infected mothers during birth. Have a doctor examine any irregularity or discomfort as soon as you detect it. Key 8.5 describes common STIs.

AIDS and HIV

The most serious STI is AIDS (acquired immunodeficiency syndrome), which is caused by the human immunodeficiency virus (HIV). Not everyone who tests positive for HIV will develop AIDS, but AIDS has no cure and

Make an educated decision about birth control.

METHOD	APPROXIMATE EFFECTIVENESS	PREVENTS STIs?	DESCRIPTION
Abstinence	100%	Only if no sexual activity occurs	Just saying no. No intercourse means no risk of pregnancy. However, alternative modes of sexual activity can still spread STIs.
Condom	85% (95% with spermicide)	Yes, if made of latex	A sheath that fits over the penis and prevents sperm from entering the vagina.
Diaphragm, cervical cap, or shield	85%	No	A bendable rubber cap that fits over the cervix and pelvic bone inside the vagina (the cervical cap and shield are smaller and fit over the cervix only). The diaphragm and cervical cap must be fitted initially by a gynecologist. All must be used with a spermicide.
Oral contra-ceptives ("the Pill")	99% with perfect use, 92% for typical users	No	A dosage of hormones taken daily by a woman, preventing the ovaries from releasing eggs. Side effects can include headache, weight gain, and increased chances of blood clotting. Various brands and dosages; must be prescribed by a gynecologist.
Injectable contraceptives (Depo-Provera)	97%	No	An injection that a woman must receive from a doctor every few months. Possible side effects may resemble those of oral contraceptives.
Vaginal ring (NuvaRing)	92%	No	A ring inserted into the vagina that releases hormones. Must be replaced monthly. Possible side effects may resemble those of oral contraceptives.
Spermicidal foams, jellies, inserts	71% if used alone	No	Usually used with diaphragms or condoms to enhance effectiveness, they have an ingredient that kills sperm cells (but not STIs). They stay effective for a limited period of time after insertion.
Intrauterine device (IUD)	99%	No	A small coil of wire inserted into the uterus by a gynecologist (who must also remove it). Prevents fertilized eggs from implanting in the uterine wall. May or may not have a hormone component. Possible side effects include increased or abnormal bleeding.
Tubal ligation	Nearly 100%	No	Surgery for women that cuts and ties the fallopian tubes, preventing eggs from traveling to the uterus. Difficult and expensive to reverse. Recommended for those who do not want any, or any more, children.
Vasectomy	Nearly 100%	No	Surgery for men that blocks the tube that delivers sperm to the penis. Like tubal ligation, difficult to reverse and only recommended for those who don't want any, or any more, children.
Rhythm method	Variable	No	Abstaining from intercourse during the ovulation segment of the woman's menstrual cycle. Can be difficult to time and may not account for cycle irregularities.
Withdrawal	Variable	No	Pulling the penis out of the vagina before ejaculation. Unreliable, because some sperm can escape in the fluid released prior to ejaculation. Dependent on a controlled partner.

Source: "Birth Control Options," December 22, 2005, Mayo Clinic (www.mayoclinic.com/health/birth-control/BI99999/PAGE=BI00005).

Sometimes, college students get involved in potentially unsafe activities because it seems like there isn't anything else to do. Use your creativity to find enjoyable activities to choose from when you hang out with friends. Check your resources: What possibilities can you find at your student union, student activities center, college or local arts organizations, athletic organizations, various clubs, nature groups? Could you go hiking? Paint pottery? Check out a baseball game? Run a 5K? Try a new kind of cuisine? Volunteer at a children's hospital ward? See a play?

Expand your horizons. List here 10 specific activities available to you:

1. _____   6. _____
2. _____   7. _____
3. _____   8. _____
4. _____   9. _____
5. _____   10. _____

results in eventual death. Medical science continues to develop drugs to combat AIDS and its related illnesses. The drugs can cause severe side effects, however, and none are cures.

HIV is transmitted through two types of bodily fluids: fluids associated with sex (semen and vaginal fluids) and blood. People have acquired HIV through sexual relations, by sharing hypodermic needles for drug use, and by receiving infected blood transfusions. You cannot become infected unless one of those fluids is involved. Therefore, it is unlikely you can contract HIV from toilet seats, hugging, kissing, or sharing a glass. Other than not having sex at all, a latex condom is the best defense against AIDS. Although some people dislike using condoms, it's a small price to pay for preserving your life.

To be safe, have an HIV test done at your doctor's office or at a government-sponsored clinic. Your school's health department may also administer HIV tests, and home HIV tests are available over the counter. Consider requiring that any sexual partner be tested as well. If you are infected, first inform all sexual partners and seek medical assistance. Then, contact support organizations in your area or call the National AIDS Hotline at 1-800-342-AIDS.

The analytical, creative, and practical thinking skills that help you improve your health are also the keys to more effective money management.

KEY 8.5 To stay safe, know these facts about sexually transmitted infections.

DISEASE	SYMPTOMS	HEALTH PROBLEMS IF UNTREATED	TREATMENTS
Chlamydia	Discharge, painful urination, swollen or painful joints, change in menstrual periods for women	Can cause pelvic inflammatory disease (PID) in women, which can lead to sterility or ectopic pregnancies; infection; miscarriage or premature birth.	Curable with full course of antibiotics; avoid sex until treatment is complete.
Gonorrhea	Discharge, burning while urinating	Can cause PID, swelling of testicles and penis, arthritis, skin problems, infections.	Usually curable with antibiotics; however, certain strains are becoming resistant to medication.
Genital herpes	Blisterlike itchy sores in the genital area, headache, fever, chills	Symptoms may subside and then reoccur, often in response to high stress levels; carriers can transmit the virus even when it is dormant.	No cure; some medications, such as Acyclovir, reduce and help heal the sores and may shorten recurring outbreaks.
Syphilis	A genital sore lasting one to five weeks, followed by a rash, fatigue, fever, sore throat, headaches, swollen glands	If it lasts over four years, it can cause blindness, destruction of bone, insanity, or heart failure; can cause death or deformity of a child born to an infected woman.	Curable with full course of antibiotics.
Human papilloma-virus (HPV, or genital warts)	Genital itching and irritation, small clusters of warts	Can increase risk of cervical cancer in women; virus may remain in body and cause recurrences even when warts are removed.	Treatable with drugs applied to warts or various kinds of wart removal surgery. Vaccine (Gardasil) newly available; most effective when given to women before exposure to HPV.
Hepatitis B	Fatigue, poor appetite, vomiting, jaundice, hives	Some carriers will have few symptoms; others may develop chronic liver disease that may lead to other diseases of the liver.	No cure; some will recover, some will not. Bed rest may help ease symptoms. Vaccine is available.

How Can You Manage Money Effectively?

According to the American Psychological Association, nearly three out of four Americans cite money as the number one stressor in their lives.[14] Adding the high cost of college tuition to the normal list of financial obligations means that, for the vast majority of college students, money is tight. Finances can be especially problematic for self-supporting students who may have to cover living and family expenses while coming up with funds for tuition, books, and other college fees.

Analyze What Money Means in Your Life

The way you handle money and the level of importance it has for you reflects your values, your goals, and your self-image. You might be a spender or a saver. You might think about money only in the present tense, or you might frequently plan for the future. You might charge everything, use cash only, or do something in between. You might measure your success in life in terms of how much money you have or define your worth in nonmaterial terms.

Approaching money management with successful intelligence can help relieve money-related stress and increase control. Engage your successful intelligence in this process by analyzing who you are as a money manager. In your analysis, consider these influences on your money management:

- **Your values.** You tend to spend money on what you think is most important.

- **Your personality.** Thinkers may focus on planning; Organizers may balance bank accounts down to the penny; Givers may prioritize spending money to help others; Adventurers may spend impulsively and deal with the consequences later.

- **Your culture.** Some cultures see money as a collective resource to be shared within families, whereas others prize individual accumulation as a sign of independence.

- **Your family and peer group.** You tend to either follow or react against how your parents and immediate family handle money. Your classmates and friends also influence your attitudes and behavior.

- **Other factors** such as ethnicity, class, level of education, and marital status can also play a role in how you manage money.

Money coach Connie Kilmark notes that you cannot change how you handle money until you analyze your attitudes and behaviors. "If managing money was just about math and the numbers, everyone would know how to manage their finances sometime around the fifth grade," she says.[15] When you take an honest look at how you feel about money, you can make more effective financial decisions based on what works best for you.

Continue to engage your successful intelligence as you use analytical, creative, and practical skills to budget and manage credit card use.

Learn to Manage Income and Expenses Through Budgeting

BUDGET

A plan to coordinate resources and expenditures; a set of goals regarding money.

Creating a practical monthly budget that works requires that you tap every aspect of successful intelligence. You gather information about your resources (money flowing in) and expenditures (money flowing out) and *analyze* the difference. Next, you come up with *creative ideas* about how you can make changes. Finally, you take *practical action* to adjust spending or earning so that you come out even or ahead.

Your biggest expense right now is probably the cost of your education, including tuition and room and board. However, that expense may not hit you fully until after you graduate and begin to pay back your student loans. For now, include in your budget only the part of the cost of your education you are paying while you are in school.

Figure Out Your Income

Add up all of the money you receive during the year—the actual after-tax money you have available to pay your bills. Common sources of income include the following:

- Take-home pay from a regular full-time or part-time job during the school year
- Take-home pay from summer and holiday employment
- Money you earn as part of a work-study program
- Money you receive from your parents or other relatives for your college expenses
- Scholarships or grants

If you have savings specifically earmarked for your education, decide how much you will withdraw every month for school-related expenses.

Figure Out What You Spend

Start by recording every check or electronic withdrawal going toward fixed expenses like rent, phone, and Internet service. Then, over the next month, record personal expenditures in a small notebook. Indicate any expenditure more than five dollars, making sure to count smaller expenditures if they are frequent (for example, a bus pass for a month, coffee or lunch purchases per week).

Some expenses, like automobile and health insurance, may be billed only a few times a year. In these cases, convert the expense to monthly by dividing the yearly cost by 12. Common expenses include the following:

- Rent or mortgage
- Tuition that you are paying right now (the portion remaining after all forms of financial aid, including loans, scholarships, and grants are taken into account)
- Books, lab fees, and other educational expenses
- Regular bills (electric, gas, oil, phone, water)
- Food, clothing, toiletries, and household supplies
- Child care
- Transportation and auto expenses (gas, maintenance)
- Credit cards and other payments on credit (car payments)
- Insurance (health, auto, homeowner's or renter's, life)
- Entertainment (cable TV, movies, eating out, books and magazines, music downloads)
- Computer-related expenses, including the cost of your online service
- Miscellaneous unplanned expenses

Use the total of all your monthly expenses as a baseline for other months, realizing that your expenditures will vary depending on what is happening in your life and even the season (for example, the cost to heat your home may be much greater in the winter than in the summer).

Evaluate the Difference

Focusing again on your current situation, subtract your monthly expenses from your monthly income. Ideally, you have money left over—to save or to spend. However, if you are spending more than you take in, use your analytical thinking skills to ask some focused questions.

- **Examine your expenses.** Did you forget to budget for recurring expenses such as the cost of semiannual dental visits? Or was your budget derailed by an emergency expense?

- **Examine your spending patterns and priorities.** Did you spend money wisely during the month, or did you overspend on luxuries?

- **Examine your income.** Do you bring in enough money? Do you need another source?

Adjust Expenses or Income

After you have analyzed the causes of any budget shortfall, brainstorm solutions that address those causes. Solutions can involve either increasing income or decreasing spending. To increase income, consider taking a part-time job, increasing hours at a current job, or finding scholarships or grants. To decrease spending, prioritize your expenditures and trim the ones you don't need to make.

Rely on your dominant multiple intelligences to plan your budget. For example, whereas logical-mathematical learners may take to a classic detail-oriented budgeting plan, visual learners may want to create a budget chart, or bodily-kinesthetic learners may want to make budgeting more tangible by dumping receipts into a big jar and tallying them at the end of the month.

Successful Intelligence Connections Online

Listen to author Sarah Kravits describe how to use analytical, creative, and practical intelligence to find the best possible part-time job for you.

Go to the *Keys to Success* Companion Website at www.prenhall.com/carter to listen or download as a podcast.

Manage Credit Card Use

College students often receive dozens of credit card offers. These offers—and the cards that go along with them—are a double-edged sword: They are a handy alternative to cash and can help build a strong credit history if used appropriately, but they also can plunge you into a hole of debt. Recent statistics from a survey of undergraduates illustrate the situation:[16]

- 42% of students in their first year of college hold a credit card. By the final year, 90% of students have at least one, and 56% have four or more.

- Students who hold credit cards carry an average outstanding balance of $2,169.

- Just under half of student credit card holders carry a balance of over $1,000. Nearly 25% of students carry over $3,000 in debt, and 7% carry over $7,000.

- 74% of students report charging school supplies on their cards. Nearly 24% report using their cards to pay tuition.

Often cash-poor, college students charge books and tuition on cards (or "plastic") as well as expenses like car repair, food, and clothes. Before they know it, their debt becomes unmanageable. It's hard to notice trouble brewing when you don't see your wallet taking a hit.

How Credit Cards Work

Every time you charge a textbook, a present, or a pair of pants, you are creating a debt that must be repaid. The credit card issuer earns money by charging interest, often 18% or higher, on unpaid balances. Debt can mount fast. To avoid unmanageable debt that can lead to a personal financial crisis, learn as much as you can about credit cards, starting with the important concepts in Key 8.6. Use credit wisely while you are still in school. The habits you learn today can make a difference in your financial future.

Managing Credit Card Debt

Prevention is the best line of defense. To avoid excessive debt, ask yourself questions before charging: Would I buy it if I had to pay cash? Can I pay off the balance in full at the end of the billing cycle? If I buy this, what purchases will I have to forgo?

The majority of U.S. citizens have some level of debt, and many people go through periods when they have a hard time paying bills. Falling behind on payments, however, could result in a poor credit rating that will make it difficult to get a future loan or finance a large purchase. Particular organizations such as the National Foundation for Credit Counseling (www.nfcc .org) or American Financial Solutions (1-888-282-5899) can help you solve credit problems. See the end of the chapter for more resources.

The most basic way to stay in control is to pay bills regularly and on time. On credit card bills, pay at least the minimum amount due. If you get into trouble, address the problem immediately to minimize damages. Call the creditor and see if you can pay your debt gradually using a payment plan. Finally, examine what got you into trouble and avoid it in the future if you can. Cut up a credit card or two if you have too many.

CREDITOR

A person or company to whom a debt is owed, usually money.

You have been thinking through all kinds of financial decisions. In a sense, your career is part of your financial decision making, because it is likely to be the primary means for earning a living. As you will see next, your earnings are only one factor in choosing a career.

How Can You Prepare for Career Success?

Your career reflects your values and talents and provides the income you need to support yourself and your family in the years ahead. As you read this section, keep in mind that all of the skills you acquire in college—thinking, teamwork, writing, goal setting, and others—prepare you for workplace success.

KEY 8.6

Learn to be a smart credit consumer.

WHAT TO KNOW ABOUT . . .	. . . AND HOW TO USE WHAT YOU KNOW
Account balance—a dollar amount that includes any unpaid balance, new purchases and cash advances, finance charges, and fees. Updated monthly.	Charge only what you can afford to pay at the end of the month. Keep track of your balance. Hold on to receipts and call customer service if you have questions.
Annual fee—the yearly cost that some companies charge for owning a card.	Look for cards without an annual fee or, if you've paid your bills on time, ask your current company to waive the fee.
Annual percentage rate (APR)—the amount of interest charged on your unpaid balance, meaning the cost of credit if you carry a balance in any given month. The higher the APR, the more you pay in finance charges.	Shop around (check www.studentcredit.com). Also, watch out for low, but temporary, introductory rates that skyrocket to over 20% after a few months. Look for *fixed* rates (guaranteed not to change).
Available credit—the unused portion of your credit line, updated monthly on your bill.	It is important to have credit available for emergencies, so avoid charging to the limit.
Cash advance—an immediate loan, in the form of cash, from the credit card company. You are charged interest immediately and may also pay a separate transaction fee.	Use a cash advance only in emergencies because the finance charges start as soon as you complete the transaction. It is a very expensive way to borrow money.
Credit limit—the debt ceiling the card company places on your account (e.g., $1,500). The total owed, including purchases, cash advances, finance charges, and fees, cannot exceed this limit.	Credit card companies generally set low credit limits for college students. Many students get around this limit by owning more than one card, which increases the credit available but most likely increases problems as well.
Delinquent account—an account that is not paid on time or for which the minimum payment has not been met.	Avoid having a delinquent account at all costs. Not only will you be charged substantial late fees, but you also risk losing your good credit rating, affecting your ability to borrow in the future. Delinquent accounts remain part of your credit record for many years.
Due date—the date your payment must be received and after which you will be charged a late fee.	Avoid late fees and finance charges by mailing your payment a week in advance.
Finance charges—the total cost of credit, including interest and service and transaction fees.	The only way to avoid finance charges is to pay your balance in full by the due date.
Minimum payment—the smallest amount you can pay by the statement due date. The amount is set by the credit card company.	Making only the minimum payment each month can result in disaster if you charge more than you can afford. When you make a purchase, think in terms of total cost.
Outstanding balance—the total amount you owe on your card.	If you carry a balance over several months, additional purchases are hit with finance charges. Pay cash instead.
Past due—your account is considered "past due" when you fail to pay the minimum required payment on schedule.	Three credit bureaus note past due accounts on your credit history: Experian, Trans Union, and Equifax. You can contact each bureau for a copy of your credit report to make sure there are no errors.

Investigate Career Paths

The working world changes all the time. You can get an idea of what's out there—and what you think of it all—by exploring potential careers and building knowledge and experience.

Explore potential careers. Career possibilities extend far beyond what you can imagine. Ask instructors, relatives, mentors, and fellow students about careers they are familiar with. Explore job listings, occupation lists, assessments, and other information about careers and companies at your school's career center. Check your library for books on careers or biographies of people who worked in fields that interest you. Look at Key 8.7 for the kinds of analytical questions that will aid your search. You may discover that a wide array of job possibilities exists for most career fields, and that within each job there lies a variety of tasks and skills.

Build knowledge and experience. It's hard to choose the right career path without knowledge or experience. Courses, internships, jobs, and volunteering are four great ways to build both.

- **Courses.** Take a course or two in your areas of interest to determine if you like the material and excel. Find out what courses are required for a major in those areas.

- **Internships.** You can get supervised practical experience in a number of professional fields through an internship. Your career center may list summer or year-round internship opportunities.

- **Jobs.** You may discover career opportunities while earning money at a part-time job. Someone who answers phones for a newspaper company, for example, might be drawn into journalism.

> INTERNSHIP
>
> A temporary work program in which a student can gain supervised practical experience in a particular professional field.

KEY 8.7 Ask questions like these to analyze how a career area or job may fit you.

What can I do in this area that I like and do well?	Do I respect the company or the industry? The product or service?
What are the educational requirements (certificates or degrees, courses)?	Does this company or industry accommodate special needs (child care, sick days, flex time)?
What skills are necessary?	Do I need to belong to a union? What does union membership involve?
What wage or salary and benefits can I expect?	Are there opportunities near where I live (or want to live)?
What personality types are best suited to this kind of work?	What other expectations exist (travel, overtime, etc.)?
What are the prospects for moving up to higher-level positions?	Do I prefer the service or production end of this industry?

You will benefit from thinking creatively, taking the initiative, and avoiding assumptions when considering careers. This woman started her own contracting company. Now the president, she stays directly involved. Here she checks the progress on a roofing project.

- **Volunteering.** Helping others in need can introduce you to careers and increase your experience. Many employers look favorably on volunteering.

Stay on top of change. The working world is always in flux, responding to technological developments, global competition, and other factors, and a growth area today may be declining tomorrow. Check the U.S. Bureau of Labor for updated statistics on the status of various careers. Be aware of trends like increased numbers of temporary employees and "quality of life" benefits such as job sharing and telecommuting. With the information you collect from the media, you can analyze what you are facing in the workplace. Based on your analysis, you can create options for yourself and take practical action.

Consider Your Personality and Strengths

Because who you are as a learner relates closely to who you are as a worker, your assessment results from chapter 3 will give you helpful clues in the search for the right career. The *Multiple Pathways to Learning* assessment on page 73 points to information about your natural strengths and challenges, which can lead you to careers that involve these strengths. Review Key 3.7 on page 86 to see majors and internships that tend to suit different intelligences, and then look at Key 8.8 to see how those intelligences may link up with various careers.

The *Personality Spectrum* assessment in chapter 3 is equally as significant, because it focuses on how you work best with others, and career success depends in large part on your ability to function in a team. Key 8.9 focuses the four dimensions of the Personality Spectrum on career ideas and strategies. Look for your strengths and decide what you may want to keep in mind as you search. Look also at areas of challenge, and try to identify ways to boost your abilities in those areas. Even the most ideal job involves some tasks that are not in your area of comfort.

Use the information in Keys 8.8 and 8.9 as a guide, not a label. Although you may not have all the strengths and challenges indicated by your dominant area, thinking through them will still help you clarify your abilities and interests. In addition, remember that you are capable of change, and with focus and effort you can develop your abilities. Use ideas

KEY 8.8   Multiple intelligences may open doors to careers.

Multiple intelligence	Look into a career as a . . .
Bodily-Kinesthetic	■ Carpenter or draftsman ■ Physical therapist ■ Mechanical engineer ■ Dancer or actor ■ Exercise physiologist
Intrapersonal	■ Research scientist ■ Computer engineer ■ Psychologist ■ Economist ■ Author
Interpersonal	■ Social worker ■ PR or HR rep ■ Sociologist ■ Teacher ■ Nurse
Naturalistic	■ Biochemical engineer ■ Natural scientist (geologist, ecologist, entomologist) ■ Paleontologist ■ Position with environmental group ■ Farmer or farm management
Musical	■ Singer or voice coach ■ Music teacher ■ Record executive ■ Musician or conductor ■ Radio DJ or sound engineer
Logical-Mathematical	■ Doctor or dentist ■ Accountant ■ Attorney ■ Chemist ■ Investment banker
Verbal-Linguistic	■ Author or journalist ■ TV/radio producer ■ Literature or language teacher ■ Business executive ■ Copywriter or editor
Visual-Spatial	■ Graphic artist or illustrator ■ Photographer ■ Architect or interior designer ■ Art museum curator ■ Art teacher ■ Set or retail stylist

KEY 8.9   Personality Spectrum dimensions indicate strengths and challenges.

DIMENSION	STRENGTHS ON THE JOB	CHALLENGES ON THE JOB	LOOK FOR JOBS/CAREERS THAT FEATURE . . .
Thinker	Problem solving Development of ideas Keen analysis of situations Fairness to others Efficiency in working through tasks Innovation of plans and systems Ability to look strategically at the future	A need for private time to think and work A need, at times, to move away from established rules A dislike of sameness—systems that don't change, repetitive tasks Not always being open to expressing thoughts and feelings to others	Some level of solo work/think time Problem solving Opportunity for innovation Freedom to think creatively and to bend the rules Technical work Big-picture strategic planning
Organizer	High level of responsibility Enthusiastic support of social structures Order and reliability Loyalty Ability to follow through on tasks according to requirements Detailed planning skills with competent follow-through Neatness and efficiency	A need for tasks to be clearly, concretely defined A need for structure and stability A preference for less rapid change A need for frequent feedback A need for tangible appreciation Low tolerance for people who don't conform to rules and regulations	Clear, well-laid-out tasks and plans Stable environment with consistent, repeated tasks Organized supervisors Clear structure of how employees interact and report to one another Value of, and reward for, loyalty
Giver	Honesty and integrity Commitment to putting energy toward close relationships with others Finding ways to bring out the best in self and others Peacemaker and mediator Ability to listen well, respect opinions, and prioritize the needs of coworkers	Difficulty in handling conflict, either personal or between others in the work environment Strong need for appreciation and praise Low tolerance for perceived dishonesty or deception Avoidance of people perceived as hostile, cold, or indifferent	Emphasis on teamwork and relationship building Indications of strong and open lines of communication among workers Encouragement of personal expression in the workplace (arrangement of personal space, tolerance of personal celebrations, and so on)
Adventurer	Skillfulness in many different areas Willingness to try new things Ability to take action Hands-on problem-solving skills Initiative and energy Ability to negotiate Spontaneity and creativity	Intolerance of being kept waiting Lack of detail focus Impulsiveness Dislike of sameness and authority Need for freedom, constant change, and constant action Tendency not to consider consequences of actions	A spontaneous atmosphere Less structure, more freedom Adventuresome tasks Situations involving change Encouragement of hands-on problem solving Travel and physical activity Support of creative ideas and endeavors

about strengths and challenges as a starting point for your goals about how you would like to grow.

Know What Employers Want

When you apply for a job, prospective employers look for particular skills and qualities that mark you as a promising candidate. Most employers require you to have a (skillset) that includes specific technical skills, but in the current rapidly changing workplace, more general life skills may be even more crucial to your success. Key 8.10 describes the particular skills

SKILLSET

A combination of the knowledge, talent, and abilities that are needed to perform a specific job.

 **KEY 8.10**

Employers look for candidates with these important skills.

SKILL	WHY IS IT USEFUL?
Communication	Good listening, speaking, and writing skills are keys to working with others, as is being able to adjust to different communication styles.
Analytical thinking	An employee who can analyze choices and challenges, as well as assess the value of new ideas, stands out.
Creativity	The ability to come up with new concepts, plans, and products helps companies improve and innovate.
Practical thinking	No job gets done without employees who can think through a plan for achieving a goal, put it into action, and complete it successfully.
Teamwork	All workers interact with others on the job. Working well with others is essential for achieving workplace goals.
Goal setting	Teams fail if goals are unclear or unreasonable. Employees and company benefit from setting realistic, specific goals and achieving them reliably.
Cultural competence	The workplace is increasingly diverse. An employee who can work with, adjust to, and respect people from different backgrounds and cultures is valuable.
Leadership	The ability to influence and motivate others in a positive way earns respect and career advancement.
Positive attitude	Other employees will gladly work with, and often advance, someone who completes tasks with positive, upbeat energy.
Integrity	Acting with integrity at work—communicating promptly, being truthful and honest, following rules, giving proper notice—enhances value.
Flexibility	The most valuable employees understand the constancy of change and have developed the skills to adapt to its challenge.
Continual learning	The most valuable employees take personal responsibility to stay current in their fields.

and qualities that tell an employer that you are likely to be an efficient and effective employee.

Employers are also drawn to candidates with high levels of emotional intelligence and social intelligence. As you learned in chapter 1, Goleman defines *emotional intelligence* as a combination of personal and social competence (see Key 1.4 on page 22), while *social intelligence* combines social awareness and social facility (see Key 1.5 on page 23). The current emphasis on teamwork has heightened the importance of emotional and social intelligence in the workplace. The more adept you are at working comfortably and productively with others, the more likely you are to succeed.

Searching for a Job—and a Career

Maximize your success by using the resources available to you, knowing the basics about résumés and interviews, and planning strategically. The information in this section will help you right away if you are one of the many who want or need to work while in school.

Use Available Resources

Use your school's career planning and placement office, your networking skills, classified ads, and online services to help you explore possibilities for career areas or specific jobs.

Career planning and placement office. Generally, the career planning and placement office deals with postgraduation job opportunities, whereas the student employment office, along with the financial aid office, has information about working during school. At either location you might find job listings, interview sign-up sheets, and company contact information. The career office may hold frequent informational sessions on different topics. Your school may also sponsor job or career fairs that give you a chance to explore job opportunities. Get acquainted with the career office early in your college career.

NETWORKING

The exchange of information or services among individuals, groups, or institutions.

Networking. The most basic type of **networking**—talking to people about fields and jobs that interest you—is one of the most important job-hunting strategies. Networking **contacts** can answer questions regarding job hunting, job responsibilities and challenges, and salary expectations. You can network with friends and family members, instructors, administrators, counselors, alumni, employers, coworkers, and others.

CONTACT

A person who serves as a carrier or source of information.

Online services and classified ads. Some of the best job listings are in newspapers. Individual ads describe the position available, including background requirements, and provide contact information. The Internet has also exploded into one of the most fruitful sources of job listings. There are many different ways to hunt for a job on the Web:

- Look up career-focused and job listing Web sites such as CareerBuilder .com, Monster.com, BilingualCareer.com, JobBank USA, or Futurestep .com.
- Access job search databases such as the Career Placement Registry.
- Check the Web pages of individual associations and companies, which may post job listings.

If nothing happens right away, keep at it. New job postings appear, new people sign on to look at your résumé. Plus, sites change all the time. Search using the keywords "job sites" or "job search" to see what sites are up (QuintCareers.com has a listing of the top 50 best job sites).

Your Résumé, Cover Letter, and Interview

Information on résumés, cover letters, and interviews fills entire books. You'll find specific sources listed at the end of this chapter. To get you started, here are a few basic tips on giving yourself the best possible chance.

Résumé and cover letter. Design your résumé neatly, using a current and acceptable format (books or your career office can show you some standard formats). Use accurate and truthful information and include keywords related to the job opening or industry. Proofread for errors and have someone else proofread it as well. Type or print it on high-quality paper. Include a brief, to-the-point cover letter along with your résumé that tells the employer what job you are interested in and why he or she should hire you.

The interview. Be clean, neat, and appropriately dressed. Choose a nice pair of shoes—people notice. Bring an extra copy of your résumé and any other materials that you want to show the interviewer, even if you sent a copy ahead of time. Avoid chewing gum or smoking. Offer a confident handshake. Make eye contact. Show your integrity by speaking honestly. After the interview, no matter what the outcome, follow up right away with a formal but pleasant thank-you note.

Be Strategic

With solid resources to support you and information about how to build a résumé and interview well, you can focus on making a practical, personal plan to achieve your career goals. First, create a time line that can illustrate the steps you plan to take toward a specific career goal you want to explore. Working with an advisor, career office employee, or mentor, establish a time frame and write in the steps when you think they should happen. Your path may change, of course; use your time line as a guide rather than as an inflexible plan.

After you establish your time frame, focus on details. Make specific plans for pursuing the jobs or careers that have piqued your interest. Set goals that establish whom you will talk to, what courses you will take, what skills you will work on, what jobs or internships you will investigate, and any other research you need to do.

Organize your approach according to what you need to do and when you have to do it. Do you plan to make three phone calls per day? Will you fill out one job application each week? Keep a record—on 3-by-5 cards, in a computer file, or in a notebook—of the following:

- People you contact
- Companies to which you apply
- Jobs you rule out (for example, a job that becomes unavailable)
- Responses to communications (phone calls to you, interviews, written communications), information about the person who contacted you (name, title), and the time and dates of contact

Keeping accurate records enables you to both chart your progress and maintain a clear picture of the process. If you don't get a job now but another opens up at the same company in a few months, well-kept records will enable you to contact key personnel quickly and efficiently.

How Can You Continue to Activate Your Successful Intelligence?

Throughout this text you have connected analytical, creative, and practical thinking to academic and life skills. You have put them together in order to solve problems and make decisions. You have seen how these skills, used consistently and balanced, can help you succeed.

You are only just beginning your career as a successfully intelligent learner. You will continue to discover the best ways to use your analytical, creative, and practical thinking skills to achieve goals that are meaningful to you. At the end of chapter 1, you completed a self-assessment to examine your levels of development in Robert Sternberg's 20 self-activators. Here are more details to remind you of these characteristics that will keep you moving ahead toward your goals. According to Sternberg, successfully intelligent people do the following:[17]

1. *They motivate themselves.* They make things happen, spurred on by a desire to succeed and a love of what they are doing.

2. *They learn to control their impulses.* Instead of going with their first quick response, they sit with a question or problem. They allow time for thinking and let ideas surface before making a decision.

3. *They know when to persevere.* When it makes sense, they push past frustration and stay on course, confident that success is in their sights. They also are able to see when they've hit a dead end—and, in those cases, to stop pushing.

4. *They know how to make the most of their abilities.* They understand what they do well and capitalize on it in school and work.

5. *They translate thought into action.* Not only do they have good ideas, but they are able to turn those ideas into practical actions that bring ideas to fruition.

6. *They have a product orientation.* They want results; they focus on what they are aiming for rather than on how they are getting there.

7. *They complete tasks and follow through.* With determination, they finish what they start. They also follow through to make sure all the loose ends are tied and the goal has been achieved.

8. *They are initiators.* They commit to people, projects, and ideas. They make things happen rather than sitting back and waiting for things to happen to them.

9. *They are not afraid to risk failure.* Because they take risks and sometimes fail, they often enjoy greater success and build their

intellectual capacity. Like everyone, they make mistakes—but tend not to make the same mistake twice.

10. *They don't procrastinate.* They are aware of the negative effects of putting things off, and they avoid them. They create schedules that allow them to accomplish what's important on time.

11. *They accept fair blame.* They strike a balance between never accepting blame and taking the blame for everything. If something is their fault, they accept responsibility and don't make excuses.

12. *They reject self-pity.* When something goes wrong, they find a way to solve the problem. They don't get caught in the energy drain of feeling sorry for themselves.

13. *They are independent.* They can work on their own and think for themselves. They take responsibility for their own schedule and tasks.

14. *They seek to surmount personal difficulties.* They keep things in perspective, looking for ways to remedy personal problems and separate them from their professional lives.

15. *They focus and concentrate to achieve their goals.* They create an environment in which they can best avoid distraction and they focus steadily on their work.

16. *They spread themselves neither too thin nor too thick.* They strike a balance between doing too many things, which results in little progress on any of them, and too few things, which can reduce the level of accomplishment.

17. *They have the ability to delay gratification.* While they enjoy the smaller rewards that require less energy, they focus the bulk of their work on the goals that take more time but promise the most gratification.

18. *They have the ability to see the forest and the trees.* They are able to see the big picture and avoid getting bogged down in tiny details.

19. *They have a reasonable level of self-confidence and a belief in their ability to accomplish their goals.* They believe in themselves enough to get through the tough times, while avoiding the kind of overconfidence that stalls learning and growth.

20. *They balance analytical, creative, and practical thinking.* They sense what to use and when to use it. When problems arise, they combine all three skills to arrive at solutions.

These characteristics are your personal motivational tools. Consult them when you need a way to get moving. You may even want to post them somewhere in your home, in the front of a notebook, or in your PDA. They will propel you on your journey, helping you to bring intention to your daily activities, take responsibility for your actions, and continue to grow.

Use the *Get Analytical* exercise on page 284 to see how you have developed your command of the self-activators over the course of the term.

Evaluate Your Self-Activators

To see how you use successful intelligence in your daily life, assess how developed you perceive your self-activators to be.

1	2	3	4	5
Not at All Like Me	Somewhat Unlike Me	Not Sure	Somewhat Like Me	Definitely Like Me

Please circle the number that best represents your answer:

1. I motivate myself well.   1 2 3 4 5

2. I can control my impulses.   1 2 3 4 5

3. I know when to persevere and when to change gears.   1 2 3 4 5

4. I make the most of what I do well.   1 2 3 4 5

5. I can successfully translate my ideas into action.   1 2 3 4 5

6. I can focus effectively on my goal.   1 2 3 4 5

7. I complete tasks and have good follow-through.   1 2 3 4 5

8. I initiate action—I move people and projects ahead.   1 2 3 4 5

9. I have the courage to risk failure.   1 2 3 4 5

10. I avoid procrastination.   1 2 3 4 5

11. I accept responsibility when I make a mistake.   1 2 3 4 5

12. I don't waste time feeling sorry for myself.   1 2 3 4 5

13. I independently take responsibility for tasks.   1 2 3 4 5

14. I work hard to overcome personal difficulties.   1 2 3 4 5

15. I create an environment that helps me to concentrate on my goals.   1 2 3 4 5

16. I don't take on too much work or too little.   1 2 3 4 5

17. I can delay gratification in order to receive the benefits.   1 2 3 4 5

18. I can see both the big picture and the details in a situation.   1 2 3 4 5

19. I am able to maintain confidence in myself.   1 2 3 4 5

20. I can balance my analytical, creative, and practical thinking skills.   1 2 3 4 5

When you complete the assessment, look back at pages 28–29 for your original scores. What development do you see? List five changes that feel significant:

1. _____

2. _____

3. _____

4. _____

5. _____

As you grow, there is always room for improvement. Choose one self-activator that you feel still needs work. Analyze the specific reasons why it remains a challenge. For example, does a need to please others lead to taking on too much work, or is it a lack of taking time to map out responsibilities and time commitments? Write a brief analysis here, and let this analysis guide you as you work to build your strength in this area.

_____

_____

_____

Successful Intelligence Wrap-Up

College pressures can be enormous—but successfully intelligent thinking gives you the power to handle that pressure by making choices that have a positive impact on your physical and mental health, financial picture, and career trajectory. You can carry this power into the rest of your college experience and beyond, where you will always have a new direction in which to grow and a new challenge to face. Live each day to the fullest, using your successful intelligence to achieve your most valued goals. Here's how you have built skills in chapter 8:

Analytical

You examined the effect that stress has on performance. You analyzed how eating, exercise, and sleeping patterns can affect your health. You explored the pros and cons of choices regarding substances and sex. You examined what money means in your life and how you manage it. You looked carefully at what promotes career success. With the *Get Analytical* exercise, you examined how you now use successful intelligence in your daily life.

Creative

Considering ways to incorporate more healthful behaviors into your life may have inspired new ideas about how to eat, exercise, adjust your schedule, or manage stress. In the *Get Creative* exercise, you brainstormed new ideas about how to have fun in safe and positive ways. You considered the perspective that asking for help in the face of an addiction isn't a sign of weakness but an act of courage. As you explored the section on careers and job searches, you may have come up with new career ideas or creative ways to look for a job.

Practical

You gathered eating, exercise, and sleeping strategies from which you can choose. In the *Get Practical* exercise, you worked through ways to improve your wellness and identified resources that can support your efforts. You considered practical ways to get help if your mental health demands it. You noted specific ways to adjust, if necessary, your use of alcohol, drugs, and tobacco. You reviewed a plan for budgeting month by month. You gathered specific strategies for managing credit card use and performing a job search. You revisited Sternberg's 20 self-activators: practical skills for living with successful intelligence.

hozh'q
(hoe-shk)

The Navajo would translate *hozh'q* as "the beauty of life, as seen and created by a person." The word incorporates many concepts, including health and well-being, balance, and happiness. The Navajo perceive that *hozh'q* can start with one person and extend outward indefinitely, having a unifying effect on other people, on the world, and even on the universe. Because the Navajo consider the unity of experience as the ultimate life goal, *hozh'q* is a way of life.[18]

Think of this concept as you reflect on yourself, your goals, your life-long education, your career, and your personal pursuits. Create your own beauty of life by seeking to improve and grow in the ways that are most meaningful to you. Share your *hozh'q* with others, extending the beauty of life as far as you can. By being true to yourself, a respectful friend and family member, a productive employee, and a contributing member of society, you can change the world.

"... the world needs you to be forever the generation of strategic optimists, the generation with more dreams than memories, the generation that wakes up each morning and not only imagines that things can be better but also acts on that imagination every day."

THOMAS L. FRIEDMAN, PULITZER PRIZE–WINNING
NEW YORK TIMES COLUMNIST

PERSONAL TRIUMPH CASE STUDY
Discovering Talents and Helping Others

JOE A. MARTIN JR.,
PROFESSOR OF COMMUNICATIONS, UNIVERSITY OF WEST FLORIDA, TALLAHASSEE

Growing up around people who've been hampered by difficulties can inspire a person to make different choices. Joe Martin made the effort to achieve as a student—but that wasn't enough for him. His main focus now is his life mission to use his abilities to help and inspire others. Read the account, then answer the questions on page 288.

I grew up in the housing projects of Miami, Florida. My mother didn't finish high school, and no one in my family even considered going to college, including me. My low GPA and SAT scores seemed to indicate I wasn't "college material."

While I was in high school, six of my friends died as a result of crime, drugs, or murder. At least 12 people I knew were in prison, five from my own family. I made a vow that if I survived the projects, I would do something constructive with my life and give something back to the community. I initially wanted to join the military, but after the recruiter told me I wasn't smart enough to go to college, I decided to prove him wrong.

I enrolled in college and, given my academic background, was shocked by my success. I ended up graduating at the top of my class, with a bachelor's degree in public relations, and was voted "Student of the Year" among 10,000 students. Competing against more than 400 other candidates, I landed a job right out of college working for the federal government. Within a year, I was able to move my mother out of the projects and afford almost anything I wanted. Life was great, but I didn't like my job and the person I was becoming.

Around that time, I heard a motivational speaker talk about the need for young professionals to give back to the community. I suddenly realized that I hadn't kept my vow. I was indulging myself, but I didn't have any passion or purpose for what I was doing with my life.

After his presentation, I asked the speaker for advice. I jotted down his suggestions on a napkin and began to implement his ideas. I discovered that I could make money doing what I do best—talking. I became a motivational speaker for students and found that my true passion was teaching. Through teaching, whether on stage or in the classroom, I discovered that I could make a difference in the lives of students who were growing up in poverty as I had.

I've given over 300 presentations and spoken to more than a quarter of a million people about student success. I've written books, recorded audio- and videotapes of my programs, and have my own television show. However, my biggest accomplishment so far has been the creation of a Web site called "Real World University." With the Web site, I'm now able to reach more than 100,000 students a month in 26 different countries.

I believe the reason many students fail is because they have no clue about their gifts and talents or about how they can use those gifts and talents to serve others. Many people are on what I call the "Treadmill Trench" of life—motivated to stay busy, but too scared to live their dreams.

My main question to students is: "If you knew you couldn't fail, what would you attempt to do professionally?" The answer to this question can help anyone find their purpose and passion in life. I also stress to students the importance of meeting a model of success—not someone you'll probably never meet, like Michael Jordan, but someone who is doing what you love to do. Then spend time with that person to find out how they did it. Once students have a clear vision of what they want to become, they're destined to succeed.

Jen Fisher, the student artist who created this drawing, discovered at an early age that art was what she enjoyed doing most. Like Joe, she realized that working in a career area she was passionate about would help her live life to the fullest. After six post-high-school years of working to save money, she is now pursuing an art degree on her way to becoming a professor of art. For more of Jen's story, please visit www.prenhall.com/carter.

SUCCESSFUL INTELLIGENCE

Think, Create, Apply

Learn from the experiences of others. Look back to Joe Martin's Personal Triumph on page 287. After you've read his story, relate his experience to your own life by completing the following on a separate sheet of paper or on a computer file:

Step 1. Think it through: *Analyze your experience and compare it to Joe's.* What was a "missing piece" in Joe's life and how did he fill it? What do you consider a missing piece in your life, and how do you think you could fill the gap?

Step 2. Think out of the box: *Imagine ways to contribute.* Think about the ways in which you could serve. How might your talents and skills give something to others? Brainstorm ideas about how you could use what you do well to help others in your community.

Step 3. Make it happen: *Make a practical plan to get involved.* Decide on a specific way to help others, then form a plan to pursue this goal. As you think about your decision, consider your missing piece: Is there a way to contribute that also somehow fills that missing piece? Write down what you intend to do and the specific steps you will take to do it.

TEAMWORK

Create Solutions Together

Actively dealing with stress. By yourself, look back at the Holmes-Rahe scale on page 256. Note the stressors you have experienced in the past year and tally your "stress score." In a discussion with your class, identify the four stressors from the scale most commonly experienced by the members of the class. Divide into four groups according to the stressor each student would identify as most important (redistribute some people if the group sizes are unbalanced).

Each group should discuss its assigned stressor and its effects on people. Then, as a group, brainstorm solutions and strategies, making sure to include ones that relate to wellness (eating, sleeping, exercise, substances). List your best coping strategies and present them to the class. Groups may want to make extra copies of the lists so that every member of the class has four, one for each stressor.

WRITING

Journal and Put Skills to Work

Record your thoughts on a separate piece of paper, in a journal, or in a computer file.

Journal entry: Your money personality. Describe who you are as a money manager, and where you think your behaviors and attitudes came from. What do you buy? Are you careful or reckless? Unattentive or detail-focused? How do you handle credit? How do you feel about how you handle money?

Real-life writing: Apply for aid. Start by reading the information on financial aid on pages xxxiv–xxxvi in Quick Start to College. Then, use Internet or library resources to find two non-federally-funded scholarships, available through your college, for which you are eligible—they can be linked to academic areas of interest, associated with particular talents that you have, or offered by a group to which you or members of your family belong. Get applications for each and fill them out. Finally, write a one-page cover letter for each, telling each committee why you should receive this scholarship. Have someone proofread your work, *send the applications,* and see what happens.

PERSONAL PORTFOLIO

Prepare for Career Success

Complete the following in your electronic portfolio or on separate sheets of paper. When you have finished, read through your entire career portfolio. You have gathered information to turn to again and again on your path to a fulfilling, successful career.

Revisit the *Wheel of Successful Intelligence.* Without looking at your assessments in chapter 1 or the wheel from chapter 4, analyze where you are after completing this course by taking the three assessments again.

Assess yourself as an analytical thinker.

For each statement, circle the number that feels right to you, from 1 for "not at all true for me" to 5 for "very true for me."

1. I recognize and define problems effectively.   1 2 3 4 5
2. I see myself as "a thinker," "analytical," "studious."   1 2 3 4 5

3. When working on a problem in a group setting, I like to break down the problem into its components and evaluate them.

1 2 3 4 5

4. I need to see convincing evidence before accepting information as fact.

1 2 3 4 5

5. I weigh the pros and cons of plans and ideas before taking action.

1 2 3 4 5

6. I tend to make connections among pieces of information by categorizing them.

1 2 3 4 5

7. Impulsive, spontaneous decision making worries me.

1 2 3 4 5

8. I monitor my progress toward goals.

1 2 3 4 5

9. Once I reach a goal, I evaluate the process to see how effective it was.

1 2 3 4 5

10. When something goes wrong, I work to find out why.

1 2 3 4 5

Total your answers here: _____

Assess yourself as a creative thinker.

For each statement, circle the number that feels right to you, from 1 for "not at all true for me" to 5 for "very true for me."

1. I tend to question rules and regulations.

1 2 3 4 5

2. I see myself as "unique," "full of ideas," "innovative."

1 2 3 4 5

3. When working on a problem in a group setting, I generate a lot of ideas.

1 2 3 4 5

4. I am energized when I have a brand-new experience.

1 2 3 4 5

5. If you say something is too risky, I'm ready to give it a shot.

1 2 3 4 5

6. I often wonder if there is a different way to do or see something.

1 2 3 4 5

7. Too much routine in my work or schedule drains my energy.

1 2 3 4 5

8. I tend to see connections among ideas that others do not.

1 2 3 4 5

9. I feel comfortable allowing myself to make mistakes as I test out ideas.

1 2 3 4 5

10. I'm willing to champion an idea even when others disagree with me.

1 2 3 4 5

Total your answers here: _____

Assess yourself as a practical thinker.

For each statement, circle the number that feels right to you, from 1 for "not at all true for me" to 5 for "very true for me."

1. I can find a way around any obstacle.   1 2 3 4 5

2. I see myself as a "doer," the "go-to" person; I "make things happen."   1 2 3 4 5

3. When working on a problem in a group setting, I like to set up the plan and monitor how it is carried out.   1 2 3 4 5

4. Because I learn well from experience, I don't tend to repeat a mistake.   1 2 3 4 5

5. I finish what I start and don't leave loose ends hanging.   1 2 3 4 5

6. I pay attention to my emotions in academic and social situations to see if they help or hurt me as I move toward a goal.   1 2 3 4 5

7. I can sense how people feel, and can use that knowledge to interact with others effectively in order to achieve a goal.   1 2 3 4 5

8. I manage my time effectively.   1 2 3 4 5

9. I find ways to adjust to the teaching styles of my instructors and the communication styles of my peers.   1 2 3 4 5

10. When involved in a problem-solving process, I can see when I'm headed in an ineffective direction and I can shift gears.   1 2 3 4 5

Total your answers here: _____

After you have finished, fill in your new scores in the blank *Wheel of Successful Intelligence* in Key 8.11. Compare this wheel with your previous wheel on page 129. Look at the changes: Where have you grown? How has your self-perception changed?

- Note three *creative ideas* you came up with over the term that aided your exploration or development:

Creative idea: _____

_____

Creative idea: _____

_____

Creative idea: _____

_____

Use this new wheel to evaluate your progress.

Rate yourself in each area of the wheel on a scale of 1 to 10, with 1 being least developed (near the center of the wheel) and 10 being most developed (the outer edge of the wheel). In each area, at the level of the number you choose, draw a curved line and fill in the wedge below that line. Be honest—this is for your benefit only. Finally, look at what your wheel says about the balance in your life. If this were a real wheel, how well would it roll?

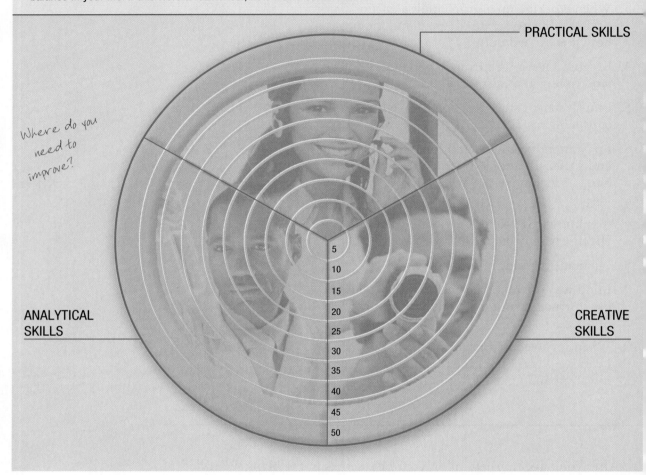

PRACTICAL SKILLS

Where do you need to improve?

ANALYTICAL
SKILLS

CREATIVE
SKILLS

5
10
15
20
25
30
35
40
45
50

Source: Based on "The Wheel of Life" model developed by the Coaches Training Institute, © Co-Active Space 2000.

- Note three *practical actions* that you took that moved you toward your goals:

Practical action: _____

_____

Practical action: _____

_____

Practical action: _____

_____

Let what you learn from this new wheel inform you about what you have accomplished and what you plan to accomplish. Continue to grow your analytical, creative, and practical skills and use them to manage the changes that await you in the future.

Suggested Readings

Beatty, Richard H. *The Resume Kit,* 5th ed. New York: Wiley, 2003.

Bolles, Richard Nelson. *What Color Is Your Parachute? 2007: A Practical Manual for Job Hunters and Career Changers.* Berkeley, CA: Ten Speed Press, 2006.

Brownell, Kelly. *The LEARN Program for Weight Management,* 10th ed. Dallas: Lifestyle, 2004.

Detweiler, Gerri. *The Ultimate Credit Handbook: How to Cut Your Debt and Have a Lifetime of Good Credit,* 3rd ed. New York: Plume, 2003.

Duyff, Roberta Larson. *The American Dietetic Association's Complete Food and Nutrition Guide.* Hoboken, NJ: Wiley, 2006.

Gifford, Allen L., Kate Lorig, Diana Laurent, and Virginia Gonzales. *Living Well with HIV and AIDS.* Boulder, CO: Bull, 2005.

Goleman, Daniel. *Working with Emotional Intelligence.* New York: Bantam Books, 2000.

Goleman, Daniel. *Social Intelligence: The New Science of Human Relationships.* New York: Bantam Books, 2006.

Grayson, Paul A., and Philip W. Meilman. *Beating the College Blues.* New York: Checkmark Books, 1999.

Kennedy, Joyce Lain. *Job Interviews for Dummies.* Foster City, CA: IDG Books Worldwide, 2000.

Kuhn, Cynthia, Scott Swartzwelder, and Wilkie Wilson. *Buzzed: The Straight Facts About the Most Used and Abused Drugs from Alcohol to Ecstasy,* 2nd ed. New York: Norton, 2003.

Selkowitz, Ann. *The College Student's Guide to Eating Well on Campus.* Bethesda, MD: Tulip Hill Press, 2000.

Walsh, Richard. *The Complete Job Search Book for College Students.* Boston: Adams Media, 2007.

Internet and Podcast Resources

The Body—The Complete AIDS/HIV Resource: **www.thebody.com/safesex.html**

Centers for Disease Control and Prevention (disease prevention and health information): **www.cdc.gov**

Career Advice podcasts (from Monster.com): **http://podcast.monster.com**

CollegeGrad.com (advice on résumés, interviews, and internships, plus a database of entry-level jobs): **www.collegegrad.com**

Consumer Credit Counseling Services (help with budgeting, money management, and credit issues): **www.cccsintl.org**

Dietary Guidelines for Americans (from the U.S. Department of Health and Human Services): **www.health.gov/dietaryguidelines**

FinancialAidPodcast.com (daily financial aid news): **www.financialaidpodcast.com**

Go Ask Alice—Columbia University's Health Q&A Internet Service: **www.goaskalice.columbia.edu**

JobWeb (career information site for college students): **www.jobweb.com**

Living Healthy podcasts: **www.livinghealthypodcast.com**

MayoClinic.com (medical information from the world-renowned medical center): **www.mayoclinic.com**

Monster.com (online job search): **www.monster.com**

The Motley Fool (money and investment advice): **www.fool.com**

Nicotine Addiction podcast: **www.podcastdirectory. com/podshows/71927**

Sexual Health Network: **www.sexualhealth.com**

Straight Talk on Alcohol and Other Drugs: **http://alcoholandotherdrugs.com**

Student Advantage (information on student discounts): **www.studentadvantage.com**

U.S. Department of Labor, Bureau of Labor Statistics—*Occupational Outlook Handbook:* **www.bls.gov/oco**

Prentice Hall Student Success SuperSite: **www.prenhall.com/success**

Endnotes

[1]Information in this section based on materials from Dr. Marlene Schwartz of the Rudd Center for Food Policy and Obesity at Yale University.

[2]Quoted in Jennifer Jacobson, "How Much Sports Is Too Much? Athletes Dislike Conferences' Efforts to Give Players More Time to Be Students," *Chronicle of Higher Education,* December 6, 2002 (http://chronicle.com/weekly/v49/ i15a03801.htm).

[3]CBS News, "Help for Sleep-Deprived Students," April 19, 2004 (www.cbsnews.com/stories/2004/ 04/19/health/main612476.shtml).

[4]"College Students' Sleep Habits Harmful to Health, Study Finds," *Daily Orange,* September 25, 2002 (www.dailyorange.com/news/2002/09/25/ Feature/College.Students.Sleep.Habits.Harmful. To.Health.Study.Finds-280340.shtml).

[5]Gregg Jacobs, "Insomnia Corner," Talk About Sleep, 2004 (www.talkaboutsleep.com/sleepdisorders/ insomnia_corner.htm); also see Herbert Benson and Eileen M. Stuart, *The Wellness Book,* New York: Simon & Schuster, 1992, p. 292.

[6]J. McGinnis and W. Foege, "Actual Causes of Death in the United States," *Journal of the American Medical Association (JAMA),* 270(18), November 10, 1993, p. 2208.

[7]National Survey on Drug Use and Health (NSDUH), "The NSDUH Report: Binge Alcohol Use Among Persons 12 to 20: 2002 and 2003 Update," August 26, 2005 (www.oas.samhsa.gov/2k5/ youthBinge/youthBinge.htm).

[8]Henry Wechsler, George Dowdall, Gretchen Maenner, Jeana Gledhill-Hoyt, and Hang Lee, "Changes in Binge Drinking and Related Problems Among American College Students Between 1993 and 1997," *Journal of American College Health,* 47(2), September 1998, p. 57.

[9]Joel Seguine, "Students Report Negative Consequences of Binge Drinking in New Survey," *University Record,* University of Michigan, October 25, 1999 (www.umich.edu/ ~urecord/9900/Oct25_99/7.htm).

[10]Darra Clark, Arizona State freshman's comments on EssayEdge.com, April 6, 2001 (www.essayedge .com/college/admissions/speakout/arizona.shtml).

[11]National Survey on Drug Use and Health (NSDUH): National Results, "Tobacco Use— College Students," 2005 (www.oas.samhsa.gov/ NSDUH/2k5NSDUH/2k5results.htm#4.6).

[12]David Stout, "Direct Link Found Between Smoking and Lung Cancer," *New York Times,* October 18, 1996, pp. A1, A19.

[13]National Survey on Drug Use and Health (NSDUH), "The NSDUH Report: College Enrollment Status and Past Year Illicit Drug Use Among Young Adults: 2002, 2003, and 2004," October 21, 2005 (www.oas.samhsa.gov/2k5/ College/college.htm).

[14]Cited in Jim Hanson, "Your Money Personality: It's All In Your Head," December 25, 2006, University Credit Union (http://hffo.cuna.org/ 012433/article/1440/html).

[15]Ibid.

[16]Nellie Mae, "Undergraduate Students and Credit Cards in 2004," May 2005 (www.nelliemae.com/ library/research_12.html).

[17]List and descriptions based on Robert J. Sternberg, *Successful Intelligence,* New York: Plume, 1997, pp. 251–269.

[18]Christopher J. Moore, *In Other Words: A Language Lover's Guide to the Most Intriguing Words Around the World,* New York: Walker, 2004, p. 85.

get focused!

time and math tests

Do the "Next Thing To Do"

Of the set of tasks required to accomplish an academic responsibility, one task is always at the top of the to-do list at any given time. If you have a test in a week, for example, your next task might be to study chapters 1 through 4 in your text. If you have a lab project due in two weeks, your next task might be to perform a particular experiment.

Deciding on, and doing, the "next thing to do" both boosts schedule awareness and inspires action. Examine your syllabi for the courses you are taking right now. Find the next responsibility pending for each course—a reading assignment, a paper, a project, a quiz, a test. Then, focus on the *next thing to do* for each. Use the accompanying table to record the information and note when the next thing is done. Use the momentum you gain to move through subsequent tasks until you successfully accomplish each responsibility.

Course	Responsibility pending (include date or due date)	Next task related to this responsibility	Done?
Example: Healthcare Management	10-page paper due November 12	Write draft of thesis statement and turn in to the TA for review	✓

Slay the Math Anxiety Dragon

A special form of test anxiety, math anxiety is based on common misconceptions about math, such as the notion that people are born with or without an ability to think quantitatively or that men are better at math than women. Students who feel they can't do math may give up without asking for help. On exams, they may experience a range of physical symptoms—including sweating, nausea, dizziness, headaches, and fatigue—that reduce their ability to concentrate and leave them feeling defeated.

The material in this segment is designed to help you deal with the kind of math-related anxiety that affects your grades on exams. As you learn concrete ways to calm your nerves and special techniques for math tests, you will feel more confident in your ability to succeed.

These test-taking tips supplement what you learned in chapter 7, "Test Taking: Showing What You Know," where you studied test taking in depth and generalized test anxiety. That chapter also includes valuable information on test preparation, general test-taking strategies, strategies for handling different types of test questions, and learning from test mistakes.

Gauge Your Level of Math Anxiety

Use the accompanying questionnaire to get an idea of your math anxiety level.

ARE YOU ANXIOUS ABOUT MATH?

Rate each of the following statements on a scale of 1 (Strongly Disagree) to 5 (Strongly Agree).

1. _____ I cringe when I have to go to math class.
2. _____ I am uneasy about going to the board in a math class.
3. _____ I am afraid to ask questions in math class.
4. _____ I am always worried about being called on in math class.
5. _____ I understand math now, but I worry that it's going to get really difficult soon.
6. _____ I tend to zone out in math class.
7. _____ I fear math tests more than any other kind.
8. _____ I don't know how to study for math tests.
9. _____ It's clear to me in math class, but when I go home it's like I was never there.
10. _____ I'm afraid I won't be able to keep up with the rest of the class.

SCORING KEY:

40–50	Sure thing, you have math anxiety.
30–39	No doubt! You're still fearful about math.
20–29	On the fence.
10–19	Wow! Loose as a goose!

Source: Ellen Freedman, *Do You Have Math Anxiety? A Self-Test*, 1997 (www.mathpower.com/anxtest.htm).

The best way to overcome math test anxiety is through practice. Keeping up with your homework, attending class, preparing well for tests, and doing extra problems will help you learn the material and boost your confidence.

Following are 10 additional ways to reduce math anxiety and do well on tests:

Use Special Techniques for Math Tests

Use the general test-taking strategies presented in chapter 7 as well as the following techniques to achieve better results on math exams:

- *Read through the exam first.* When you first get an exam, read through every problem quickly and make notes on how you might attempt to solve the problems.

- *Analyze problems carefully.* Categorize problems according to type. Take the "givens" into account, and write down any formulas, theorems, or definitions that apply before you begin. Focus on what you want to find or prove.

- *Estimate before you begin, to come up with a "ballpark" solution.* Work the problem and check the solution against your estimate. The two answers should be close. If they're not, recheck your calculations. You may have made a calculation error.

- *Break the calculation into the smallest possible pieces.* Go step-by-step and don't move on to the next step until you are clear about what you've done so far.

- *Recall how you solved similar problems.* Past experience can provide valuable clues.

- *Draw a picture to help you see the problem.* Visual images such as a diagram, chart, probability tree, or geometric figure may help clarify your thinking.
- *Be neat.* Sloppy numbers can mean the difference between a right and a wrong answer. A 4 that looks like a 9 will be marked wrong.
- *Use the opposite operation to check your work.* Work backward from your answer to see if you are right.
- *Look back at the question to be sure you did everything.* Did you answer every part of the question? Did you show all required work?

Decide How Well These Techniques Work for You

Use what you just learned about yourself and math to answer the following questions:

- What did you learn from the math anxiety questionnaire? Describe your current level of math anxiety:

  _____

  _____

- If you are afraid of math, what effect do you think it will have on your future?

  _____

  _____

  _____

- Which suggestions for reducing math anxiety are you likely to use? How do you think they will help you feel more comfortable with math?

  _____

  _____

  _____

  _____

- Which suggestions for improving your performance on math tests are you likely to use?

  _____

  _____

  _____

  _____

- In what other ways can you improve your math performance?

  _____

  _____

  _____

INDEX